The Study of Animal Behaviour

The Study of Animal Behaviour

FELICITY HUNTINGFORD

Department of Zoology
University of Glasgow, UK

LONDON   NEW YORK

Chapman and Hall

First published 1984 by
Chapman and Hall Ltd
11 New Fetter Lane, London EC4P 4EE
Published in the USA by
Chapman and Hall
733 Third Avenue, New York NY 10017

© 1984 Felicity Huntingford

Photoset by Enset Ltd.
Midsomer Norton, Bath, Avon
and printed in Great Britain by
J.W. Arrowsmith Ltd., Bristol

ISBN 0 412 22320 1 (hardback)
ISBN 0 412 22330 9 (paperback)

British Library Cataloguing in Publication Data

Huntingford, Felicity A.
　The study of animal behaviour.
　1. Animal behavior
　I. Title
　591.51　　　QL751

　ISBN 0-412-22320-1
　ISBN 0-412-22330-9　Pbk

Library of Congress Cataloging in Publication Data

Huntingford, Felicity A. (Felicity Ann)
　The study of animal behaviour.

　Bibliography: p.
　Includes index.
　1. Animal behavior.　I. Title.
　QL751.H757　1984　　　591.51　　　83-19002
　ISBN 0-412-22320-1
　ISBN 0-412-22330-9　(pbk.)

To Tim and Anne,
without whom this book
would not have been written,
and to Joan and Jessica,
without whom it might have
been written sooner

Contents

Preface

The aim of this book is to identify the main areas of active discussion about, and research into, the biology of animal behaviour, to describe and assess ways in which these can be studied and using selected examples, to illustrate the kinds of results which are emerging. It is not intended to provide an exhaustive review of all we know about animal behaviour, although the examples have been chosen to cover as many as possible of the things that animals do.

Acknowledgements

I would like to thank C. Swann, M.L.N. Murthy and the Superbrain for typing the manuscript; Linda Partridge, Pat Monaghan, Douglas Fraser and Richard Wilson for constructive criticism of earlier drafts; Alan Crowden for help in planning and producing the book and, particularly, Tim Huntingford for help and encouragement at all stages of its production. Acknowledgements are gratefully made to Jim Tulley for producing plates 1, 2, 3, 7 and 12 and to Michael Hansell for the remainder.

List of plates

CHAPTER 1

Introduction

1.1 The ethological approach to the study of behaviour

In 1951, Tinbergen published a book called *The Study of Instinct* in which he integrated a substantial body of information about animal behaviour into a coherent theoretical framework and outlined the main problems awaiting investigation; in doing this, he shaped the future of research into the subject. The approach to the study of behaviour which Tinbergen advocated, and which he defined very simply as the biological approach to behaviour, is usually called *ethology* (Thorpe, 1979). The main characteristics of ethology which distinguish it from other approaches to the study of behaviour such as comparative psychology, anthropology or neurophysiology, stem in part from this biological background and in part from the fact that many of its early exponents grew up as natural historians.

Thus, a key feature of ethology is the belief that animals must be studied in natural conditions if useful questions about their behaviour are to be asked and answered. Such a study should start with a period of unobtrusive but precise and careful observation; ethologists believe that many questions about behaviour can be answered without experimental interference. Any experiments which may eventually be performed should be kept simple and, wherever possible, carried out in the field.

It is not just the priority given to observation over experiment at the initial phase of a study that characterizes the ethological approach; the way in which data are collected is also important. Ethologists tend to describe what animals do in terms of relatively simple components of behaviour, such as movements and postures, and to give these descriptive rather than interpretive labels; a chimpanzee shows a bared toothed open mouth face rather than a submissive gesture. The early ethologists were impressed by the fact that behaviour does lend itself to description in such discrete terms and that a given species tends to show a characteristic repertoire of behaviour patterns. The aim of much early ethological investigation was to produce inventories of such actions (ethograms) for a range of animal species, just as an anatomist might painstakingly describe the bones that make up the skeletons of the same animals. This comparative aspect of ethology was a legacy from zoology, as was the tendency to view behaviour in the framework of evolutionary theory; studies of the ways in which behaviour contributes to fitness and how behaviour has changed during the course of evolution have a special place in the ethological literature. Thus it is the observation of the detailed movements that animals display in their natural habitats and the application of evolutionary theory to this behaviour that gave ethology its special flavour and which still tends to characterize the way zoologists study the behaviour of their subjects.

An archetypal example of an investigation in the ethological tradition is Tinbergen's study of egg-shell removal in the black-headed gull (*Larus ridibundus*). Prolonged observation of the breeding behaviour of these birds showed that shortly after each chick hatches, one of its parents picks up the broken egg shell and drops it at some distance from the nest; this brief action is performed without fail by all black-headed gull parents. From his knowledge of the general biology of this species, Tinbergen suggested several possible functions; removal of the shells might protect the young against disease, against damage or against the attentions of predators. Comparison of the behaviour of different species revealed that egg shells are only removed by those gulls in which protection of the young depends on camouflage. This tended to support the last suggestion, although of course it does not rule out the others. Tinbergen then carried out a series of simple experiments in which he placed broken egg shells beside some artificial nests in a gull colony while, as a control, only disturbing others. A significantly greater number of eggs were taken by visually hunting predators, such as crows, from the nests with broken shells beside them; this indicates that by removing the broken egg shells after hatching the gulls do indeed reduce the chances of their brood being killed by predators (Tinbergen *et al.*, 1962). Thus, prolonged, careful observation of gulls in their natural habitat pinpointed an interesting question and cross species comparison suggested a number of possible answers. Simple experiments carried out in the field confirmed at least one of these.

The strengths of the ethological approach stem from these special characteristics; patient observation of animals under natural conditions reduces the chances that rare but important behaviour patterns will be overlooked and that artefacts in the behaviour of animals kept in the laboratory will be taken as normal. At the same time it highlights biologically important questions and is a fruitful source of hypotheses, especially where questions about the functions of behaviour are concerned. An additional claim made for the ethological approach is that straightforward description of the movements that animals make, as free as possible from preconceived interpretation as to their significance, encourages an open mind about how behaviour is organized and what it is for. Provided that the movements concerned are carefully described, this method of recording behaviour should facilitate replication. Finally, description of a range of species makes it possible to look for general principles about animal behaviour, although zoological experience indicates that extrapolation should be done cautiously.

However, the ethological approach has a number of weaknesses. To overstate the case somewhat, observation of simple movements tends to overemphasize the importance of discrete, stereotyped actions, which can be seen or heard and to underemphasize the importance of more variable movements and the production of scents. As a result, ethological research has tended to concentrate on the behaviour of animals such as insects, fish and birds which use predominantly visual and auditory signals. In addition, description of behaviour in terms of form alone, often stated as an ideal of ethological research, may result in important aspects of behaviour being ignored; for example, it may be useful to distinguish pecking at food from pecking at nest material, which introduces something about the behaviour's relationship to the environment into the description. Nor is the ideal of an open minded observer faithfully reporting all an animal does realistic in practice. Of necessity, since we can never record everything, decisions must be made about what to include in a behavioural study and the process by which this is done depends heavily on the observer's interests and preconceptions about what is important. This is not necessarily a bad thing, but the claim of objective open mindedness which is sometimes made for the ethological approach leaves an impression of complacency. Even with all this filtering, conscious or otherwise, there is still a danger of collecting large masses of unwieldy data which are of little interest, simply because these are there to be collected. This tendency to record everything sometimes results in overemphasis of techniques of data collection and analysis at the expense of ideas.

In the early literature at least, although many of the experiments were attractive in their naturalness and simplicity, this very simplicity sometimes led to weaknesses in experimental design. To give just one example, having observed that male three-spined sticklebacks *(Gasterosteus aculeatus)* develop red bellies in the breeding season and that they preferentially attack conspecifics, Tinbergen conducted his famous experiments to determine what elicits this response. To do this he presented male fish with a series of stimuli ranging from an entire dead, non-breeding stickleback to very crude models of various shapes, with or without a red spot. All the sticklebacks in his study attacked most strongly those models with red on their lower surface, regardless of shape. This led him to conclude that in male sticklebacks the fighting response is critically dependent on the stimulus 'red belly underneath' (Tinbergen, 1953). Having designed his experiments around the natural behaviour of sticklebacks and since the males generally go red in the breeding season, not yellow or green, he did not investigate their response to models of other colours. An experimental psychologist would have considered this control to be essential before the conclusion described above could be considered valid. In fact, when sticklebacks were exposed to models of different colours, although all sticklebacks attacked coloured models more than silver ones, they did not all attack the red model most vigorously (Muckensturm, 1968); in the light of subsequently discovered variation in the breeding colours of these fish, this result is an interesting one. This is not to belittle the importance of

Tinbergen's results, but to illustrate the point that simple and apparently natural are not always best where experimental design is concerned.

Impressed as any field naturalist must be by the apparent precision with which animals are adapted to their environments, ethologists were especially interested in the functions of behaviour. This interest has led to many useful insights into the selective forces acting on behaviour but can turn into uncritical acceptance of what Lewontin (1978) calls the adaptationist paradigm (the assumption that everything an animal is or does is an adaptive product of natural selection). This has meant that other sources of evolutionary change tend to be ignored in much of the ethological literature, although not in Tinbergen's own writings. In addition, since by definition only inherited characteristics can evolve, the weight placed on behaviour as the product of selection led the early ethologists to overemphasize the importance of genotype and to ignore the profound and complex effects of the environment on the development of behaviour.

These then are the claims made for and against the ethological approach itself, as opposed to the body of theory developed to account for the results it produced. The theoretical framework outlined in *The Study of Instinct* centres on a few key concepts which will be outlined briefly here, without much in the way of supporting evidence; some of the relevant evidence will be discussed in later chapters but for a more detailed account, the reader is referred to *An Introduction to Animal Behaviour* by Manning (1979).

1.2 A brief outline of classical ethological theory

According to classical ethological theory, an animal's behaviour consists of a series of regularly repeated, stereotyped movements or combinations of movements which are as characteristic of the species concerned as any of its structural features. These are called *fixed action patterns* and are elicited by one or a few key aspects of the environment or *sign stimuli*; for example, the red belly of a rival elicits the fixed action patterns used in attack by breeding male sticklebacks. While some sign stimuli are very simple, others are complex, configurational affairs; the red only elicits attack if it is underneath. Where more than one sign stimulus triggers a response, their effects were believed to combine additively, a property which is summarized in the *Law of Heterogeneous Summation*; a male stickleback with a red belly and in a head down posture elicits more attack than one in a horizontal position. The specificity with which a fixed action pattern can be released by the appropriate sign stimulus was seen as the result of mechanisms in the central nervous system specific to the response in question which detect the presence of a particular configuration of stimuli and activate the appropriate response; these mechanisms were called *Innate Releasing Mechanisms.*

Observation of undisturbed animals made it clear that a given stimulus does not always elicit the same response; male sticklebacks do not attack red models outside the breeding season. Ethologists therefore stressed the fact that an animal's internal state or *motivation* is extremely important in determining what behaviour it shows. The behavioural repertoire of a given species was believed to consist of a number of distinct groups of fixed action patterns, the members of which usually serve the same overall function and are controlled by one specific internal factor. Such internal factors, or *drives*, were thought to represent an accumulation of *action specific energy*, whose level determines how likely the animal is to show a particular set of fixed action patterns. At any given time the animal will display fixed action patterns controlled by that drive whose action specific energy is at the highest level. In order to explain precisely how the occurrence of fixed action patterns varies with time, the hypothetical properties of these drives were often represented in the form of motivational models. In this context, a model is an analogy in which the behaviour of animals, which is not understood, is compared to the output of some structure or system which is understood in an attempt to clarify the properties of the former. The two most famous of these, Lorenz's Psychohydraulic Model (1950) and Tinbergen's Hierarchical Model (1951), are summarized in Fig. 1.1. Between them, these two models account for the way in which the effectiveness of a particular stimulus in releasing a given response changes with time. In addition they explain such bizarre behavioural phenomena as the performance of a fixed action pattern in the absence of the appropriate stimulus (vacuum activities) and in a functionally irrelevant context (displacement activities) when an animal is presented simultaneously with stimuli eliciting incompatible responses. A characteristic feature of both models is their use of the concept of motivational energy with drives being said to accumulate, to flow from one place to another, to spark over and so on.

In addition to studying how fixed action patterns are elicited and controlled, early ethologists also addressed the question of how they develop. Classical ethological theory was quite clear on this point; fixed action patterns are inherited, genetically determined and do not require specific environmental contingencies for their final expression. This picture of the way fixed action patterns develop was based on a number of observations: animals tend to perform the fixed action patterns typical of their species, the more closely related two species are, the more similar their behaviour tends to be, behaviour often appears to be clearly adapted by natural selection to the animal's needs and it may appear fully formed at the first performance in the absence of any opportunity for learning. For example, breeding male sticklebacks reared without any experience of conspecifics in nuptial colours attack rivals with red breasts on the first occasion that they encounter them (Cullen, 1960). To give an even more striking example, hand-reared garden warblers (*Sylvia borin*) show migratory restlessness at the appropriate season, heading in the correct south-westerly direction for about a month and then changing to a course which would prevent their being lost over the Atlantic on a real migratory flight (Gwinner and Wiltschko, 1978).

In spite of this belief that the development of fixed action patterns is independent of environmental influence, one particular way in which behaviour can be modified by experience received considerable attention from classical ethologists. Lorenz noticed that newly hatched geese follow the first moving object that they encounter; this is usually their mother but for hand-reared birds was often himself. He suggested that long-term social and sexual preferences are formed at a critical stage in development in the absence of any conventional reinforcement by a process called imprinting (Lorenz, 1937). Thus while the movements involved in following by young goslings and those used in subsequent sexual activity may be inherited, the stimulus to which these

Figure 1.1 (opposite) Two influential models of the causes of behaviour from classical ethology. (a) Lorenz's psychohydraulic model: this represents the critical features of a drive as Lorenz sees them. After a fight, for example, energy specific to aggressive behaviour is gradually produced inside the animal as water drips out of the pipe (1) and accumulates, as in the reservoir (2). As a result, pressure builds up on the piston (3) which gradually moves to the right. This movement is augmented by weights in the pan (4) (representing the sign stimuli eliciting aggression) until the piston passes the hole (5). This allows the water to flow out of the reservoir into a sloping trough (6) with holes (7) at different heights; water falling through these represents performance of the different action patterns of fighting (8). The fuller the trough, the more complete the aggressive sequence. When the reservoir is empty, the behaviour comes to an end. Various combinations of water pressure (= drive strength) and weights (= stimulus strength) are sufficient to move the piston past the hole. When the pressure is very high, it is sufficient to move the piston in the absence of any weights at all (the animal shows vacuum activity). (After Lorenz, 1950.) (b) Tinbergen's hierarchical model: the motivational system underlying a major instinct is a hierarchical arrangement of neural centres controlling increasingly specific aspects of behaviour. Action specific energy accumulates in each centre as a combined result of the action of external stimuli, intrinsic motivational processes, and input of energy from higher centres. Energy flow between centres is prevented by blocks which are removed when the relevant sign stimulus activates the appropriate innate releasing mechanism. Increasingly specific stimuli are required to remove blocks lower on the hierarchical scale. Activation of higher centres causes general restlessness and appetitive behaviour; only when the lowest centres of all are activated are fixed action patterns performed. The proposed sequence of events leading to a biting attack in breeding sticklebacks is as follows: under the influence of increasing temperature and day length, the centre (1) controlling reproductive behaviour as a whole is activated. This causes the stickleback to migrate to shallow water. Sign stimuli provided by a suitable territory remove the block (2) between the reproductive centre and the territorial centre (3), energy flows in and the fish settles. The aggressive centre (5) is activated when the sign stimulus 'red male intruding' removes the block (4) and the resident swims towards the intruder. The sign stimulus 'intruder bites' removes the final block (6), allowing energy to flow down to the lowest level centre controlling biting (7), finally to be dissipated in performance of the fixed action pattern (8). If action specific energy accumulating in a centre reaches a high level in the absence of the appropriate sign stimulus, it can spark over to another centre and activate a different fixed action pattern (displacement activity). If two centres at the lowest level are activated simultaneously, mixtures of, or alternation between, fixed action patterns may be seen.

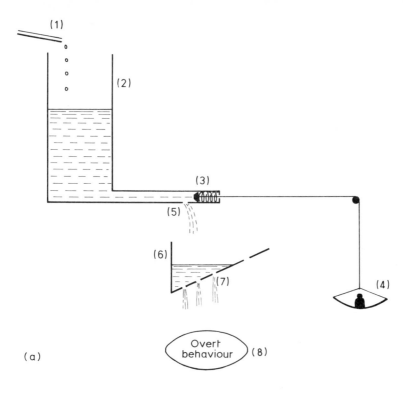

(1)

(2)

(3)

(5)

(6)

(7)

(4)

Overt behaviour (8)

(a)

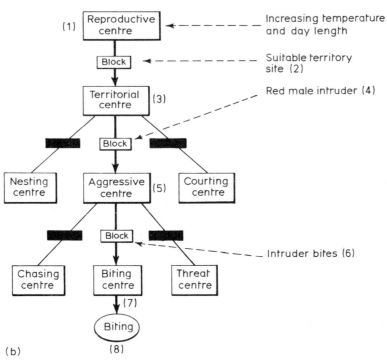

(1) Reproductive centre ←----- Increasing temperature and day length

Block ←----- Suitable territory site (2)

Territorial centre (3) ←----- Red male intruder (4)

Nesting centre

Block

Aggressive centre (5)

Courting centre

Chasing centre

Block ←----- Intruder bites (6)

Biting centre

Threat centre

(7)

Biting

(8)

(b)

responses are directed is influenced by experience. A considerable amount of research has been devoted to identifying the properties of this imprinting process.

Thus the fixed action pattern was seen as a stereotyped combination of movements elicited by specific features of the environment in conjunction with a filtering mechanism and, together with other fixed action patterns serving the same function, controlled by action specific energy within the animal concerned. The form of the fixed action pattern and the filtering mechanism are both inherited but development of the orientation of the response may be influenced by the environment. This list summarizes the properties of the *instinctive behaviour pattern* and the title of Tinbergen's book illustrates the importance of this concept in classical ethological theory.

Observations and experiments on animals in their natural habitats suggested that behaviour serves a variety of functions such as avoiding predators, obtaining food, attracting mates and rearing young. It was usually taken for granted that such adaptive responses are the product of evolution by natural selection. In the absence of any satisfactory fossil evidence, attempts to trace the course of this evolution relied heavily on comparison of the behaviour of living species and concentrated on the evolution of displays since these are relatively easy to observe and describe. For example, comparison of fixed action patterns used by related species during courtship indicated that these may often have evolved from behaviour shown when two or more incompatible drives are simultaneously activated. To quote a famous example, during courtship, domestic cocks (*Gallus domesticus*) show similar movements and calls to those used to attract other birds to a new food source (scratching, stepping back, pecking the ground, picking up pebbles); this was interpreted as a displacement activity which apparently also served to attract females. In a related species, the Impeyan pheasant (*Lophophorus impeyanus*), the male bows rhythmically before the hen with wings and tail expanded. The peacock pheasant (*Polyplectron bicalcaratum*) scratches the ground and bows to the female with its wings and tail spread, while the peacock (*Pavo pavo*) erects and shakes its elaborately coloured tail in front of the female, then takes several backward steps and bows (Schenkel, 1956). Thus, according to classical ethological theory, behaviour originally shown as a result of a motivational conflict undergoes a series of changes whereby its effectiveness as a signal is enhanced. These changes involve increasingly exaggerated and stereo-typed movements, loss of dependence on the original motivational conflict and the evolution of bright colours; they were summarized by the term *ritualization* and were believed to have occurred in the evolution of many displays.

1.3 The modern study of animal behaviour

Following Tinbergen's synthesis, ethology existed as a coherent body of theory, elegantly explaining many known facts relating to the immediate causes, development, function and evolution of animal behaviour. The ideas he discussed stimulated a great deal of research which, inevitably, resulted in alteration and extension of many early concepts. Perhaps the most obvious difference between the research of the early ethologists and that of modern students of animal behaviour is the enormous increase in the complexity of the exercise; techniques of data collection have become much more sophisticated, pencil and paper having largely given way to the multichannel event recorder, analysis of large blocks of multivariate data is commonplace and a highly complex body of theory has been developed, which itself requires precise quantitative results to test its predictions. These developments all feed on one another and whereas Lorenz boasted that he had never published a paper with graph in it (1975), ethology is now very much a quantitative subject. To illustrate this change with just one example, extracts from two papers about courtship in sticklebacks, published in 1953 and 1974, are presented below.

'Each male (stickleback), if ready to receive a female, reacts to them by performing a curious dance towards and all around them. Each dance consists of a series of leaps, during which the male first turns as if going to swim away from the females, then abruptly turns towards them with its mouth wide open. ... a (mature) female ... turns towards the male, at the same time adopting a more-or-less upright attitude ... The male now immediately turns round and swims hurriedly towards the nest.' (From Tinbergen, 1953.)

'As a last example of an inhomogeneous process of a renewal structure, we shall look at the zigzag behaviour of the stickleback. For further use let us introduce the notation $Z(t)$ for the mean number of zigzags per time unit or zigzag intensity ... The zigzag frequency is not a simple linear function of E and T ... (and) ...

$$Z(t) = Ce^{q^c}$$

where $C = b_{2E} E + b_{2T} T$,
E = excitation
T = threshold'

(From H. Metz, 1974.)

Extensive analysis of complex data and sophisticated theoretical treatment are not new to ethology, Russel, Mead and Hayes (1954) and Nelson (1965) being forerunners in this respect, nor have they been universally welcomed (Lorenz, 1975). However, to proceed beyond a certain point in understanding the more recent literature on animal behaviour and to carry out original research in this area, at least an intuitive grasp of some fairly sophisticated techniques and concepts is necessary.

Another change which has come about since the 1950s, and one anticipated in *The Study of Instinct*, is increasing exploitation of the common ground shared by the various other disciplines which involve behaviour. Ethologists have many objectives in common with comparative psychologists, endocrinologists, neurophysiologists, ecologists, geneticists and evolutionary biologists, not to mention sociologists, anthropologists and psychiatrists. Interchange of ideas, techniques and results between these different areas of study is difficult but is being attempted more frequently and often with useful results. For example, the idea (borrowed from engineering via neurophysiology) that an animal has an internal representation of what its sensory input from the environment should be and adjusts its behaviour in an attempt to achieve this state, has elucidated the motivational mechanisms underlying complex social interactions such as courtship and fighting (Toates, 1980). The observational techniques of ethology as well as its ideas about motivational conflict have been applied to the problem of childhood autism, with some success (Tinbergen and Tinbergen, 1972). While such exchange of ideas and techniques has been and continues to be fruitful, it extends the range of subjects that the would-be student of behaviour needs to know about. It also means that the boundaries between disciplines break down; our current understanding of animal behaviour owes as much to psychology, physiology and evolutionary biology as it does to ethology and it is often hard to recognize a distinct field of research to which the term can still be applied. However, much modern research into animal behaviour has an ethological flavour in the form of observation of fine grained movements and an interest in evolutionary questions.

A final change reflected in the more recent literature, is an increasing awareness of the practical applications of ethology, in areas ranging from animal husbandry and veterinary medicine to psychiatry. This is partly a reflection of the current harsh economic climate but is also a stage that most disciplines reach after a certain body of theory has been developed; like any other group of people, ethologists wish to be useful.

1.4 An outline of the book

The aim of this book is to discuss the techniques and theories which are currently being applied to the question of why animals behave in the way that they do and to see how our present picture of animal behaviour compares with that presented in *The Study of Instinct*. Chapter 2 looks at the way in which animal behaviour can be described and measured and the implications this has for analysis and interpretation. Chapter 3 is about the immediate causes of behaviour, discussing the ways in which the internal and external factors controlling behaviour can be investigated and the picture of motivation which emerges. Chapter 4 deals with the development of behaviour, while Chapters 5–7 discuss behaviour and evolution, considering in turn the effects of the process of natural selection on behaviour, the phylogenetic history of specific behaviour patterns and the influence of behaviour on the evolutionary process. The techniques for studying the inheritance of behaviour are discussed in Chapter 8. Finally, Chapter 9 looks at the ways in which the understanding of animal behaviour outlined in the previous sections can be applied to practical problems; the question of why humans behave as they do is included among the practical issues to which a knowledge of animal behaviour may have a contribution to make.

CHAPTER 2

The description and measurement of behaviour

It is not a simple matter to provide the reliable and unambiguous accounts of what animals actually do that the ethological approach requires or the precise measurements demanded by modern theory. The question of exactly how the two exercises of describing and measuring behaviour should be carried out has therefore received considerable attention.

Behaviour is the result of continuous changes in the body muscles which we see as an uninterrupted stream of postures and movements; these have a series of consequences for the relationship between the animal and its environment. Thus, following a complex sequence of neurophysiological events, an incubating goose extends its neck towards an egg which has rolled out of its nest, lowers its bill and retracts its neck towards its body; as a result, the egg is returned to the safety of the nest. In order to describe what the bird does, and before any analysis of this behaviour can be carried out, this continuous stream of movements must be condensed in some way, and divided up so that words or some other essentially discrete labels can be applied to it. There are two rather different ways in which this can be done; the labelling can refer either to the actual movements the animal performs (the goose extends its neck and so on) or to their influence on the environment (the egg is returned to the nest). In other words, we can use form or function in characterizing what the animal does (Hinde, 1970).

2.1 Describing behaviour by its function

Describing behaviour in terms of its environmental consequences or function has the great advantage of providing a concise, economical account of what may be a very complicated activity. In addition, in some cases it is possible to achieve a high degree of objectivity by this method; while there may be disagreement about exactly how far the goose's neck was extended, observers are likely to agree about whether or not the egg is back in the nest. For many kinds of study, it is the consequence of behaviour which is important and not the precise form which it takes; if we wish to understand the selective forces acting on incubating geese, it may be more important to know how quickly and reliably the egg is returned than whether this is done with the head or the feet.

However, there are circumstances in which it is necessary to know not only the results of an animal's behaviour but also how these were brought about. By recording exactly how a grey lag goose retrieves its eggs, in particular how the inward movement is determined by the position of the egg, it was shown that the action itself and its orientation are controlled by separate mechanisms (Lorenz and Tinbergen, 1938). In addition, if the consequences of behaviour are not immediately obvious or if these are numerous and complex, describing behaviour in functional terms may involve lack of objectivity and risk of error. Ethologists therefore tend to concentrate on describing the form of behaviour patterns, although in practice, the two methods of description are often combined. For example, many lizards show a movement called a 'signature bob' when they meet a conspecific, the 'bob' referring to the form of the movement and the 'signature' to its supposed function.

2.2 Describing behaviour by its form

2.2.1 BEHAVIOUR DESCRIBED AS A CONTINUOUS PROCESS

Since all behaviour is the consequence of muscle activity, recording this activity seems a logical way to describe what an animal does. Traces of the electrical activity in the muscles themselves (electromyographs or EMGs) provide a clear and unambiguous record of their pattern of contraction and thus represent one way of describing what animals do. Figure 2.1(a) shows the activity of eight muscles in the head of the fish *Petrotilapia tridentiger* recorded while they were scraping algae from vertical surfaces and directing biting attacks on other fish in an attempt to determine the relationship between these two activities. The form of the movements are broadly similar, but during biting the upper jaw is protruded more, suction is minimized and while the mouth is being closed the upper jaw is retracted earlier and the lower jaw later producing a strong, pincer-like movement. The difference in muscle activity which brings about these functional changes is that during biting the epaxial muscle is opposed by only weak levels of activity in the *adductor mandibulae,* the *levator* and *adductor arcus palatini* and the *dilator operculae* remain silent for the most part and during closing of the mouth the *adductor mandibulae* muscles fire in a different sequence (Liem, 1980).

Thus, continuous recording of the activities of a number of muscles provides a powerful tool in the fine scale analysis of behavioural sequences; however, it is obvious that it generates an enormous amount of data which may be at too fine a level of detail for the needs of many studies. In addition, the restrictions imposed by the recording electrodes may interfere with the free movement of the animals concerned. Behaviour is therefore usually described at the level of the overt movements; these may be recorded in the form of a continuous record of the position of various parts of the body, as in Fig. 2.1(b) which shows two fragments of a behavioural record of a lizard (*Anolis limnifrons*) in which the height of the

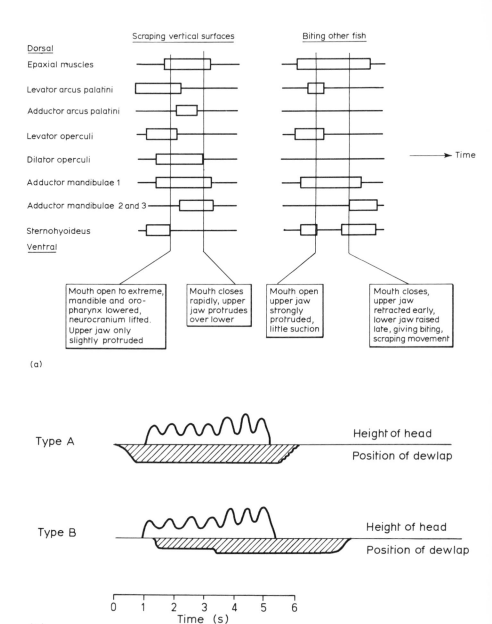

Figure 2.1 Describing behaviour as a continuous process. (a) Firing pattern of 8 jaw muscles in *Petrotilapia* during scraping vertical surfaces and biting other fish (after Liem, 1980); (b) two-dimensional representation of a sequence of behaviour of an anole lizard (after Hover and Jenssen, 1976); (c, *opposite*) three-dimensional representation of grooming movements in a 3-day-old mouse (from Fentress, 1976).

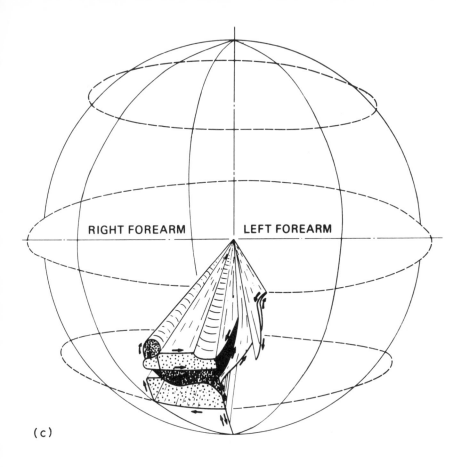

RIGHT FOREARM | LEFT FOREARM

(c)

head above the ground and the extent to which the dewlap was lowered were measured simultaneously during frame by frame analyses of social encounters (Hover and Jenssen, 1976a). In an attempt to provide an accurate description in three dimensions of movements of parts of an animal's body, Golani (1976) and various collaborators have adapted a system of notation used by choreographers (the Eshkol–Washman system). Briefly, the body is seen as a series of connected limb segments, the end of each of which describes movements on the surface of a sphere which are described in terms of their initial and final positions and the trajectory of the movement between these. Figure 2.1(c) shows the results of such an analysis on the grooming movements of young mice in which the animal's own body was used as the frame of reference (Fentress, 1976).

2.2.2 BEHAVIOUR DESCRIBED AS A SERIES OF DISCRETE EVENTS
This last figure gives an accurate record of how the mice moved their arms and one which emphasizes the essentially continuous nature of behaviour. However, collecting and analysing this sort of data is extremely time consuming; in addition,

the results do not lend themselves to simple description or measurement of behaviour. It is a fundamental assumption of ethology that the apparently continuous stream of behaviour can be seen as a series of discrete events. On this picture, the behavioural repertoire of an animal consists of a limited number of combinations of movements and postures which always occur in the same form and which differ from other such combinations. In other words, natural units of behaviour exist which can be used to describe and measure what animals do; the problem of producing a behavioural record reduces to that of identifying these regularly repeated actions and recording them as they occur.

Tinbergen (1959) spelled out clearly the principles involved in identifying such behavioural units, and the following text quotes in full his description of three (out of 14) display postures shown during social interactions by various kinds of gull.

Choking. The bird squats and bends forward. The tongue bone is usually lowered, the neck is held in an S bend and the bill is pointed down. In this position the head makes rapid downwards movements, usually, however without touching the ground. The carpal joints are often raised and the wings may even be raised and spread and kept stationary for a few seconds. A muffled, rhythmic sound is given, which may or may not be in time with the pecking movements. The breast is 'heaving' strongly, particularly in the large gulls. Often the lateral and ventral feathers are raised. The bird may be facing another bird or facing away from it or take up an intermediate orientation.

Forward. The body is about horizontal and the neck is stretched to varying extents. The bill is pointed horizontally forward or slightly up; it can be slightly open or closed. The carpal joints are often raised. It may be given without sound but more often a muted version of the long call note is given. In this posture . . . a bird can face another bird, stand parallel to it or take up an intermediate position; it can even face away from the other bird.

Oblique. The neck is stretched obliquely forward and up with considerable . . . variation in the vertical plane. The carpal joints are usually raised. In this position the bird utters a loud, long drawn call with the bill wide open. In herring gulls the head is first pointed obliquely forward and slightly up in which position the usually hoarse call is given. Then the head is jerked down and one or two muffled high pitched calls are given. Finally, it is thrown up with a jerk and a series of long calls begins; with each call the head is lowered a little so that the bird ends in an almost horizontal position. This display is not directed at any specific animal.

(Tinbergen, 1959.)

A number of different criteria were used in identifying these variable but distinct patterns of behaviour:

1. While the same structures may be involved in different actions, the complete set of body parts involved is distinct.

The Study of Animal Behaviour

2. When the same structures are used these take different positions or are moved in different ways; for example, the neck is in an S bend and the head jerked forward during choking while the neck is stretched and the head jerked upwards in the oblique posture.

3. The displays consist of constellations of postures and movements, which may be performed simultaneously or sequentially; in the latter case, the sequence may vary between displays.

4. The orientations of the displays differ, choking and forward being directed at specific individuals while oblique is not.

5. The displays may differ in the context in which they are shown, including aspects of the performer's own behaviour, such as vocalizations and feather erection.

Thus recognizing the actions which make up an animal's behavioural repertoire involves identifying associations between different components, computing the average form of a particular movement and assessing variability. Recognizing such spatiotemporal patterns is something the human brain is particularly good at; however, it is becoming increasingly common to use formal analytical techniques, often run on a computer, to help with this procedure.

(a) *Associations between simultaneously occurring components*
Table 2.1 summarizes the various things that a flamingo (*Phœnicopterus chilensis*) can do with different parts of its body, based on interactions between these birds (Davies, 1978). If, of all the possible combinations of states of these seven characteristics, only a few ever occur, these combinations represent natural units of behaviour. In order to determine whether this is the case and, if so, what the observed combinations are, 100 frames of film were selected at random and the state of the seven characteristics determined for one bird. The associations between the states were measured in order to find out whether they varied independently. The process starts with the 100 frames and selects the pair of frames from all possible pairwise combinations which is most similar on the basis of the seven features of interest. Selection is based on a measure of the information lost as a result of each possible combination, calculation of which is outlined very simply in the table. Intuitively, if two frames have identical scores for all seven features, then no information is lost by replacing either by the average configuration of the two. This process is repeated using the 99 frames left after the two most similar have been replaced by their average value until all the items are combined, a measure of the information lost as a result is calculated at each stage. A selected set of results is also presented in the table; this shows that the amount of information lost by successively combining the most similar frames is small until seven clusters are reduced to six and again when four are reduced to three. Taking this latter reduction for the purposes of illustration, this means that the various features recorded in this study do not vary independently; in fact there

Table 2.1 Using statistics to identify regular associations between movements and postures of different parts of the body (after Davis, 1978).

The seven components of body posture:
1. The angle of the bill to the horizontal
2. The angle of the neck to the horizontal
3. The angle of the line joining neck and leg to horizontal
4. Whether neck is straight or bent
5. Angle of body to horizontal
6. Whether walking or standing still
7. Distance from neck to tip of bill

Calculation of similarity between frames
Loss of information resulting from combining frame A with frame B for a single attribute
  $=$ (score in frame A−average score for frames A+B)^2
  $+$ (score for frame B−average score for frames A+B)^2
Summing over all 7 attributes gives the total amount of information lost

Information lost by combining frames in the final stages of the analysis

Number of clusters	Information lost
8	6.08
7	12.25
6	8.30
5	4.19
4	12.74
3	46.16

are four major combinations or postures. The average value of the seven features for each of the four groups provides the 'typical configuration' of each posture; while one of these had been identified previously by unaided observation, the cluster analysis was needed to show up the distinction between the remaining three. A discriminant function analysis was carried out to find which combination of the seven variables best separates the frames belonging to the four categories and to provide a compound score which can be used to assign any new observation to one of them. Thus, as well as identifying and describing four distinct patterns of behaviour used by the flamingos, the analysis provides an objective criterion on which to base subsequent decisions about what a flamingo is doing (Davies, 1978).

(b) *Sequential or temporal associations between components*
In the previous example, behavioural units were identified on the basis of simultaneously occurring static postures. However, the regularity of apparently fixed action patterns may lie in sequential relationships between postures and movements. Thus, referring back to Fig. 2.1(b), two types of display are recognized on the basis of head and dewlap movements. In type A dewlap extension occurs before the first head bob, while in type B, dewlap extension

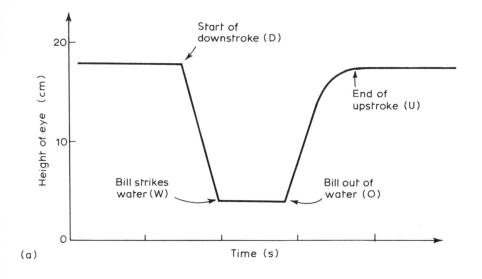

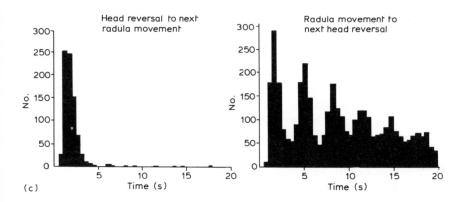

Figure 2.2 Using statistics to identify regular sequential and temporal associations between behavioural components (after Dawkins and Dawkins, 1974). (a) A typical record of eye height in chicks during a period of drinking; (b) the frequency with which each component is followed by each of the others; (c) frequency distributions of intervals between radula movements and head reversals in a feeding snail (from Dawkins, 1974).

starts later in the head bob series. In this case the regular sequential associations can be identified by visual examination of the behaviour profiles but where these are less obvious, statistical analysis of sequential associations may be necessary. The head movements of chicks drinking from a water surface were studied by recording the height of the eye above the ground in successive frames of film. A computer was programmed to recognize four features of this movement which are sufficiently regular to be used as landmarks; these are shown in Fig. 2.2 which also shows the frequency with which each landmark is followed by each of the others. As might be expected, in the majority of cases the chick lowers its head to the water surface, puts it into the water, takes it out and raises its head again. However, down–up transitions ('aborted downstrokes') and up–water transitions (the head obviously is lowered, but this is too gradual for the computer to recognize) do occur. Thus formal sequence analysis has demonstrated the regular sequence in which the components of drinking are performed but has also identified some rare but interesting departures from this (Dawkins and Dawkins, 1973).

Often, however, it is not just the sequences in which the components occur which is typical of a given unit of behaviour but the details of their timing. Again, while such regularly occurring features may be easily identified by eye (the type A display of *Anolis limnifrons* is characterized by a first head bob one second after dewlap extension, followed by bobs at approximately half second intervals thereafter), some sort of statistical analysis may be necessary. The feeding movements of the snail *Lymnea stagnalis* consist of two main components, radula movements which occur regularly at intervals of about three seconds and side-to-side movements of the head. The possibility of a regular temporal relationship between these two movements was tested by measuring the interval between each head reversal and the next radula scrape, and vice versa. Figure 2.2 shows the frequency distributions of these two intervals; head reversal and radula scrapes never coincide but a head reversal is likely to be followed by a radula scrape at an interval of 2–3 seconds. Radula movement is likely to be followed by a head reversal after an interval of 1, 5, 8 or 12 seconds. This analysis has thus identified regularly occurring temporal relationships between the two components of the feeding movement (Dawkins, 1974).

Where an action consists of a series of regularly repeated movements, such as the head bobbing in lizard displays, it is not always obvious when one action ends and another begins. For example, chicks tend to direct a series of pecks at a particular object; perhaps the whole series rather than each individual peck is the true unit of behaviour (Machlis, 1977). This possibility was investigated by measuring all the intervals between pecks from a film of chicks exposed to objects of different colours. For each interval category, the percentages of all the recorded intervals which were of that length or shorter were calculated to produce what is called a survivorship curve; Fig. 2.3 shows this curve, with the percentages expressed as logarithms. If the length of the intervals between pecks

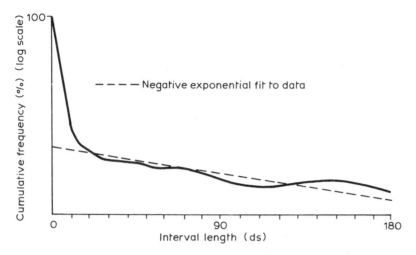

Figure 2.3 Using statistics to identify bouts of behaviour; log survivorship curve for intervals between pecks in chicks (after Machlis, 1977).

depends on a random process, the survivorship curve will be a negative exponential and the log survivorship curve a straight line. If pecks do come in clearly defined clumps, there should be more short intervals than expected on a random model and a small but regular number of long intervals. This would show up as a kink in the log survivorship curve and the interval at which this kink occurs would be an objective criterion for deciding when one bout ends and the next begins. Although the figure clearly rules out a random model for the generation of interpeck intervals, there is no sharp discontinuity in the curve. A computer program was used to find combinations of curves which best fit the observed one. Briefly, the intervals are such that the chick appears to be in one of three states: a pecking state during which pecks are given rapidly, at short intervals (producing the bouts which are obvious to the unaided eye), a between-bouts state in which the chick is paying attention to the stimuli but not actually pecking (this is the cause of the medium length intervals) and finally the non-pecking state during which it ignores the stimuli and does other things (this is the cause of the long intervals between pecks). This analysis produced an objective criterion for identifying a bout of pecking; this is a series of pecks whose modal interval is three seconds and with 94% of the intervals of less than ten seconds.

(c) *Regularity of context*
Another aspect of the displays described by Tinbergen, sometimes incorporated into their definition, is the context in which these are shown. The importance of this kind of parameter in identifying items of behaviour is reflected in the existence of categories such as 'courtship fanning' in the repertoire of sticklebacks. This kind of contextual information was analysed systematically to identify

groups of postures in black headed gulls. Four aspects of body posture were considered, including the angle of the body axis and the position of the wings, each of which could be in one of 3–5 states. Of the 240 possible combinations of characters and states, only 49 were observed to occur at all frequently, indicating that the components do not vary independently. In an attempt to determine whether any postures were sufficiently similar to be combined into a single category, a number of other characteristics of each posture were recorded; these included their frequency of occurrence and how this changed with the time of year and whether the postures were accompanied by vocalizations and followed by attack. Similarities between pairs of postures were determined from the correlation between their scores on 17 such properties; on the basis of these correlations, groups of related postures were identified using a hierarchical, agglomerative, single linkage cluster analysis. Such an analysis starts with the 49

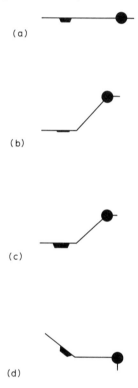

(a)

(b)

(c)

(d)

Figure 2.4 Using statistics to investigate the context in which behaviour patterns are shown (after Van Rhijn, 1981). Commonest form of posture, (a) forward: cluster contains 4 postures, tail, body and bill horizontal, carpals raised to varying extents; (b) oblique in: cluster contains 1 posture, carpals close to body; (c) oblique out: cluster contains 6 postures, carpals raised to varying extents, tail usually but not always horizontal; (d) choking: cluster contains 15 postures, tail always up and bill down, carpals usually but not always raised.

22   *The Study of Animal Behaviour*

separate postures, selects a high level of similarity and groups together any postures with that degree of similarity (hence it is agglomerative). Similarity at this level with any member of an existing group is sufficient qualification for membership of that group (hence single linkage). The analysis then selects a lower level of similarity and repeats the clustering procedure on the groups defined at the previous level as well as the remaining ungrouped postures. The process is repeated until all the postures have been combined (hence the term hierarchical). The analysis recognized 17 groups of postures, four of which resemble Tinbergen's categories discussed above and are described in Fig. 2.4. A distinction is made between two versions of the oblique posture (with and without raised carpals); while choking occurs in a number of different forms, these are all similar in terms of the context in which they occur. The analysis has therefore allowed a reduction in the number of behavioural items which require further analysis and has also pinpointed a difference in the way the birds use the two forms of oblique display (Van Rhijn, 1981). However, it should be noted that a different technique of cluster analysis might have produced different results.

(d) *Independent support for the identity of a unit of behaviour*
Although for the purposes of description and measurement it is not necessary to know how the different features of a recognizable behaviour pattern are controlled, if these do depend on a single mechanism, this provides independent evidence that it does represent a discrete unit of behaviour. For example, electrical stimulation of a single group of neurones in the CNS reliably produces the complete escape movements of the sea slug *Tritonia* (Willow *et al.*, 1973). Alternatively, if a unit of behaviour recognized by any of the criteria described above turns out to be controlled by a single genetic mechanism, this too can be used to confirm the original identification. For example, in hybrid male doves, the head lowered phase of the bow–coo display is typical of the species of one parent while the head raised phase resembles that of the other parent (Davies, 1970). Thus if control by a single genetic mechanism is a valid criterion for identifying units of behaviour, then bow–cooing represents two units rather than one.

(e) *Variability of units of behaviour*
Tinbergen incorporated a verbal indication of variability into his descriptions of gull displays and recently this aspect of supposedly fixed action patterns has been analysed systematically. For example, male goldeneye ducks (*Bucephala clangula*) show two characteristic displays while swimming round the female; in 62% of all wingstretch displays the male spreads the wing on the side facing the female while in 69% of the observed head rub displays the head was rubbed on that side (Dane and Van der Kloot, 1964).

Most quantitative studies of variability of behaviour measure duration, since this is easier to record than orientation or amplitude. Male sage grouse (*Centrocerous urophasianus*) perform a complex display involving a series of inflations of the oesophageal sac accompanied by movements and sounds. To the unaided eye, the display appears highly stereotyped. The mean duration of the display in a number of male grouse, taken from films and tape recordings, is 1.7 seconds and the coefficient of variation (standard deviation/mean) is 1.1. These figures strongly confirm the impression that duration of this display is almost invariant (Wiley, 1973). By way of contrast, the duration of the signature display of the lizard *Anolis nebula* is very constant when the displays of individual males are considered separately; however, it is quite variable between males (mean = 2.2, coefficient of variation = 7.95), which may facilitate individual recognition, as its name implies (Jenssen, 1978).

(f) *Determining repertoire size*

Tinbergen described 14 displays in his comparative account of the behaviour of gulls but pointed out that these may not represent the complete repertoire of these birds. This question can be tackled systematically to produce objective criteria for deciding whether a catalogue of behaviour patterns is complete. Figure 2.5 shows the number of identified actions which were observed with different levels of frequency during a study of human children. The curve can be extrapolated to give an estimate of the number of actions whose frequency is zero

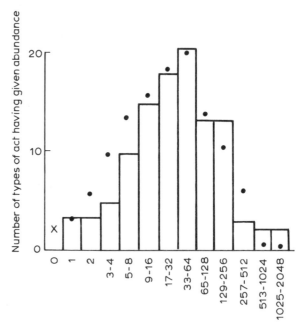

Figure 2.5 Using statistics to determine repertoire size; observed behavioural–abundance distributions for human children, expected abundances, on log normal Poisson model (•) and extrapolated value for the number of categories which exist but have not been observed (×) given this sample size (after Fagen, 1978).

The Study of Animal Behaviour

in the sample; this can then be used to correct the observed repertoire size to an estimate of the actual repertoire size. In this case, the observed repertoire of 111 categories is corrected to 113 ± 2.7 (Fagen, 1978).

2.3 Describing and measuring the relationship between an animal and its environment

The examples discussed so far have been concerned with the problem of describing and measuring the actual movements which an animal performs; however, many important questions about animal behaviour can only be answered by studies of an animal's relationship with its social or non-social environment. Thus a complete account of behaviour often involves not only what an animal is doing but where it is doing it and to whom. There is an enormous literature on this subject and it is not possible to give more than a brief description of some of the ways this question can be approached.

2.3.1 DESCRIBING THE WAY A SINGLE ANIMAL USES SPACE

The starting point of an analysis of an animal's movements is often a series of records of the position in which it was seen, trapped or located by radiotracking. How can the information in such a record be used to describe and measure the way an animal uses the space available to it? The simplest piece of information which can be obtained from such a record is the area within which the animal restricts its movements, or its home range. The easiest way to estimate both the shape and the size of an animal's home range from a series of sitings it to join up the most peripheral points. There are a number of problems with this approach which can be met by taking into account the distribution of points as well as the overall area they cover as discussed by Macdonald, Ball and Hough (1980).

Measurements of home range area, however carefully calculated, do not make the fullest use of the information in a set of sitings, since they give no indication of whether some parts of the range are used more than others. The simplest way to use such data is to represent the home range as a grid with the frequency of sitings in different sections indicated by histogram columns. Again, there are many ways of presenting, measuring and testing the significance of such information; Fig. 2.6 shows the space use pattern of two rodent species using just one of the techniques available. The home range of these species is very similar in size, but the pattern of space use within this differs, *Dipodomys agilis* males confining their movements more sharply to a small core area than do *Rattus exulans* males (Ford and Krumme, 1979).

In all these examples, the sitings are analysed regardless of the time at which they were made, although sequential sitings can provide data on the movement patterns of the animal concerned. For example, a series of radiotracking fixes were taken of individual bushbabies (*Galago senegalensis*) at ten minute intervals

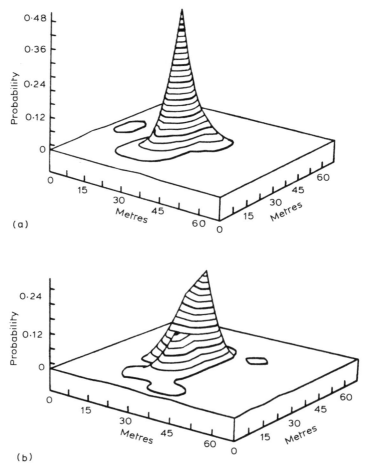

(a)

(b)

Figure 2.6 Measuring the intensity with which animals use different parts of their home range. On the basis of trapping or siting data for a number of individuals of a given category, the minimum area within which an average animal is found with different probabilities can be calculated. (a) *Dipodomys agilis* males; (b) *Rattus exulans* males; (after Ford and Krumme, 1979).

for as long as possible. The information from these fixes was used to identify the route along which the animals travelled (Bearder and Martin, 1980).

Although most studies of movement patterns are at this simple level of description, the ways in which animals move are amenable to quantitative analysis. For example, the movements of thrushes *(Turdus philomelos)* were recorded as a series of points; the distance between each successive pair of points and the angle through which the path changed at each point was measured. Figure 2.7 shows the frequency distributions of these lengths and angles; the modal move length was 21–30 cm but the distribution was skewed with longer movements overrepresented. The frequency of distribution of the path angles showed a marked peak at 0 degrees, falling off symmetrically. In order to detect any relationship between successive move lengths, these were classified into longer or shorter than the mean and the lengths of pairs of successive movements compared. There was a significant tendency for moves to occur in pairs which are of similar length; there was also a weak second-order effect, indicating that longer sequences of moves of similar length occurred. Analysis of path angles, classified into right and left handed turns, showed a significant tendency for the direction of turns to alternate, again with a weak second order effect. The birds' feeding path can therefore be described and measured as follows: it consists of a series of roughly linear moves, the distribution of whose lengths is positively skewed. Moves of similar lengths tend to occur in runs extending at least two moves back in time. The distribution of turn angles is symmetrical about the direction of the previous move; turns of opposite sign tend to alternate and this sequential dependence of turn direction extends back two or more moves. The alternating sign of the angle and the tendency to move straight ahead means that there will be little overcrossing of the path. Thus raw data in the form of a string of points in space have been condensed into a clear, quantitative description which invites functional interpretation and which can be used in further analyses (Smith, 1974).

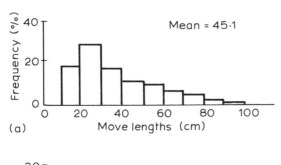

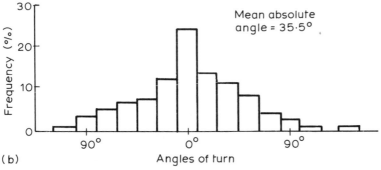

Figure 2.7 Analysing patterns of movement. Frequency distributions of move lengths and turn angles from records of feeding thrushes (after Smith, 1974). (a) Lengths; (b) angles.

(a) *Coefficients of dispersion, nearest neighbour distances and sociograms*
Some of the techniques for investigating, describing and measuring the way in
which animals use space can be applied to their relationships with conspecifics.
The raw data again often come in the form of a map of places where animals were
sited with no information about behaviour, but in this case it refers to simultaneous sitings of many animals rather than to sequential sitings of the same
animal. How can this data be used to tell us about the social interactions between
animals? The first step in answering such a question is to study the distribution of
the animals, since certain kinds of distribution are only compatible with particular
types of social organization; while a clumped distribution is not necessarily the
result of social attraction between conspecifics, it rules out the possibility of
mutual avoidance. The techniques for identifying and quantifying distribution
patterns from a series of quadrat readings or nearest neighbour distances are
basic to quantitative ecology and are described in most textbooks on the subject
(Southwood, 1978; Pielou, 1974). For example, Fig. 2.8 shows the distribution of
the polychaete *Armandia* on the sea floor, together with its index of dispersion

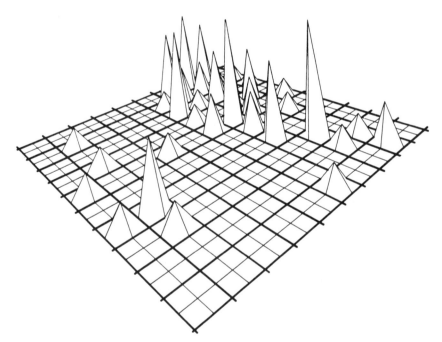

Figure 2.8 Describing distribution patterns of a number of animals. The number of
individuals of the polychaete *Armandia* in each cell of a grid of one-inch square samples;
index of dispersion (variance/mean) = 2.570 (from Jumars, Thistle and Jones, 1977).

which is significantly greater than one, indicating that this species tends to occur in fairly tight clusters. Larger scale patterning can be discovered by comparing the density of animals in one locality with that in neighbouring localities. To use the same example, the existence of clusters at a level larger than the quadrat size would show up as a tendency for the density in nearby quadrats to be similar. The observed correlation between the number of *Armandia* in diagonally adjacent cells is 0.186 ($p < 0.001$) but drops off for cells further apart, indicating that the worms live in clumps of approximately 2 quadrat lengths across (Jumars, Thistle and Jones, 1977).

Nearest neighbour distances have been used to quantify the organization of fish schools and bird flocks. These dense collections of animals have attracted a great deal of attention but answering many of the questions which have been asked about them requires some measure of the strength of the flocking or schooling response. The distribution of animals in 3-D space can be compared with a random distribution to find out whether a number of individuals are clumped. However, this is often so obviously the case that this stage of the analysis is omitted and effort is concentrated on describing and measuring the internal structure of the group. Once the positions of all the fish in a school have been found, the distribution of distances between each one and its nearest neighbour provides a measure of the compactness of the school; for a school of pilchards, 80% of all fish were between 3 and 6 cm of each other, with a mean nearest neighbour distance of 4.4 cm (Cullen, Shaw and Baldwin, 1965). The direction of the nearest neighbour gives more precise information about the way the fish pack themselves into the school. Figure 2.9 shows the frequency with which the nearest neighbour was found in a specific bearing from the reference fish in schools of minnows (*Phoxinus phoxinus*); there is a weak tendency for minnows to position themselves between 15 and 45 degrees above or below the horizontal plane of their nearest neighbour (Pitcher, 1973). These measurements were used to determine the effect of current speed on the internal structure of minnow schools; an increase in current brings the nearest neighbour bearings closer to the horizontal plane. Thus even such a complex structure as a school of fish can be described and measured.

Pielou (1974) warns against the use of frequency distributions to suggest causes of departures from randomness: 'It is a delusion to suppose that mysterious mathematical manipulations will reveal a full blown theory lurking unsuspected in a modest column of numbers'. In a behavioural context, this means that however strong the evidence that animals are clumped or dispersed, proof that this depends on social responses can only come from observation of how the animals concerned interact with each other. In some cases, this kind of information can be extracted from simultaneous records of the positions of the animals concerned. The positions in three dimensions of minnows in small schools at successive time intervals were used to determine the degree to which a change in speech or direction by one fish affected that of another. This involved

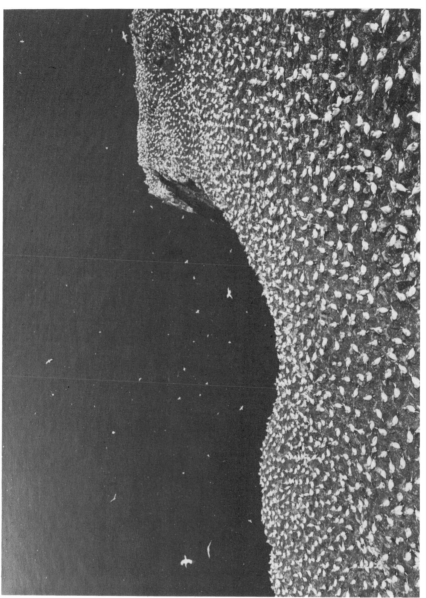

Plate 1 Non-random spacing in animals; a colony of breeding gannets.

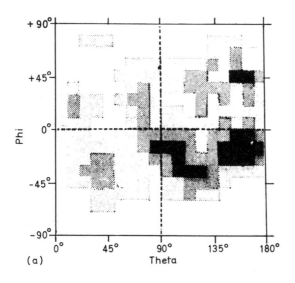

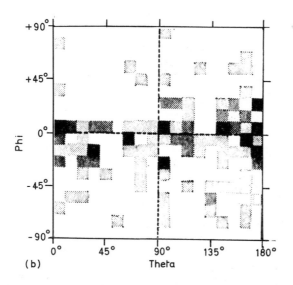

Figure 2.9 Describing and measuring the internal structure of fish schools; the frequency with which a minnow's nearest neighbour is situated at different horizontal (theta) and vertical (phi) bearings at different current speeds. The more frequently occurring bearings have heavier shading (after Pitcher, 1973). (a) Slow current; (b) fast current.

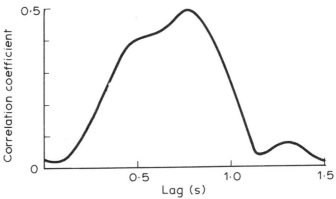

Figure 2.10 Describing and measuring interactions between individuals within a social group; correlations between the speed of movement of two minnows at time lags of 0–1.5 seconds (after Partridge, 1980a).

calculating correlations between their speed and direction of movement at different time lags. Figure 2.10 shows that a fish in a pair responded to a change in velocity of its companion by matching with a lag of less than one second (Partridge, 1980a). Thus by extending the precise measurement of position of a number of fish to a series of fixes, social interactions can be identified and measured.

Such studies tend to treat all animals as interchangeable and techniques are needed which identify and quantify associations between particular animals, whether these are identified merely by age or sex or are recognized individually. Information about social structure can be gained from records of associations between particular individuals regardless of what they are actually doing. There are various ways of analysing and presenting such data; one of the simplest is the sociogram in which individuals or categories of animal are represented by circles joined by lines whose thickness provides a rough guide to the frequency of associations between the animals involved. Figure 2.11(a) summarizes observations on how often various bushbabies were seen together and indicates that this species tends to occur in social groups consisting of a male, a number of females and an assorted collection of young (Bearder and Martin, 1980).

Where large numbers of recognized individuals are involved, this method of analysis and presentation of data becomes difficult to use and it is commonly

---

Figure 2.11 Describing and measuring association between specific individuals. (a) A sociogram summarizing the pattern of association between 31 bushbabies; position of circles represents centre of sleeping area, thickness of lines represents strength of association (from Bearder and Martin, 1980); (b) a dendrogram summarizing the patterns of association during feeding between 61 jackdaws, produced by a single linkage cluster analysis. Horizontal axis represents level of similarity. Bracketed groups represent birds which nest close together (from Röell, 1978).

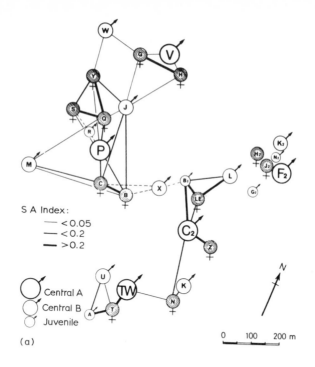

S A Index:
— <0.05
— <0.2
— >0.2

◯→ Central A
◯→ Central B
◯ Juvenile

N

0   100   200 m

(a)

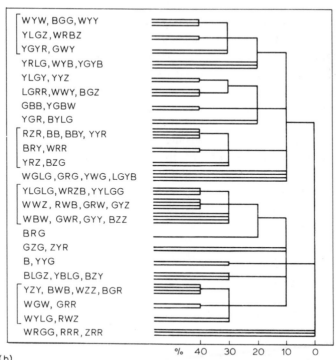

WYW, BGG, WYY
YLGZ, WRBZ
YGYR, GWY
YRLG, WYB, YGYB
YLGY, YYZ
LGRR, WWY, BGZ
GBB, YGBW
YGR, BYLG
RZR, BB, BBY, YYR
BRY, WRR
YRZ, BZG
WGLG, GRG, YWG, LGYB
YLGLG, WRZB, YYLGG
WWZ, RWB, GRW, GYZ
WBW, GWR, GYY, BZZ
BRG
GZG, ZYR
B, YYG
BLGZ, YBLG, BZY
YZY, BWB, WZZ, BGR
WGW, GRR
WYLG, RWZ
WRGG, RRR, ZRR

% 40   30   20   10   0

(b)

replaced by multivariate analysis, usually a cluster analysis of some kind (Morgan *et al.*, 1976). For example, in order to test the possibility that jackdaws which are known to nest at the same site also tend to forage together, the frequency with which each of a number of marked male birds was observed feeding with each of the other birds in the group was recorded. An index of association between any pair of birds was calculated from the number of times that pair was seen feeding together (expressed as a percentage of the product of the total number of observations of each one, since some jackdaws were seen more often than others). Groups of birds which regularly associate together were identified by a hierarchical, agglomerative, single linkage cluster analysis, the results of which are shown in Fig. 2.11(b) in the form of a dendrogram for groupings obtained at the 10%, 20%, 30% and 40% levels of association. The clusters identified at the 30% level link jackdaws which are known to nest together. Thus 'The data do suggest that the total resident population in the study area can be divided into a number of more-or-less separate social units or colonies composed of resident birds which nest and feed together.' (Röell, 1978).

Data on the spatial proximity of individuals can thus provide considerable information about social organization, but a complete picture requires a knowledge of what the animals are doing to each other.

(b) *Sequence analysis and information theory*

Speculation about social interactions is usually based on the fact that performance of a particular action by one animal is regularly followed by a specific change in the behaviour of a second one. The data often take the form of a list of the actions performed by each animal; the way in which such a behavioural record can be analysed to elucidate the interaction between the two animals concerned is best illustrated with an example. Dane and Van der Kloot (1964) filmed the behaviour of small groups of goldeneye ducks to establish, among other things, whether particular actions performed by male ducks triggered specific responses on the part of the females. If this is the case, transitions between the male and female behaviour patterns concerned should be relatively common in the behavioural record. If there is no sequential relationship between particular male and female actions, the frequency of a given transition will depend only on how common the two actions are. A chi-squared test is frequently used to test the significance of departures from expected frequencies, although the assumptions on which this test depends are not often met (Slater, 1973). The observed transitions in the goldeneye sequences differ from those expected on a random model indicating that the male's behaviour does influence subsequent responses of the female. For example, 22% of headthrow-bowsprits by the male are followed by dip by the female. Thus what the female does is not independent of what the male does, but his influence takes the form of a shift in probability rather than an all-or-nothing effect.

A sequence in which the probability of observing a given event at a particular point is dependent on the immediately preceding event is called a first order Markov process; where there is no dependence, the sequence is a zero order Markov process and where probability depends on the two previous events, it is a second order process and so on. There are many examples in the literature where the behaviour of two animals has been analysed as a Markov process and in which first order and higher dependencies have been identified. However, while this approach allows sequential regularities in the behaviour of two animals to be identified, these are rarely clearcut and do not provide a concise description or a method of measuring the interactions between the animals concerned. In 1965, Altmann applied the technique of Information Theory, developed for the study of man-made communication systems, to interactions between rhesus monkeys living in small social groups. A simple-minded account of the technique will be given here; Losey (1978) and Steinberg (1977) provide more detailed discussions.

If there are just two actions (P and Q) in an animal's behavioural repertoire, only one yes–no question (Is it behaviour P?) is needed to determine exactly what the animal did on a particular occasion. In information terminology, one bit of information is provided by a statement of what behaviour was performed. Obviously, no animal has such a limited range of behaviour; if an animal has a repertoire of ten equally common acts, the amount of information gained, or uncertainty removed, by finding out what it did (usually called H_{max}) equals $\log_2(10)$ bits. This figure is larger than the amount of information gained by finding out which of two actions was performed; intuitively it is easier to predict correctly how the animal will behave if it can only do one of two things. The significance of the subscript max is that the information gained by finding out what was done on a given occasion only has this value if all the acts are equally probable; if this is not the case, for example if one act of the ten is much commoner than the others, less uncertainty is dispelled by finding out that it has occurred. The amount of information acquired is a function both of the size of the behavioural repertoire (which depends in part on how the behaviour is classified in the first place) and on the relative probabilities of the various acts in the repertoire (which depends in part on how these were defined). There is a close relationship between information and variability; a more variable sequence, both in terms of the number of acts involved and in the extent to which their probabilities differ, is one for which a great deal of uncertainty is reduced by a knowledge of what actually happens and which therefore has a high information content. The information content of a series (X) of observations of behaviour (the difficulty involved in predicting that precise sequence) is calculated as follows:

$$H(X) = -\sum_{i=1}^{n} p(i) \log_2 p(i)$$

where i represents the various acts in the repertoire and $p(i)$ the probability of the *i*th act, usually estimated from the relative frequency of act *i* in the complete sequence.

How can these concepts be used to identify and measure communication between animals? Given a behavioural record consisting of a series of actions by an animal A and series of following acts by an animal B, the information content of the series for each animal alone can be calculated by the formula shown above to give $H(A)$ and $H(B)$ respectively. From the transition matrix, the information contained in the whole set of pairs of successive acts ($H(A,B)$) can be calculated in a directly analogous way. The conditional uncertainty (the information present in the distribution of frequencies of acts performed by B if the preceding actions of A are known) can be calculated according to the formula:

$$H(B/A) = -\sum_{i,j} p(i,j) \log_2 p(j/i)$$

where $p(i,j)$ is the joint probability of the two act sequence $A = i, B = j$ and $p(j/i)$ is the conditional probability of $B = j$, given $A = i$.

This figure measures the average amount of uncertainty about the behaviour of animal B which remains when the preceding actions of A are known; if the behaviour of B is completely determined by what A does, then $H(B/A)$ will equal 0. The difference between $H(B)$ and $H(B/A)$ is called the transmission or $T(A,B)$ and provides a measure of the information transmitted from A to B. It ranges

Table 2.2 Identifying and measuring communication between two animals; results of an information analysis of inter-male behaviour in grasshoppers (from Steinberg and Conant, 1974).

	Actions of initiator (I) followed by those of respondent (R)		Actions of respondent followed by those of initiator
Uncertainties			
$H(I)$	2.94		3.04
$H(R)$	2.02		1.78
Conditional uncertainties			
$H(R/I)$	1.58	$H(I/R)$	2.68
Transmissions			
$T(I/R)$	0.44	$T(R/I)$	0.36
Normalized transmissions			
$t(I/R)$	0.22	$t(R/I)$	0.12
Contributions to t of specific actions			
e.g. Approach	0.163		0.024
Flick	0.025		0.091
Continues to do nothing	0.144		0.135

from 0 when the actions of the two animals are completely independent to a high positive value when B is strongly influenced by A. Since the values of $H(A)$, $H(B)$ and $H(A,B)$ are dependent on how the behavioural repertoire of the animals is originally defined, the transmission is usually expressed as a fraction of $H(B)$ to give the normalized transmission or the percentage by which uncertainty about B is reduced as a result of knowing what A does. In addition, it is possible to calculate the contribution of a particular action on the part of A to the overall normalized transmission. Table 2.2 shows the results of an information analysis of aggressive interactions between grasshoppers (*Chortophaga viridifasciata*) taking transitions between actions of the initiator and those of the respondent separately from transitions in the reverse direction. The normalized trans-missions of 0.22 and 0.12 bits respectively indicates that the animals influence each other's behaviour, and that the initiator of the fight has the stronger effect; the preceding act, Approach, makes a large contribution to this effect (Steinberg and Conant, 1974). Thus the normalized transmission provides a statistic which can be used to identify and measure the dependence of the behaviour of one animal on precisely what its partner does and thus to quantify the process of communication.

There are a number of problems in the use of transition matrices (of whatever order) to study communication, some of which can be solved by judicious use of information theory. In the first place, valid statistical analysis of the matrices requires very large sample sizes; these can be obtained by combining the data for several sets of individuals and by using long sequences. However, a different problem then arises, since the important assumption that the relationship between variables is constant for all the interactions which go into a single transition matrix (i.e. that the sequence is stationary) is very likely to be violated. Where there is reason to believe that the assumption of stationarity is not met, one course of action is to split long sequences up at appropriate points and to carry out separate analyses on the different parts. Thus in a study of aggressive interactions between female iguanas (*Iguana iguana*) Rand and Rand (1976) analysed the first act in each encounter separately from all the others. In the case of shorter sequences, and provided there is sufficient data, it is preferable to consider each transition in the sequence separately (Oden, 1977).

Schleidt (1973) has stressed the importance of temporal aspects of interaction sequences, by pointing out that the length of time an action lasts may alter its effect on the behaviour of a partner and that the nature of any such effects may vary with time. For example, Fig. 2.12(a) shows the frequency with which roosters crow in the period after a companion has done the same; the initial crow has a short-term inhibitory effect and a long-term stimulatory effect. The frequency distribution of time intervals between consecutive acts shown by male and female newts (*Triturus vulgaris*) during courtship are shown in Fig. 2.12(b). There is a very sharp increase in probability that the female will approach within half a second of a retreat display by the male. The end of a fanning bout also

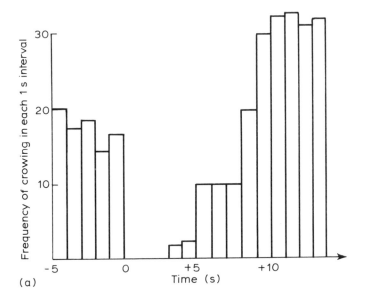

(a)

Retreat ⟶ approach   Fanning ends ⟶ approach

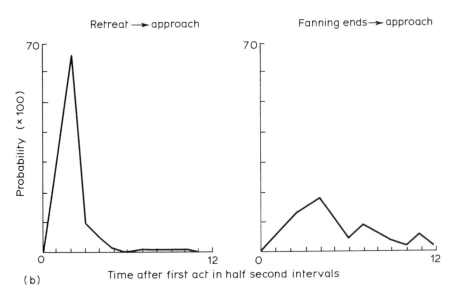

(b)   Time after first act in half second intervals

Figure 2.12 Incorporating information about time into a sequence analysis. (a) The frequency of crowing by roosters in the period following a stimulus crow (modified from Schleidt, 1973); (b) frequency distributions of time intervals between two actions of male newts (retreat and fanning ends) and a subsequent approach by a female (after Halliday, 1975).

increases the probability that the female will approach, but this effect is slower and more variable. These differences in temporal relationships imply differences in the nature of the interaction (Halliday, 1975).

Losey (1982) developed a modified information analysis to study aggressive interactions in midas cichlids (*Cichlasoma citrinellum*) using filmed records of hour-long encounters. The fights were divided into segments on the basis of behavioural landmarks (for example, the period from the initial encounter to the first withdrawal); the segments were analysed separately, thus reducing the problem of non-stationarity. Transitions were recorded between each reference act on the part of one fish and every act that its opponent performed in the preceding 6 second interval (chosen on the basis of Heiligenberg's studies of temporal patterning of behaviour in another cichlid (Heiligenberg, 1976, and see page 56). The resulting transition matrix allows for the fact that behaviour patterns differ in duration and for the fact that any effect on the behaviour of an opponent may occur after a time lag. However, detecting significant departures from randomness of a transition matrix generated in this way requires complicated simulation techniques.

It is not always possible to record the behaviour of two animals as a sequence of point events representing alternating responses; one animal may continue to show the same activity while its partner makes a series of behavioural changes. At a practical level, this problem can be solved by including a category of 'no change' in the analysis. In aggressive interactions between grasshoppers, the action 'continues to do nothing' made a large contribution to the information transmitted between the respondent and the initiator (0.135 bits in a total of 0.36, see Table 2.2), implying considerable communicative importance (Steinberg and Conant, 1974).

Using matrices of transitions between the actions of two individuals in this way assumes that all changes in behaviour on the part of one animal are the result of what its partner does; this ignores the possibility that they may be the result of some alteration within the animal itself, perhaps set in train by earlier responses of its partner. Information theory can be used to tease apart these two kinds of effect and to measure their relative importance. Van der Bercken and Cools (1980a) envisage the behaviour of each of a pair of animals as a series of states which occur at points in time, each with a given probability. The data is expressed in terms of variability rather than of information (as mentioned above, these two concepts are closely related) and an analysis of covariance used to determine the interacting effects of earlier behaviour of an animal and those of its partner on its present activities. Put simply, the analysis takes the sequence of states of each individual and calculates the amount of variability at one stage in a series that can be accounted for by what occurred in the preceding stage of the same series; this measures the extent to which each action in the sequence depends on the preceding act of the same individual and is called the auto-covariability. The extent to which performance of each act in the sequence for one animal depends

The description and measurement of behaviour   39

on the preceding act of its partner is then calculated in a similar way, to give the cross-covariability. These two processes are equivalent to carrying out separate information analyses of the within animal and between animal transition matrices. However, it is possible that a change in the behaviour of one animal is an indirect effect of the activities of its partner at an earlier point in the sequence; in order to tease apart these various, complex effects, the amount of variability in what an animal does at any given time that can be predicted from a combined knowledge of the preceding acts of the animal itself and its partner (the total sequential covariability) is calculated. If the two preceding acts are not independent (i.e. if the kind of influence described above occurs), then the total sequential covariance will deviate from the sum of the auto- and cross-covariabilities. This difference is called the interaction covariance and can be used to correct the auto- and cross-covariance terms to give estimates of the exclusive effect of the animal's own preceding action and of the preceding action of its partner. The latter provides an unambiguous statement about the communication between the animals concerned. Some details of the method are given below.

An encounter between two animals I and J is described in terms of a series of observations of the sort K_{It} indicating that animal I showed behaviour K at time t; M categories of behaviour exist. The probability of this occurrence is denoted $p(K_{It})$ and is estimated from the observed sequences.

Total individual variability (the information in the observed behaviour sequence of one animal)

$$H(I_t) = -\sum_{K=1}^{M} p(K_{It}) \log_2 p(K_{It})$$

Auto-covariability (the degree to which I's previous responses determine its behaviour)

$$T(I_t : I_{t-1}) = H(I_t) + H(I_{t-1}) - H(I_t I_{t-1})$$

where the last term represents variability in the distribution of combinations of preceding and following actions by I.

Cross-covariability (the degree to which partner's previous responses determine the behaviour of I)

$$T(I_t : J_{t-1}) = H(I_t) + H(J_{t-1}) - H(I_t J_{t-1})$$

where the last term represents variability in the distribution of combinations of preceding acts of J and following actions by I.

Total sequential covariability (the amount of correlation between I_t and both I_{t-1} and J_{t-1})

$$T(I_t:I_{t-1}J_{t-1}) = H(I_t)+H(I_{t-1}J_{t-1})-H(I_tI_{t-1}J_{t-1})$$

where the second term represents the joint variability of the simultaneous states of I and J at $t-1$ and the third term represents the variability of particular combinations of preceding acts by I and J and current act by I.

Interaction covariability (the extent to which specific combinations of previous acts by I and J determine the behaviour of I)

$$P(I_t:I_{t-1}J_{t-1}) = T(I_t:I_{t-1})+T(I_t:J_{t-1})-T(I_t:I_{t-1}J_{t-1})$$

Partial auto- and cross-covariabilities (the exclusive effects of previous acts by I or J)

$$P(I_t:I_{t-1}) = T(I_t:I_{t-1})-P(I_t:I_{t-1}J_{t-1})$$

$$P(I_t:J_{t-1}) = T(I_t:J_{t-1})-P(I_t:I_{t-1}J_{t-1})$$

The method was tested on the behaviour of small groups of java monkeys (*Macaca fascicularis*) with 49 behaviour patterns being recorded. They found a cross-covariability of 1.14, an interaction covariability of 0.34 and thus a partial cross-covariability of 0.80. Thus about 30% of the original cross-covariability is not unambiguously due to inter-individual effects and this figure gives an inflated picture of the communication in progress (Van der Bercken and Cools, 1980b).

Where it is not possible to divide what an animal does into discrete, unitary acts, a complete behavioural record requires simultaneous observations of the movement and orientation of a number of parts of the body. Arnold (1972) analysed interactions between male and female salamanders during courtship to test the suggestion that in *Plethodon jordani*, where females seem to be more successful at picking up spermatophores, sexual partners influence each other's behaviour more than do courting *Ambystoma maculatum*; in other words he is predicting a difference in the communication system of the two species. The state of 10 components or parts of the body (for example, the angle of the tail, whether the head was moving and which parts of the male's body were in contact with that of the female) were recorded for each member of the pair whenever there was any change in behaviour. The complete behavioural sequence consisted of a series of 800 such events and information theory was used to determine the extent to which the state of each component could be predicted from the state of any or all the components of the partner in the immediately preceding act. Briefly, taking the behaviour of the male by way of example, the observed uncertainty for each male component (M) was calculated as outlined above. This is expressed as a fraction of the maximum information, had all states for that component been equally probable. Still considering each component separately, the conditional uncertainty for each male component M was calculated given that a particular state had occurred in the female component F. Summing over all states of F gives the average uncertainty of M when the state of component F is known, the average amount of information transmitted from the female's F component to the male's M component can then be calculated from the difference between the absolute and the conditional uncertainty. Summing over all female components F gives the total information transmitted from the female's behaviour to a particular male component in the next act. Expressed as a proportion of the total uncertainty of the male component to give a normalized transmission, this figure ranges from 0 when the female's behaviour has no influence to a figure of greater than 1 when uncertainty about the state of a particular component in the male is reduced by a knowledge of what the female did in the previous act. The procedure is described in more detail below.

The data comprise a series of records of the state of 10 components (M and F) of body posture for males and females. Calculating the information transmitted between partners:

1. For a single male component,

$$\text{Observed uncertainty } H(m) = -\sum_i p(M)_i \log_2 p(M)_i / H_{Mmax}$$

where $p(M)_i$ represents the probability of M being in state i and where H_{Mmax} represents the uncertainty if all states are equally common

Conditional uncertainty
(a) given state j has just occurred in female component F,

$$H(M/F_j) = -p(F)_j \sum_i p(M_i/F_j) . \log_2 p(M_i/F_j)$$

where $p(F)_j$ represents the probability of F being in state j and $p(M_i/F_j)$ the probability of M being in state i given F was previously in state j
(b) summed over all states of component F,

$$H(M/F) = -\sum_j p(F)_j \sum_i p(M_i/F_j) . \log_2 p(M_i/F_j)$$

Information transmitted
(a) from any one female component

$$T(F, M) = H(M) - H(M/F)$$

(b) from all female components (normalized transmission)

$$T(\overline{F}, M) = \sum_F T(F,M)/H(M)$$

2..For all male components to give the extent to which the behaviour of the female in previous act determines the male's actions

$$T(\bar{F},\bar{M}) = \sum_{M} T(\bar{F},M)$$

Table 2.3 shows some of the results for both males and females. The means and standard errors were calculated by taking the figures for the various components as replicates, a procedure which is questionable, since if the components are influenced differentially, real effects might disappear in the averaging process. These statistics show that in neither species do the two sexes differ in the extent to which they influence each other's behaviour; however, *P. jordani* females affect their partner's subsequent behaviour more than do *A. maculatum* females.

Table 2.3

	$T(F,M)$	$T(M,F)$	Information transmitted/ spermatophore deposition
Plethodon jordani	0.568	0.608	221.53
Ambystoma maculatum	0.243	0.446	86.46

The average rate of information transfer was calculated from the product of the number of acts per minute and the number of bits transferred per act. The product of this figure and the average time to deposit one spermatophore gives the amount of information transferred per spermatophore deposition; these are also shown. For each spermatophore deposited, *P. jordani* pairs affect each other's behaviour three times as much as *A. maculatum* pairs and the original hypothesis is therefore supported.

Although in this example various parts of the body were considered separately, their movement is still represented as a series of discrete states. Fentress and others (1976) have argued that many subtle aspects of communication are missed as a result of this 'snapshot' approach. In an attempt to look for rules in social interactions between Tasmanian devils (*Sarcophilus harrisi*), Golani (1976) described movements of the whole body of the animals using the Eschol–Wasmann notation described on page 15, with the body of the partner as a frame of reference. Figure 2.13 summarizes the movements of the male's body with reference to that of the female. The female alternates between movements

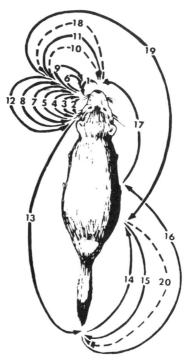

Figure 2.13 Analysing communication when discrete units of behaviour cannot be recognized; summary of the continuously changing relative positions of a male and female Tasmanian devil during social interactions. Continuous arrows represent changes in position of the contact point between male and female due to movement by the female. Broken arrows represent those due to movement by the male. Numbers represent the serial order of the shifts (from Golani, 1976).

towards and away from the male, initially maintaining the point of contact towards the front of her body then moving away. This sort of analysis can potentially identify subtle and important aspects of social interactions. However, verbal descriptions derived from them often seem trivial and, given that this technique and others described above are extremely time consuming, it seems appropriate to ask what such complex analyses have achieved.

2.4 What is the point of all this sophisticated analysis?

'A description does not acquire scientific respectability just because it has been based on something which has been counted. Highly quantified descriptions based on irrelevant parameters of a situation can be more barren than observations which are not quantified at all.' (Marler and Hamilton, 1966).

The following points can be made in favour of complexity:

1. Although Davies (1978) spent a considerable time carefully watching flamingos, his unaided eye only identified two postures while the computer picked out four. Similarly, Machlis (1974) only recognized the 'attending' phase of her chicks after the computer had drawn it to her attention. Using statistical analyses to recognize regularities can therefore save time and avoid mistakes.

2. As mentioned in Chapter 1, the kinds of questions which are being asked about behaviour are becoming more complex and answering them often requires precise measurement of behaviour. A common way to determine how intensely an animal performs a particular behaviour pattern is to set up a running total which is increased by one each time it is observed, on the assumption that if the action looks more-or-less the same on different occasions, we are seeing examples of the same kind of thing. To be confident that this is the case it is necessary to know the normal levels of variability within a category. Even if a behaviour pattern is sufficiently regular in its general form to be accepted as the same on different occasions, if its performance varies in intensity or duration, then accurate measurement of the behaviour concerned requires a record of how strongly it is shown and how long it lasts. To give an example of the implications of choosing one definition of a behavioural unit rather than another, in assessing the strength of the preference of chicks for green stimuli over yellow, the average number of pecks per bout was found to differ only slightly; on the other hand, the number of bouts of pecking directed at an object was markedly greater when this was green than when it was yellow (Machlis, 1974). Units of behaviour must therefore be identified and described as accurately and as publicly as possible; this may but does not necessarily mean that the techniques must be complicated.

3. Detailed analysis of the coordination, patterning and timing of the various components of behaviour may produce useful information in its own right, as well as providing a basis for accurate measurement. For example, the timing of head and radula movements in feeding snails suggested that a particular neuro-physiological mechanism was involved (Dawkins, 1974), the extreme stereotypy of the strut display of the sage grouse suggested hypotheses about its control and development (Wiley, 1973) and the variability of the signature bob of anole lizards supported the existing proposals about its function (Jenssen, 1978).

4. If these complex, quantitative aspects of behaviour patterns are important to the animals concerned, students of behaviour need to know about them. For example, if lizards really do use differences in display duration to identify individual conspecifics (Jenssen, 1978) or if red deer stags (*Cervus elephas*) use the rate of repetition of roars to judge the fighting ability of their opponents (p. 202) (Clutton-Brock *et al.*, 1979), then an understanding of the social interactions in these species requires that these aspects of behaviour be measured.

Easily obtainable and accurate descriptions of bird song have been available for many years in the form of sound spectrograms; sophisticated analysis of fine details of behaviour is therefore the rule rather than the exception in this field. It is no coincidence that many important advances in our understanding of the control and development of behaviour have been based on studies of bird song.

Thus while there is no virtue in complexity for its own sake, the precise quantitative analysis of specific behaviour patterns is often a necessary preliminary to useful research. In all cases, however, the success of both these exercises depends on precisely what is chosen for measurement and this can only be decided after a period of careful observation.

CHAPTER 3

The study of the causes of behavioural change

An animal's behaviour is constantly changing: it may respond to different stimuli in its environment on different occasions (a stickleback concentrates on food in the winter and on nest material early in the breeding season), it may react to different intensities of the same stimulus (a stickleback ignores all but the most gravid female early in the breeding season but courts any moving object later on), it may react to an identical stimulus with different intensities of the same response (a gravid female is courted only weakly late in the breeding season) or even with quite different responses (after the end of the breeding season, females elicit a schooling response). These changes in responsiveness are not random; the animal performs coordinated sequences of actions which often have some obviously adaptive consequence (territories are defended, nests are completed and filled, tubifex worms are located, caught and eaten) and generally carries one sequence through to completion before changing over to another. The aim of a causal study of behaviour is to understand how such coherent behavioural sequences are brought about.

3.1 What constitutes a causal explanation of behaviour?

An explanation of what causes a given pattern of behaviour to occur at a particular time must provide an economical theoretical framework which accounts for all the known facts; in other words, it should reconstruct the behavioural sequences which are known to occur. It must also allow accurate prediction of how the animal would behave in situations which have not yet been studied; comparing predicted behaviour with that of real animals is the acid test of whether the explanation is correct.

3.2 The different kinds of causal explanation

There is disagreement about the extent to which we can and should draw on physiological facts in attempting to arrive at causal explanations. According to one school of thought, since all behaviour ultimately depends on events in the nervous system, it is to physiological concepts that we should look for real explanations of what animals do. The processes within the animal which control its behaviour must eventually be studied by relating behavioural to physiological states. In the age of computers, this is often called the 'hardware' approach, since such explanations of behaviour depend on a knowledge of the actual mechanisms involved.

Others argue that, since whole animals are so very much more sophisticated than even the most elaborate neural circuit, it is philosophically unjustified and/or practically impossible to explain behavioural change in terms of physiological events. This being the case, we can only find out about the factors which control behaviour by careful observation of the actions of intact animals under a range of different conditions. Deductions can then be made about the properties of the mechanisms which control their expression. This is called the 'black box' approach, for obvious reasons, or the 'software' approach, by analogy with the fact that we can understand how a computer program works even if we know nothing about the actual mechanisms inside the machine on which it is run. Some published comments on the relative merits of hardware and software explanations of behaviour are presented below.

De Ruiter: 'If one could unravel the structure and the physiological properties of the information processing networks of the brain one could predict its behavioural output without ever observing the behaviour at all.'

Marler and Hamilton: 'Behaviour is the product of physiological processes. We may hope eventually to explain it in physiological terms.'

Pringle: 'Behavioural models should incorporate the properties of naturally occurring input and output elements if they are to be useful to the biologist. A model which merely performs computations on given information is unlikely to bear much resemblance to events in the nervous system and can contribute little to the understanding of natural animal behaviour.'

Manning: 'It is true that ultimately we shall hope to be able to explain behaviour in terms of the functioning of the basic units of the nervous system – the neurons ... (but) ... Many of the most important aspects of neural organization can be expressed only in behavioural terms. Even if we knew how every neuron operated in the performance of some pattern of behaviour, this would not remove the need for us to study it at the behavioural level also ... Trying to describe the nest building behaviour of a bird in terms of the action of individual neurons would be equivalent to trying to read a page of a book with a microscope.'

Baerends: ' ... the ethologist may use the common knowledge that the black box contains receptors and effectors, but for the rest he should refrain from all temptations to be guided in his analysis by his knowledge of physiological mechanisms ... (although) ... his findings should be formulated in such a way as to appeal to the physiologist and warrant an unbiassed approach by the latter.'

Colgan: 'As the apparently insuperable problems of executing a comprehensive analysis of behaviour using a physiological approach become more obvious, one realises that ... holistic models are the only viable options for the full investigation of ethological phenomena.'

Dawkins: ' ... the physiologists nirvana: the complete wiring diagram of the nervous system of a species, every synapse labelled as excitatory or inhibitory, presumably also a graph for each axon of nervous impulses as a function of time during the course of each behaviour pattern ... would not constitute an understanding of behaviour in any real sense at all.'

There is no right or wrong answer to the question of whether or not we should include physiological mechanisms in our explanations of short-term behavioural changes, although some combination of the two approaches seems appropriate. At the very least, software models should take sufficient account of endocrinological and neurophysiological knowledge not to violate our existing understanding of animal physiology. On the other hand, a detailed study of organization at the behavioural level should precede any physiological study since this is the only way we can identify and characterize the phenomena which require explanation in hardware terms.

3.3 Motivational models

Thus any study of the causes of behaviour requires investigation at the behavioural level even if this is merely a stepping stone on the way to a physiological explanation. Since the software approach relies heavily on the use of motivational models, it is important to discuss what this term means.

In this context, a model is a special sort of hypothesis or analogy which is used as an aid to clear thinking about a difficult subject. In using such models, we try to represent the key properties of an animal's motivational system, which we do not understand, in terms of some other, simpler concepts or mechanism which we do understand, whether this is a mathematical relationship or some mechanical or electronic device. Thus a set of hypothetical entities is postulated whose characteristics are sufficiently clearly defined to allow us to work out how they would interact. If such interactions reproduce all the known behavioural properties of the subjects, then the essential components of their motivational system may be similar to those of the model. While all motivational models conform to this broad pattern, they come in many different forms.

At its simplest, motivational modelling consists of fitting mathematical equations to data in order to provide a precise and economical summary of behaviour. For example, the distribution of lengths of intervals between pecks in chicks in Machlis's experiments (1977, and see page 20) can be fitted by three distinct Poisson processes (Fig. 3.1). At a more complex level, the relationships between seven behaviour patterns shown by breeding male cichlid fish (*Haplochromis burtoni*) can be described accurately in terms of four independent processes with levels fluctuating over periods of minutes and hours (Heiligenberg, 1976, and see page 69). As depicted here, these are descriptive models which summarize but do not explain what is going on. Explanatory motivational models also describe observed behaviour in an economical way but, in addition, attempt to explain it in terms of proposed entities within the animal. To the extent that they go beyond what is directly indicated by the data, there is a creative element in the construction of such models; the success of the modelling exercise depends on the informed insight which allows potentially useful analogies to be recognized. For example, Lorenz's psychohydraulic model of motivation (1950, and see page 6) equates the factors controlling a particular aspect of behaviour, such as fighting, with a set of components in a hydraulic system; he suggests that the animal behaves as if it contains a tank in which lipid gradually accumulates and so on.

This distinction is not completely clear, since elements of hypothesis and explanation may go into descriptive models. Thus the analysis used by

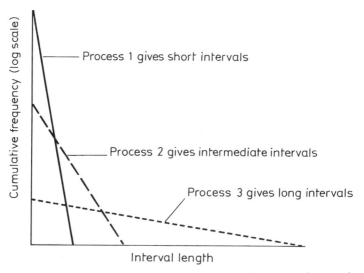

Figure 3.1 Descriptive motivational models; the intervals between pecks given by chicks can be described by 3 distinct Poisson processes, generating mainly long, medium and short intervals (after Machlis, 1977).

The Study of Animal Behaviour

Heiligenberg to identify the four factors controlling behaviour in cichlids (the method of principal components: see page 68) makes the strong assumption that the factors are independent. Machlis's suggestion that the three processes could be used to describe the distribution of pecking intervals in chicks arose from the idea that the birds can be in one of three states, a pecking state during which rapid bouts of pecks at short intervals occur, a between-bout state during which the chick is attending to the stimulus prior to initiating a bout of pecking and a not-pecking state in which other behaviour patterns occur; in other words, she has proposed an explanatory model of the decision making process of chicks.

3.3.2 GENERAL, THEORY-BASED AND SPECIFIC, DATA-BASED MODELS

A related distinction is between models such as Heiligenberg's, which are developed as a result of analysis of very precise data and refer to a single species and Lorenz's, which represent a broad theory about the organization of behaviour based on less precise observation of a wide range of animals. Lorenz is trying to provide a general theory of motivation which can be applied to different behavioural systems in a range of species; Heiligenberg's model, while it may suggest ideas which could be tested in other cases, refers to attack in one species of cichlid.

3.3.3 DETERMINISTIC AND PROBABILISTIC MODELS

In Lorenz's model, whenever a particular water level and weight coincide, the water always flows out of the reservoir; in terms of real behaviour, whenever an animal with a particular level of agression-specific energy encounters a stimulus of a certain strength, attack, and attack only, occurs. The model is therefore a deterministic one; given sufficient information about the animal and its environment we can predict precisely how it will behave. In Heiligenberg's model, on the other hand, the state of the hypothetical entities merely influence the probability of attack; under certain conditions this may be very high but it never reaches unity. Such probabilistic models are used if it is felt that an element of true randomness underlies behavioural events or when our ignorance of the variables influencing the behaviour forces us to treat in probabilistic terms a system which is ultimately deterministic.

3.4.4 ASSESSING MODELS

Once a model has been constructed, it is necessary to decide whether it provides a satisfactory explanation of the causes of behaviour; in the first place, this involves considering how well the model accounts for the known facts. The model must be internally consistent, with the proposed properties of any one component compatible with those of all others; logical deductions arising from these properties must indeed reconstruct the data on which it was based.

In addition, the model's assumptions must be compatible with knowledge in other areas; for example, Tinbergen's hierarchical model of motivation (1951, and see page 6) was phrased in terms of neural structures in which energy 'accumulated' and between which it 'flowed'. We now know that the nervous system does not work in this way and certain aspects of the model are thus inconsistent with physiological knowledge and have been rejected for that reason.

Usually the extent to which a model accounts for the data on which it is based is assessed in qualitative terms; Lorenz's model provides a mechanism whereby animals may sometimes respond to suboptimal stimuli, while Tinbergen's allows for the occurrence of apparently irrelevant, or displacement, activities. However, quantitative measures of the goodness of fit between the reconstructed behaviour and observed data can be derived; Fig. 3.2 shows how well the observed correlations between behaviour patterns in *Haplochromis* agree with those predicted by models incorporating different numbers of factors. The difference between the observed and expected values fell markedly when four rather than three factors were used but the fit was not improved greatly by incorporating any more; hence the inclusion of four slow processes in the model.

Given a number of models which correctly embody the properties of a particular motivational system, some sort of aesthetic judgement about their originality, interest and elegance may be appropriate. As an explanation of the facts about animal fighting as he presented them, Lorenz's model is simple, clever and accounts elegantly for many aspects of this behaviour. By contrast, Fig. 3.17 shows another model of the control of aggression in vertebrates which

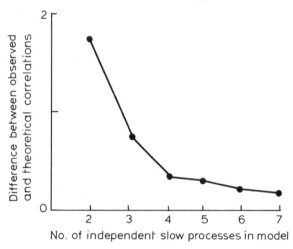

Figure 3.2 Measuring how well models reproduce known behavioural facts: the sum of the squared differences between observed time-lagged correlation curves and those calculated on the basis of various numbers of hypothetical slow processes (after Heiligenberg, 1973).

The Study of Animal Behaviour

have a red underside, red was identified as a 'sign stimulus' of key importance in triggering aggression in this species. This approach can be extended in two main directions: firstly, increasingly sophisticated dummies are used to identify in more detail the role of various components of a natural stimulus in eliciting particular behaviour patterns; secondly, the physiological basis of such selective responsiveness can be investigated by presenting stimuli and recording electrical activity in various parts of the relevant sensory pathways. To illustrate these trends, three examples will be considered in some detail.

3.4.1 PREY CATCHING IN TOADS, BEHAVIOURAL STUDIES

Ewert and his collaborators (Ewert, 1980) have carried out an intensive study of the stimuli eliciting prey catching and predator avoidance in toads, as a preliminary to physiological analysis of the sensory mechanisms involved. Toads show feeding responses (orientation, tracking and snapping) to a variety of small moving objects, mainly at ground level; anti-predator avoidance responses are shown towards larger moving objects, approaching from above. To identify the stimuli involved in eliciting these responses, simplified dummies in which different aspects of the natural stimulus were systematically manipulated were presented to the toads on a moving visual field. Figure 3.3 shows the number of orienting movements per minute made by the toads towards a variety of black stimuli moved horizontally across a white background. They responded maximally to a moving black stripe with its long axis in the direction of the movement; this is called the worm configuration. A black stripe with its long axis perpendicular to the direction of movement releases very little orientation; this is the anti-worm configuration. The response given to a black square of increasing edge length is intermediate and appears to be the result of summation of the stimulating effect of the movement of its horizontal edge and the inhibiting effect of the movement of its vertical edge. Similar results were obtained for vertically moving stimuli, for stimuli oriented at various degrees to the horizontal and moved jerkily rather than smoothly and to white objects on a black background.

These experiments show that prey catching in toads is elicited by a stimulus elongated in the direction of movement and inhibited by a stimulus which is extended in a direction perpendicular to the movement; the latter also elicits anti-predator responses. The excitatory effects on prey catching of a worm-like stimulus combine, possibly additively, with the inhibitory effects of an anti-worm stimulus when these are presented simultaneously. This selectivity is apparently common to all the toads and experiments on a related species have shown that experience of live prey is not necessary for development of the specificity of responsiveness (Ewert and Burghagen, 1979). However, the details of the stimuli which are most effective in eliciting prey catching are influenced by experience; to give just one example, repeated presentation of an effective stimulus results in

The study of the causes of behavioural change 55

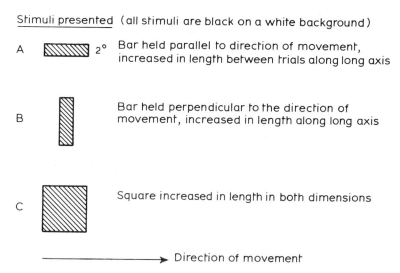

Stimuli presented (all stimuli are black on a white background)

A   2°   Bar held parallel to direction of movement, increased in length between trials along long axis

B   Bar held perpendicular to the direction of movement, increased in length along long axis

C   Square increased in length in both dimensions

⟶ Direction of movement

Strength of elicited response

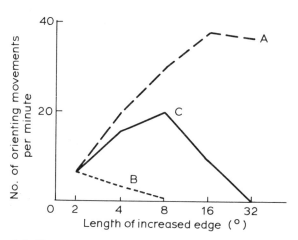

Figure 3.3 Characterizing the effects of external stimuli on behaviour; the prey catching response given by toads to various stimuli moved across their visual field (after Ewert, 1980).

habitation of the prey catching response to that particular stimulus and others similar to it (Ewert and Keul, 1978).

3.4.2 ATTACK IN *HAPLOCHROMIS BURTONI*

In the previous study, the behaviour under investigation was directed towards the dummy which elicited it, an experimental set up which favours the detection of

56   *The Study of Animal Behaviour*

immediate effects of the stimulus on behaviour directed towards the dummy itself at the expense of longer term influences and on behaviour directed towards other features of the environment. These were studied in the cichlid *Haplochromis burtoni*, a species in which breeding males defend territories against conspecific rivals, by presenting dummies to the adult males and recording their effect on the rate at which the males attacked blinded juvenile fish with which they were housed (Heiligenberg, 1976). Figure 3.4(a) shows the effect of a 30 second presentation of a dummy with a black eye bar (a colour pattern shown by breeding males of this species at least under laboratory conditions). The fish showed a sudden, dramatic increase in attack rate which had largely but not completely disappeared within a few minutes; after this the attack rate returned slowly to its prestimulus level. This change in response to the stimuli presented by the juvenile fish can be interpreted as the combined effect of two separate incremental influences of the dummy, one large and short-term and the other small and long-term. The nature of the short-term influence was investigated by comparing the relationship between the attack rate of individual fish in two

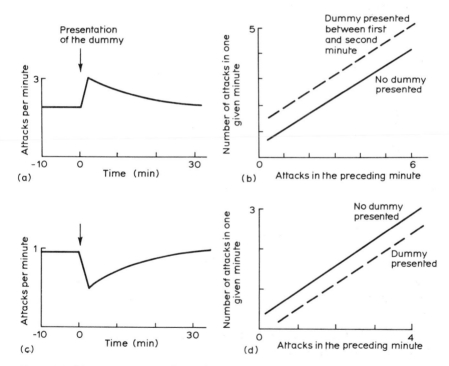

Figure 3.4 Characterizing the effects of external stimuli on behaviour; attack rates of male *Haplochromis burtoni* before and after presentation of a dummy with a black eye bar or with orange spots (from Heiligenberg, 1976). Eye bar dummy (a) attack rate versus time, (b) attack rate in successive minutes; spot dummy (c) attack rate versus time, (d) attack rate in successive minutes.

Plate 2 Behaviour of gulls at the nest; relief of an incubating kittiwake by its partner.

successive minutes taken at random with that for the minutes immediately preceding and following presentation of the dummy; the lines are parallel (see Fig. 3.4(b)), which indicates that the stimulus adds the same amount to the attack rate regardless of the initial level (though Houston and McFarland (1976) question whether measurement is of a sufficiently high level to justify this sort of conclusion). The figure also shows equivalent results for dummies with orange spots on the pelvic fins (typical of territory holders in this species). The spots produce a marked, short-term decrease in attack rate, which again is added to whatever base level exists. In dummies with eye bars and spots, the effects combine additively to determine the attack rate.

3.4.3 INCUBATION IN HERRING GULLS

Perhaps the most intensive study of the effects of external stimuli on behaviour is that of Baerends and his collaborators on incubation responses in herring gulls. Three major sources of stimuli can potentially cause these responses, namely the landmarks provided by the nest site, the nest itself and the eggs it contains, three being the normal clutch size. The relative importance of these different aspects of the environment was indicated by fairly unsystematic observation. For example, after a disturbance gulls may return to the nest site even if the nests have been removed and they subsequently prefer a strange nest in the right place to their own nest and eggs when these are placed at some nearby site. When eggs are removed from the nest, an incubating bird will rarely retrieve them if they are more than about 15 cm away. 'From all this we tentatively conclude that the nest site itself is the most important component of the nest situation, that the eggs are next and that the actual nest structure has a low releasing value for settling.' (Baerends *et al.*, 1970.)

A systematic study was carried out to investigate the importance of stimuli from the eggs in the control of incubation. Figure 3.5(a) summarizes various aspects of the behaviour of gulls on artificial clutches of different sizes. The presence of normal eggs in the nest bowl is important in eliciting settling and staying but there is apparently no difference between nests containing 1–3 eggs. Since the level of resettling is lowest for clutches of 3, as opposed to 1, 2 or 4, eggs, the natural clutch size seems to represent the optimum stimulus for maintaining uninterrupted incubation. Thus cues from the eggs are important in initiating and maintaining incubation but they do not influence all aspects of this behaviour in the same way.

Tactile, thermal and visual cues could all potentially exert an effect on incubation behaviour. Possible effects of the temperature of the eggs were investigated by placing in the nests of incubating birds artificial eggs whose temperature could be made colder or hotter than the natural 35–37 degrees. Figure 3.5(a) shows that birds are more likely to leave eggs which are hotter than normal but less likely to leave those which are colder. Resettling is not altered by cooling the eggs but is increased by heating them. Thus 'egg temperature is one of the feedback stimuli regulating incubation behaviour in herring gulls.' (Drent, Postuma and Joustra, 1970). The importance of tactile and visual stimuli in initiating and maintaining incubation is shown by the nature of the response of the birds to glass eggs as opposed to normal eggs. Since fewer birds settle on 3 glass eggs than on clutches of 1–3 normal eggs, visual cues must be important in initiating incubation. However, birds brooding glass eggs do not resettle more often and there is no difference in readiness to retrieve an egg between birds sitting on normal and glass eggs; the effect of a clutch of eggs in maintaining incubation and controlling retrieval must be mediated by tactile cues.

The stimulus parameters of the egg which elicit retrieval were investigated by placing two models on the nest rim and observing which one was retrieved first. The birds tend to collect larger eggs before smaller ones, speckled before plain, green and yellow before blue, red and grey and eggs with rounded before those with sharp corners; the last effect is a weak one (Baerends and Drent, 1982). In all these tests, the birds showed a temporary, weak tendency to retrieve first the egg in a particular position in the nest, regardless of what it looked like. This position preference was used to provide a scale against which to compare the effectiveness of different dummies. For example, the size of a dummy necessary to overcome the bird's preference for a smaller one at the preferred site can be used to put a figure on the relative importance of size in controlling retrieving. The effect of altering some other parameter such as shape or colour on the value of an egg of a particular size can then be used to determine how incubating gulls weigh up the different visual cues that an egg on the nest rim provides. Figure 3.5(b) summarizes some results of a series of experiments in which the effectiveness at eliciting retrieval was measured (by the 'titration' method outlined above) for models of various sizes after changing either the colour (from brown to green), the pattern (from speckled to plain) or the shape (from egg shape

Figure 3.5 (opposite) Characterizing the effects of external stimuli on behaviour; incubation in gulls. (a) Strength of settling, leaving and resettling responses produced by various artificially manipulated clutches (after Baerends *et al.*, 1970 and Drent, Postuma and Joustra, 1970). (b) The relative importance of colour, pattern, size and shape in determining whether an egg is retrieved from the nest rim (after Baerends, Blokzijl and Kruijt, 1982). The reference scale is determined by trading off size against position preference for models of normal eggs (brown, speckled, egg-shaped) ranging from 5/8 to 14/8 natural size. The relative values of different sized models with other features (green colour, no speckling, block shaped) are determined by finding the minimum size of a normal model retrieved before the unknown model when the latter is in the least preferred position. The circles represent the average position of the various categories of model, the numbers in the circles represent the size of the model and the lines give the best parallel fit joining models of the same size with one altered feature. (c) The relative effectiveness of stimuli of different colours in eliciting 4 responses in gulls (simpified from Baerends and Kruijt, 1973).

Nest	Normal eggs					Glass	Cold	Normal	Hot
contents	0	1	2	3	4	eggs	eggs	eggs	eggs
Percentage of birds settling	60 < 98		97	98		>23			
Percentage of sitting birds leaving	72 > 8		3	6.8	3	14	4	<21<	66
Resettling bouts per hour		14.5 10.8 > 4.0		> 1.08< 12.2		2.66	2.96	2.61 < 18.30	

< > represent direction of significant differences.

(a)

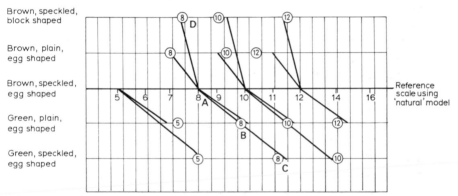

Brown, speckled, block shaped

Brown, plain, egg shaped

Brown, speckled, egg shaped

Green, plain, egg shaped

Green, speckled, egg shaped

Reference scale using 'natural' model

(b) Value of model as retrieval-eliciting stimulus

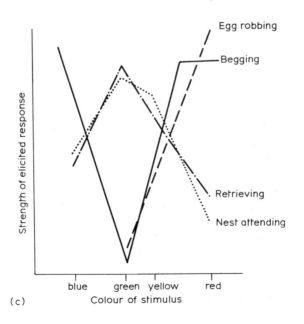

(c)

Colour of stimulus

to block shape). Various combinations of visual stimuli elicit retrieval but the effects of altering the different features are not equally important. Thus changes in size and colour have a strong effect on the probability of retrieval (compare the horizontal positions of A and C), changes in speckling less so (compare B and C) and changes in shape very little (compare A and D). The figure also shows a number of sets of parallel lines drawn between the standard model and the various altered models at different points in the size range. The points representing the mean positions of each dummy type lie approximately on these lines. This means that the effect of changing shape, colour or pattern is the same regardless of the size of the model. Similar results were obtained when colour, shape and pattern were manipulated systematically. Thus 'the information processing mechanism involved ... computes the value of each feature distinguished independently of the value of other features...'. The data are not sufficiently precise to determine whether the effects of the different parameters combine additively or according to some more complex rule (Baerends, Blokzijl and Kruijt, 1982).

Gulls do other things to eggs besides incubating them, for example they may eat them. Figure 3.5(c) shows the relative sensitivity of these birds to stimuli of different colours when they are showing different responses to eggs. The effect of colour is not the same in these different cases, which would suggest that selective responsiveness is the result of separate, possibly central releasing mechanisms specific to the different responses. However, since there is a negative correlation between the curves, the effect of colour in eliciting different responses may depend on a single mechanism, possibly part of the visual pathways, which acts on retrieving and eating eggs in opposite ways (Baerends and Kruijt, 1973).

3.4.4 PREY CATCHING IN TOADS; PHYSIOLOGICAL STUDIES

A great deal of research has been aimed at determining the neurophysiological basis of selective responsiveness identified at the behavioural level. The kind of techniques which have been used and some representative results can be illustrated by Ewert's study of the prey–enemy discrimination of toads. The visual system of the toad has been thoroughly described at the anatomical level; axons from the retinal ganglion cells project to the thalamic pre-tectal region of the contralateral side of the brain from which fibres pass to the optic tectum. Extracellular recordings were made of the activity of single cells in these three regions when various stimuli were placed in the visual field of immobilized but conscious toads. In this way it was possible to identify the nature of the stimuli which influence the firing rate of particular cells in the visual pathway. If these correspond to those which release prey catching in intact toads, the units concerned may provide the physiological mechanism whereby the behavioural specificity is attained (see page 55).

The retinal ganglion cells have circular receptive fields with central excitatory and peripheral inhibitory regions. Different types of ganglion cell have receptive fields of different diameter but all respond maximally to moving objects. One type of cell in the thalamic pre-tectal region (TP1) has a more or less circular receptive field with a diameter of about 46 degrees which is activated by relatively large, dark moving objects on a light background with no directional sensitivity. Figure 3.6(a) shows how the activity of these cells is influenced by the worm and anti-worm bars used in Ewert's behavioural studies. The activity of TP1 cells does not change when a square stimulus is elongated in the direction of movement but increases when the stimulus is elongated perpendicular to the direction of movement (the anti-worm stimulus).

In the optic tectum, two broad classes of cells were detected; both have approximately circular receptive fields about 27 degrees in diameter which are sensitive to moving objects. T1 cells show no change in firing rate when the stimulus is expanded in a direction perpendicular to the direction of movement but an increased firing rate when the stimulus is expanded in the opposite direction. T2 cells show increased activity to worms but decreased activity to anti-worms.

There are clear similarities between the stimuli which activate these various cells and those which control prey catching and predator avoidance. In order to clarify the prey–enemy discrimination and to study more systematically the relationship between behavioural selectivity and neural activity, a number of correlations were calculated. In the first place, for both the behavioural and the physiological results, the shape of the curves relating strength of response to stimulus length when this was extended in the worm and the anti-worm direction were compared for the three cell types by Pearson's waveform correlation (Fig. 3.6(b)). For cell type T2 only, the response curve for worm and anti-worm are negatively correlated. In addition, for each cell type and for worm and anti-worm separately, the curve relating stimulus length to firing rate was compared to that relating stimulus length to behaviour using the same statistic. Again, for cell type T2 only, the physiological response curve is positively correlated with the curve relating prey catching to bar length, for both worm and anti-worm. In other words, 'The response specificity of the T2 neurons reflects approximately the probability that the configuration of a moving stimulus fits the category "prey" rather than "predator".' (Borchers and Ewert, 1979.)

A model of the prey–enemy recognition system in toads was developed on the basis of the assumption that increase in firing of the T1 cells on presentation of a worm-like stimulus activates the T2 cells while the increase in firing rate of the TP1 cells on presentation of an anti-worm stimulus inhibits them (Fig. 3.6(c)). Very simply, the process of discrimination begins in the retina where size, velocity and contrast of a stimulus are determined by the extent to which it activates the different kinds of ganglion cell. The TP1 and T1 neurons act as form filters, detecting the presence of features typical of anti-worms and worms respectively. Interaction between these two filters via their effect on the T2 cells allows a distinction to be made between a stimulus signalling prey and one signalling predator. If elongation in the direction of movement outweighs that per-pendicular to it, the firing rate of the T2 cells increases, the stimulus is categorized as prey and the mechanisms of orientation activated. On the other hand, if elongation in the perpendicular direction exceeds a certain amount the firing rate of the T2 cells is reduced, the stimulus is categorized as unsuitable for food, prey catching is inhibited and predator avoidance facilitated. This idea is supported by the fact that the firing rate of certain cells in the optic tectum is reduced by electrical stimulation in the thalamic pretectum and that lesion of the same area results in a complete lack of discrimination of the prey catching response (Ewert, 1980).

3.4.5 THE ROLE OF EXTERNAL STIMULI IN THE CONTROL OF BEHAVIOUR

1. External stimuli can exert long term motivating effects as well as short term releasing effects (as in the case of the cichlid's eye bar).

2. Various aspects of the natural stimulus, in a number of modalities, may contribute to its influence on behaviour (tactile and thermal cues influence resettling, while size, colour, shape and pattern influence retrieval of eggs by herring gulls). These may be subtle, configurational stimuli (toads orient towards a bar lying in the direction of movement but avoid one perpendicular to it).

3. The behavioural effects of different aspects of the natural stimulus apparently act independently but some aspects of the natural stimulus are of greater importance than others (size outweighs colour, which outweighs shape for retrieving gulls). The parameters which have the greatest effects on behaviour tend to correspond to the important features of the natural stimulus (worms are flat and low but, to a toad, striking snakes are upright and high).

4. In some cases, there is an optimal strength of stimulus above and below which the response is less marked (thus 2 and 4 eggs are less effective than 3 in maintaining incubation in gulls).

5. Selective responsiveness may be a product of sensory mechanisms which are common to a number of different aspects of behaviour rather than to a response-specific releasing mechanism (the effect of colour on strength of various activities in gulls follows one of two, negatively correlated curves).

Figure 3.6 (opposite) Investigating the physiological basis of selective responsiveness; analysis and interpretation of the electrical activity recorded in single cells of the visual system of toads when presented with various moving stimuli. (a) Firing rate of 3 cell types in response to worm and anti-worm bars (stimuli A and B in Fig. 3.3; after Ewert, 1980); (b) Pearson wave form correlations between physiological response to worm and anti-worm bars and between overt behavioural effects and physiological responses for three cell types (after Borchers and Ewert, 1979); (c) highly simplified version of Ewert's model of the physiological basis of prey–enemy recognition in toads (after Ewert, 1980).

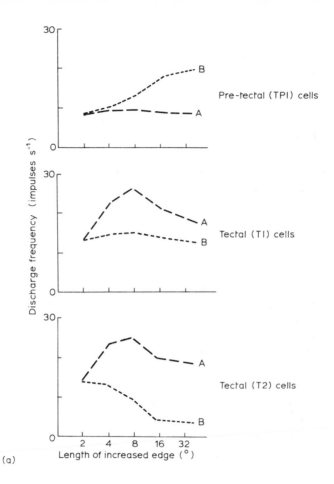

(a)

(b)

Cell type	Worm/ anti-worm	Behaviour/physiology	
		Worm	Anti-worm
TP_1	0.8	0.9	−0.9
T_1	0.6	0.8	0.0
T_2	−0.6	0.7	0.9

(c)

6. In many cases, response selectivity is the result of a series of information processing steps occurring as neurons converge at different points in the sensory pathway; these gradually extract the pertinent features of the natural stimulus (prey–predator discrimination in toads involves cells in the retina, the thalamus and the tectum).

7. While many examples of selective responsiveness develop in the absence of exposure to the natural stimulus, individual experience is not without effect (the orientation response in toads habituates to stimuli which are presented repeatedly).

Thus the ethological picture of one or a few sign stimuli playing a key role in eliciting particular responses has stood up well to more intensive study. On the other hand the concept of the innate, response–specific releasing mechanism has largely outlived its usefulness. Experience does often influence how animals respond to stimuli and therefore the term 'innate' is not appropriate, releasing is only one of the ways in which external stimuli control behaviour and the mechanism whereby the selectiveness for a particular response comes about may be a result of the physiology of sensory pathways common to a number of behaviour patterns.

3.5 Studying internal influences on behaviour

This section considers how the properties of the motivating factors within an animal can be deduced from a complete, accurate account of an animal's behaviour.

3.5.1 IDENTIFYING GROUPS OF CAUSALLY RELATED ACTS

(a) *Coincidence in time*

If two behaviour patterns are controlled by the same internal factor, their rates of occurrence will correlate when different samples are compared, whether these come from different sexes, different individuals or different time periods; both acts will occur frequently in samples taken when the internal factor is at a high level but infrequently when its level is low. Thus one indication that behaviour patterns may be causally related is the existence of correlations between some measure of their strength, while lack of correlation or weak correlation suggests that at least some of their causal factors are distinct. This source of evidence on the nature of the internal factors controlling behaviour requires measurement of the strength of various activities. This is not as easy as it sounds (Houston and McFarland, 1976); to simplify a complex issue, it is possible to determine whether an animal does more of a particular behaviour at one time than another but our interpretation of the size of this difference depends on how the behaviour is defined and on the rules (usually quite unknown) whereby internal state is translated into behaviour in the animal concerned. Ideally, such measurements should be treated as ordinal rather than interval.

Figure 3.7 shows the number of minutes of interruptive behaviour (resettling, building and preening) observed in gulls incubating single eggs in a 90 minute period after a disturbance. There is a clear and significant decrease, followed by an increase, in the time spent in interruptive activities over this period; since there has been no systematic change in environmental conditions, something inside the birds must have changed. The three activities which make up the category interruptive behaviour all show a similar pattern of change with time. On the arguments outlined above, these three actions share a common causal factor whose level falls and then rises again over 90 minutes. The curves are not perfectly parallel, building increasing in occurrence more markedly than re-settling and preening in the last 30 minutes. It could therefore be argued that while these three activities share some common internal factors, their causal mechanisms are not identical (Baerends *et al.*, 1970). However, if the different levels of each behaviour are measured on an ordinal scale as advocated by Houston and McFarland, the correlation between them is perfect.

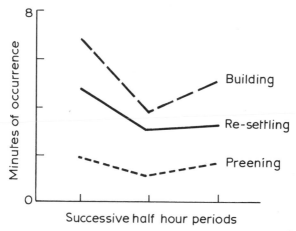

Figure 3.7 Using correlations to identify related behaviour patterns; the time spent by incubating gulls in 3 different activities in the three half-hour periods following a disturbance (after Baerends *et al.*, 1970).

In a study of the factors controlling courtship in newts, Halliday (1976) observed and measured the responses of males to a standard female for 5 minutes on 40 successive days. A breeding male newt eventually responds to the approach of a female by performing what is called a retreat display, during which he frequently whips his tail towards the female. Following the retreat display the male creeps slowly away from the female, stops, quivers and, if the female touches his tail, deposits a spermatophore and pushes her back onto it with his tail; he may then return to the female and recommence the retreat display. The number of completed sexual sequences in the five minute period decreased across the 40 days; this behavioural variability was used to investigate the causal relationships between the actions described above. Eight measures of behaviour for each completed sequence were used: duration of retreat display, number of whip displays, number of whips per 100 seconds (whip rate), number of turns back, number of quiver sequences, number of pushes back, seconds elapsing from last creep to spermatophore deposition and seconds elapsing from spermatophore deposition to next display.

Correlations between these measures as they varied over the 40 days were calculated, giving a total of 28 figures. To help in interpreting these, a principal components analysis was carried out. This is a technique whereby the information contained in a set of multivariate observations can be condensed and described economically with minimum loss of significant information. In this case, the eight scores for each courtship sequence can be summarized in a single point in eight dimensional space, the axes of which represent the original behavioural variables; the whole data matrix for one male then forms a cloud of 40 points in this space. The relative positions of these points can be expressed equally well by any set of axes in the space and the analysis provides a new set of axes (or components) according to two simple rules: each successive axis must account for as much as possible of the variation in the data (it must provide the closest possible fit to the cloud of points, passing along its longest axis) and the set of axes must all be at right angles with each other, or orthogonal. If, as is often the case, the first few components account for a large proportion of the variation in the original data, these can provide an adequate description of the important differences between the samples. In addition to setting up these new axes, the analysis describes each of them in terms of a set of loadings which reflect its correlation with the eight original variables; in geometrical terms, these pinpoint the position in space of the new axis with reference to the original ones. Behaviour patterns which are positively correlated with each other have high loadings on the same component, those which are negatively correlated have loadings in opposite directions on the same component, while uncorrelated variables load on different components. The loadings for the components which account for sizeable proportions of the original variance thus provide a concise summary of the relationships between all the original variables. Finally, by taking projections of the original data points onto the main components, the analysis provides a set of compound scores for each sexual sequence which tell us all we need to know about it.

Figure 3.8 presents the loadings for the eight behavioural measures for one male on the first component, which accounted for 46% of the total variance (as opposed to 14% for the second). One score, whip rate, is positively loaded on this component, with all the others loading in the opposite direction. This means that at least seven of the eight variables are mutually correlated and therefore may be controlled by the same factor within the newt. This interpretation depends on our

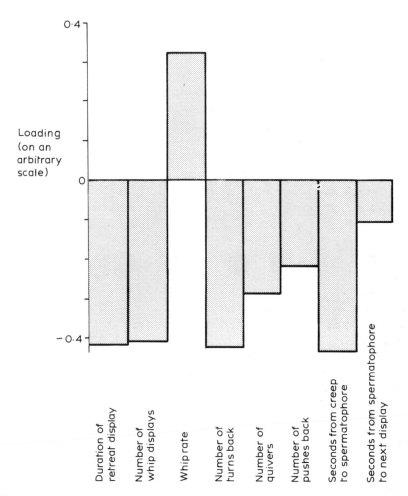

Figure 3.8 Using multivariate analysis to summarize the frequency correlations between a number of behaviour patterns; loadings on the first component emerging from a Principal Component Analysis of the courtship behaviour of newts (after Halliday, 1976).

being confident that the correlation coefficients on which the analysis is based are the result of common internal causes. Whip rate is known to be positively correlated and the other scores to be negatively correlated with the number of spermatophores a male will deposit; the common causal factor for these correlations may therefore be identified as a reflection of the male's sexual potential or 'libido' (Halliday, 1976).

To give an example on a finer time scale, Heiligenberg (1976) observed the reactions of undisturbed breeding male cichlid fish towards blinded juveniles, recording in each second whether or not each of seven behaviour patterns occurred; these were feeding, digging, attacking, courting, approaching, chafing

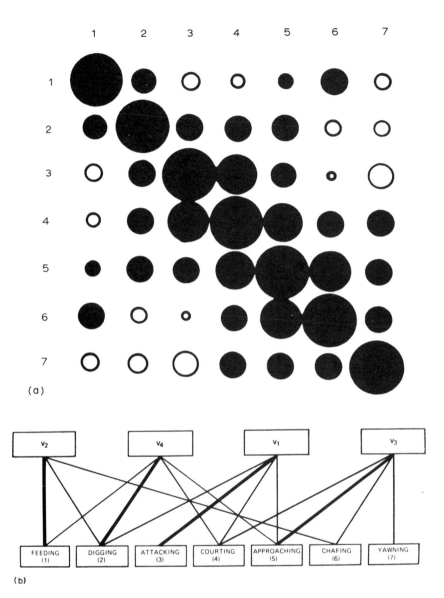

Figure 3.9 Using multivariate analysis to summarize frequency correlations between a number of behaviour patterns; the results of a factor analysis on the behaviour of male cichlids (from Heiligenberg, 1976). (a) Correlations between frequency per hour of seven behaviour patterns; the diameters of the circles represent absolute values of correlation coefficients, open circles represent negative and closed circles represent positive values respectively. (b) Summary of the main loadings of the first four factors v_1-v_4, identified as basic slow processes within the animal controlling behaviour; the thickness of the line that connects process and behaviour is proportional to the magnitude of the influence of the process on that behaviour.

and yawning. In order to characterize the internal factors responsible for the marked long-term changes in behaviour which occurred in these constant conditions he calculated the correlations between the number of observations per minute of each action and that of each other action; these are shown in Fig. 3.9(a). Three groups of mutually correlated actions can be identified by eye but these relationships were analysed more systematically using a factor analysis. This is a modification of principal components analysis in which the main components are rotated to new positions so that the variance of the loadings for the seven variables on any one component (or factor as they are now called) and the variance of the loadings on all the factors for any one behaviour is as high as possible, while retaining orthogonality. In this way, the differences in structure between the factors are emphasized to increase the chance that biologically meaningful dimensions will be identified, if these do indeed exist. The variability in the original data can be described accurately and economically in terms of the first four factors (see page 52) whose structures are shown in Fig. 3.9(b). In contrast to the previous example of newt courtship, the factors do not correspond to distinct functional systems; nevertheless, the analysis has identified groups of activities which may share, at least in part, the same causal factors within the fish.

(b) *Sequential relationships between behaviour patterns*
The different actions that an animal performs rarely occur in a random order but tend to show sequential patterning. According to one line of reasoning, behaviour patterns which have similar internal causes will tend to occur at adjacent points in a behavioural sequence at times when these causal factors are strong. Alternatively, it can be argued that if actions are so similar in their causal background as to be interchangeable, it is unlikely that they will occur in sequence.

Baerends (1970) used the sequential relationships between different behaviour patterns to investigate the control of behaviour in incubating herring gulls (Fig. 3.10(a)). The number of times each of the 16 actions was preceded by each of the other 15 was observed and the frequency of each type of transition that would be expected if there were no sequential dependencies was calculated from the observed frequency of each behaviour pattern as the preceding or following act (the row and column totals) and the total number of all transitions (the grand total). The two sets of figures were then used to determine the differences between observed and expected frequency for each transition. The similarity between any two of the 16 actions in terms of their position in the behaviour sequence was assessed by calculating rank order correlation co-efficients between these deviations; actions which have a similar pattern of probability of being preceded by each of the other 15 are positively correlated. Figure 3.10(b) summarizes the significant correlations; these are highly complex and a factor analysis was used to condense the information in this table into a form in which it can more readily be interpreted. Figure 3.10(c) also summarizes the loadings of each behaviour pattern on the first three factors (which together account for 70% of the total variance in the original data). There are two distinct groups of behaviour patterns which are similar in terms of the sequences in which they occur. One of these comprises re-settle, peck, pick up, sideways building; the other consists of trimming, head shaking, shaking, scratching, yawning, looking around and looking down. The actions in these two groups load in opposite directions on factor II; this suggests either that they are controlled by two antagonistic causal factors or that a single causal factor influences them in opposite ways.

A study of higher-order sequential dependencies can also throw light on the internal organization of behaviour. Groups of related actions involving either the front or the back of the body were identified in grooming flies (*Calliphora erythrocephala*) on the basis of their sequential relationships by a method similar to that used by Baerends. The transitions between these groups were investigated, to test the possibility that the details of within group transitions were independent of prior transitions in a different group; this is part of a more general model of motivation which will be discussed below (page 79). While there are significant sequential dependencies for acts within a group, this is not the case for transitions between groups; the suggestion does therefore seem to be correct, although the sample size is very small (Dawkins and Dawkins, 1976).

(c) *Temporal relationships between behaviour patterns*
In addition to using frequency correlations in different time periods and sequential dependencies to elucidate the relationship between preening, nest building and resettling in incubating gulls, Baerends analysed the temporal relationships between these three activities; for example, Fig. 3.11 shows the percentage of gulls which showed either preening or nest building in the fifteen one minute time units preceding and following a resettling bout. Resettling is regularly preceded by an increase in the frequency of both preening and nest-building but only the latter shows an increase in frequency after the resettling bout. This sort of data provides powerful information about the precise motivational relationships between these three activities.

'The fact that the occurrence of re-settling is foreshadowed by a rise in preening and building, whereas only building shows a high level afterwards, indicates a basic difference between preening and building in their relations to resettling. Preening shares with resettling only the situation of an imminent

---

Figure 3.10 (opposite) Using sequential relationships to identify groups of related behaviour patterns in incubating gulls (from Baerends *et al.*, 1970). (a) The actions recorded in the analysis; (b) correlations between pairs of acts in the relative frequencies with which they were preceded by each of the other 15 acts; (c) the loadings for each action on the first 3 factors (axes I, II and III). The 16 actions are represented by straight lines whose angles are inversely proportional to the correlations between them; those with high loadings on a particular factor have small angles with that axis.

72   *The Study of Animal Behaviour*

1. Sitting on nest
2. Looking down while sitting on nest
3. Re-settling
4. Pecking at nest material
5. Picking up nest material
6. Sideways nest-building
7. Yawning
8. Mandibulating
9. Head-shaking
10. Shaking
11. Trimming
12. Scratching
13. Looking down while not on nest
14. Looking around while standing on nest
15. Looking around while standing elsewhere
16. Walking and flying

(a)

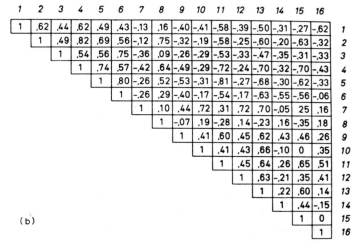

	1	2	3	4	5	6	7	8	9	10	11	12	13	14	15	16	
1	1	.62	.44	.62	.49	.43	-.13	.16	-.40	-.41	-.58	-.39	-.50	-.31	-.27	-.62	1
2		1	.49	.82	.69	.56	-.12	.75	-.32	-.19	-.58	-.25	-.60	-.20	-.63	-.32	2
3			1	.54	.56	.75	-.36	.09	-.26	-.29	-.53	-.33	-.47	-.35	-.31	-.33	3
4				1	.74	.57	-.42	.64	-.49	-.29	-.72	-.24	-.70	-.32	-.70	-.43	4
5					1	.80	-.26	.52	-.53	-.31	-.81	-.27	-.68	-.30	-.62	-.33	5
6						1	-.26	.29	-.40	-.17	-.54	-.17	-.63	-.55	-.56	-.06	6
7							1	.10	.44	.72	.31	.72	.70	-.05	25	.16	7
8								1	-.07	.19	-.28	.14	-.23	.16	-.35	.18	8
9									1	.41	.60	.45	.62	.43	.46	.26	9
10										1	.41	.43	.66	-.10	0	.35	10
11											1	.45	.64	.26	.65	.51	11
12												1	.63	-.21	.35	.41	12
13													1	.22	.60	.14	13
14														1	.44	-.15	14
15															1	0	15
16																1	16

(b)

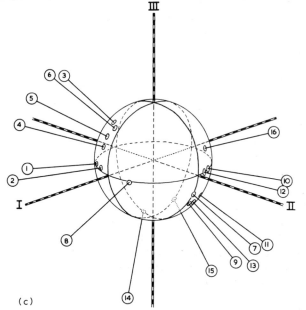

(c)

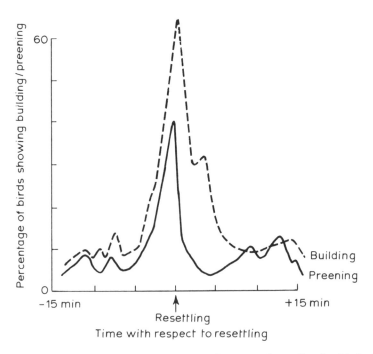

Figure 3.11 Using temporal relationships to identify groups of causally related behaviour patterns; the occurrence of preening and building in the 15 minutes preceding and following a re-settling bout in incubating gulls (after Baerends *et al.*, 1970).

interruption of incubation, whereas building shows a much stronger link with resettling, with high levels of occurrence both during the phase of interruption and the phase of resumption of incubation.' (Baerends *et al.*, 1970.)

(d) *Studying the causes of behaviour when discrete units cannot be identified*
All these techniques for identifying groups of causally related behaviour patterns depend on our being able to subdivide the behaviour of the animals concerned into clearcut, mutually exclusive units, involving the whole body. Where this is not the case, working out the rules determining how an animal puts together its behaviour has to start with an investigation of the coordination between different parts of the body. This could be done by identifying correlations between continuous variables such as limb angle or body height; however, software studies of the control of behaviour in the absence of discrete units is easier if regularly identified landmarks in the movements can be identified. For example, the movement of an animal's leg can be condensed into a record of when it was on and off the substrate. Figure 3.12 shows for each pair of legs of a freely walking crayfish (*Astacus leptodactylus*) the proportion of all the steps in a sequence for which it was in contact with the ground at a given time (after reducing all steps to a standard length and using the fifth leg as a reference). The three legs are raised in

a regular sequence from front to back and lifting a given leg appears to be suppressed until the one behind it is in a supporting position. This possibility is confirmed by the fact that loosely tying the fourth leg so that it is free to swing but cannot make contact with the ground has no effect on its own rhythm but disrupts that of the leg in front (Kidd and Barnes, in prep.).

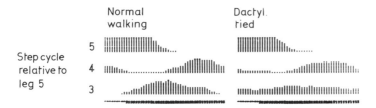

Figure 3.12 Identifying causally related movements when discrete units of behaviour cannot be recognized; the movements of the third, fourth and fifth legs on one side of a walking crayfish. The step cycle of each leg is divided into 50 equal intervals, starting when the fifth leg is lifted off the ground; the histograms represent the percentage of all steps for each leg which are off the ground as the fifth leg completes its full cycle in normal walking and with the fourth leg tied (from Kidd and Barnes, in prep.).

3.5.2 THE ROLE OF INTERNAL FACTORS IN THE CONTROL OF BEHAVIOUR

These different kinds of study make it clear that internal factors are of critical importance in determining the behaviour shown by animals and that an observed sequence of behavioural events represents a complex interaction between the immediate effect of external stimuli and the results of longer term changes within the animal. Software evidence of the kind discussed above often indicates that groups of behaviour patterns are controlled by the same internal mechanism. However, unlike the drives of classical ethological theory, these internal mechanisms may not lend themselves to functional classification (the slow processes identified in the behaviour of territorial cichlids cannot be given functional labels), do not represent simple, unitary systems (frequency correlations indicate that resettling, building and preening in gulls share common causal factors which change in level over a period of half-hours, but fine scale temporal analysis indicates that other factors differentiate their causal backgrounds) and are not specific to a single group of actions (slow process 4 in territorial cichlids is of primary importance in determining the level of attacking, but also has causal influences on courting and approaching). The classic ethological concept of specific, unitary drives controlling functionally related groups of behaviour has given way to a more complex picture of motivation.

The study of the causes of behavioural change   75

3.6 What is the nature of the mechanisms which cause behavioural change?

Having discovered from observation of intact animals that a given number of distinct internal factors must be involved in the control of behaviour, further understanding of motivation requires a knowledge of how these work and of the relationship between then and the external stimuli which elicit behaviour. In other words, models of the motivational system must be constructed.

3.6.1 A PROBABILISTIC MODEL

Figure 3.13 shows a model developed by Heiligenberg (1976) to account for changes in attack rate in cichlids: the influence of the two external stimuli was deduced directly from the result of dummy presentations; the additive interaction between their short term effects arose from the results of presenting models with both eye bar and spots; the fact that these short term effects combine additively with the base level of attack rate was deduced from comparison of successive minutes with and without presentation (page 56); finally, the existence of four internal slow processes whose effects also combine additively was suggested by the factor analysis of the frequency correlations between actions shown by undisturbed fish (page 69). The model goes beyond the data at one point, in the suggestion that the long-term increment in attack rate resulting from presentation of a dummy with an eye bar acts through an influence on the slow process 4.

Heiligenberg (1974) developed a more generally applicable model embodying his ideas about how behaviour is controlled. Briefly, a particular action, for example, attack in a cichlid fish, occurs when the level of a causal factor inside the animal crosses a threshold value for a period long enough for the action to be

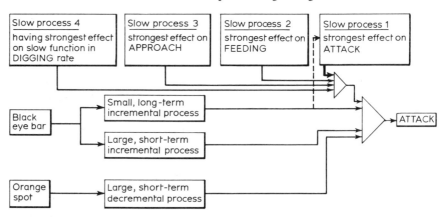

Figure 3.13 Motivational models; Heiligenberg's probabalistic model of the control of attack in *Haplochromis burtoni*. Continuous lines represent identified and dotted lines represent postulated relationships respectively (after Heiligenberg, 1976).

performed. The level of this internal factor varies under the influence of long term changes within the animal, of random events inside and outside the animal and of events in the external environment. Thus presentation of a dummy with an eye bar results in a marked increase in the base level of the factor and thus a rise in the probability that random effects will push it across the threshold; the behavioural result is an increase in attack rate. The internal variable then drops within minutes to slightly above its prestimulus level, taking several hours to return to normal; during this period, the threshold is crossed only slightly more frequently than before the stimulus occurred. A stimulus such as a dummy with an orange spot produces a marked, transient decrease in the level of the internal variable, resulting in less frequent crossing of the threshold and in a lowered attack rate. The model therefore accommodates long term as well as short term influences and both inhibitory and excitatory effects of external stimuli on behaviour. Although it is discussed here in the context of attack in cichlids, this (probabilistic) model could potentially be applied to a broad range of systems and species.

3.6.2 A DETERMINISTIC MODEL

Baerends (1970) constructed a model for the motivational system underlying incubation in gulls which incorporates the various results discussed above, along with a few others. The main feature of the model, which is shown in Fig. 3.14, is its hierarchical nature. At the right hand side are the 27 behaviour patterns which the birds show during incubation; groups of these are controlled by the higher level systems (incubation, settling, building, locomotion, trimming and bathing) which are activated by internal factors relevant to nesting, escape and preening and by specific stimuli such as the approach of a predator. This part of the model is based on the observation that groups of behaviour patterns covary with time and/or are similar in their sequential relations. The model departs from a strict hierarchy in that certain behavioural elements (turning and stooping), are controlled by the two separate systems (building and settling). Covariance and sequential relationships also allow identification of higher order systems controlling all nest related behaviour, escape responses and preening. The hierarchical arrangement is further complicated by the fact that interaction occurs between units at the same level, with the three major systems having mutually inhibitory effects on each other; observation indicates, for example, that the tendency to escape is lowered when the nesting impulse is strong but that incubation can be interrupted by a sufficiently strong escape-eliciting stimulus. A final departure from a simple hierarchy is a closed feedback loop (see page 80) in the top right hand corner in which information passes from lower to higher levels as well as in the opposite direction. Briefly, the bird is assumed to have some sort of internal representation, or mental picture (EC), of what stimuli the clutch should be providing with which it compares the actual sensory input it receives (FB). When input

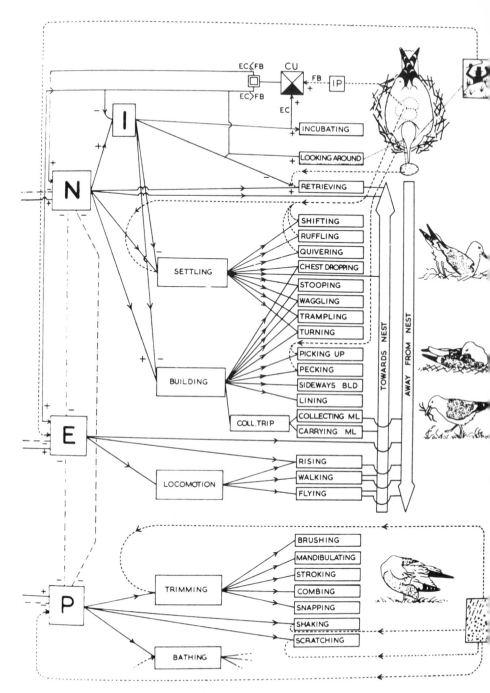

Figure 3.14 Motivational models; Baerends' deterministic model of the control of behaviour in incubating gulls. N, I, E and P represent systems controlling nesting, incubation, escape and preening (from Baerends, 1970).

from the clutch equals or exceeds this expected value, the nesting system and subsequently the incubation system are activated. When stimuli from the clutch fall below this critical value, the nesting system is inhibited and looking around activated; the causes of the discrepancy can then be identified and the discrepancy corrected by an appropriate response.

This model accounts for the observed relationships between the 27 actions and the way in which these are influenced by external stimuli, by means of a deterministic system reflecting the complex, interacting nature of the causal mechanisms controlling behaviour. It goes beyond the hard data in the relationships which it postulates between the higher centres and the proposed feedback loop based on the stimuli expected from an optimal clutch. The details of the model are obviously specific to this behavioural system; however, Baerends believes that it embodies some generally applicable behavioural principles.

3.6.3 MODELLING MOTIVATION AS A HIERARCHY OF DECISIONS

Dawkins (1976) elaborated this hierarchical picture of behavioural control in a model which sees the sequence of acts performed by an animal as the result of a series of (binary) decisions at successively finer levels (Fig. 3.15). For example, a fly may be in a state in which it is certain to groom rather than to do anything else but any part of the body may receive attention; at this point a decision at a high level (1) has been made. The fly may then change to a state in which it is certain to groom the front of its body rather than the back but whether this will involve rubbing the front legs, the middle legs with the front feet, the head or the tongue is uncertain; a decision at level 2 has been made. Further decisions in favour of middle legs, head and tongue rather than front legs (decision level 3), between head and tongue rather than middle legs (decision level 4) and finally between head grooming and tongue grooming (decision level 5) are made before the fly shows the overt behaviour of grooming its head. A single grooming bout is the result of a series of decisions at levels 2–5, with the fly switching to other behaviours within a decision group or moving back up the hierarchy and entering a different group. The model predicts sequential constraints between the acts within a particular group but not between those in different groups.

The model was put to an empirical test by analysing the sequential relationships between eight grooming movements in flies; this confirmed the existence of clusters of actions whose position in the behaviour sequence is more-or-less interchangeable and (less convincingly) demonstrated the independence of transitions between groups (Dawkins and Dawkins, 1976). A similar analysis of grooming by crickets *(Teleogryllus oceanicus)* also showed that the grooming movements form clusters of elements with similar sequential relationships, corresponding to the anterior and posterior regions of the body with significant dependencies within but not between clusters. This analysis extends the original model by postulating a random length of time spent within decision groups at

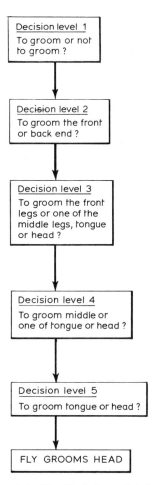

```
┌─────────────────────┐
│ Decision level 1    │
│ To groom or not     │
│ to groom ?          │
└─────────────────────┘
          │
          ▼
┌─────────────────────┐
│ Decision level 2    │
│ To groom the front  │
│ or back end ?       │
└─────────────────────┘
          │
          ▼
┌─────────────────────┐
│ Decision level 3    │
│ To groom the front  │
│ legs or one of the  │
│ middle legs, tongue │
│ or head ?           │
└─────────────────────┘
          │
          ▼
┌─────────────────────┐
│ Decision level 4    │
│ To groom middle or  │
│ one of tongue or head ? │
└─────────────────────┘
          │
          ▼
┌─────────────────────┐
│ Decision level 5    │
│ To groom tongue or head ? │
└─────────────────────┘
          │
          ▼
┌─────────────────────┐
│ FLY GROOMS HEAD     │
└─────────────────────┘
```

Figure 3.15 Motivational models: Dawkins' deterministic model of a hierarchy of decisions; the model referring to grooming in flies.

each level, a suggestion which is supported by observation of the number of acts per cluster and the number of clusters per grooming bout (Lefebvre, 1981).

3.6.4 CONTROL THEORY MODELS OF MOTIVATION

(a) *Basic concepts*
It is a matter of general observation that animals tend to keep their internal state within fairly narrow bounds; in other words, they maintain homeostasis. Constancy of internal state could be achieved by many possible mechanisms; the principles embodied in control theory, developed by engineers for analysis of self-regulating systems, represent just one of these. The key concept in this approach is that of the closed negative feedback loop. According to this principle,

the current state of a particular controlled variable is compared to a reference value, which is some stored representation of the set point at which the system is designed to maintain itself. If there is a discrepancy, mechanisms are activated which decrease and eventually remove the discrepancy, bringing the system back to the correct state; the strength with which these mechanisms are activated often depends on the size of the original discrepancy. Correction of the deviation may be by physiological means (a drop in body temperature may be corrected by an increase in metabolic rate) or by behaviour (the animal may seek out a warmer place). In the latter case, departure from an optimal internal state acts as a motivating factor for behaviour.

Motivational models based on control theory therefore draw an analogy between the mechanisms within an animal which control its behaviour and the components of a man-made self-regulating system working on the set point principle. To give a very simple example, a model might propose that an animal is designed to maintain its body temperature at a certain, optimal level. Whenever temperature falls below this level, a behavioural system is activated which causes the animal to find and stay in a warm place; heat is absorbed by the body, raising its temperature, removing the discrepancy and switching off the mechanism which activates heat-seeking behaviour.

The logic of control theory is usually made explicit in the form of a block diagram in which the functional components of the system are depicted as a series of boxes connected by arrows representing the variables in the system. Associated with each box is a transform function describing the operations it performs on the input to produce its output. Thus the verbal account of a temperature regulating mechanism given above would be represented as shown in Fig. 3.16. The first box (1), represents the precise way in which a shortfall of a given size in body

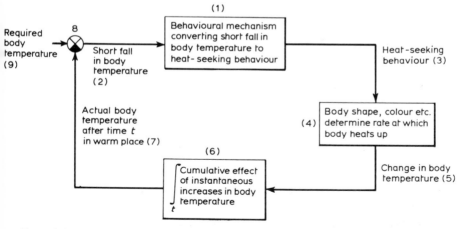

Figure 3.16 Motivational models using control theory; a block diagram representing a very simple model for the behavioural control of body heat; ⊗ represents a comparator, subtracting actual body temperature from required body temperature.

temperature (2) is converted into behaviour (3); the next box (4) represents the physiological and environmental features which determine how quickly body temperature changes (5) as a result of the heat-seeking behaviour (4). The last box (6) is an integrating component in which this rate of change is converted to the final body temperature after a certain time spent in the warm place (7). The feedback component of the model is represented in the block diagram by a comparator unit (8) in which the actual body temperature is subtracted from the required temperature (9) to determine the size of any discrepancy (2) and thus the instruction sent to the behavioural mechanism.

In many cases, control theory models do account for existing facts and make testable predictions; they thus have all the hallmarks of a good model. However, there are a number of problems in the application of control theory in this (and other) biological contexts.

(b) *Is all behaviour controlled by departure of an internal variable from a set point?*
The concept of a fixed set point on a single dimension inside the animal, deviation from which controls the start, the strength and the stopping of behaviour, is too simple for many behavioural contexts. Homeostasis may keep the body within

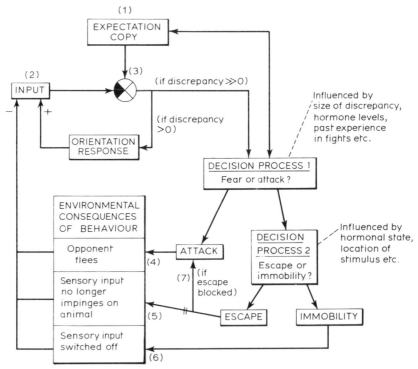

Figure 3.17 Motivational models using control theory; a simplified version of a control theory model of aggression and fear in vertebrates (Archer, 1976).

certain limits rather than at a precise set point, and these limits may vary, for example, with the seasons. More seriously, to use feeding as an example, on a fine time scale, there is no simple relationship between any single measurable deficit and changes in feeding behaviour. It has proved necessary to make a distinction between primary motivation which is a response to an obvious deficit and secondary motivation, as when a satiated animal eats appetizing food. This distinction is an acknowledgement of the fact that the tendency to feed is influenced by many factors; a drop in blood glucose level may be one but other nutrients, external stimuli, social status and past experience also play a part.

A set point or reference value may refer not to the level of some internal factor but to an expectation of what the state of the environment should be. For example, Fig. 3.17 shows the main features of a model of the motivation of aggression and fear in vertebrates in which an internal representation, expectation copy or neuronal model of the environment based on experience (1) is compared (3) with the actual environment in which the animal finds itself (2). Any discrepancy between these, whether this results from the presence of a conspecific rival or the sensation of pain, activates behavioural systems which alter the level of the discrepancy. Small discrepancies activate orientation towards the relevant stimuli; larger ones activate decision process 1, which determines whether attack or fear will be shown, depending on the size of the discrepancy, hormone levels, past experience etc. If this process decides in favour of fear, decision process 2 determines whether the animal will flee or freeze, depending on the nature of the stimulus producing the discrepancy and the state of the animal. Whatever the response, the discrepancy is corrected, by driving off (4) or escape from (5) its source or by cutting off (6) all input from the environment. If escape is activated but blocked, the attack system is triggered (7), thus allowing for the so-called cornered rat behaviour. This model, which is based on general observations of a range of vertebrate species, fails to account for some of the fine details of animal fights; for example, it does not explain precisely the sequence of actions during a fight nor does it accommodate the fact that fear and aggression can be activated simultaneously in some species. However, it does provide a much needed unifying framework in terms of which many facts about aggression can be interpreted (Archer, 1976).

(c) *Is strength of response proportional to the size of the discrepancy?*
Nor is the strength of a response necessarily proportional to the size of the deficit which activates it. Figure 3.18(a) shows a model of the control of feeding in rats in which feeding starts when the rate at which energy enters the blood stream falls below a critical value (Toates and Booth, 1974). Most of the model concerns the time course of feeding and digestion and thus the rate at which energy enters the blood following a meal and how this interacts with energy release from the fat stores. The lower box embodies the hypothesis about how the net rate of energy change activates behaviour; very simply, when this reaches a critical threshold

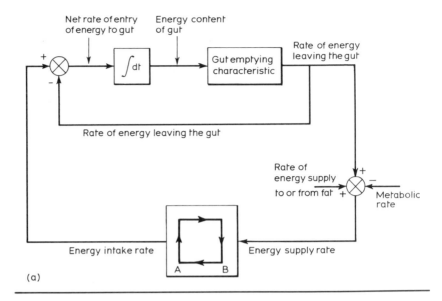

Figure showing block diagram with labels:
Net rate of entry of energy to gut
Energy content of gut
Rate of energy leaving the gut
∫ dt
Gut emptying characteristic
Rate of energy leaving the gut
Rate of energy supply to or from fat
Metabolic rate
Energy intake rate
Energy supply rate
A B
(a)

	Dark phase		Light phase	
	Real rat	Model rat	Real rat	Model rat
Total intake (g/12 h)	17.3 ± 3.4	13.3 ± 1.6	5.1 ± 1.3	6.4 ± 0.9
Size of meal (g)	3.1 ± 2.2	2.1 ± 0.4	1.6 ± 1.2	2.2 ± 0.9
Meal–meal interval (min)	160	100 ± 15	218	282 ± 72
Correlation between meal size and post-meal interval	0.84	0.76	0.65	0.98

(b)

Figure 3.18 Motivational models using control theory; (a) a model for the control of feeding in rats (from Toates, 1980); (b) feeding measures predicted by model and those observed in feeding rats *(Rattus norvegicus)* (mean ± standard error).

(*A*) feeding starts at a fixed speed, as a result the rate at which energy enters the blood increases until it reaches a second threshold (*B*) when feeding stops. The rate of energy intake gradually falls to *A* again, feeding starts up at the same, fixed speed, and so on. Figure 3.18(b) shows the values of a number of behavioural measures predicted from this model together with observed values. Although the predicted values depend heavily on assumptions about the physiology of the system, the fit is good; this indicates that the model, in which behaviour occurs at a constant rate independent of the size of the deficit, accurately reflects the properties of this motivational system.

(d) *Positive and feedforward loops*

Even if behaviour is initiated as the result of a physiological deficit, it may be brought to an end in some other way. For example, dogs with oesophageal fistulae will eventually stop feeding even though no food reaches their body; stimuli from the mouth can therefore bring feeding to an end. In addition, animals are well able to learn the physiological consequences of performing particular actions; they can thus potentially predict that a deficit will occur and avoid it. In this case, behaviour is activated not by the deficit itself but by anticipation of it, a mechanism which is called feedforward control. For example, drinking in mammals is usually activated when the body fluids (extracellular and intracellular) fall below a critical level. However, rats often drink during a meal even when this is not the case, an example of feedforward control whereby the animals anticipate the water deficit which results from feeding and drink to avoid it (Oatley and Toates, 1969).

Classic control theory assumes that the performance of the deficit-activated behaviour reduces the tendency to perform that behaviour; however, behaviour is often self-enhancing. For example, in many species rate of food intake increases during the early stages of a meal as does attack rate in a fight. In order to accommodate this kind of phenomenon, control theory models have to incorporate a positive feedback loop in which some consequence of behaviour promotes its maintenance.

Figure 3.19 shows a simplified version of a model of the control of mating in male rats. In this species, sexual interactions start when a female in oestrus is encountered and take the form of an accelerating series of intromissions culminating in ejaculation which is followed by a refractory period. The excitatory effects of external stimuli combine additively with a variable representing the level of internal arousal (1) to give actual arousal (A) whose level depends on the excitability of the nervous system (2). If (A) reaches a critical level (T_1) intromission occurs; stimuli received by the male as a result (3) have a positive effect on arousal level (integrated over the time spent in copulation, 4). There is thus a positive feedback loop whereby performance of intromission increases the level of A and thus the probability that further intromission will occur. Finally, A crosses a second threshold (T_2) at which point ejaculation occurs; this causes a sharp decrease in arousability (5) and thus puts the rat in a refractory period. Here again, the beginning and end of behaviour are controlled by different mechanisms (external stimuli and a negative feedback loop respectively) and strength of performance is independent of the precise level of A, provided it is higher than the relevant threshold. The variable whose level determines the course of the behaviour sequence (A) does not correspond to any simple physiological factor whose level requires regulation; indeed its physiological basis is almost totally unknown. Even so, the engineering principles of positive and negative feedback have produced a model which gives an elegant explanation of many features of the sexual behaviour of rats (Toates and O'Rourke, 1978).

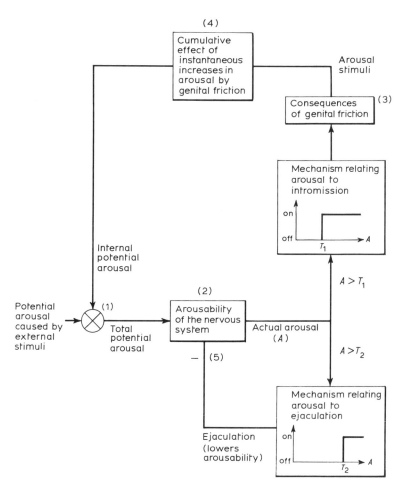

Figure 3.19 Motivational models using control theory; a model of the motivation of sexual behaviour in rats (after Toates and O'Rourke, 1978).

(e) *Control theory applied to social interactions*

The final stage of courtship in newts involves three behaviour patterns, retreat display, creep and spermatophore deposition (see above, page 67). Several spermatophores can be deposited in a single courtship bout; early on the three behaviour patterns are performed in this straightforward sequence but after several spermatophores have been deposited the male tends to alternate between retreat and creep before eventually depositing another spermatophore. In addition, the rate of display in a courtship bout is correlated with the total number of spermatophores which is eventually deposited. Figure 3.20(a) shows in a simplified form a control model developed to account for these behavioural details. The behaviour shown by male newts is assumed to be controlled by three variables;

these are the initial amount of sperm (S; this is taken as proportional to the number of spermatophores eventually deposited), the apparent sexual state of the female (F) and some index of oxygen requirements (O). At the start of a courtship sequence the male's response to the female depends on the state of a variable called 'hope'; this is the combined consequence of S and F and represents 'the male's assessment of the sexual state of the female' (McFarland and Houston,

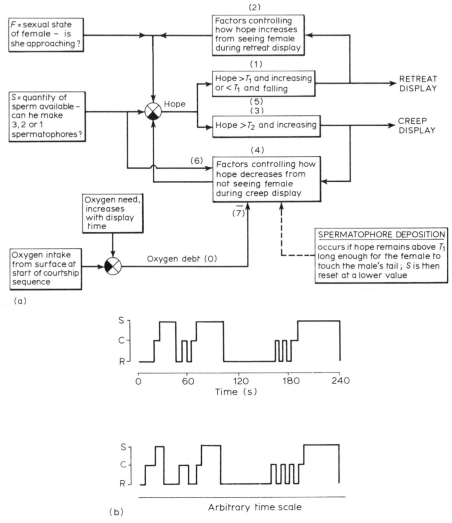

Figure 3.20 Motivational models using control theory; (a) a model to explain the sequence of actions performed by male newts during courtship (after Houston, Halliday and McFarland, 1977); (b) occurrence of retreat (R), creep (C) and spermatophore deposition (S) during a courtship sequence for real newts (Halliday, 1976) and as generated by the model (from Houston, Halliday and McFarland, 1977).

The study of the causes of behavioural change   87

1981). If hope reaches the threshold T_1 the male performs retreat display (1); in the process he is able to see the female approaching and therefore the level of hope rises through the effect of the positive feedback loop (2). When a second threshold (T_2) is reached retreat display gives way to creep (3). In order to do this, the male turns his back on the female and as a consequence information about her state is no longer available (the F input is cut off) and hope decreases (4). The male continues to perform creep as hope falls back below T_2 and until it reaches T_1, when he switches back to retreat display (5). Thus in this model, the effect of crossing the two thresholds depends on whether hope is decreasing or increasing. The rate at which hope decreases during the creep display is slow when S is high (when a male has enough sperm to deposit several spermatophores) but fast when it is low (6). In the former case tail touch by the female (which triggers spermatophore deposition and is assumed to require a fixed, minimum period of creeping) occurs before T_1 is reached and therefore courtship takes the form of a simple retreat-creep-deposition sequence. Following spermatophore deposition, S is reset at a lower value. When S is low, hope falls quickly and T_1 is reached before tail touch occurs; creep and retreat display therefore alternate. It is also assumed that during the course of a long courtship bout the oxygen need (O) increases; this has the effect of reducing the rate at which disappointment sets in during creep display (7) and therefore allows the sequence eventually to continue through to the spermatophore deposition phase (Houston, Halliday and McFarland, 1977; MacFarland and Houston, 1981).

This scheme does not have the elegant simplicity of some of the more conventional control theory models but its complexity is commensurate with that of the behaviour which it is designed to explain. It accounts cleverly for the broad sequence of events in courtship in newts and the way in which these vary with sperm availability. The results of computer simulations using this model and a summary of the behaviour of real animals are shown in the figure; the fit is impressive. The model also predicts that the form of the courtship sequence will depend on the male's oxygen balance and this is borne out. Increasing oxygen debt (by replacing air above the tank with nitrogen) decreases the length of the courtship sequence; decreasing oxygen debt by providing extra oxygen lengthens the sequence. This indicates that this model does accurately reflect the mechanism controlling this complex behaviour. Thus an expanded version of control theory can provide insight into the motivational bases of complex, non-homeostatic behaviour involving more than one animal as well as the more obvious candidates such as feeding or drinking.

3.6.5 SPACE–STATE MODELS

(a) *Outline of the model*
In the control theory models discussed above both the input to the system and the relevant consequences of behaviour are represented by one or a few variables

although the causes and effects of the behaviour concerned are known to be highly complex. In an attempt to accommodate this complexity while making use of the powerful concepts of control theory, McFarland and his collaborators (McFarland and Houston, 1981) have developed the space–state approach to motivation. The aim is to provide a theoretical framework which can explain changes in the tendency to perform particular kinds of behaviour and the ways in which these interact for a range of species and behavioural systems.

To simplify (Fig. 3.21), according to this theory, an animal's behavioural repertoire consists of a set of mutually exclusive actions which compete for the machinery whereby movement is produced. Functionally related groups of actions have specific motivational bases which depend on complex interactions between the animal's internal state and stimuli from its environment. At any particular time, the physiological state of an animal which is acclimatized to its environment can be depicted as a point in multidimensional space whose axes represent all the independent physiological variables to which the animal is subject. The origin of this *physiological space* is the optimal value for all the variables; departure from this activates physiological and behavioural mechanisms which tend to move the animal's position in space towards the origin.

Not all physiological variables are amenable to behavioural influence, either as a result of properties of the animal itself (the level of a substance which the animal does not absorb cannot be altered as a result of feeding) or because of the nature of the environment (if no water is ever available in an animal's natural environment, departure from an optimal water level can only be corrected by conservation of metabolic water); a subspace of physiological space therefore exists with axes representing only those variables whose levels can be influenced by behaviour. This space is called *motivational space* since departure from the (optimal) origin of this space is what motivates the animal to perform the particular behaviour patterns which will correct the imbalance; the similarities with classical control theory are obvious but in this case input to the control system is the summed effect of deviation on several axes, and the consequences of behaviour take the form of movement in several dimensions of motivational space. The theory obviously relates most directly to behaviour which maintains homeostasis but can potentially be applied to systems for which this is not the case.

On this scheme, one cause of the behaviour of an animal in a given environment is the set of physiological needs represented by departure from the origin of motivational space. A second determinant of behaviour is the stimuli which impinge on the animal from its environment and how these are interpreted; these can be represented in *cue space*, in which all independent, behaviourally relevant aspects of the environment have a separate axis. Using Baerends' study of egg retrieval in gulls as an example (see page 59), since the effects of the different visual stimuli provided by the egg itself appear to combine to determine the value

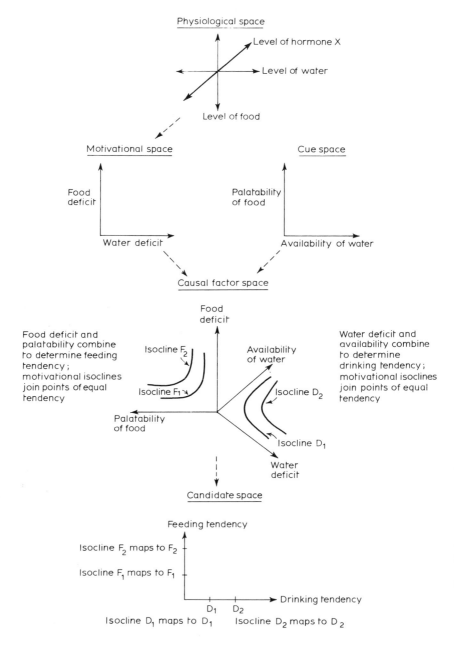

Figure 3.21 The space–state model of motivation; the relationship between the various spaces in an animal adapted to its environment with access to food and water but with no means of altering hormone X by behavioural means.

of the egg as a stimulus eliciting retrieval, this can be represented on a single axis in cue space. The effect of contextual cues such as the number and state of the eggs in the nest are independent of what the displaced egg looks like and therefore require a separate axis if cue space is to describe completely the effect that external stimuli are known to have on retrieving.

The interacting effects of external and internal events in the control of behaviour are accommodated by combining cue space (of x dimensions) and motivational space (of y dimensions) into a single *causal factor space* (of $x+y$ dimensions); the position of an animal in this space controls in a deterministic way what behaviour it shows. A particular state in this space always results in the same behaviour but different combinations of cue strength and internal imbalance can have the same behavioural product; surfaces in causal factor space which join such points are called motivational isoclines and their shape reflects the relative importance of the different causal factors which influence behaviour. When the trajectory representing an animal's changing position in causal factor space crosses such an isocline the strength of its tendency to perform the various actions in its repertoire is altered. Thus what the animal does and when is controlled by the relationships between the axes of causal factor space and by the trajectory of the animal's state through this space.

At any one time the animal's state is likely to deviate from optimum on several axes of causal factor space and therefore the animal may well be simultaneously motivated to perform a number of actions which are incompatible by definition. The way in which the animal assigns priorities in such a situation can be examined by constructing yet another space, the *candidate space* whose axes represent the strength of its tendency to perform each possible type of behaviour; the sections of this space in which each of these is shown can then be determined.

Finally, the space–state representation of motivation proposes that there is a cost to the animal in terms of an increased risk of death when it is not in its optimal state with respect to one or more of the axes of physiological space; there is also a cost associated with performing the behaviour necessary to remove the discrepancy. These can be combined by integrating the cost of the various deviations and behaviours (combined according to some rule which must be discovered or guessed at) over the time a behaviour sequence lasts. It is possible to identify the sequence of responses which minimizes this overall cost function; this is the optimal sequence in the sense that animals behaving in this way rather than any other have the greatest fitness. This optimal sequence can then be compared with what animals actually do in order to determine the extent to which behaviour has been moulded by natural selection.

Although the computations involved in applying the space–state approach make use of matrix algebra, which allows all the factors influencing a specific type of behaviour to be varied simultaneously, the theory is usually described graphically; this necessarily means restricting discussion to two or at most three dimensions. A real reduction in dimensionality is often necessary in the early stages of such an analysis in order to keep its complexity within reasonable limits; for example, animals may be given just one sort of food in which case differential intake of various nutrients is impossible and, if the animal is acquainted with the experimental set up, a single axis of motivational space controls eating. However, the approach is potentially most powerful in its ability to handle complex multivariate systems.

(b) *Applying the space–state model: time sharing and dominance boundaries*
The space–state model therefore provides a clear framework in which the complex causes of behaviour can be investigated but it is not immediately obvious how it can be applied to real animals. The most direct approach would be to identify all the axes of causal factor space, precisely what behaviour is shown by an animal whose state is at any point in the space and how this is altered as a consequence of what the animal does. A combination of physiological manipulation and behavioural observation would go some way towards achieving this; however, a number of practical and theoretical problems make this very difficult in real life, even for systems whose dimensionality has been reduced by placing the animal in a simplified environment. An easier way to find out about causal factor space is to look at the way animals allocate their time to different activities and to work back from this to the structure of causal factor space.

Although each item of behaviour is usually pursued to its adaptive endpoint, in a long bout of behaviour complete actions serving different functions may alternate; food and water deprived animals switch between bouts of feeding and drinking rather than concentrating on feeding until the food deficit is removed and then changing to drinking. Figure 3.22 gives an example from an experiment in which Barbary doves (*Streptopelia risoria*) were trained to peck keys in a Skinner box for small food and water rewards (Sibly and McCleery, 1976). In this highly simplified, constant environment only two aspects of physiological space can be altered by behaviour; therefore, providing the doves are adapted to and have learned about the environment, causal factor space has just two dimensions, namely food deficit and water deficit. The doves were deprived of food and water, placed in the box and allowed to peck at the keys until they stopped. Since the birds did not lose weight during the experiment, it was assumed that this occurred when their state was optimal with respect to nutrients and water; the total amount eaten and drunk per session thus represents the size of the original deficits. In the figure the behavioural sequence is summarized in a trajectory in two dimensional causal factor space between the point representing the original deficit (O) and the origin (S). Feeding (represented by a change in state on the horizontal axis) and drinking (which shows up as a change on the vertical axis) alternate as the animal brings its state back to the optimum.

It is possible to use such a sequence to identify the line in causal factor space which separates points for which the feeding tendency is strongest from those resulting in a stronger drinking tendency. The position and shape of this switching line provides information about the properties of causal factor space and thus about the way in which feeding and drinking are controlled. If the behaviour whose motivational tendency is strongest is always expressed, as suggested by traditional ethological theory, then an alternating sequence of feeding and drinking such as that shown in the figure arises as a result of successive competition and the switching line can be found by simply drawing a line between the points in causal factor space at which feeding and drinking occurred.

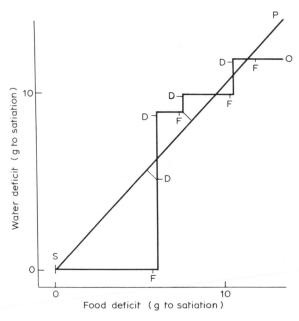

Figure 3.22 Applying the space–state model; movement in two-dimensional causal factor space in barbary doves feeding and drinking in a Skinner box. F represents points for which feeding is dominant, D represents points for which drinking is dominant, O represents the original state, S the satiation point and SP the dominance boundary (from Sibly and McCleery, 1976).

However, when the tendency to perform mutually incompatible actions is simultaneously present, it is not always the case that the one with the strongest tendency is performed; classical ethological theory recognized that animals sometimes show activities for which the motivating factors appear to be weak or absent but, as the term displacement activity implies, these were considered rather special cases. Later theory suggested that displacement activities represent behaviour which is normally inhibited by a high priority activity; this inhibition is removed when the latter is itself opposed by another strong drive. Recently, McFarland (1974) has proposed that such removal of inhibition, or disinhibition, occurs quite commonly when motivational systems interact and not just when two major tendencies are in competition. A switch from one behaviour to another may occur if the one with the strongest tendency is self-terminating and thus from time to time permits the expression of behaviour with a lower tendency; the latter thus gains overt expression without being in control of its own timing. Such a relationship between incompatible actions is called time-sharing; the behaviour whose level of motivation controls the sequence of events is called the dominant behaviour while the disinhibited behaviour is called subdominant.

Time-sharing can be identified by measuring or manipulating the causal factors for two behaviour patterns and studying the effect on the sequence of behaviour. If the timing and the length of bouts of one behaviour are independent of the level of its causal factors, this indicates that it is the sub-dominant behaviour in a sequence controlled by time-sharing. Where time-sharing is suspected, the dominant and subdominant systems can be identified by judicious interruption of the behaviour sequence. Suppose an animal which has switched from feeding to drinking is prevented from showing either behaviour; if the switch occurred as a result of competition following a rise in the causal factors for drinking to a level above those for feeding, the animal should go on drinking when the interruption comes to an end. On the other hand, if the animal returns to feeding after the interruption, the initial switch must be the result of disinhibition of drinking. If the interruption is short, the subdominant behaviour may continue, but for a period less than its normal length by an amount equal to the length of the interruption.

Food deprivation does not influence the relative timing of feeding and mating in rats and feeding tends to occur at times when sexual motivation is low; these results indicate that the alternation of these two activities is the result of time-sharing, sexual behaviour being dominant (Brown and McFarland, 1979). The most thorough investigation of this phenomenon in conditions approximating normal concerns the interaction between courtship and nest activity in breeding male sticklebacks. The fish were kept in long tanks with a nest at one end, a female at the other and a compartment in the middle in which they were kept for various intervals following a switch from one activity to another. It was shown that at any particular time the behavioural sequence was determined by one dominant behaviour; the time at which switching to the subdominant behaviour occurred was not influenced by the level of its causal factors and interruption of the one behaviour, the dominant, was always followed by performance of the same behaviour. Interruption of the other, subdominant, behaviour for short periods was followed by bouts of that behaviour shortened by an appropriate amount; a return to the dominant behaviour occurred after longer interruptions. However, nest activity was dominant on some occasions while courtship was dominant on others; independent evidence (such as the rate at which each activity was performed) indicated that the behaviour which was dominant in a particular sequence was the one with the higher level of motivation (Cohen and McFarland, 1979).

Where an animal is alternating between two activities as it moves towards a satiation point for both, it may be possible to identify a line in causal factor space on one side of which one behaviour is dominant and on the other side of which the other is dominant. The existence and position of such a line (the dominance boundary) provides information about the rules which relate current causal factor state to behaviour. To pursue the example shown in Fig. 3.22, whenever a switch in behaviour occurred, the dove was interrupted by removal of reward for a period long enough to mask subdominant behaviour in this system; if the behaviour continued, it was dominant, if not, it was subordinate. The points on the trajectory through causal factor space for which feeding and drinking are dominant are shown in the figure. It is possible to draw a straight line (SP) through the origin, leaving most feeding dominant points to one side and most drinking dominant points to the other, although the trajectory does not follow this line absolutely. The angle of this line varies between individuals but remains remarkably constant for the same individual on different occasions. Therefore the dominance boundary appears to be a real landmark in causal factor space; the fact that the boundary is straight indicates that in this experimental set up, feeding tendency is proportional to food deficit and drinking tendency to water deficit. Although this conclusion is the same as that reached by many less sophisticated theories of motivation, it is not self evident and is more valid in the present instance since it is not based on the assumption of simple competition between behaviour systems (Sibly and McCleery, 1976).

The same experimental set up was used to test the suggestion that the strength of a dove's tendency to feed is determined by the product of deficit (its deviation from the origin of an axis of motivational state) and its expectation of reward or incentive (an axis of cue space). Doves were deprived of food and water for varying lengths of time (to give a range of food and water deficits) and were trained to give different numbers of key presses to get a reward (in order to alter incentive). As in the previous experiment, the birds were allowed to feed for a time and the dominance boundary in deficit space identified by the interruption technique. The incentive value of the food rewards was then altered, with each subject as its own control and the position of the dominance boundary reassessed; a typical result is shown in Fig. 3.23. Increasing incentive makes the slope of the line steeper, indicating that feeding is dominant over drinking for a larger part of the space and therefore that feeding tendency has been increased. To identify the precise nature of this effect, the ratio of the slopes of the two lines (y) was measured for a number of different changes in incentive (measured by the ratio of the reward rates x). The following calculations demonstrate how a simple prediction ($y = x$) can be derived from the hypothesis that feeding tendency is equal to the product of deficit and incentive.

If $T_f = D_f I_f$ and $T_d = D_w I_w$, at the boundary, where feeding tendency = drinking tendency $D_f I_f = D_w I_w K$.

T_f is feeding tendency, D_f is food deficit, I_f is incentive to feed, T_d is drinking tendency, D_w is water deficit, I_w is incentive to drink and K is a constant to equate units and thus to ensure that the slope of the dominance boundary

$$= D_w D_f^{-1} = I_f I_w^{-1} K^{-1}$$

Therefore the ratio of the slopes before and after changing the food incentive from I_{f1} to I_{f2} at food deficits of D_{f1} and D_{f2} respectively while keeping the drinking incentive I_w constant

$$= \frac{D_{w1} D_{f1}^{-1}}{D_{w2} D_{f2}^{-1}} = \frac{I_{f1} I_w^{-1} K^{-1}}{I_{f2} I_w^{-1} K^{-1}}$$
$$= I_{f1}/I_{f2}$$

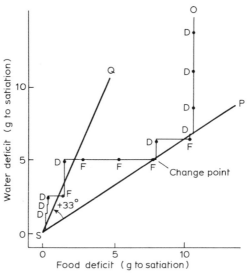

Figure 3.23 Applying the space–state model; the position of the dominance boundary in doves before and after an increase in the maximum rate at which food rewards could be obtained (from Sibly, 1975). SQ represents the dominance boundary after change of incentive, otherwise symbols are as for Fig. 3.22.

Thus if the hypothesis is correct, the ratio of the slopes of the two dominance boundaries equals the ratio of the two food incentive levels. The observed relationship between y and x confirms this prediction. Thus by using the dominance boundary as a landmark in causal factor space, it can be shown that feeding and drinking tendencies are an increasing function of both deficit and incentive and that the animal performs the one with the highest product of incentive and deficit. A considerable amount has been discovered about the way in which motivational and cue space interact and how the animal assigns priority to feeding or drinking without any direct physiological manipulation of the subjects (Sibly, 1975).

These are pioneering studies in the use of the space–state approach to motivation; however, they show that by formally defining a mathematical framework in which the complex network of influences on behaviour can be represented, phenomena which were previously oversimplified or considered too complex for study can be analysed. Thus the multiple, interacting internal and external factors which influence a given category of behaviour, the interactions between different functional systems and the causal background underlying complete behavioural sequences can potentially be identified. In addition, by defining the cost of different trajectories in causal factor space, behaviour sequences which maximize fitness can be identified; the approach therefore has important implications for the study of the adaptive significance of behaviour.

3.7 Studying the physiological bases of behavioural change

The space–state model of motivation illustrates how far the software approach can potentially go in identifying the mechanisms controlling behaviour when it takes the form of powerful theory and careful observation. At present, theory has outstripped data and while there are many ideas about how behaviour might be controlled, there are relatively few cases in which we have a completely satisfactory software explanation of behavioural change. Even where detailed motivational models are available which accurately account for the behavioural phenomena, as in the case of the courtship of newts, these explanations are sometimes considered unsatisfactory in that they lack any information about the physiological nature of their important variables; what exactly is 'hope' in a courting male newt?

As far as hardware studies of the physiological bases of behaviour are concerned, the situation is almost the reverse. Techniques for measuring and manipulating physiological parameters are continually being improved and extended. As a result there is an enormous body of data on how particular endocrinological or neurophysiological changes influence specific behaviour patterns in one species or other. On the other hand there is little in the way of a general theory to integrate these results and to explain the way whole animals behave. There are of course specific cases about which an enormous amount is known; to pick just a few, for some nematode worms something close to a complete wiring diagram of the nervous system is available and behavioural effects of alterations in specific regions have been identified (Ward, 1977); neurotransmitter-specific pathways in the vertebrate brain have been mapped and behavioural consequences of precise biochemical changes in them characterized (Meyerson and Malmnas, 1978); structural, physiological and behavioural effects of altered levels of androgens in development and in adult life have been found in many species of mammal (Johnson and Everitt, 1980), while the complex two-way interaction between hormonal state and behavioural change during the breeding cycle of ringdoves (*S. risoria*) has largely been identified (Lehrman, 1964; Cheng, 1979).

All these are important developments which must eventually be relevant to our attempts to understand what controls the complex behaviour of animals in their natural habitats. However, with some notable exceptions, the nature of the problems being studied by ethologists (using the word as a short hand for people studying the behaviour in intact animals) and physiologists and the way these are tackled and discussed are so different that useful interaction between the two disciplines is still limited. Rather than reviewing the techniques used and results

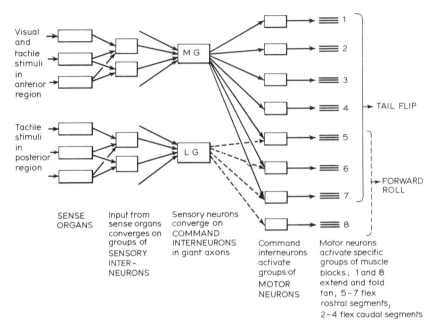

Figure 3.24 Explaining behaviour in neural terms; a simplified wiring diagram of the neural network which controls rapid escape responses in crayfish. Visual or tactile stimulation at the front of the body produces a rapid tail flick, involving flexion of all the abdominal segments and with the tail fan spread. Tactile stimulation of the rear end produces a rapid forward somersault, involving flexion of the rostral abdominal segments only and with the tail fan folded. The former response is controlled by the medial giant axons of the abdominal nerve cord (MG) which are activated by sensory interneurons receiving input from sensory receptors at the anterior of the body. The latter response is controlled by the lateral giant axons (LG) activated by sensory interneurons receiving input from sensory receptors at the posterior of the body. A further system of non-giant interneurons (not shown) mediates slower responses and the sustained tail flips of swimming. Both escape responses are inhibited when the crayfish is out of water; this change in responsiveness is mediated by a descending pathway which inhibits firing in MG and LG (after Wine and Krasne, 1982).

obtained by physiologists in their search for the mechanisms underlying behaviour, this short section on the hardware approach to behaviour will concentrate on areas where some progress has been made in integrating these two approaches.

3.7.1 PHYSIOLOGICAL EXPLANATIONS OF COMPLEX BEHAVIOUR

In a few cases, physiologists have provided detailed and satisfying explanations of behavioural change at a level which interests ethologists. For example, neuro-anatomical and neurophysiological study of the escape movements in crayfish (*Procambarus clarkii*) has identified a network of specific neurons with known properties. This provides an almost complete account of the way external stimuli bring about escape responses in these animals (Wine and Krasne, 1982) and is summarized in Fig. 3.24. At a different level of analysis, by investigating the precise behavioural effects of brain stimulation and lesion and of hormonal manipulation in songbirds, it has been possible to locate the parts of the nervous system

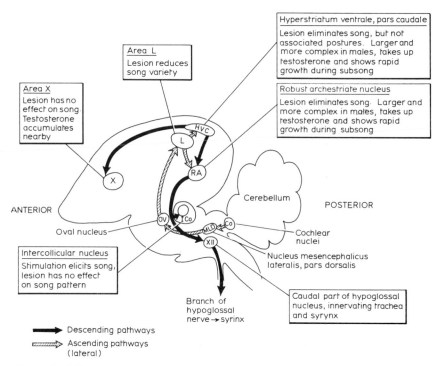

Figure 3.25 Explaining behaviour in neural terms; brain pathways which play a role in song production in canaries. ICo appears to be responsible for motivation of song system; HVC receives input from auditory processing pathways and, via its descending projections through RA and XII nucleus of the midbrain, generates the patterned movements of the syrinx which produces sound (after Nottebohm, 1980).

involved in song production, from the ear to the brain and out to the syrinx, to describe their neural architecture and to determine how they influence singing. The results are summarized in Fig. 3.25; this is far from being a complete wiring diagram of the neural system controlling birdsong, but it comes close to providing a physiological explanation of what causes birds to sing and how integrated song sequences are put together (Nottebohm, 1980).

3.7.2 ALTERATION IN BEHAVIOURAL THEORY AS A RESULT OF PHYSIOLOGICAL RESEARCH

In other cases, the results of physiological studies have caused ethologists to modify their theories. Both Tinbergen's hierarchical model and Lorenz's psychohydraulic model were rejected as satisfactory explanations for the control of behaviour on the grounds that they were incompatible with more recent information about the physiology of the nervous system. Similarly, electro-physiological studies of sensory pathways, as illustrated by Ewert's (1980) study of visual processing in toads (see page 62), showed that sensory processing takes place at a number of different levels in the nervous system, as a result of the way neurons are connected together; the same sensory pathways process stimuli eliciting different components of behaviour. In the light of these results, among others, the ethological concept of the central, reaction-specific innate releasing mechanism has been discarded.

3.7.3 IDENTIFYING FRUITFUL TOPICS FOR PHYSIOLOGICAL STUDY BY BEHAVIOURAL ANALYSIS

On the other hand, careful descriptive and analytical studies at the behavioural level can identify questions that need physiological investigation and can suggest fruitful lines of attack. Heiligenberg's observations on cichlid fish (1976) defined the precise time course of the effects of environmental stimuli and identified four independent factors inside the fish which change over periods of hours in the absence of any systematic alteration in the environment. These carefully identified properties of the behavioural system controlling attack in cichlids invite an investigation into their physiological nature; Heiligenberg suggests that sensory adaptation and hormonal change are likely candidates.

3.7.4 ETHOLOGICAL CONCEPTS AND TECHNIQUES CAN IMPROVE THE QUALITY OF PHYSIOLOGICAL RESEARCH

Ethological techniques can improve the quality of research into the physiological bases of behaviour and its relevance to real animals. Observation of free-living rats indicates that males of this species live in territories containing several females and juvenile males; other adult males are driven from the territory but outside it fighting is minimal. Koolhaas and his collaborators (Koolhaas, Schuurman and Wiepkema, 1980) have carried out a series of experiments designed to elucidate the endocrinological and neurophysiological basis of aggression in rats in which they used this behavioural information. In contrast to many physiological studies where animals are exposed to a standard opponent in just one environment, the rats were observed both in their own territory and in an unfamiliar cage and in the presence of oestrus females and subordinate males as well as other dominant males. To give just two sets of results, castration only reduced the ability of the rats to dominate a rival in the unfamiliar environment. 'The hormone appears to be particularly relevant during offensive behaviour performed in an unfamiliar environment in the presence of an obtrusive opponent, suggesting that testosterone plays a role in establishing or expanding a territory. The hormone is less important in maintaining a territory. Here experience with the environment might become the important factor.' Lesion of the posterior ventro-medial hypothalamus produced a marked increase in level of offensive behaviour in the presence of a subordinate opponent but not in the presence of a dominant male or an oestrus female. '. . . a posterior VMH lesioned animal is well capable of adapting its offensive behaviour to the type of opponent that intrudes in its territory . . . We may conclude, therefore, that the lesioned brain structure is not involved in a mechanism that allows male–female and subordinate–dominant male recognition.'

In this study, the behaviour of the rats was recorded in terms of twenty specific movements such as rear, scan, sniff and clinch. Although the sequential relationships between these actions were investigated as a preliminary to the experiments, the effect of the various manipulations on these relationships was not studied. In contrast, Veening (discussed in De Ruiter, Wiepkema and Veening, 1974) analysed sequential dependencies between eleven behaviour patterns shown by male rats in the presence of food and an oestrus female before and during electrical stimulation of the VMH. In this way, the precise behavioural effects of the manipulation could be identified (Fig. 3.26). The overall level of sexual behaviour was reduced by the stimulation, an effect which would have been detected using much cruder behavioural techniques. However, the different components of the sexual response were altered differentially and their sequential relationships were also changed, with scanning taking up a central position in the flow of behavioural events. Veening suggested that rather than simply determining the level of sexual behaviour, the brain region concerned plays a complex role in the decision making process of rats and that stimulation disrupts this process; to oversimplify, the scanning rats are simply unable to make up their mind about what to do.

These two studies involve a degree of precision in the way behaviour is elicited, quantified and analysed which is unusual in physiological studies and this precision has paid off; the results are clearcut, interesting and make sense in the light of what we know of the behaviour of rats in their natural habitats.

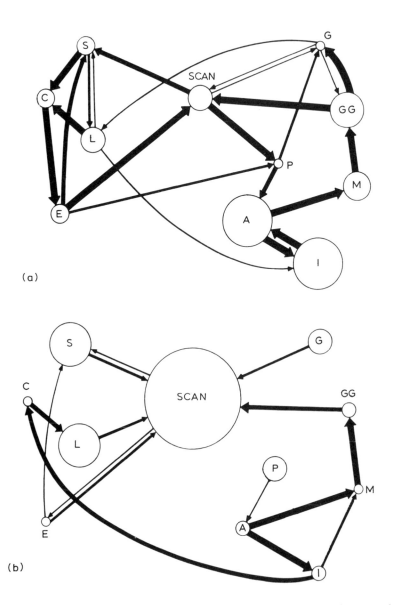

Figure 3.26 Application of ethological techniques in physiological studies; changes in the sequential organization of behaviour in rats following stimulation of the ventromedial hypothalamus (from de Ruiter, Wiepkema and Veening, 1974). SCAN represents scanning, L locomotion, S sniffing, C carrying food, E eating, P attending to partner, A approaching partner, I investigating partner, M mounting, G grooming and GG genital grooming. The size of the circle indicates the time spent in each behaviour, the arrows indicate transitions occurring significantly more often than random. (a) Structure of normal behaviour of male rats in the presence of food and an oestrus female; (b) structure of behaviour during unilateral stimulation of the ventromedial hypothalamus.

Finally, the ideas developed by ethologists may suggest new kinds of explanation for physiological results; for example, in an experiment along classical endocrinological lines, Erickson and Martinez-Vargas (1975) investigated the effects of castration and androgen replacement on various components of the breeding behaviour of male ring doves. Rather surprisingly, behaviour patterns performed early in the sequence required higher levels of gonadal hormones for their performance than those later in the sequence; the reverse is the case for females (Cheng, 1979). These results were interpreted in the light of ideas about mate choice currently under discussion by students of the adaptive significance of behaviour (Trivers, 1972, and see page 221); specifically, it was suggested that this hormonal arrangement allows the female ring dove to determine at an early stage in an encounter whether or not a potential mate will be able to copulate successfully, although it is not immediately obvious why it should be in the male's interest to provide this information.

CHAPTER 4

The development of behaviour

A full understanding of behaviour requires a knowledge of the processes whereby, under normal circumstances, a fertilized egg develops into an adult animal with a complete behavioural repertoire. For example, closely related passerine birds sing songs which vary in overall pitch, in the pattern of sounds involved and in their degree of complexity. Species also vary in the number of song types they sing; a chaffinch (*Fringilla coelebs*) has just one song type, a marsh wren (*Cistothorus palustris*) may use upwards of one hundred song types, while sedge warblers (*Acrocephalus shoenebaenus*) produce '. . . a seemingly endless stream of constantly varying song types'. (Catchpole, 1979.) Individual birds may produce variations on their species specific theme in the form of local dialects (Marler and Tamura, 1962) and may have repertoires of different sizes (Catchpole, 1979). What sorts of process could account for the development of behaviour patterns like this which are at once sufficiently constant to be a recognizable attribute of the species concerned and yet which vary between individual animals?

4.1 Problems with the instinct-learning dichotomy

The proposition that it is possible and useful to construct a dichotomous classification of adult actions into innate behaviour which is the result of a fixed programme of maturation under the influence of the genes and learned behaviour acquired as the result of experience has been strongly criticized on many occasions; Lehrman (1970), Bateson (1981a) and Hinde (1982) provide a representative selection of reviews. Only the main arguments against this instinct-learning dichotomy will be mentioned here.

4.1.1 INSTINCTS ARE DEFINED BY EXCLUSION

The main distinctive feature of instinctive behaviour is a negative one, namely the unimportance of learning in its development. As a category, it is therefore likely to be heterogeneous. This is not a problem in itself but can become one if all instincts are presumed to depend on identical developmental processes.

The logic of the deprivation experiment, the key source of evidence used to identify instinctive behaviour, is clear. An animal is reared in the absence of certain stimuli or without the opportunity to practice certain movements. If it fails to react to such stimuli or to show such movements when adult, then the behaviour of normally reared animals of this species must be influenced by the experience of which the experimental animal was deprived. If the behaviour of the isolated animals is normal, this particular experience cannot be essential for for the development of the behaviour. This last sort of case, in which animals deprived of what seems to be the relevant experience behave in a normal manner, however striking, does not mean that the behaviour is the result of maturational events under the influence of the genes without input from the environment.

(a) *Has the subject been deprived of relevant experience?*
The animal may itself provide stimuli on which learning is based; for example, ducklings incubated in isolation from all conspecifics respond preferentially to the maternal call of their own species immediately after hatching. According to the theory outlined above, this is an instinctive response, clearly adaptive in nature and with a developmental history which does not involve direct learning about the sounds which other ducks make. However, if ducklings are prevented from making noises inside their eggs, the preferential response to calls of their own species is much less marked (Gottlieb, 1971).

Information acquired in one context may influence the development of behaviour shown in another. Thus rats build normal nests in the absence of any practice provided that they have the opportunity to carry some object, such as solid food, around; in the absence of this possibility, for example when fed on powdered food, nest building does not develop normally (Riess, 1954).

(b) *Alternative developmental routes*
Even if an animal has genuinely been deprived of all sources of information relevant to a specific pattern of behaviour, the fact that it responds normally when adult does not necessarily mean that the features of the environment which have been removed play no part in its development under natural conditions. It is theoretically possible, and known to be the case in several instances, that alternative developmental routes to the same adult behaviour exist. Early weaned kittens play more per minute of active time than late weaned kittens, possibly by way of compensation for the fact that they are receiving less stimulation from their mother; normal adult behaviour may thus develop through interactions with the mother or with siblings and inanimate objects (Bateson, 1981b). There appear to be self-correcting mechanisms in the processes underlying development of behaviour. This is an interesting phenomenon, implying that the normal behaviour is of importance to the animal concerned, but it complicates inter-

pretation of negative results in deprivation experiments. To borrow an analogy, the fact that travellers are forced to use bikes during a fuel shortage does not mean that cars run without petrol (Bateson, 1981a).

Another problem in opposing learned to instinctive behaviour is that this overlooks the many ways other than learning in which the environment can influence the course of behavioural development. For example, Arizona juncos (*Junco phaeonotus*) do not develop their full song if reared in isolation; however, young birds reared in groups, which hear and make noises but have no experience of adult song, vocalize normally when adults. In this case, general auditory/social stimulation rather than direct learning from the adult song appears to be necessary for the normal development of this complex behaviour (Marler, 1975). At a more general level, a single exposure to white light is sufficient for normal development of various visually guided responses in chicks (Vauclair and Bateson, 1975), while nutrition level can influence development of the whole behavioural repertoire. Thus the environment plays a role in behavioural development which varies from highly specific influences on particular behaviour patterns to general effects on almost all aspects of an animal's life. It is artificial to draw a line across this continuum dividing conditions necessary for life in general from environmental effects specific to a given behaviour.

4.1.4 THE INSTINCT-LEARNING DICHOTOMY CONFOUNDS THREE DISTINCT CONSEQUENCES OF BEHAVIOURAL DEVELOPMENT

The most serious objection to the classification of adult behaviour patterns into clear and mutually exclusive categories of instinctive and learned is that this fails to distinguish between three quite different developmental phenomena. These are the origins of fully formed behaviour patterns in an adult animal, the origins of adaptive behaviour and the origins of behavioural differences between animals.

(a) *The processes which give rise to adult behaviour patterns*
There is abundant evidence that an alteration in the genetic material of the zygote can change the behaviour shown by the animal into which it ultimately develops (Chapter 8). However, proof that genetic factors influence the course of development of a particular character does not mean that the same character is not also influenced by the environment. For example, the condition of phenyl-ketonurea with its attendant mental disorders depends on substitution of one allele for another at a single autosomal locus, the affected condition being recessive to the normal one. However, the condition can be greatly ameliorated by a diet low in phenylalanine and rich in tyrosine (the normal substrate and

product of the enzyme which is inactive in the mutant form). Laughing gulls (*Larus atricilla*) peck at their parent's bill for food from the first day of hatching but the eliciting stimulus is modified over subsequent days as a result of reinforcement; in this case, an initially unlearned behaviour responds flexibly to environmental conditions after its first appearance (Hailman, 1967). Conversely, while development of normal song in canaries (*Serinus canarius*) depends on learning from conspecific adults, the success of selection for vocal ability in this species indicates that there is a degree of genetic control over this characteristic.

At a different level of analysis, recording from the visual cortex of kittens as soon as they open their eyes shows that cells in this region have normal orientation and direction specificity and a normal pattern of occular dominance, although they are generally less active. Cortical cells of adult cats reared in the dark also have most of these properties. These results imply that development of the major neural connections in the visual pathway, and of the resulting behavioural selectivity, is independent of visual input. However, depriving one eye of visual input has profound effects on subsequent behaviour, physiology and anatomy. Thus the cats show impaired depth perception and abnormal scanning movements, the cells in the visual cortex fail to respond to stimulation of the deprived eye and the size and shape of the cells at various points in the pathway are abnormal. Similarly, depriving the kittens of various aspects of patterned visual input, for example by allowing them to see only vertical lines, also affects their behaviour and physiology as adults. In this case, the kittens fail to respond to horizontal lines and cortical cells with horizontal receptive fields are rare or absent. These effects can be produced by visual deprivation lasting no more than a few days, provided this occurs within the first few weeks of life (see review by Lund, 1978). Normal development of full visual acuity and the underlying neural pathways thus depend on both inherited growth patterns and experience of the visual environment.

In all these cases, two quite independent kinds of question have been asked about the behaviour concerned and both have been answered positively. It is simply not possible to categorize the result of behavioural development (the actions and responses shown by individual adult animals) into those dependent on the environment and those dependent on heredity; any characteristic of an adult animal is the end product of a continuous and complex interaction between the genetic material present in the zygote and various features of its internal and external environment during development.

It is true that some behaviour patterns are relatively stable in the sense that they develop normally in a variety of environments while others are labile, depending critically on particular kinds of experience. However, stability is not always the product of genetic determination. Behaviour whose final form depends on learning can be highly stable and species specific, provided that the features of the environment on which the learning is based are regular. For example, under normal conditions a duckling always hears its own voice when inside the egg

(Gottlieb, 1971) and a laughing gull chick is normally fed by parents of the same species. Although the final form of the behaviour depends on experience, development is stable and all undisturbed ducklings hatch with a strong preference for maternal calls of the appropriate species just as all three day old laughing gulls peck preferentially at the heads of conspecifics.

(b) *The processes which result in adaptive behaviour*

The adaptive properties of a particular behaviour may be a result of an individual learning by personal experience (animals discover for themselves which are good food sources and how to exploit them), by cultural transmission of information (animals learn good food sources and how to exploit them by watching their parents feed) or may be the results of natural selection acting in the past (individuals with an inherited preference for a particular kind of feeding area and for a particular foraging technique leave more offspring than those with different feeding responses). Thus demonstration of the adaptive nature of a behaviour pattern is not proof that learning or some other environmental influence plays no part in its development. Even where natural selection is implicated, this only requires that offspring resemble their parents in the trait in question. Development of the trait must be stable but, as discussed above, this may come about through learning in a regular environment as well as by the rigid unrolling of the effects of genes.

(c) *The processes which result in behavioural differences between animals*

Any given adult characteristic is the end product of interaction between many different genetic and environmental factors and therefore items of adult behaviour cannot be classified as dependent on either heredity or environment. However, it is perfectly possible for a particular behavioural difference to be the result of one or other of these sources of influence acting alone. Thus while it is nonsense to ask whether a particular item of behaviour depends on genes or on the environment, it is valid to ask whether a given difference in behaviour is a consequence of genetic differences between the zygotes from which the animals concerned developed or of a difference in the environment in which this took place.

4.2 Why is the term innate still used?

There are clearly many good reasons for discarding the dichotomous classification of adult behaviour patterns into innate or learnt, yet the former term is still frequently used. This reflects the fact that observers still, quite rightly, marvel at the appearance of fully formed acts in animals reared without any opportunity for learning and at the astonishing capacity of the developing animal to compensate for environmental (and genetic) deficits. It is extraordinary that young warblers reared in isolation 'know' their migratory route to Africa

(Gwinner and Wiltschko, 1978) and that as little as 15 minutes exposure per day to peers can produce rhesus monkeys (*Macaca mulatta*) with a more or less normal repertoire of social responses (Harlow and Harlow, 1965). The term innate has not dropped out of use in spite of the recognized sterility of the instinct-learning dichotomy because it reflects this very real adaptive stability of much behavioural development and no satisfactory alternative has been proposed.

4.3 Describing the ontogeny of behaviour

Unravelling the process of behavioural development for any particular species involves two main exercises. In the first place the behavioural events that occur as the fertilized egg develops into an adult animal must be characterized and related to important events in the animal's life history such as birth, weaning and dispersal. The next step is to identify the factors which influence the course of this development and to work out how these exert their effects.

4.3.1 THE EMERGENCE OF RECOGNIZABLE BEHAVIOUR PATTERNS IN YOUNG ANIMALS

(a) *Development of behaviour in the chick embryo*
The movements of chicks inside the egg have been intensively studied by embryologists and frequently reviewed (Oppenheim, 1974; Broom, 1981). Briefly, the first discernible movements appear spontaneously 3 to 4 days after incubation starts in the form of slight, unilateral contractions of the neck musculature at regular intervals of more than a minute. This movement gradually spreads down the body, becoming more frequent and taking the form of S-shaped waves passing along the long axis of the embryo. Around 9 to 11 days, these movements of the whole body are replaced by irregular, jerky movements of individual parts of the body, which increase in frequency to a peak at 12 to 13 days and then become less common. Simultaneous, integrated movements of several parts of the body are occasionally observed; for example the chick may flex and extend its legs while moving its wings. These coordinated movements, which gradually shift the embryo's position, increase in frequency until just before hatching when they occupy 90% of the chick's time. At hatching the chick makes a hole in the egg shell by a series of movements of the head and bill, emerges from the egg by means of regular movements of the legs and wings and, after a short time, starts to walk around and peck.

(b) *Development of song in the chaffinch*
The chaffinch is one of a number of song birds whose vocal behaviour has received considerable attention; the broad course of its development appears to be typical of a number of passerine species. It is usual to divide the noises made by adult song birds into short and relatively simple calls and the longer and more

complex songs which give this group of birds their common name. An egg bound chick starts to produce calls soon after its beak pierces the air space in the egg and continues to do so after hatching, giving food begging calls when hungry. Initially these are complex and variable in structure and are named onomatopoeically as 'cheep' calls. In older, fledgling birds the feeding call becomes more stereotyped, consisting of two fundamental frequency bands which rise and fall with time. These are characterized as 'chirrup' calls and are initially associated with food

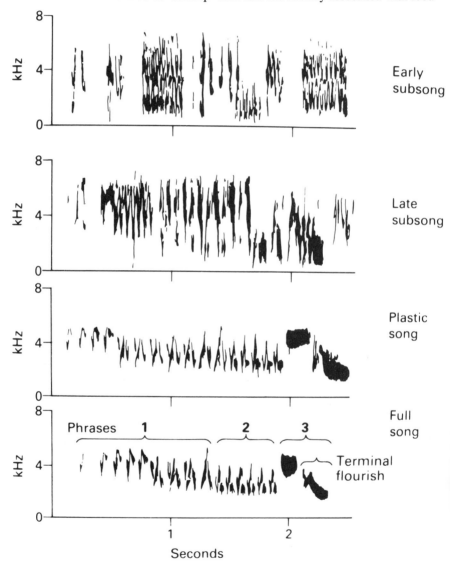

Figure 4.1 Describing the ontogeny of behaviour; sound spectrograms of vocalizations produced by chaffinches at different stages. (From Thorpe, 1961, after Catchpole, 1979).

deprivation; after the young birds become independent of their parents this link with hunger breaks down, the calls being given in social contexts. From about five weeks after hatching the feeding call gradually changes into a more rambling type of sound consisting of loose aggregations of chirps and other simple notes at low volume and continuing for some minutes, often while the bird dozes. This is called subsong (Fig. 4.1) and reappears after a winter's silence in the bird's first spring. During this latter period, the subsong becomes more complex with the addition of a new element, the rattle. Over a period of about a month variable fragments resembling adult song appear in the subsong, which becomes longer and more consistent in form; at this stage it is called the plastic song. Finally the plastic song takes on the definitive form of the full adult song, with its complex note structure and three phrases; this final process in song development is called crystallization (Thorpe, 1961).

4.3.2 THE TIME OF APPEARANCE OF BEHAVIOUR PATTERNS
DURING DEVELOPMENT

Once recognizable units of behaviour have been identified in an animal's repertoire, the next phase in the description of the ontogeny of behaviour involves determining the times at which they appear and, in some cases, disappear. For example, Fig. 4.2 lists the ages at which various activities appear in the repertoire of young cichlids of the species *Etroplus maculatus* (Wyman and Ward, 1973). This is not a complete description of behavioural development since during the period in which a particular behaviour pattern is performed it may change in various ways. Thus the form of the movement may alter, while staying sufficiently similar to be classified as the same; for example, in the period following the first appearance of overhand grooming as a recognizable unit in mice, a progressive increase occurs in the velocity, size and smoothness of the strokes (Fentress, 1981). The variability of the movement may change; for example, the movements used by squirrels to open nuts become more regular as time progresses (Eibl-Eibesfeldt, 1951). In contrast, the position of the bore hole made in the shells of prey animals by the predatory gastropod *Natica gualtieriani* becomes more variable as the animal gains in age and experience (Berg, 1978). Finally, a behaviour pattern can change in the readiness with which it is shown during the course of ontogeny. Figure 4.2 also shows the changes in frequency with age of various acts shown by *Etroplus maculatus*. Each behaviour follows a particular pattern of change in frequency with age and the ontogeny of behaviour as a whole is a combined effect of all these separate effects. However, the different behaviour patterns do not all follow the same developmental trajectory; glance and micronip gradually decrease with age, chafe and quiver increase and then level off while ram and charge increase steadily (Wyman and Ward, 1973). Thus it is possible to recognize different groups of behaviour patterns in terms of the way their frequencies change with age.

Behaviour pattern	Day of first appearance
Chafe	21.00
Glance	21.00
Frontal display	21.00
Micronip	21.50
Quiver	22.25
Charge	25.63
Ram	33.00
Carousel	34.00
Lateral display	36.00
Pendulum	38.50
Mouthfight	54.62
Tail beat	64.13

(a)

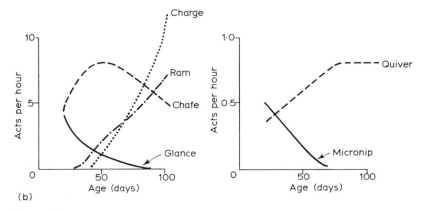

(b)

Figure 4.2 Describing the ontogeny of behaviour in young cichlids (after Wyman and Ward, 1973). (a) Mean date of first appearance of 12 behaviour patterns in the behavioural repertoire; (b) changes in frequency with age of selected behaviour patterns.

4.3.3 THE DEVELOPMENT OF MOTIVATIONAL SYSTEMS

Chapter 3 discussed the fact that certain groups of actions are controlled by common causal factors; it is of interest to know when and how these motivational relationships between behaviour patterns develop. This can be discovered by studying correlations between different behaviour patterns, their sequential relationships and their stimulus response relationships at different stages of development.

Developmental trajectories of movements used during play in cats indicated that a period of rapid change occurs around week 7; during this time most activities used during play decrease in frequency but object contacts increase. In order to investigate this more fully, the correlations between the frequency of the various play actions were calculated across individual kittens for the period before and after week 7. In the younger group, there were no negative correlations and the mean correlation was 0.35. These positive associations disappear in the 8–12 week period, several correlations being negative and the mean correlation being

Plate 3 Development of behavioural sequences; certain elements of play in cats become incorporated into predatory sequences.

0.18 (Barrett and Bateson, 1978). The results of a similar study in which predatory movements as well as play behaviour were investigated are shown in Fig. 4.3. Again correlations between the different play acts drop out at about 7 weeks; at the same time, the predatory sequence becomes more rigid some items of play (paw) becoming more closely associated with predatory behaviour as the kittens grew older while others (rear) become less (Caro, 1981).

Grooming movements in adult mice tend to occur in one of a few relatively fixed sequence patterns, for example, multiple single strokes followed by overhand (Fentress and Stilwell, 1973). Figure 4.4 shows how this adult sequence gradually emerges in young mice by a progressive decrease in the length of pauses between single strokes and an increase in the number of strokes per bout (Fentress, 1978).

These studies of frequency correlation and sequential relationships indicate that as development proceeds groups of behaviour patterns come under the control of a certain number of more or less specific systems. It is also of interest to know when and how these groups of causally related actions take on the relationship with external stimuli and antecedent conditions typical of adult motivational systems.

To give just a few examples, in adult mice, grooming usually occurs in gaps between locomotion and sitting. In young mice the occurrence of grooming seems more capricious in that an animal may start to groom in the middle of a bout of locomotion if it accidentally touches its face with its hand (Fentress, 1981). In young jungle fowl (*Gallus gallus spadiceus*) hopping, a juvenile version of the leap used by adults to start a fight, appears 1–3 days after hatching. At this stage it is not directed at or released by other individuals although hopping chicks may clash accidentally. At about 1 week hopping gradually begins to be directed towards, though not elicited by, other chicks and other behaviour patterns such as pecking are added to the fighting repertoire. At this stage fighting is not facilitated by the proximity of other individuals as it is in adults; hopping still shows its earlier association with walking and running while pecking is enhanced by hunger. In addition, fighting in chicks is strongly suppressed by escape, which is not the case in adults. Thus not only the form of aggression but also the way in which it is controlled by internal and external factors change during the process of development (Kruijt, 1964).

Figure 4.3 (opposite) Describing the ontogeny of behaviour; correlations between the frequency of various activities performed by litters of kittens of two different age categories (from Caro, 1981). (a) Significant correlations between different items of predatory behaviour; (b) significant correlations between different items of social play; (c) correlations between social play and predation, the number of correlations with predatory actions which increased and decreased in the second age category for each item of social play.

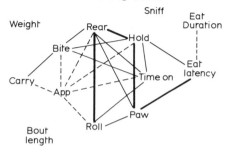

4-7½ Weeks

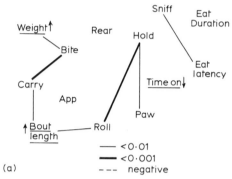

8-12 Weeks

——— <0·01
▬▬▬ <0·001
- - - negative

(a)

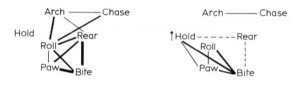

4-7½ weeks   8-12 weeks

——— <0·05
▬▬▬ <0·01
▬▬▬ <0·001
- - - negative

(b)

	Number of correlations with predatory acts which	
Social play item	Increased	Decreased
Approach	6	2
Sniff	3	5
Paw	5	3
Hold	7	1
Bite	5	3
Roll	3	5
Rear	2	6
Arch	1	7
Chase	1	7

(c)

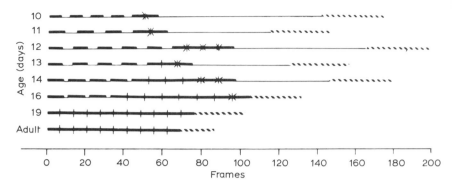

Figure 4.4 Describing the ontogeny of behaviour; the development of sequential relationships between grooming movements typical of adult mice. Full bars represent single strokes, hatched bars represent overhand and X represents the failure to alternate between limbs (from Fentress, 1978).

4.3.4 PHYSIOLOGICAL CHANGES ACCOMPANYING BEHAVIOURAL DEVELOPMENT

It is outside the scope of this book to provide a comprehensive review of the enormous literature on the development of the nervous system, although this is of obvious relevance to the question of behavioural development. Discussion of this subject will therefore be mainly confined to a few selected examples in which descriptions of the development of the animal's physical and physiological state accompany detailed accounts of their behavioural development.

In young male rats, mounting appears abruptly in the repertoire (unheralded by any obvious pre-mounting play) along with a preference for females as play partners around 30 days of age (Meaney and Stewart, 1981); this corresponds to the time at which testosterone levels begin to rise and the subsequent increase in mounting frequency corresponds to the age of first penile erection (Sachs and Meisel, 1979).

Neural activity in the chick embryo commences at an early stage, and by 7–8 days, frequent and coordinated bursts of electrical activity can be detected in the nerve cord. On a day-to-day basis, there is a correlation between development of these discharge patterns and the emergence of the simultaneous, irregular movements of several parts of the chick's body described above. On a finer time scale, bouts of movement are regularly associated with bursts of neural activity in the spinal cord (Oppenheim, 1974). Recordings of the electrical activity of specific muscles allow more detailed investigation of the development of the neural mechanisms underlying coordinated behaviour in this species. For example, at a behavioural level, there is no obvious relationship between the jerky, uncoordinated movements shown by very young chick embryos, the later coordinated pre-hatching movements and the hopping of a newly hatched chick.

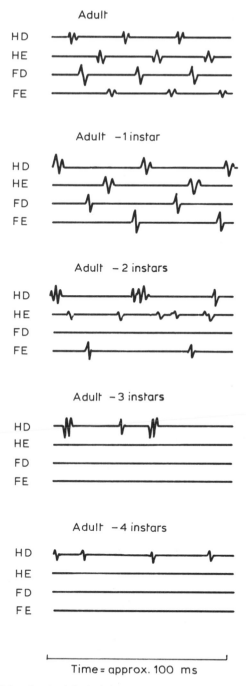

Figure 4.5 Describing the physiological changes accompanying behavioural development; electrical activity in the motor neurons of the elevator (E) and depressor (D) muscles in the fore (F) and hind (H) wings of crickets during the four instars preceding the final moult (after Bentley and Hoy, 1970).

However, EMG recordings from various muscles in the hind limbs show, for example, that contractions of the flexor and extensor muscles of the ankle alternate on the very first occasion that overt movements occur (6–7 days) with the same phase relationships as those observed during both pre-hatching movements and post-hatching locomotion, although their relationship is relatively imprecise in very young chicks. The coordination between activation of muscles moving the ankle and knee joints typical of these later movements can also be seen in the irregular, jerky movements of chicks 9 days after the onset of incubation. Finally, although in very young chicks the firing of the muscles of the two hind limbs are uncoordinated, they alternate regularly in both pre- and post-hatching movements. Thus the muscles of the limbs show a similar pattern of activation during these overtly very different movements, although with gradual refinement in their temporal patterning (Bekoff, 1976, 1978, 1981).

The development of flight in the cricket *Teleogryllus commodus* has been carefully studied from hatching to the final moult (of eleven). At a behavioural level, flight in adult crickets involves lifting up the first and second pairs of legs and holding the third pair backwards, stiffening the abdomen and flapping the wings with the hind pair slightly in advance of the front. Up to the 6th moult, nymphs never show flying movements; from the 7th moult they will assume the flight posture if suspended without support but this becomes easier to elicit as the animals get older. The development of the neural patterns underlying flight movements were investigated by recording from the depressor and elevator muscles of the hind and forewings. Figure 4.5 shows the activity of these motor units in the four instars leading up to the final moult. At −4, single spikes occur occasionally in the hindwing depressor but the other units are silent. These single spikes gradually turn into sustained bursts while the hindwing elevator and forewing units gradually become active. The adult rate of firing does not develop until the final moult because it depends on sensory feedback from the wing. Thus this study describes '. . . a physiological substrate which bridges (the gap between) . . . descriptions of the ontogeny of insect behaviour and the anatomy of the developing nervous system.' (Bentley and Hoy, 1970.)

4.4 Characterizing the factors which influence the development of behaviour

Having described the behavioural events which occur as a zygote develops into an adult animal it is now necessary to explain them; in other words, we need to identify the factors which determine the course of development and to discover how they exert their effects.

4.4.1 DEDUCTIONS FROM DESCRIPTIVE STUDIES

Although accounts of the kind mentioned above are strictly descriptive it is possible to make deductions from them about the processes determining the course of development.

(a) *Deductions from the form of the movements shown at different stages*
It is an assumption of much of the literature that development is a continuous process whereby early movements are eventually transformed into adult behaviour patterns. Studies of the form of movements at different ages can tell us whether this is an accurate picture of behavioural development and if so how one movement changes into another. From descriptions of the behaviour of chick embryos at various ages, it does seem to be the case that fully formed, integrated acts emerge gradually from the uncoordinated movements performed at earlier stages; the similar pattern of muscle activation in their limbs during the movements shown at different ages supports this conclusion. However, in other cases, complex behaviour patterns such as mounting in rats appear in the repertoire in their complete, final form without any obvious precursors in earlier movements; the development of actions with these different histories must be distinct.

Accounts of the changing form of behaviour with age can sometimes suggest possible processes underlying behavioural change during development. For example, the gradual replacement of uncoordinated, jerky movements by coordinated ones in chick embryos suggests that the early movements may be necessary for the normal development of later behaviour. Similarly, the appearance of fractions of adult song in the plastic song of young chaffinches raises the possibility that they may be imitating songs that they have heard. On the other hand, the abrupt appearance of mounting and its coincidence with a sharp rise in testosterone level in rats indicates that the neural mechanisms underlying this behaviour may develop in the absence of performance of any obviously similar movements (though not necessarily of any movement at all), possibly being activated by a threshold level of circulating androgen.

Once differentiated movement patterns have appeared in the repertoire, it is possible by observation alone to identify a series of changes during development from one form to another and thus, possibly, to understand how the adult actions emerge as the behavioural repertoire develops. Such attempts to arrange behaviour patterns in a developmental sequence raise problems as to how derivatives of actions performed at earlier stages are to be identified. There is no simple answer but certain guidelines can be used: an act which arises later on in ontogeny may have its developmental origins in an earlier one if the two are similar in form or linked by an intermediate version or if they have similar correlational and sequential relationships with other items of behaviour (i.e. appear to be controlled by the same mechanisms); if they also serve a similar function the identification receives further support (Chalmers, 1980). However, it is quite possible for an act which is genuinely derived from an earlier one to take on different control (as in the case of the various play movements in cats) and functions (as in the case of the hatching and walking movements of chicks).

The development of the repertoire of adult responses has been thoroughly described for the cichlid fish *Etroplus maculatus*. Two behaviour patterns appear at an early stage in these fish, initially directed towards the parents and are believed to give rise to all the behaviour patterns which appear later. These two movements are the glance (in which a moving fish holds its fins close to its curved body, propelling it towards another fish and then away, tracing a circular path) and the micronip (in which one fish approaches another directly as if to glance but nips it in the side with its mouth, the fins being spread at this point). Five actions shown by older fish, all of which involve arcing the body and subtle changes in fin posture with the mouth closed, are believed to be derived from the glance as a

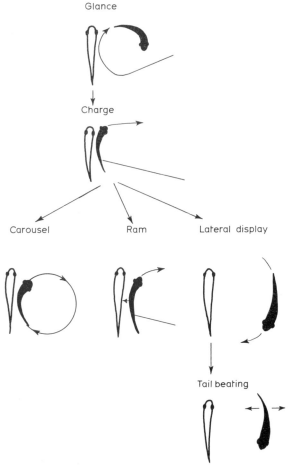

Figure 4.6 Hypothesis for the development of the repertoire of adult behaviour patterns in *Etroplus maculatus*; patterns originating from the glance (after Wyman and Ward, 1973). The black fish is the performer and the white fish is the opponent.

result of emphasis on different parts of the circular movement (Fig. 4.6). Thus in the charge (which appears around day 26) the component in the direction of the other fish is stressed; this is emphasized still further in the ram. In the carousel the whole circular movement is maintained but without contact with the partner while in lateral display the movement is held at the outermost extent of the circle. These three movements all appear around 35 days. Tail beat appears at 64 days by adding sideways movements of the tail to the lateral display. A further three patterns involving the mouth together with elevation of the paired and medial fins are thought to derive from the micronip. Frontal display appears on day 21 as a result of freezing the forward movement, pendulum arises at about 38 days by addition of a backward and forward movement, while mouth fighting, which does not appear until 54 days, is the result of holding the bite of the micronip. Observation of the circumstances in which the young cichlids interact suggests that these changes depend on experience of dominance interactions during competition for space (Wyman and Ward, 1973).

However, it is misleading to treat the course of behavioural ontogeny simply as a process by which functional adult behaviour patterns are constructed, although these are obviously one of its end products. The developing animal must function effectively at all stages, and the behaviour necessary for survival and growth at one stage may not be the same as that necessary at another. Therefore the things that immature animals do at various points in their development from growth to adult may represent adaptations to the developing animals' needs rather than the quickest and most effective way of assembling adult behaviour. In some cases, actions necessary to meet the requirements of the young animal and those required for the development of adult behaviour are the same; for example, the coordinated movements shown by chicks during hatching meet the needs of the young animal at that age, namely to get out of the egg, but they also serve as practice of the walking movements of older chicks and adults. However, in other cases, these needs are conflicting and the behaviour shown in development must be seen as a response to immediate need rather than precursors from which later behaviour develops. For example, red squirrels (*Tarnia scurus hudsonicus*) start life crowded together in nests where their primary need is to locate their mother and to gain and maintain contact with a nipple; this is achieved by pushing forward and head swinging. On leaving the nest, the animals fend for themselves and these actions disappear and since they now need to move around in the branches the quite different behavioural patterns of forward and backward hopping and hanging upside down appear in the repertoire (Ferron, 1980).

(b) *Deductions from developmental trajectories*
A knowledge of when various acts appear and disappear from the repertoire and how their frequency changes with age can be used to characterize the underlying processes which dictate the course of behavioural ontogeny. For example, in young olive baboons (*Papio ambis*) acts such as mounting, mouth and wrestle,

riding dorsally on the mother's back and bipedal standing, are shown for the first time around 6 to 8 weeks. The time at which these apparently distinct behaviour patterns appear in the repertoire may therefore depend on a single process; the ability to maintain postural control while balancing, which develops at about this age, is a likely candidate (Chalmers, 1980).

The actual pattern of change in frequency can also be used to generate hypotheses about developmental processes. When several behaviour patterns are considered simultaneously, it is sometimes possible to identify periods of rapid behavioural change which may be related to internal and external events. Thus in kittens of about 7 weeks many behaviour patterns (play and predatory) all show rapid changes in frequency, some increasing and others decreasing. This fact, together with the change in their pattern of correlations, indicates that various actions shown during play by young kittens are coming under the control of different adult motivational systems; for example, arch is incorporated in the aggressive system while hold and bite join the prey catching group (Caro, 1981). Weaning normally occurs at around six weeks and therefore the change from social play to object contact play and the subsequent rearrangement of behaviour control may be triggered by the experience of weaning. It is equally possible that the influence works the other way round, with the early stages of a behavioural reorganization causing weaning to occur (Bateson, 1981b).

4.4.2 EXPERIMENTAL STUDIES OF BEHAVIOURAL DEVELOPMENT

Thus observational studies can suggest that certain factors may play a part in the control of behavioural development; however, in order to determine for certain whether this is so and how the effects are exerted experimental manipulation is necessary. Controlled variation of such a factor will alter behavioural development, producing adult animals whose behaviour differs from normal. The experimental paradigm is therefore to rear groups of animals in conditions which differ with respect to the factor under study; if animals in the various treatment groups differ in certain aspects of their adult behaviour, then the factor concerned must have an effect on the course of development.

For example, in order to test the suggestion that performance of early movement is necessary for the normal development of coordinated behaviour in chicks, embryos were paralysed for various periods of time at an early stage of development; this resulted in permanent atrophy of the limb muscles and malformation of the joints. The possibility that weaning may be a cause rather than an effect of the behavioural reorganization which occurs in kittens at about 7 weeks was tested experimentally by weaning kittens early and monitoring the frequency of the various movements used during play over the subsequent weeks. In early weaned kittens the various changes in frequency and correlations of these actions did indeed occur at an earlier age than normal. '. . . it does seem reasonable to infer that the change in organization of play is induced by some aspect of weaning.' (Bateson, 1981.)

This experimental approach of subjecting developing animals to different conditions and comparing their behaviour can be used whether the factor in question is part of the environment in which the zygote develops or a genetic one, such as the presence of one allele rather than another at a particular locus. An enormous amount of natural genetic variation exists and a number of techniques are available for relating this to behavioural differences in adult animals in order to identify genetic determinants of behavioural differences. In addition, direct experimental manipulation of the genotype of animals, by judicious breeding schedules and by mechanical reorganization of embryos, allows this issue to be studied directly (Chapter 8).

The *hyperkinetic* condition in *Drosophila melanogaster*, in which walking is slightly jerky and the legs twitch violently when the flies are etherized depends on a recessive allele at a single locus (Hotta and Benzer, 1972). Some progress may be made towards finding out how the mutant allele produces this behavioural abnormality by comparing various structural and physiological features of mutant and normal flies. However, such effects may be hidden within the fly's body or too subtle to be readily detected and even if *hyperkinetic* flies regularly showed abnormality in the physiology of their legs, for example, this may be the result of abnormal muscles, nerves, ganglia or brain tissue. It is possible to tease apart these effects by constructing genetic mosaics. An abnormal (ringed) X chromosome of *Drosophila* exists which is often lost from the nucleus during cell division; in a zygote which is female (the homogametic sex in flies) the descendants of the cells in which the ring X is lost have the constitution XO rather than XX. This means that any recessive alleles on the remaining X chromosome are exposed and the resulting individual is therefore a genetic mosaic. The ring X may be lost at various stages and therefore individuals with varying amount of mutant tissue can be formed. Genetic markers with visible effects on the body surface can be introduced onto the normal X chromosome and various body structures can thus be identified as mutant or normal in a large number of genetic mosaics. The frequency with which two adult characteristics are both mutant or both normal provides an index of how close their primordia are on the blastoderm. Similar measurements for a large number of different structures allow a complete fate map to be constructed for the surface structures; if the markers are biochemical ones this map can be extended to include the primordia of the internal tissues. The technique can be used to determine the focus of recessive mutant alleles which alter behaviour by introducing the mutant together with the markers onto the normal X chromosome. It is then possible to determine whether the behaviour exhibited by the mosaic flies corresponds to the normal or the mutant genotype in particular body regions and thus to find the focus of the mutant on the fate map. The morphological features whose blastoderm sites are at or near the focus are likely to be those through which the mutant exerts its effects. When this procedure is applied to the *hyperkinetic* mutant, shaking of a given leg pair usually occurred when its cuticle was abnormal; however, shaking was occasionally observed in legs whose cuticle was normal. Thus the mutant allele has three different foci each lying near, but slightly ventral to, the primordia of the cuticle for a particular pair of legs in the region which ultimately gives rise to the ventral nervous system. This analysis shows that the *hyperkinetic* mutant probably exerts its effect by altering the development of the thoracic ganglia; histological investigation of this part of the CNS in mutant flies may identify the nature of the change (Hotta and Benzer, 1972).

Since controlled manipulation of the environment is easier than controlled manipulation of the genone, much more work has been done on the former lines and discussion will now be concentrated on the results of this kind of experiment. No attempt will be made to review the enormous literature which all this research has generated. Having introduced a wide range of examples into the preceding sections, the rest of this chapter follows the traditional expedient of concentrating on the two most intensively studied systems, namely the development of song in passerines and the development of social preferences in galliform birds. These examples illustrate well the kinds of experiments that can be carried out to identify and characterize the factors influencing the development of behaviour and the sort of results they produce.

4.4.3 EXPERIMENTAL STUDIES OF THE DEVELOPMENT OF SONG IN PASSERINES

Descriptions of the normal development of song in chaffinches suggested that young birds imitate the songs of adult conspecifics. The appropriate environmental manipulation to test this possibility is to rear chaffinches without the opportunity to hear adult song; Fig. 4.7(b) shows the song produced in their first breeding season by chaffinches raised in groups of contemporaries in sound proof cages. The duration of the song, its average frequency and tonal quality are within the normal range (Fig. 4.7(c)) and it has a fairly complex structure including something of the terminal flourish; however, the song is clearly abnormal with little evidence of the three phrases typical of wild chaffinch song. This result indicates that young chaffinches must be exposed to adult conspecifics if song is to develop normally.

The nature of this effect can be defined more precisely by further deprivation experiments. Figure 4.7(a) also shows the song produced by chaffinches reared alone, in complete social isolation; in this case all they ever hear is the sound of their own voice. Again, the song is more or less normal in duration, average frequency and tonal quality but the structure is even less like the typical chaffinch song, being very simple with no sign of any phrasing at all. This result, together with the fact that individuals reared together in groups tend all to sing the same

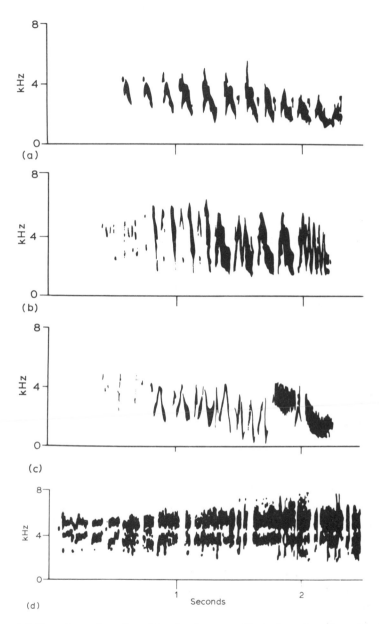

Figure 4.7 Experimental studies of the development of behaviour; the effect of various manipulations on the song of chaffinches (from Thorpe, 1961 and Nottebohm, 1968, after Catchpole, 1979). (a) The song of chaffinches reared in isolation (Thorpe, 1961); (b) the song of chaffinches reared in groups without adults (Thorpe, 1961); (c) the song of chaffinches normally reared (Thorpe, 1961); (d) the song of chaffinches deafened at an early age (Nottebohm, 1968).

song, suggests that song development is also influenced by the sounds produced by juvenile companions.

Finally, the figure shows the songs produced by chaffinches deafened at an early age and thus deprived of experience of any sounds including their own vocalizations. While the average frequency corresponds roughly to that of wild chaffinch vocalizations, the song is completely abnormal in duration and in tonal quality, lacks any phrasing and sounds like a harsh screech (Thorpe, 1961).

Similar experiments have been carried out on other passerine species, with the almost uniform result that birds reared in social isolation produce songs which are recognizably different from, and usually simpler than, the normal song of their species, although the magnitude of this effect varies. Isolated white crowned sparrows (*Zonotrichia leucophrys*) produce very abnormal song (Marler, 1975); zebra finches (*Taeniopygia guttata*) given the same treatment produce phrased songs with a typically complex note structure and more or less normal temporal patterning but with fewer notes and of fewer types (Price, 1979). Song sparrows (*Melospiza melodia*) reared in isolation sing almost normally but have a smaller repertoire (Marler, 1975), while certain strains of canary, bred for frequent singing, show completely normal song following the same treatment. In complete contrast, brown headed cowbirds (*Molothrus ater*) raised in social isolation sing songs which are more complex than normal (West and King, 1980). Since these birds are brood parasites and rarely encounter conspecific adults when young, the fact that isolated birds sing the full song is not surprising; it is not clear why these should actually be more elaborate than usual.

In most species, birds reared in groups of juveniles also sing abnormally, although as in chaffinches, this is usually less marked than in birds reared in complete isolation. However, group reared Arizona juncos produce songs which are more-or-less normal; in this case the presence of companions seems to be sufficient for normal song development, even when these do not produce songs (Marler, 1975).

The results of deafening on song development are also variable; in white crowned sparrows and song sparrows this has a severe effect (Konishi, 1965). On the other hand, red-winged black birds (*Agelaius phoeniceus*) deafened at 9 days sing almost normally (Marler, 1975) and canaries deprived of the sound of their own voices produce songs which resemble closely those of normally reared birds; the individual notes and their immediate sequential relationships are similar but higher order relationships in the normal song are impaired in deafened birds (Güttinger, 1981).

Thus experience of adult birds, of juvenile companions and of their own vocalizations all play a part in the normal development of song in chaffinches and in many other passerines. In order to understand these effects, it is necessary to know just what features of the experience are responsible, at what stage in development they act, the precise nature of their effects and the mechanisms whereby these are brought about.

An obvious possibility is that the sounds produced by other chaffinches are the relevant factors; isolated juvenile chaffinches exposed to tape recordings of normal chaffinch song show normal song development and eventually sing like the 'tutor', as they also do if played a tape in which the components of the normal song are mixed up. If they are exposed to recordings of the song of other species, they only learn to sing the tutor song if it is similar in tone to chaffinch song, otherwise they sing like isolates which have no experience of adult song. Finally, when exposed to tapes which are a mixture of chaffinch and some other, tonally different song, young chaffinches only copy the notes of the former. Thus chaffinches do appear to copy songs which they hear when young, provided that these resemble normal chaffinch song (Thorpe, 1961).

Similar selectivity in song learning has been demonstrated for white crowned sparrows and for swamp sparrows but song sparrows are less selective. Red winged black birds exposed to taped sounds of conspecifics and another species which commonly nest in similar habitats, learn elements of both songs. The fact that this does not appear to happen in the wild suggests that responses to the characteristic colour of these birds may add selectivity to the learning process under natural conditions (Marler, 1975). Zebra finches reared by Bengalese finches (*Lonchura striata*) produce perfect copies of the song of their foster parents, although if exposed simultaneously to adults of both species they learn the song of the zebra finch (Immelmann, 1969). In all these cases, some sort of selectiveness is apparent in what is learned, whether this is a response to the nature of the sounds themselves or to other aspects of the potential models including their social relationship with the young bird.

In an attempt to find out at what stage in the period from hatching to first breeding the environmental effects described above exert their effects, experimental manipulations (isolation, exposure to taped songs and deafening) were performed on chaffinches of different ages. In the wild, juvenile chaffinches experience adult songs in their first autumn and then again the following spring; during these periods they are producing subsong and, later on, plastic song until crystallization of the full song just before breeding starts. Chaffinches caught in the autumn when they are already a few months old and subsequently reared in isolation develop normal songs, as do birds isolated from hatching and exposed briefly to taped chaffinch song during the autumn. Birds exposed to adult song for a short time when they were just a few days old and then reared alone sing like complete isolates and isolates only exposed to taped song in their first spring show limited effects of this experience. Clearly there is a period spanning the birds' first autumn, and possibly extending into the following spring, when chaffinches can learn from adult songs, even when they hear these for a fairly short time. The memory is sufficiently strong to influence the birds' behaviour after an intervening winter and for the rest of their lives (Thorpe, 1961).

The consequences of deafening at various ages are quite different; chaffinches deafened at any age up to the middle of their first spring give abnormal screeches of the type described above. If deafened during plastic song, this gradually degenerates to a similar, highly abnormal, condition; deafening after crystallization produced no alteration in song. Thus normal development of song in chaffinches only occurs if they are able to hear themselves during the period when they are producing subsong and plastic song up to the appearance of full song (Nottebohm, 1968). Similar results have been obtained for a number of species, although the time in which learning occurs (the sensitive period) may vary; it ends before the first winter in white crown sparrows but some species are capable of learning throughout their lives.

In all these examples, the duration of the sensitive period but not its internal structure has been studied. The precise readiness to learn across the whole sensitive period has been determined for the long billed marsh wren, a species with a large repertoire of song types. The ease (sensitivity) of learning is measured quantitatively by recording the number of song types learned from a tutor tape at different times (Fig. 4.8). The sensitive period lasts from 10 to 80 days, but has a gradual onset and termination, peaks in the effectiveness of tutoring occurring at about 35 and 50 days (Kroodsma, 1978, 1981). It is known that the birds retain some ability to learn in their first spring if exposed to live adults rather than to taped songs and that in natural conditions, young hatched late in the year experience fewer adult songs before moulting and migrating. It may be that the young birds are able to delay the end of their sensitive period if they hatch at a time when there is little opportunity for learning. This possibility was tested by rearing hatchlings of the same age in a photoperiod typical of June

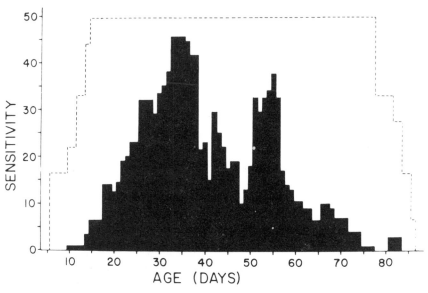

Figure 4.8 Experimental studies of the development of behaviour; characterization of the sensitive period for song learning in the long-billed marsh wren (from Kroodsma, 1978).

or August. The latter group moulted earlier, had a shorter period of subsong and displayed earlier migratory restlessness. They learned slightly fewer songs than birds in the 'June' group although this learning occurred over the same period of time; however, while none of the June group learned any songs in the following spring, half the August group did so. Similarly, birds exposed to a smaller number of songs retained the ability to learn in the spring. Thus the degree of exposure to adult song and the photoperiod in which this is heard determine when the sensitive period ends in this species (Kroodsma and Pickert, 1980).

From these studies the following hypothetical sequence of events during song learning in chaffinches has been proposed (Marler, 1976). Song learning involves two processes, with the birds first learning what to sing and then learning how to sing it.

Learning what to sing mostly occurs during the first autumn of the young bird's life as a result of hearing the songs of adult birds of the same species. Chaffinches possess an internal representation of roughly what the species song should sound like (the neural template) and will only learn songs which conform reasonably well to this pattern. As a result of learning, the neural template is modified to provide a representation of the tutor song; in the wild this will be the full song of nearby conspecific males. In the absence of any appropriate tutor during the sensitive period the template remains rudimentary.

In the late autumn and early spring, during subsong, young chaffinches learn how to sing by gradually matching the sounds they make to the model provided by the neural template. If unable to hear themselves at this stage, matching is impossible and the birds therefore develop a song which is far cruder even than the untutored template. Once the song has crystallized, the birds no longer need to match their vocal output to the template, some permanent memory having been formed of the motor commands necessary to produce the appropriate song. This memory cannot be further modified and does not depend on auditory feedback for its maintenance; hence the lack of effect of deafening after full song has developed.

This model accounts neatly for the observed facts about song development in chaffinches and can be modified to represent the same process in different species. For example, in birds such as the song sparrow whose song develops relatively normally in isolation, the untutored template must be a fairly complete representation of the species' song. However, there are facts which cannot be accommodated in this scheme. For example, red-winged blackbirds and canaries deafened at an early age produce relatively normal songs when adult (Marler, 1975; Güttinger, 1981). Similarly, although early deafening does sometimes result in grossly abnormal song in swamp (*M. georgiana*) and song sparrows, the deafened song may retain normal elements. In addition, differences between the natural songs of these two species (the song sparrow produces longer songs with larger repertoires) can also be detected when the vocalizations of deafened birds are analysed in detail (Marler and Sherman, 1983). These facts are not compatible with the suggestion that all structure in the song of birds is the result of a process of matching vocalizations to a mental picture of how song should sound. In these species, the template may be in the form of a proprioceptive rather than an auditory model; alternatively, development of the motor commands necessary to produce song may not depend entirely on experience.

In addition, even where the model does fit, there are still many things we do not know about song development, such as what causes the beginning and end of the sensitive period, the exact physiological nature of the auditory template and its modification during learning and crystallization.

The pathways in the brain which are involved in song production are fairly well known (see page 99). The caudal ventral hyperstiatum (HVC), which has a critical role in song production, projects onto the robust archistriate nucleus (RA nucleus) which is itself linked to the hindbrain regions which supply motor nerves to the syrinx. Both the HVC and the RA are closely opposed to and receive projections from the region of the forebrain (area L) in which the auditory pathways terminate (Nottebohm, 1980).

In most passerines, only the males sing and all these structures are markedly larger in males than females. In addition, the cytoarchitecture differs in the two sexes; for example, in male zebra finches the neurons in the RA nucleus are larger, with longer processes and more dendritic spines than those of their female counterparts. The route of the efferent projections is the same in the two sexes but better developed in males. Treatment of young females with testosterone masculinizes their behaviour (unlike normal females, when adult they sing following testosterone injections) and their neuroanatomy (Gurney, 1981). Thus genetic maleness causes the birds to develop a nervous system which is built to produce song, via an early effect of circulating testicular androgens.

There is evidence that the left HVC dominates the right in song production; severing the tracheosyringeal branch of the left hypoglossus nerve in normal adult birds seriously impairs song production; severing the right results in loss of just a few elements. If these procedures are carried out in young birds, normal song development is possible, presumably because the right hemisphere takes over control of singing.

The period in which young canaries are producing subsong and plastic song corresponds with the time at which growth of the HVC and RA is most rapid. It is thus possible that this practice singing occurs at a time when auditory experience can influence the growth of neural pathways in this region. This suggestion is supported by the fact that lesion of the area L, the auditory projection nucleus underlying the HVC, results in reduced song complexity and that the HVC and RA are better developed in songbird species in which song development involves vocal learning (Nottebohm, 1980).

The formation of social preferences in galliform birds has been intensively studied and at least some of the multiple factors which determine how these develop have been identified and characterized. In order to proceed further with the analysis of such systems, the interaction between these factors must be investigated. This exercise is complex and quantitative models may be useful as aids to clear thinking. One of the few studies in which such a mathematical model has been used to investigate the effects of interaction between several factors influencing behavioural development concerns sexual imprinting in birds (Bateson, 1978a).

The term 'imprinting' refers to the process (or processes) by which social preferences are narrowed as a result of experience. In the most famous example, soon after hatching young chicks and ducklings will follow almost any moving object which they encounter; after a short exposure to one particular object, other moving objects are ignored or avoided. The young birds are said to be (filially) imprinted on the object which first elicited the following response; in nature, this will usually be their parent or their siblings. This process takes place most readily during a certain, sensitive, period of the young bird's life; in the case of chicks and under normal conditions this covers the time from a few hours to a few days after hatching. It was originally thought that this early social bond was carried over into the adult animal in the form of a preference for a particular category of animal as a mate. Although early experience in a sensitive period can indeed influence subsequent choice of a sexual partner, these two processes of filial and sexual imprinting are at least partially distinct (Bateson, 1978a).

In Bateson's model, the results of a large body of research on all aspects of the imprinting process are condensed into a few mathematical terms which determine ultimate sexual preferences. The model envisages an animal (presumably a bird) exposed to an imprinting stimulus (B) for a particular, variable length of time at a particular, variable age. Before this period, the bird is kept in a condition described as stimulus A, to which it is returned for a variable time before its ultimate preference is assessed. The subject does not generalize between these two stimuli; their strengths (SA and SB) are variable (although remaining constant during any one 'experiment'), which allows for the fact that not all objects are equally effective as imprinting stimuli.

Since it is known that there is an age before which any imprinting is impossible, the model assumes that a restriction in preference as a result of exposure can only occur if a factor within the animal, called its intrinsic responsiveness (i), is above a critical level. The model also makes assumptions about how i changes with age; in the simplest case, it increases gradually to a ceiling level.

The essence of imprinting, that exposure to one stimulus reduces responsiveness to others, is represented in the model by postulating that on responding positively to one stimulus, the level of response to all different objects is reduced by a specified amount; the size of this acquired reduction in responsiveness (n) depends on the level of i and on the strength of the stimulus which is eliciting the positive response. More specifically, following a positive response to A the acquired reduction in responsiveness to B (nB) is increased by the product of SA and i, magnified by a weighting factor Z ($Z > 1$) to allow for the fact that this depressing effect overrides the effects of habituation to the other stimulus. Enforced exposure to an unfamiliar object may overcome the tendency to avoid it; in the model the strength of this habituation effect again depends on the level of i and the strength of the stimulus concerned. Thus in a bird familiar with stimulus A but exposed to stimulus B and unable to avoid it, nB is reduced by the product of i and SB, with the constraint that it can never reach zero. The model ignores the attractive effects of slight novelty.

The essence of the model is that overall responsiveness to a given stimulus (r) at a particular time (t) is determined by the strength of the stimulus concerned, the animal's intrinsic responsiveness and the size of the reduction in responsiveness to that stimulus acquired as a result of all that has gone before. A bird will show a preference for B over A if its responsiveness to B (rB) is greater than that to A (rA); the strength of this preference will depend on the size of the difference. The precise calculations are summarized below.

$$r B_t = SB(i_t - nB_t)$$

where

$$nB_t = nB_{t-1} + (rA_{t-1}Z) - (SBi_{t-1})$$

The model is developed by working out the strength of the ultimate preference for B while altering some components and keeping others constant. For example, Fig. 4.9(a) shows the effects of varying both the age at which exposure to B starts and the strength of B; a preference for B only results if exposure to this stimulus occurs within a certain range of ages, the length of this period depending on the strength of the imprinting stimulus. In other words, the model reconstructs the sensitive period and the fact that the length of this period is variable rather than fixed.

In addition, the model was used to study the effects of simultaneous variation in length of exposure to B and its strength; Fig. 4.9(b) shows the range of values of SB and length of exposure which resulted in a preference for B. However strong the stimulus, no preference is formed if exposure is too short and however long the exposure, below a certain value of SB no preference develops. Neither of these results is self evident from the literature and therefore both constitute testable predictions of the model.

Thus a relatively simple model of the way different factors interact to determine the effect of previous experience on subsequent preferences does simulate correctly the known behaviour of birds. It therefore provides a candidate explanation for the processes involved which can be put to the test by investigating the accuracy of its predictions.

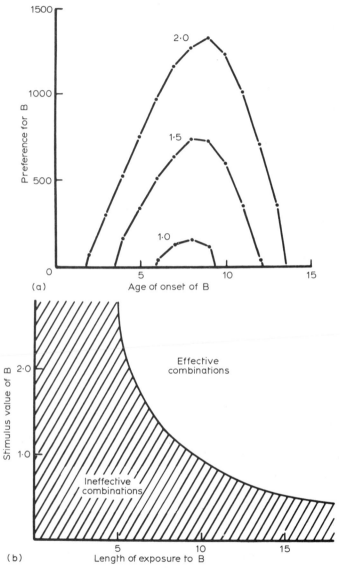

Figure 4.9 Predictions from Bateson's model (1978a) regarding the development of social preferences in birds. (a) The effects on preference for B at 50 days of altering the age of onset of exposure to B (for a fixed number of days) for stimulus values of 2.0, 1.5 and 1.0 compared to a stimulus value of 1.0 for A; (b) the combinations of stimulus value and length of exposure which result in a preference for B over A at 50 days.

4.5 Classifying the factors which influence the development of behaviour

Thus, some of the factors which influence the development of song in passerine and of social preferences in galliform birds have been identified and their properties described in considerable detail. It is clear that a range of different factors, both internal and external in origin and acting in a variety of ways play a part in behavioural development even when just these two examples are considered. When this list of processes is expanded to include other behaviour in other species, it becomes enormous and no generally applicable theory of behavioural development can be constructed until some kind of order can be imposed upon these many and diverse examples. In an attempt to provide a preliminary classification, Bateson (1978b)) has specified three dimensions along which influences on behavioural development can vary (Table 4.1).

Table 4.1 A three-way classification of the kinds of process which can influence the way behaviour develops. (After Bateson, 1978b).

Origin of influence	Nature of influence	Nature of consequence
Genome	Inducing	Specific ⟷ General
	Facilitating	Specific ⟷ General
	Maintaining	Specific ⟷ General
Environment	Inducing	Specific ⟷ General
	Facilitating	Specific ⟷ General
	Maintaining	Specific ⟷ General

In the first place, influential factors may originate in the genome (differences in song between canary breeds are genetic in origin) or may impinge on the animal from its external environment (dialects in chaffinches in different geographical regions are the result of learning from neighbouring conspecifics). Secondly, both internal and external factors may exert specific effects (in *hyperkinetic Drosophila*, the legs twitch but wing movements are almost normal; chaffinches mimic the actual notes of tutor songs) but their effects may also be of a more general nature (mutant alleles influencing the physiology of the retina in *Drosophila* and exposure to light in chicks alter the development of a range of visually guided behaviour patterns). Finally, following Gottlieb (1976), three distinct kinds of effects on behavioural development can be recognized. The most dramatic are those which have a determining effect, producing a radical switch from one developmental pathway to another and thus making a qualitative difference in the behaviour of the resulting adult animal. These are the so-called *inducing variables* and in their absence the trait concerned is absent or abnormal. The presence of testosterone in the blood just after hatching in canaries and feedback from singing during subsong in chaffinches are examples of factors with an inductive effect on the development of bird song. In contrast, *facultative variables* exert a quantitative effect, speeding up development processes which can proceed normally, if slowly, in their absence; they thus produce quantitative differences in the adult behaviour. For example, experience of auditory input from parent, from siblings or from their own pre-hatching vocalizations enhances the strength of the preference for maternal calls of the appropriate species which even devocalized ducklings show. Lastly, the development of behaviour may be influenced by factors which keep the behavioural system intact during periods of stability, in which case they are said to be *maintaining variables*. Absence of such factors results in retrograde development. As a very general example, an adequate food supply is essential for the processes of development to continue, while whatever triggers off growth of the joints in chick embryos, movement within the egg is necessary to maintain this development.

No clear distinction can be made between these three kinds of process; for example, under certain circumstances the effects of a maintaining variable may resemble those of a facultative one, while a strong facultative variable may produce a qualitative difference in adult behaviour, especially if some threshold is involved. However, this classification does make explicit the variety of ways in which the course of behavioural development can be influenced. It also provides a framework within which examples dependent on similar processes can be identified; scrutiny of their common properties may provide insight into the mechanism by which they work. The scheme obviously does not imply that a given trait is subject to just one type of influence. 'It seems reasonably likely that many patterns of behaviour of complex long-living animals will be determined by a combination of conditions from all the categories. This is a daunting prospect for anyone who wants to understand the origins of behaviour.' (Bateson 1981a.)

4.6 Some general features of behavioural development

The examples discussed illustrate a number of general features about the development of behaviour which are worth mentioning here.

4.6.1 SENSITIVE PERIODS

Several of the examples demonstrate the existence of periods in which the developing organism is particularly susceptible to specific kinds of influence. While this susceptibility may lie in the state of development of the nervous system at the time (Nottebohm, 1980), the original view that such sensitive periods are rigidly fixed and that an animal which fails to receive the necessary experience at the right time will be permanently deficient in behaviour is no longer accepted. The end of a sensitive period may be a consequence of what happens in the period itself and therefore is open to modification; thus failure to learn an adequate repertoire of song types extends the sensitive period for song learning in marsh wrens, as does exposure to a suboptimal imprinting object in young chicks.

4.6.2 CONSTRAINTS ON LEARNING

Some constraints on what animals will learn are of a rather obvious kind; thus if an animal is more sensitive to certain stimuli it can be conditioned to them more easily and if certain movements pose a strain on its physical equipment these will not readily be learned. However, selective song learning in chaffinches and other passerines is not a simple consequence of the birds being better able to hear nor of their being better able to sing particular notes; in this and in many other cases constraints on learning seem to be more subtle and interesting. For example, rats can be taught readily to avoid visual cues if these are associated with a shock and to avoid certain tastes if negative reinforcement comes in the form of emetic-induced vomiting. The converse pairings, with visual cues negatively reinforced by vomiting or taste with shock, do not readily modify behaviour; there is thus a constraint on which reinforcers can be used to modify the response to particular stimuli (Garcia, Ervin and Koelling, 1966). Breeding male sticklebacks quickly learn to swim through a ring or to bite a rod if their reward is the opportunity to attack a rival and will learn to swim through a ring for the opportunity to court a gravid female. However, it is almost impossible to train them to bite a rod in order to gain access to a gravid female. In this species, biting is a component of the aggressive response and aggression and sex are incompatible motivational systems. When the male is in a state in which the opportunity to court a female would act as a reinforcer, he is inhibited from biting the rod and when his motivational state allows him to bite the rod, a female is of no interest to him. Here the constraint is between which response can be strengthened by which reinforcer (Sevenster, 1973). As already mentioned, such constraints on what an animal will learn in a given situation represent one process whereby regular development can be assured. In addition, they often make obvious adaptive sense; rats would do well to remember which tastes made them sick and thus avoid dangerous food sources while too fierce an attack on a female stickleback, however gravid she may be, will drive her away.

4.6.3 FUNCTIONAL ASPECTS OF BEHAVIOURAL DEVELOPMENT

This raises the last general issue, that the influence to which a developing behaviour pattern responds may itself be the adaptive product of natural selection. There are many cases in which the details of behavioural ontogeny make sense in functional terms; for example, it is obviously adaptive for young red squirrels to show behaviour patterns which get them to the nipple when they are dependent on their mother's milk and to move efficiently in an adult manner when they come out onto the branches of the trees in which they live. Equally, since young cowbirds do not encounter conspecifics until they are grown up, normal song development in the absence of exposure to the song of their own species is essential. To give a more complex example, it has been suggested that learning to sing by improvization rather than by imitation as in the sedge warbler is an adaptation to a fluid breeding system in which interaction with particular individuals rarely lasts for more than a few weeks; learning by imitation occurs where the breeding structure is more stable. Birds which return to the same site each year to breed (for example the white crowned sparrow and the marsh wren) will tend to interact with the same individuals for long periods of time. If singing the same songs improves the efficiency of communication, it would pay these species to have a sensitive period for song learning which terminates during the first year of life. Where the population within a single breeding season is constant but the social environment may vary radically on occasions, as in the case of the indigo bird, the ability to learn throughout life may be at a premium (Kroodsma, 1981).

As a final example, it has been suggested that quail (*Coturnix coturnix*) and possibly other birds including chicks mate preferentially with individuals which are similar to but not identical with their siblings and that this intermediate level of inbreeding is adaptive (Bateson, 1979 and see page 227). The sensitive period for formation of this preference occurs within the first few weeks of hatching in quail, around the time when they start to take on their adult plumage. On the other hand, in chicks, which develop adult plumage at a later age, sexual imprinting occurs at 5–6 weeks. It is therefore possible that the sensitive period in these species is adapted to ensure that sexual preferences form at a time when siblings are beginning to take on their final adult appearance; the birds can thus learn what their close relatives will look like as adults before dispersing (Bateson, 1979). However, as Bateson points out, in this example, as in all the other cases where adaptive consequences are proposed for the details of the developmental process, there is nothing to go on but speculation.

CHAPTER 5

The adaptive significance of behaviour

There are three distinct questions which can be asked about evolution and behaviour. These are: Does an animal's behaviour influence its chances of surviving and/or reproducing and if so how? By what phylogenetic route has the behaviour evolved? and Does behaviour have a special role in the evolutionary process and if so what is it? This chapter is about the first of these questions; the other two are discussed in Chapters 6 and 7 respectively.

Hinde (1975) distinguishes between two meanings of the word function as it applies to behaviour; the term may refer either to any beneficial consequence of behaviour, the weak meaning of the word, or to the critical consequence through which selection acts to maintain the character in its present form; this is the strong sense of the word in Hinde's terminology. Although all the consequeces of performing a particular behaviour, beneficial or otherwise, will influence the fitness of the animal concerned to some extent and thus determine the response of the trait to natural selection, it is often possible to identify one consequence which apparently outweighs all others in this respect. For example, the function the lekking behaviour of male ruffs (*Philomachus pugnax*, see page 208) is to obtain mates (Van Rhijn, 1973) but they may derive other benefits such as the exchange of information about other resources (Kruijt, de Vos and Bossema, 1972). It may also be useful to distinguish between the present-day function of a behaviour and that responsible for its original evolution; thus, group foraging in great blue herons (*Ardea herodias*) probably evolved originally because it reduced vulnerability to predation but may now be maintained because it increases foraging efficiency (Krebs, 1974).

In order to understand the adaptive significance of a particular behaviour it is necessary to know whether it does, in fact, enhance fitness in the sense that individuals showing some different response do less well. If this is the case, we also need to find out to what broad aspect of the environment it is an adaptation (it may improve the performer's chances of obtaining food or of finding a mate) and how it exerts this effect (it may improve detection or enhance effectiveness of competition). Finally, we need to measure the size of the fitness advantage that the behaviour gives to the animal concerned and whether it represents the best possible solution to the problem.

5.1 Sources of evidence about the adaptive significance of behaviour

5.1.1 DEDUCTION FROM THE THEORY OF NATURAL SELECTION

The evidence quoted in support of a claim that a given behaviour pattern is of adaptive significance often amounts to little more than a declaration of faith in the ubiquitous influence of natural selection, especially when the behaviour concerned is expensive in some way, whether in time, energy or risk of some sort. While there are many cases in which this faith in the Darwinian process is justified, on its own it does not prove that a given behaviour is of adaptive significance; there are a number of evolutionary processes which could result in the appearance and maintenance of behaviour which is not adaptive (page 272).

5.1.2 THE CONTEXT IN WHICH BEHAVIOUR IS SHOWN

Additional support for the contention that a given pattern of behaviour enhances fitness, together with information about how it does so, comes from studies of the context in which the behaviour is shown. The elaborate songs produced by male sedge warblers are only heard before the birds acquire mates or if they lose their partner. This result suggests that the song functions to attract a mate (Catchpole, 1980) although alternative interpretations are possible.

5.1.3 THE SHORT-TERM CONSEQUENCES OF BEHAVIOUR

Observation of the usual short-term consequences of performance of a particular behaviour pattern can help in determining whether, how and, perhaps, how much, it contributes to fitness. For example, Cade (1979) noted that female crickets (*Gryllus integer*) often alight beside calling males and suggested that calling serves the function of attracting potential mates, a conclusion which is almost certainly correct (page 232). However, calling very often attracts flies as well as females and, on the basis of short term consequence of calling, one could argue that it serves to attract flies for food. This is unlikely since the crickets are herbivorous and the flies parasitic, but it does indicate that a common short-term consequence is not always a reliable indicator of the function that a behaviour pattern serves.

5.1.4 COMPARISONS BETWEEN SPECIES AND POPULATIONS

A great deal of information about whether and how particular behaviour patterns enhance fitness comes from attempts to correlate differences in behaviour, either between species or between populations of the same species, with ecological conditions or some other aspect of biology. For example, in wrens, males of polygamous species sing more complex songs than do males of monogamous species in which competition for mates may be less severe. This correlation between song complexity and the degree of competition for mates suggests that singing complex songs may serve the function of attracting females or repelling other males (Kroodsma, 1977).

However, a number of other explanations are possible for such a correlation between behaviour and ecology. In the first place, unless the choice of taxonomic unit for the comparison is carefully made, the correlation may be the result of phylogenetic constraints. To use a much quoted example, the existence of a correlation between polygyny and a marshland breeding habitat in wrens was used to support a theory that females mate preferentially with males defending high quality territories; since marshland is patchy, territories will differ in quality and the few males with a high quality area will attract most of the females (Verner and Wilson, 1966 and see page 211). However, of the 14 species used in the comparison, 9 belonged to the same family. It may therefore be that polygyny is not so much an adaptive consequence of living in a marsh habitat as a character-istic which happens to be common to all members of this group of wrens, which also and independently tend to breed in marshes. One solution to this problem is to treat each group of related species as a single unit for the purposes of comparison, selecting that taxonomic level which shows maximum variability in the behaviour concerned. An alternative solution is to compare behaviour and ecology only in very closely related animals, on the assumption that any phylo-genetic constraints of the kind mentioned above will act equally on all the units.

This assumption is best met in the case of populations of the same species. Thus, Seghers (1974) exploited the fact that guppies (*Poecilia reticulata*) live in isolated populations exposed to different environmental conditions to study the adaptive significance of schooling in this species. He measured the schooling response of guppies from several such sites and found a clear correlation between the strength of this response and the level of predation in both wild-caught and laboratory-reared guppies. In this species, therefore, living in groups may function as an anti-predator device.

Another problem in interpreting such correlations is that many features of the environment are variable and it is not always easy to decide to which of these the behaviour concerned might be an adaptation. For example, the areas from which Seghers collected his guppies also differed in visibility, the slower moving streams in which predators were found having clearer water. It may therefore be that guppies from low predation sites school less strongly because they cannot see each other well in their natural environments rather than as an adaptation to increased predation pressure (Liley and Seghers, 1975; Farr, 1975).

These problems with the comparative approach can often be solved by the use of common sense and by a knowledge of the biology of the species concerned. However, there are also a number of statistical techniques which can be used to unravel some of the complexities. One of these is the partial correlation co-efficient; in Seghers' study of guppies, given a sufficient number of populations, it would be possible to distinguish between the effects of visibility and predation level by estimating the correlation between the level of predation and strength of schooling for populations with the same visibility. If this was still positive then Seghers' original conclusion that the differences in schooling response were related to predation pressure is supported; if not, the key factor determining schooling tendency would appear to be the clarity of the water. Where species differ in a number of respects, morphological or ecological, to which a particular behaviour may be an adaptation, it may be possible to tease apart their interacting effects by using some form of multivariate analysis. Discriminant function analysis can be used if the behaviour concerned comes in discrete categories such as polygamy versus monogamy; multiple linear regression is appropriate if it is measured as a continuous variable such as strength of schooling. Both these techniques are discussed in more detail in the next section.

5.1.5 MEASURING THE FITNESS OF INDIVIDUALS WHICH DIFFER IN THEIR BEHAVIOUR

Natural variation among individuals within the same population can be used to determine the function of the behaviour, by relating the fitness of individuals to the behaviour they show. In Fig. 5.1 an estimate of the complexity of the song of male sedge warblers (the number of different syllable types produced in ten songs) is plotted against the date on which each male paired, a measure of its success in attracting females. The strong inverse correlation indicates that males with larger repertoires attract females and pair before their rivals and therefore that the function of song is to attract females (Catchpole, 1980).

Once again, there are problems; to prove that a complex song repertoire increases fitness, it is necessary to demonstrate not only that it results in early pairing but that as a result more eggs are produced, and these must be fertilized by the male in question. It is also necessary to know that more of these eggs survive to adulthood and that the chances of the parent's surviving to subsequent breeding seasons is not decreased by early breeding. Different measures of reproductive success might give different answers to the question of whether and how much a behaviour contributes to fitness. Table 5.1 shows the percentage of eggs hatched and fledged and of young surviving beyond their first winter in kookaburras (*Dacelo gigas*) breeding in pairs or in larger family groups; depending on which measure of reproductive success is used, a different picture is obtained of which breeding system is best and by how much (Parry, 1973). This problem of deriving measures of fitness is exaggerated in the case of behaviour which is not directly concerned with breeding, since there are so many intervening steps

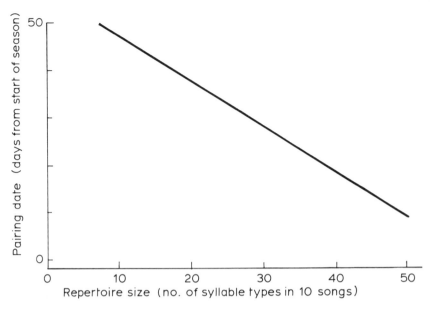

Figure 5.1 Measuring the fitness of naturally occurring behavioural variants; the relationship between song repertoire size and date of pairing in sedge warblers (after Catchpole, 1980).

between a behavioural difference and the lifetime reproductive output of the individuals concerned. The usual solution is to assume that some positive relationship exists between fitness and a more immediate beneficial consequence of the behaviour concerned and to concentrate study on the latter. This allows identification of behaviour patterns which enhance fitness and of the ways in which they do so, but unless the relationship between immediate consequence and lifetime fitness is positive and linear, estimating the extent to which fitness is enhanced, and therefore whether this is maximal, is difficult.

Table 5.1 Different measure of fitness; breeding success in single pairs and family groups of kookaburras measured at egg, fledgeling and juvenile stages (from Parry, 1973).

	% eggs hatching	% eggs fledged	% eggs surviving beyond winter
Pairs	71	50	0
Families	62	54	28

In order to interpret the consequences of such naturally occurring behavioural variation, it is also important to know how the differences arose. For example, the negative correlation between song complexity and pairing date in sedge warblers might arise because males which are weaker sing less complex songs and also, but independently, attract fewer females. Even if a complex song repertoire does clearly enhance success in attracting females, there are a number of different ways in which this may come about; the complex songs themselves may be selected by females or these may enable males to establish better territories, which are preferred by females. Catchpole distinguished between these two possibilities by using partial correlations. The full correlation between success in attracting females (pairing data) and repertoire size is −0.77; the partial correlation when territory quality is held constant is −0.87; when repertoire size is held constant the strong negative correlation disappears. Thus '. . . territory quality has little effect on female choice which is primarily influenced by complexity of the song.' (Catchpole, 1980.)

Given these complexities, studies of the adaptive significance of behaviour often require information about many properties of the animals concerned and of their environments. However, interpretation of such data is complicated and analytical techniques which identify and summarize the interactions between a large number of simultaneously varying factors are often necessary. Vehrencamp (1978) studied the adaptive significance of communal breeding in the groove-billed ani (*Crotophaga sulchirostris*) by recording habitat (pasture or marshland), the availability of food, the size of territory, and the number of males, females and helpers in the group; these are the independent variables, which might possibly influence fitness. In addition, she noted whether or not the brood was predated and the average number of juveniles reared per female; these are the dependent variables, the measures of fitness for which explanations are sought. The first of these (whether or not the brood is predated) is a discrete variable and was therefore analysed by discriminant function analysis. Briefly, this technique finds that combination of independent variables which best predicts the state of the dependent variable; more importantly in the present context, it also provides a measure of how important each independent variable is in discriminating between groups whose nests succumb to or avoid predation. The possibility that the differences in predation were the result of differences in the age of the broods or in territory quality was therefore allowed for by including these as variables in the analysis. Table 5.2(a) shows the results of such an analysis; in the pasture habitat, and during the eggs stage, multi-pair groups have greater breeding success regardless of age of eggs and quality of territory.

The average number of juveniles fledged per female, a continuous variable, was analysed by multiple linear regression. This technique attempts to predict the state of the dependent variable by successively adding to the equation that independent variable which correlates best with it. The effect of this variable is then controlled statistically and the procedure repeated until all variables which correlate significantly with the dependent variable have been included. The resultant model indicates what proportion of the variability in the number of juveniles per female can be predicted from the state of each of the independent variables. Table 5.2(b) gives just a few figures from such an analysis, for the pasture data only. The average number of juveniles reared per female increases with group size and when food supplies are abundant but decreases markedly with the number of laying females in the group.

Table 5.2 Using multivariate analysis to identify behavioural parameters which influence fitness in the groove-billed ani (from Vehrencamp, 1978).

(a) Multiple discriminant analysis with successful and predated nests as the dependent variable.

| | Percentage of variance in whether or not predation occurred predicted by each significant variable in | |
	Pasture	Marshland
Stage at which nest was found	17.8	63.8
Presence or absence of helpers	18.2	
How late in breeding season	20.0	−22.6
Insect biomass	12.3	
Number of females	16.4	
Extent of cover	−15.4	
Nest density		−13.6
Territory quality	No significant effects in either habitat	

*Negative score indicates variable is negatively correlated with success.

(b) Stepwise multiple linear regression with number of juveniles fledged per female as the dependent variable; significant effects in birds nesting in pasture.

Variable	Direction of effect	Magnitude of effect
Number of females	−	51.0
Abundance of othoptera	+	33.7
Group size	+	15.3

5.1.6 EXPERIMENTAL MANIPULATION OF THE CONSEQUENCES OF BEHAVIOUR

These sophisticated techniques provide a means of allowing for the effects of a number of variables when these cannot be controlled. However, since they are based on correlations, cause and effect are hard to unravel. For example, although number of young per female is designated the dependent variable and attempts are made to predict it from other factors, it is theoretically possible that orthoptera biomass, which features in the results of the multiple linear regression analysis as a good predictor of success, correlates with the number of young per female because orthoptera are attracted by the droppings of the young birds. These alternatives can only be separated by experimental manipulation of the consequences of performing a particular behaviour pattern. The classic example of such an experiment, Tinbergen's study of the function of egg shell removal in the black headed gull, has already been described (see page 2). In contrast to this simple field experiment, Gray, Kenney and Dewsbury (1977) investigated the adaptive significance of the precisely timed and complex sequences of male copulatory behaviour in meadow voles (*Microtus pennsylvanicus*) by a series of manipulations in the laboratory. Females of this species are induced ovulators and it is possible that the elaborate mating sequence stimulates ovulation in the female. The amount of copulation performed by the males was therefore varied experimentally, some being allowed to complete the full copulatory sequence while others were removed at an earlier stage. The *corpora lutea* in the females were then counted. Table 5.3 gives the percentage of females in the two groups which had ovulated. On this measure at least, reproductive success is greatest following the normal, complex copulatory sequence; this supports the suggestion that the adaptive significance of the elaborate pattern of copulatory behaviour in the male meadow voles derives from the stimulation required to induce ovulation in the female.

It is tempting to assume that because some neat manipulation has been performed, results obtained by the experimental approach are somehow more conclusive; to a certain extent this is true since it allows a distinction to be made between cause and effect in a way which is impossible where correlations alone are used. However, experimental manipulation presents its own problems, especially if the natural behaviour of the subjects is not well known. The mating behaviour of voles in the wild is unknown and the multiple intromissions whose adaptive significance was studied in this experiment may be something that these animals only do in captivity. Even if multiple intromissions are part of the natural behavioural repertoire of this species, they will only enhance fitness of the male if his sperm fertilize the eggs whose release they stimulate; a detailed study of the

Table 5.3 Experimental studies of the adaptive significance of behaviour; the effects of varying the amount of copulatory stimulation received on ovulation and implantation in young female meadow voles (from Gray, Kenney and Dewsbury, 1977).

	Unmated	One ejaculatory series	Complete ejaculatory series	
Number of *corpora lutea*	0	4.57	6.10	$p < 0.01$

breeding system of voles is necessary to find out whether this is the case. Finally, removing male voles during copulation may disturb the female as well as reducing the length of copulation and the subsequent reduction in frequency of ovulation may reflect an accidental consequence of the disturbance rather than an adaptive effect of the normal behaviour. While these problems do not invalidate an experimental approach to the adaptive significance of behaviour, they do mean that results need to be interpreted with caution.

5.1.7 DEDUCTIONS FROM THE GENETIC ARCHITECTURE OF BEHAVIOUR

A further source of evidence which is sometimes used in attempts to elucidate the way selection has acted on behaviour in the past comes from studies of the genetic mechanism controlling behaviour (Broadhurst, 1979). Heritability in the narrow sense is defined as the proportion of the total phenotypic variance which depends on additive genetic effects, as opposed to non-additive genetic effects or environmental influences (see page 305). The value of this statistic in the present context is that differences in heritability in characters within a single population are believed to reflect the way in which selection has operated on them. Where a character is important to fitness, directional selection is thought to stabilize it at high level by means of dominance and epistatic effects, reducing the additive genetic variance of the trait in question and thus its heritability. Therefore, if a character has low heritability and uni-directional dominance in its favour, this is often taken as evidence that natural selection has favoured it during evolution. For example, a series of crosses between inbred strains of *Drosophila melanogaster* which differed in the speed at which mating occurred produced a low heritability estimate and found strong dominance effects in favour of more rapid mating (Fulker, 1966). On the argument outlined above, these results suggest that in the past selection favoured males which mate rapidly and therefore that quick mating is of adaptive significance in modern flies.

If these arguments are valid, genetic architecture provides a very powerful source of evidence, since the effects of natural selection can be read directly in the genetic mechanism of the behaviour concerned. However, the situation is very complex and while a high uni-directional dominance effect may mean that a behaviour has been the subject of directional selection in the past, the absence of such an effect does not necessarily mean that it is without adaptive significance. A similar series of crosses found a high heritability and no dominance effects for the inter-pulse interval (ipi) of *Drosophila* courtship song (Cowling, 1980). This could mean that stabilizing selection has favoured intermediate ipis (although anti-directional dominance would then be expected), that antagonistic selection on pleiotropic effects has hindered the evolution of dominance or that differences in ipi of 5 msec (the difference between the parental strains) have no implications for fitness.

5.1.8 MODELS OF THE ADAPTIVE SIGNIFICANCE OF BEHAVIOUR

All the techniques discussed so far start with a behavioural difference and then look for evidence as to what function it might serve. Another approach, deductive rather than inductive, is to postulate a function for a particular behaviour and on the basis of this proposed function and the known or assumed properties of the system to derive logical predictions about what behaviour is to be expected under various circumstances. If real animals behave as predicted, this suggests that the behaviour in question does indeed serve that function. Such formal statements of the proposed function of behaviour and how it works are called models. The distinction between the deductive and inductive approach to the adaptive significance of behaviour is not always clearcut. Thus Seghers did not compare the schooling behaviour of different populations of guppies without having an idea that it served an anti-predator function. Equally, models are often constructed after the event in order to account for data already collected.

Three examples of the modelling procedure, all concerned with the question of why animals live in groups of a particular size, will be discussed to illustrate the ways in which it can be used, the sorts of answers it can provide about the adaptive significance of behaviour and some problems of the approach.

(a) *Foraging constraints on group size in antelopes; Jarman, 1974*
Jarman suggested that in antelopes, formation of groups reduces vulnerability to predation, which therefore sets a lower limit on group size. However, if feeding style is such that neighbouring animals do better feeding at a distance, along different paths or at different speeds, coordination between animals will break down and groups will fragment. Food dispersal will therefore place an upper limit on group size. These two suggestions represent the creative idea in Jarman's model.

The facts that he used in developing his model are summarized in Table 5.4. Foraging on food items which are dispersed and which, because of the selectivity of the animals concerned, are used up entirely in a single feeding episode limits the number of individuals which can associate and still feed efficiently; antelopes of type A should therefore live in very small groups. If the food supply is continuous and the foraging technique is unselective, animals can feed in large groups without unduly influencing each other's food supply; antelopes of type D and E are expected to live in large groups. Type B and C antelopes which are intermediate both in the distribution of their food plants and in the depletion of food supply resulting from one feeding episode will live in groups of intermediate size. Data on the actual group size of antelopes of types A to E are summarized in the table; the predictions outlined above are met very well, thus supporting the suggestion that the upper limit on group size is determined by feeding pattern.

This model is designed specifically to explain antelope social organization, although the hypothesis it embodies could be applied to other groups, and is very

The adaptive significance of behaviour 147

Table 5.4 Models of the adaptive significance of behaviour; group size as an adaptation to feeding habits in antelopes (after Jarman, 1974).

Feeding style	Example	Distribution of food before grazing	Effect of feeding on food distribution	Predicted group size and structure	Observed group structure
A. Highly selective as to plant part; feed on range of browse species	Steinbok	Small, scattered discrete food items	Removes whole plant; followers get none	Avoid grazed areas; groups separate	Feed singly or in pairs
B. Selective as to plant part; feed on range of browse and on grass	Bushbuck	More continuous but still patchy	Animals at rear suffer some reduction in food availability	Large groups disperse	3–6
C. Rather selective on range of grass and browse	Thomson's gazelle	More continuous but still patchy	Animals at rear suffer some reduction in food availability	Large groups disperse	6–60; large groups disperse
D. Selective as to age, unselective as to species	Wildebeeste	Continuous	Gradually reduced by successive bites; food abundance lowered but distribution stays the same; followers get a little less	Large groups maintained	9–several hundred; may aggregate into herds of several thousand during migration
E. Unselective on wide range of grass and browse	Eland	Continuous	Gradually reduced by successive bites; food abundance lowered but distribution stays the same; followers get a little less	Large groups maintained	Permanent herds of many hundreds to several thousands

closely grounded in known facts. It is really little more than a clever idea, clearly and logically developed to derive testable predictions, which happen to be correct. The term model may seem unnecessarily grandiose, but the underlying principles are the same as in the most complex mathematical model.

(b) *The selfish herd; Hamilton, 1971*

The most famous of all models designed to answer questions about the adaptive significance of behaviour is Hamilton's 'selfish herd', which was developed to discover whether natural selection acting on individuals to minimize predation risk could account for the fact that many animals live in groups. The model depicts an extremely simple system in order to clarify the issues involved; a number of frogs take shelter at the periphery of a circular pond from which a frog-eating snake emerges daily and eats the frog which is nearest to it. Each frog lives in a domain of danger, which is that section of the pond edge for which it will be nearest to the snake and therefore will get eaten. Frogs attempt to reduce their domain of danger by remaining where they are unless the gap in which they sit is larger than those beyond their two neighbours, in which case they jump into the smaller of these. In order to work out what results to expect from such a system, Hamilton started with a situation in which 100 frogs are randomly spaced around the pond, and calculated how many frogs would be found in each 10 degree sector of the pond in 20 successive rounds of movements in which each frog takes up a position according to the rules outlined above. In one representative case, after 4 moves the frogs were beginning to cluster in a few sections, after 10 rounds, only 9 of the 36 sections had any frogs in and by 16 rounds, 6 stable groups had formed.

This model is based entirely on ideas and refers to any species that behaves like the hypothetical frogs. It tells us that if animals attempt to reduce their own risk of predation by using others as cover, social groups will result; it is therefore not necessary to postulate any more complex selective process to explain the existence of animal groups although the model cannot prove that these do not apply. This conclusion, which represents the main theoretical contribution of the model, does not depend on the precise assumptions about the properties of the system. However, these can be put to some sort of test by seeing whether those prey animals which do live in groups behave in a frog-like way and whether their predators act like Hamilton's snake. Group living species often close in when predators appear and animals on the outside of groups do try to obtain positions on the inside; in addition, predators do often direct their attacks selectively at outlying animals. Thus in spite of its simplicity, Hamilton's selfish herd model has provided a general insight into the question of why animals might live in groups and, perhaps, why some actually do.

(c) *Group living as a protection against detection by predators; Treisman, 1975*

Treisman (1975) developed a series of models to test the same suggestion, that the dispersal patterns of animals represent an adaptation to predation, in this case postulating that vulnerability is lowered by reducing the chance of detection. In the simplest model, he considers an aerial, visually hunting predator searching alone for ground-living prey whose only defence is crypsis and which are either randomly distributed or form a circular clump. The model assumes that the predator scans the environment completely in a fixed period of time and if it locates prey it captures one while the rest escape; group living thus provides an element of safety in numbers. If the predator fails to locate prey within a given period, the predator stops searching; all other things being equal, clumps of prey are harder to detect than randomly distributed prey and group living increases the chance that the predator will give up and go elsewhere. However, in this model, all other things are not equal, in that groups of prey present a larger surface area for detection, although they are not more conspicuous in any other way.

An important feature of Treisman's model is the way it treats the relationship between stimulus area and detectability, this being based on known properties of the perceptual mechanisms of real animals. In humans, the probability that a stimulus will be detected increases linearly with its area (with a slope dependent on its inherent conspicuousness) but only up to a certain critical point; beyond this, further increase in area does not increase the probability of detection. The predator in his model is assumed to have the same perceptual quirk and thus beyond a certain point, the larger surface area presented by animals in groups ceases to affect their probability of detection.

Treisman developed his model by derived formulae relating the two proposed beneficial consequences of group life (reduced probability of detection due to clumping and reduced chances of being taken after detection) and its dis-advantageous consequence (increased surface area) to the number of animals in a group. The probability of detection in groups of different sizes was then cal-

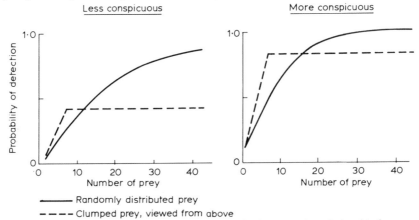

Figure 5.2 Models of the adaptive significance of behaviour; the relationship between detectability and abundance calculated from Treisman's model for prey with different degrees of conspicuousness and different distribution patterns.

culated for prey with different degrees of conspicuousness (Fig. 5.2). The aim is to identify the conditions in which the probability of detection is lower for clumped than for randomly distributed animals and thus to predict when animals will live in groups if the adaptive consequences of this behaviour are as he suspects.

Over a certain critical prey number ($N = 10$ and $N = 15$ respectively) animals clumped in a circle are less easily detected than randomly dispersed prey when viewed from above; these are the critical group sizes below which the prey should disperse. While increased conspicuousness raises the probability of detection for prey in both distributions, this effect is more marked when they are clumped. Thus the critical group size at which clumped prey is less vulnerable is greater when they are more conspicuous; prey are therefore less likely to be found in groups because they cannot exploit the advantage of clumping. For prey whose degree of conspicuousness is intermediate, large groups are beneficial while small groups are not.

(d) *How models can elucidate the adaptive significance of behaviour*
Between them, these three models illustrate the various ways in which models can help determine whether, how and how much behaviour contributes to fitness.

1. All three models make explicit the facts and assumptions upon which their deductions depend. They thus show up their own weaknesses and invite improvement; Treisman's is just one of the many models expanding on Hamilton's selfish herd.

2. They also make their logic, whether this is verbal or algebraic, public and therefore available for critical assessment and improvement. The use of mathematical models allows realistic complexities to be accommodated in the model, but demands careful presentation if this beneficial publicity is to be retained.

3. Models can suggest the way in which selection could potentially act on behaviour; if the model proposed is simple, it can eliminate the need for more complex explanations. Thus, since these models postulating benefits to individual animals predict that animals will sometimes live in groups there is no need to postulate the action of selection on groups to explain the fact that they often do so (see page 257).

4. Finally, such models provide testable predictions which can be compared with the behaviour of real animals. Potentially, therefore, they allow us to determine whether the picture they present of the way selection works does indeed reflect reality in any given case. This is the most powerful application of the modelling procedure but it depends critically on the nature of the predictions.

As discussed in the context of motivational models (see page 53), useful predictions must be unique to the model concerned in the sense that different models do not predict the same thing. Treisman's model predicts that animals should

The adaptive significance of behaviour 151

form groups provided these exceed a certain critical size: however, this would also follow if groups of animals above a certain size mount more effective counterattacks. The model also predicts that increased conspicuousness will raise the critical size at which group life becomes adaptive; if groups serve to enhance active defence the reverse might be expected. Treisman also made quantitative predictions about the precise group size above which clumping will be favoured; the alternative suggestion, that group life enhances the effectiveness of communal defence, is unlikely to make exactly the same prediction. These thus constitute unique and therefore useful predictions for assessing the picture of selection on which the model is based. However, the critical group size calculated from Treisman's equations (which are relatively simple) is dependent on his estimates of the key parameters, in this case the precise relationship between area and detectability and how this changes with conspicuousness. Unless these are accurately assigned, quantitative agreement between observed and predicted behaviour does not mean the hypothesis is right and disageement does not mean it is wrong. As discussed in Chapter 3 (see page 53), models could be designed for robustness in the face of altered parameter values but almost by definition a model which accurately reflects the way behaviour adapts animals to the many features of their environment is likely to produce predictions which depend critically on the values assigned to its parameters. Using only those models whose predictions are robust may therefore rule out those which are potentially the most useful in elucidating the adaptive significance of behaviour. Therefore in the present state of the game, the best predictions are probably qualitative but counter intuitive ones.

5.2 Difficulties in studying the adaptive significance of behaviour

Thus each source of evidence on the adaptive significance of behaviour has its own special problems; in addition, however, there are a number of general difficulties which complicate the exercise of determining how selection acts on behaviour.

5.2.1 MULTIPLE BENEFITS

Behaviour may be answerable to more than one selection pressure and therefore even if one or more of the techniques above has shown that some action contributes to fitness in a particular way, this need not be its only contribution. 'How' questions require more than one answer and 'how much' questions require the various contributions to fitness to be combined. For example, for groove-billed anis living in pastures, dominant females benefit from communal breeding, both as a result of reduced predation and as a result of increased breeding success. This raises the problem of how these disparate effects are to be combined to estimate the overall impact of communal nesting on fitness; how is a reduction in predation risk to be equated with an increase in breeding success, and should these two contributions to fitness be combined additively or multiplicatively?

5.2.2 COSTS, BENEFITS AND OPTIMALITY MODELS

As an extension of the previous point, where behaviour is influenced by a number of selective forces, their influences may not all be in the same direction; thus behaviour often carries costs as well as benefits. For example, subordinate female groove-billed anis gain protection against predation from breeding communally but this is offset by a reduction in breeding success. 'How' questions therefore need qualification and 'how much' questions require costs and benefits to be combined in some way to give a measure of overall fitness.

The exercise of finding out whether the advantages of performing a particular pattern of behaviour outweigh its disadvantages is commonly referred to as the cost–benefit approach to behaviour. It is often combined with attempts to find out whether the way an animal behaves provides the best possible solution to the problem for which it is presumed to be an adaptation. This question can only be solved by means of models and, in particular, the rather specialized ones of optimality theory. It can be argued from the theory of natural selection that an animal species existing for a sufficiently long time in a particular environment will acquire characteristics which are optimal in the sense that they maximize the fitness of the animals concerned. Optimality models take a hypothetical function of a particular behaviour pattern, and use this to generate testable predictions about how an animal should behave in order to maximize its fitness. The aim is not to test whether or not natural selection maximizes fitness but to use the assumption that it does do so to test a specific hypothesis about the nature of the selection pressures acting on behaviour.

The steps in developing an optimality model of behaviour are:

1. Specification of the different behaviour that an animal could potentially show in particular conditions. For example, an animal may have a number of different ways of feeding. In what is omitted from this set of competing solutions, constraints are put on the system.

2. Deciding what is to be maximized, or choosing the currency in which costs and benefits are to be calculated. Ultimately, this should be a lifetime contribution to subsequent generations but since this is extremely difficult to measure, it is usual to assume that the immediate consequences of behaviour will have an impact on fitness and to guess at precisely what fitness-related consequence is being maximized. This represents the hypothesis about the way selection acts on behaviour which the model is to test. For example, feeding behaviour could be adapted to maximize the rate of intake of energy during a foraging period or the rate of intake of some other nutrient. It should be possible to derive predictions to distinguish between these two possibilities.

The adaptive significance of behaviour 153

3. Estimation of the costs and benefits of employing the various behavioural options, based on a knowledge of the animals concerned, so that the relationship between behavioural variation and the chosen currency can be determined.

4. Development of the model, usually mathematical, to identify that behavioural option which produces the highest pay-off in terms of the chosen currency. This is the behaviour that the animal should show if natural selection has acted on it in the way suggested. It therefore constitutes a prediction which can be used to test the hypothesis about the adaptive significance of behaviour embodied in the model.

In an early application optimality theory was used to investigate the adaptive significance of copulation duration in dungflies (*Scatophaga stercoraria*) (see Parker, 1978) in which species males compete intensively for females arriving at fresh cowpats to mate and lay eggs. On finding a female a male copulates with and then guards her, often until she lays her eggs, before going off in search of another female. Every minute that the male spends with one female increases the chances that his sperm will fertilize her eggs, but at the same time it reduces the time available for finding other females. Parker was interested in what determines how long males spend *in copula* and whether this is the optimal solution to their dilemma.

The behavioural options are the various possible copulation times and the proposed currency in which gains are measured is the proportion of eggs fertilized per unit of time spent in both finding and mating with females (which is assumed to bear some direct relationship to fitness). The costs of the various components of behaviour were determined as follows: the average rate of encountering females (140 minutes per female) was estimated directly from field data, as was average time spent guarding females between copulation and oviposition (16.5 minutes); these two figures give a total search time (S) of 156.5 minutes. The benefit (G) in terms of the number of fertilized eggs accruing from the various copulation times (I for investment) was calculated from laboratory experiments using males with labelled sperm, on the assumption that a certain proportion of wild females have mated before and that all females are of equal value in terms of egg production. Figure 5.3(a) shows the relationship between the proportion of eggs fertilized and copulation time. The longer a male copulates, the more eggs he fertilizes because his sperm (which are assumed to cost nothing to produce) displace those of any previous male.

What copulation time would maximize the proportion of eggs fertilized per unit time? Intuitively, the male should remain *in copula* as long as the future gain rate expected from doing so exceeds that from withdrawing to search for another female; when this ceases to be the case he should leave. In mathematical terms, this equilibrium is reached when the rate of fitness gain (which simplifies to $G/I+S$) is maximum and is found quite simply by differential calculus. Graphically, the maximum overall rate at which fertilized eggs can be gained from the system shown in the figure is found by producing the abscissa beyond the

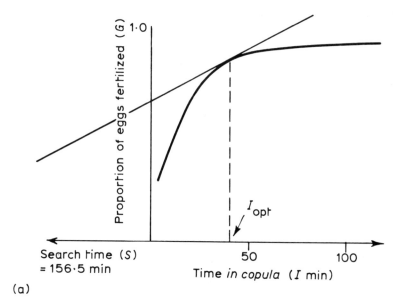

(a)

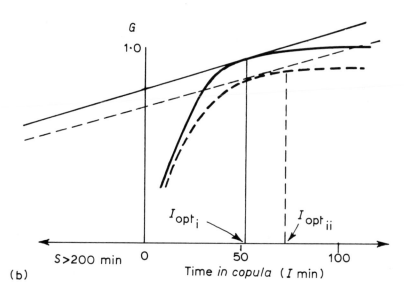

(b)

Figure 5.3 Using optimality theory to investigate the adaptive significance of copulatory behaviour in dungflies (after Parker, 1978). (a) Derivation of optimal duration of copulation using realistic parameters; (b) the effect of altering search time and gain rate.

origin by a distance S and drawing the tangent from this point to the curve $G(I)$. It is clear that the optimum copulation time (Iopt) is not that which gives maximum gain in a single copulation (Imax); the possibility of acquiring other females reduces the optimum value. As Fig. 5.3(b) shows, an increase in the time taken to search for females (S) and thus the costs of finding a new mate decreases the extent to which a male can benefit from leaving; it therefore pays him to stay with a given female for a longer time (Iopt increases). Iopt also increases if the slope of the $G(I)$ curve is small (the rate of gain per unit of investment is slow). The predicted Iopt in Fig. 5.3(a) is 41.4 minutes; the mean copulation time observed in the field is 35.5 minutes. These two figures are in sufficiently close agreement for the hypothesis that copulation time maximizes the number of eggs fertilized per unit time to be provisionally accepted. Thus, if the G/I curve has been calculated accurately this model represents correctly the nature of the selective forces acting on one aspect of behaviour in dungflies and illustrates the potential of the optimality approach.

However the fit is not perfect, and this can be corrected by modifying two assumptions (sperm now cost something to produce and females which have recently laid eggs are worth less) and reassigning one parameter value (the estimation of the proportion of virgin females in the wild used to convert the experimental data into gain rates is increased). These changes are biologically reasonable and improve the fit between the observed and predicted copulation times. However, the discrepancy could be real, in which case the model should be rejected in favour of an alternative. Thus, fertilization rate might be maximized over the whole breeding season rather than over the lifetime of a single pat (which would give a shorter optimum copulation time). Alternatively, dungflies may not be able to measure the passage of time very accurately, or some conflicting selection pressure such as the need to avoid being trodden on by cows might reduce the optimum copulation time. Parker's model could be extended to include such complexities. However, it may be that dungflies are unable to measure the passage of time very accurately and there is also a real possibility that natural selection has not produced perfectly designed flies. Such problems with optimality theory are discussed in more detail on page 180.

5.2.3 FREQUENCY DEPENDENT COSTS AND BENEFITS; GAMES THEORY

The costs and benefits associated with performance of a particular behaviour pattern often depend on environmental conditions; for example, communal nesting protects groove-billed anis against predation in pastures but not in marshes. This is a practical problem, to be solved by studying the animals concerned in a range of habitats. However, a rather special case arises when the environmental circumstances which modify the consequences of behaviour are other animals of the same species, in which case costs and benefits are often frequency dependent. In such circumstances, special methods are necessary to clarify the effects of selection on the behaviour concerned, and one which has been widely used in this context is an extension of optimality models called Games Theory. This is a branch of mathematics developed for analysing two-way human conflicts, the essence of which is to predict which of a number of possible strategies is the best one for an individual to use taking into account what the opponent does. It was first applied to the problem of the evolution of animal behaviour by Maynard Smith (see Maynard Smith, 1979 for a review).

As with other optimality models, the analysis starts by specifying the various forms of behaviour that the hypothetical animal could show in each situation in which it finds itself: these are called strategies but the term does not imply that the animals make conscious choices about what to do. The pay-off resulting from employing each strategy, given each possible behaviour of the opponent, is then assessed, in some currency ultimately related to fitness. Development of the model then involves working out the frequency of the different kinds of encounter and thus the overall pay-offs to the different strategies. In order to do this, the animals concerned are usually assumed to be part of an infinite population and to encounter each other at random. Assuming further that the strategies are represented in successive generations with frequencies proportional to their overall pay-off in the previous one, the relative frequencies of individuals using the different strategies over a number of generations are calculated. It is therefore possible to determine the fate of the hypothetical strategies as natural selection exerts its effects. Although the pay-off in any single encounter depends on the strategy adopted by the opponent, it is possible that certain strategies exist which cannot be displaced once they predominate in a population. These are the evolutionary stable strategies (or ESSs) towards which the model population should evolve: if the hypothesis about the adaptive consequences of each strategy is correct and the assumptions of the model valid, they represent the behaviour which real animals should show.

The classic example of the use of games theory to unravel the effects of selection on behaviour concerns fighting between conspecifics. Suppose that an animal can show three forms of aggressive behaviour; it may fight viciously in every contest (the hawk strategy), it may use only conventional signals in a fight, withdrawing at the first signs of dangerous fighting in its opponent (the dove strategy) or it may display conventionally against a dove but retaliate against a hawk (the retaliator strategy). The opponent-dependent costs and benefits of each strategy depend on a set of rules for the outcomes of encounters; thus when two hawks or a hawk and retaliator meet, they have an equal chance of winning and of getting severely injured. When doves and/or retaliators meet both participants waste time in conventional display and have an equal chance of winning. When a hawk meets a dove, the encounter is short, the hawk always wins while the dove retreats and may receive a slight injury in the process. If V is the benefit gained from winning, D is the cost of serious injury, S the cost of minor injury and T the cost of wasting time, these rules can be converted into pay-offs for the two participants in each kind of encounter, as in Table 5.5. In calculating

Table 5.5 Using games theory to investigate the adaptive significance of behaviour; the pay-off matrix for a game played between hawks, doves and retaliators (from Maynard Smith, 1974).

| | In a contest against: | | |
Pay-off to:	Hawk	Dove	Retaliator
Hawk	$1/2(V-D)$ (equal chance of winning or being injured)	V (opponent always retreats)	$1/2(V-D)$ (opponent acts like a hawk)
Dove	$-S$ (never wins and may get slight injury)	$V/2-T$ (wins half of fights but always spends time)	$V/2-T$ (opponent acts like a dove)
Retaliator	$1/2(V-D)$ (acts like a hawk)	$V/2-T$ (acts like a dove)	$V/2-T$ (both participants act like a dove)

V is the value of winning, D is the cost of serious injury, S is the cost of slight injury and T is the cost of spending time in display.

the pay-offs of a given strategy, items measured in different units (however one measures benefits of winning, risk of damage, waste of time) are being compared; thus the analysis assumes that the various consequences of a particular action have some direct relationship with ultimate fitness.

How would selection act on a population of hawks, doves and retaliators? For any strategy to be an ESS, the overall fitness of animals playing that strategy must be greater than that of animals playing any other strategy. Consider a population consisting of hawks, in which a mutant dove arises; because most hawks meet hawks, their average pay-off is $1/2$ $(V-D)$. Most doves also meet hawks so their average pay-off is $-S$. Provided that $-S > 1/2(V-D)$ (which will be the case if serious injury is expensive) doves will do better on average than hawks and therefore increase in frequency, even though they never win any fights. In the reverse situation, doves will mostly encounter doves giving them an average pay-off of $V/2-T$: hawks will mostly meet doves and get a pay-off of V, and will therefore do better than doves. Therefore in this game, neither hawk nor dove is an ESS. The situation is more complex in the case of retaliators; if $D > V$ and if T is small, retaliators have a higher average pay-off than hawks, because they do not incur serious injury so often and do better than doves because they win against hawks on 50% of the occasions on which they encounter one. Thus, a population of retaliators cannot be invaded by hawks or doves and retaliator is therefore an ESS; if the conditions assumed in this model prevail in real life, animals should therefore use conventional displays and escalate only in retaliation to overt attack.

Had hawk and dove been the only two strategies in the game, there would be no ESS. However, given certain parameter values a specific proportion of hawks and doves exists for which the overall pay-offs for the two strategies are equal. This proportion represents an evolutionarily stable, mixed strategy and may come about either because every individual plays the two strategies in ESS proportions or because individuals playing just one of the two strategies occur in these proportions.

Even with such simple assumptions about the way animals fight, by identifying evolutionarily stable strategies, games theoretical models indicate the kind of behaviour to be expected if selection favours characteristics which maximize fitness. Thus, game theory has shown that we do not need to invoke arguments about the good of the species to explain why much animal fighting is ritualized (see page 194). Because of the enormous problems involved in measuring costs and benefits and of combining these to produce a realistic pay-off matrix, precise, quantitative predictions which can be tested against hard data are not to be expected. However, the hawk–dove model does produce counter-intuitive qualitative predictions such as the existence of mixed populations of equally successful escalated and conventional fighters against which the behaviour of real animals can be compared.

Games theory runs into a number of difficulties, for example when the genetic mechanisms underlying the strategies are made more realistic. These are discussed in more detail below (see page 193).

5.3 The state of the art

Notwithstanding the sophisticated arguments of cost–benefit analysis and optimality theory, the actual techniques available for collecting hard data on whether, how and how much behaviour contributes to fitness are broadly the same as those available when Tinbergen wrote *The Study of Instinct*. So are the problems these involve, although use of multivariate analysis has helped in resolving some of these. What is different is the nature of the behavioural phenomena about which the questions are asked. In the classic study of egg shell removal in the black-headed gull, Tinbergen *et al.* (1962) studied the consequences of the presence or absence of a given behaviour pattern. Seghers (1974) studied the effect on fitness of different levels of a given response, namely schooling. Catchpole (1980) investigated the functional significance of the complexity of behaviour, in the form of song repertoires of different sizes. Several authors have speculated on the adaptive significance of the motivational background of behaviour; for example, Heiligenberg (1976) found that in male convict cichlids, black eye bars increase attack readiness while orange fin spots depress it. In the laboratory at least, males which already have territories and which therefore are unlikely to attempt a take over have orange spots; males without territories have eye bars only. It was therefore suggested that the way the fishes' motivational state is influenced by external stimuli makes them attack most those males which present the greatest threat. Yet others have speculated about the adaptive significance of interactions between different motivational systems. Roper (1978) suggests that a time sharing relationship between feeding and drinking (see page 94) would be the most efficient form of motivational organization when food and water are found at different places. The space–state approach to motivation (see page 88) has been extended to allow identification of complete sequences of behaviour which maximize fitness in animals whose state departs from optimum on more than one axis of physiological space (Sibly and McFarland, 1976). Finally, the way in which behaviour is modified by experience may be of adaptive significance; thus Bateson suggests that development of social preferences as a result of experience during a sensitive period influences subsequent mate choice so as to ensure optimum levels of inbreeding (Bateson, 1981b and see pages 137 and 227).

These, then are the kinds of techniques that can be used to study the adaptive significance of behaviour, the problems they pose and the kinds of behavioural phenomena to which they have been applied. In the light of their results, can we sustain the view that most, if not all, aspects of behaviour are the result of natural selection acting on individual animals in favour of those characters which maximize fitness? Theories about the ways in which behaviour contributes to fitness have changed so much in the last decade or so, that before attempting to answer this question (see page 270), current theory on adaptive significance of the main aspects of behaviour will be briefly discussed; to consider these fully would require a much longer book than this one.

5.4 The adaptive significance of the way animals pattern their behaviour in time

5.4.1 RHYTHMS OF BEHAVIOUR

Over and above the irregular fluctuations in responsiveness whose internal basis was discussed in Chapter 3 and whose possible adaptive significance was mentioned in the previous section, the behaviour of many animals undergoes regular cycles; these have periods ranging from hours (voles (*Microtus arvalis*) show cycles of feeding with a period of about 2 hours, Daan and Slopsema, 1978) to several years (some cicadas emerge from their eggs at regular intervals of about 15–17 years, Lloyd and Dybas, 1966). The most widely studied rhythms are those which correspond to geophysical cycles such as the earth's rotation on its own axis. Figure 5.4 shows the number of *Drosophila melanogaster* emerging from their pupae at various times of day; there is a clear peak in the early morning (Konopka and Benzer, 1971). Rhythms may also fit in with the moon's movements; the shore crab, *Carcinus maenus*, is one of many marine creatures which show tidal rhythms of activity (with a period of about 12 hours) emerging

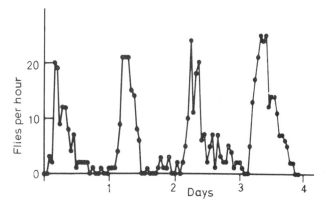

Figure 5.4 An endogenous circadian rhythm; eclosion rates in *Drosophila melanogaster* expressed in numbers of flies emerging per hour (from Konopka and Benzer, 1971).

regularly from hiding at high tide (Naylor, 1958). The marine midge (*Clunio marinus*) lays its eggs at the lowest part of the intertidal zone which is uncovered only at spring tides. The adults eclose, mate and lay their eggs within the few hours that the larval sites are exposed; they therefore show a semi-lunar rhythm, with a period of about 14 days (Neumann, 1975). Lunar cycles of activity with a period of about 29 days are also quite common; for example, the ant lion (*Myrmeleon obscurus*) shows a rhythm of pit building with peak activity at full moon (Youthed and Moran, 1969). Rhythms have also been described which fit in with the earth's annual cycle of movement around the sun. The golden mantled ground squirrel (*Citellus lateralis*) shows an annual activity rhythm, hibernating in the winter and emerging each spring (Pengelley and Asmundson, 1971). One species of animal may be subject to several rhythms of different periodicity; for example, shore crabs show both diurnal and tidal rhythms, the former manifesting itself in a larger tidal peak at night than in the daytime (Naylor, 1958). In marine midges, the onset of pupation has a semi-lunar rhythm, but emergence only occurs during the daytime spring low tide, keeping to a daily rhythm.

In many, though by no means all, cases, these rhythms have been shown to persist under constant conditions. Thus *Drosophila melanogaster* still shows peak levels of eclosion at 24 hour intervals in constant darkness; the tidal rhythms of shore crabs, the semi-lunar rhythms of marine midges and the lunar rhythms of ant lions persist under constant conditions while ground squirrels continue to hibernate at annual intervals in the absence of any regular environmental changes. Some rhythms disappear after a few cycles in constant conditions (the activity rhythm of the shore crab is a case in point) but others, such as the eclosion rhythm in *Drosophila*, may persist for hundreds of cycles. In the latter case, while the cycle persists, its period changes slightly from almost exactly 24 hours under normal light conditions to a period of 25 hours 5 minutes in constant light. For this reason the pattern is called a circadian rhythm, having a period of about a

The adaptive significance of behaviour   161

day. Activity rhythms which are not dependent on the existence of regularly occurring environmental events must depend on some factor within the animal and are therefore called endogenous rhythms.

Much of the enormous literature on this subject is aimed at unravelling the mechanisms underlying the rhythmicity. To summarize very briefly, two main properties are characteristic of endogenous rhythms; they are extremely resistent to perturbation by environmental changes and in natural conditions, the endogenous cycle often runs synchronously with (or is entrained to) some rhythmic features of the environment such as the light–dark cycle. The readiness with which this entrainment occurs is itself the result of an internal cycle of sensitivity. A great deal is known about the properties of these endogenous cycles in a few intensively studied species; no one has yet found the structure(s) which controls them (the so-called biological clock).

5.4.2 THE ADAPTIVE SIGNIFICANCE OF BEHAVIOURAL RHYTHMICITY

Shore crabs reared in the laboratory in the absence of any stimulation with a 12 hour periodicity only require a single, brief exposure to a lowered temperature in order to start showing tidal rhythms of activity (Williams and Naylor, 1967). Similar results for other endogenous rhythms including the eclosion rhythm of *Drosophila* indicate that these may well represent inherited characteristics of the animals concerned. In addition, both the potential for showing rhythmicity and the period of the cycles can be modified by genetic change. For example, crosses between local strains of *Clunio* show that details of the phase relationships between the circadian and tidal rhythms are inherited under the influence of just a few genes (Neumann and Heimbach, 1979). Populations of *Drosophila* respond to artificial selection for early and late eclosion (Clayton and Paietta, 1972) while mutants exist in these flies whose eclosion rhythm is lost or its period altered (Konopka and Benzer, 1971). All these results indicate that different patterns of rhythmicity may depend on genetic differences and are therefore potentially subject to natural selection. However, very little work has been carried out on the question of whether the way animals pattern their behaviour in time contributes to fitness and if so how it does so.

This is partly because the search for the biological clock has proved absorbing but also because it is usually taken as self-evident that such an elaborate characteristic must be of adaptive significance. For example, many of the flowers from which bees collect pollen and nectar open and close at different times of day. Bees time their foraging trips so that they visit each type of flower only when it is open and it hardly seems necessary to conduct experiments to find out whether this regular pattern of behaviour improves the bees' foraging efficiency. However, the answer is not always so obvious and functional questions can usefully be asked about the presence of the rhythm, why it should be internally programmed rather than dependent on external circumstances, why it should be self-sustaining and why the details of the mechanism should be as they are.

(a) *Why show rhythmic behaviour?*
It is intuitively obvious that the regular and profound changes in an animal's environment which result from geophysical cycles must have implications for its survival and reproductive success; one would therefore expect natural selection to act on animals in such a way as to make them active at the most suitable time. In many cases, consideration of the adaptive significance of activity rhythms goes no further than this. However, there are a few cases in which the evidence is more compelling. For example, different species of *Drosophila* with different transpiration rates show peak eclosion at different times of day; this observation, together with the fact that *Drosophila* emerging from the pupae in dry conditions often fail to survive, suggests that the rhythm ensures that eclosion occurs at the correct humidity (Pittendrigh, 1956). This is supported by the fact that *Drosophila* species living in subtropical forests where humidity is high have more flexible activity rhythms than those found in open country (Taylor and Kalmus, 1954). Thus at least one factor shaping the temporal patterning of an animal's activity is the need to avoid dessication.

Rhythmic activity can also be an adaptation to biotic factors. Thus, most young guillemots (*Uria lomvia*) jump off the ledges on which they hatch between 20.00 and 24.00 hours. This peak, which occurs when it is still light, coincides with the time when the risk of predation is at its lowest, partly because gulls are not very hungry and partly because synchronized jumping swamps the predators (Daan and Tinbergen, 1979). In a long series of laboratory and field studies, Daan and Slopsema (1978) showed that during the day, voles alternate between surface feeding and subterranean resting at approximately two hour periods and that the rhythms of different individuals are synchronized. Cross species comparisons among voles and lemmings, which are related and have similar life styles, showed a positive correlation between weight, and therefore presumably the amount of food that can be taken in at one meal, and the period of the activity rhythm. This indicates that the timing of the activity cycle is adjusted to the metabolic needs of the animal concerned, although food intake and digestion are not necessary for the rhythm to manifest itself. From observations of the hunting success of kestrels (*Falco tinnunculus*) in the study area in relation to the relative abundance of voles, it is possible to calculate the relative vulnerability to predation of voles which are active at different phases of the daily cycle. At times when most of the population is inactive, predators pick on any which are on the surface making the risk incurred very high at these times. Thus while the existence of a two hour rhythm has primarily to do with digestive efficiency, the synchrony of the cycles of different individuals is probably an anti-predator device.

Synchronization of rhythms may serve other functions; *Dacus tryoni*, a species of fruit fly, is active for a period of several hours but both sexes restrict their mating activity to a period of just thirty minutes at dusk in the wild and at the equivalent time under constant conditions in the laboratory. A second species, *Dacus neohumeralis*, has a similar pattern of overall activity but shows mating behaviour over a much longer period of about seven hours, with a peak at midday. In large laboratory populations, either mixed or separate, *D. tryoni* increases in numbers much more rapidly than does *D. neohumeralis*. In both species males locate females by random copulation attempts; however, *D. tryoni* males have a much higher proportion of successful to unsuccessful mating attempts which may well be the result of the highly synchronized receptivity in the two sexes. Assuming that individuals of the two species are receptive for the same length of time within the period of mating activity, this could account for the higher rate of population increase in *D. tryoni*. The fact that these two species which are closely related and have very similar courtship behaviour mate at different times of day reduces the chance of hybridization between them (Gee, 1969; Tychsen and Fletcher, 1971).

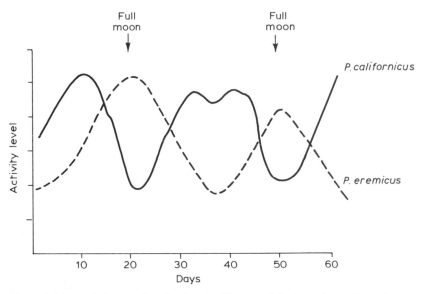

Figure 5.5 Speculation on the adaptive significance of rhythmically varying behaviour; activity patterns of two closely related species of deermouse (simplified from Owings and Lockard, 1971).

Other kinds of competition may also be reduced by appropriate activity rhythms; Fig. 5.5 shows lunar cycles of activity in two closely related species of *Peromyscus* which live in similar places and eat similar food. The very different pattern of activity of these two species may serve to reduce competition although it may also be related to a difference in vulnerability to predation (Owings and Lockard, 1971).

(b) *Why have self-sustaining, endogenous rhythms?*

On theoretical grounds, rhythms of behaviour which are internally controlled rather than a direct response to environmental changes are expected when it is necessary to prepare in advance for some regularly occurring event (such as the laying down of fat prior to hibernation), if information about important environmental changes is not immediately available to the animal (as for a vole in its burrow) or if such information is not sufficiently precise and reliable to ensure that an animal does the right thing at the right time. For example, willow warblers (*Phylloscopus trochilus*), which overwinter near the equator where changes in day length are not marked, have an endogenous migratory rhythm; chiff chaffs (*P. collybitta*) which overwinter further north use the fairly obvious photoperiodic changes to time migration and have no endogenous rhythm (Gwinner, 1971). The rhythmic emergence of the marine midge illustrates a number of similar points; emergence at spring tide must be preceded by a 3–5 day period of metamorphosis and therefore some degree of anticipation is necessary if the adults are to be ready to breed at the right time. The semi-lunar emergence rhythm is indeed endogenous and in most populations is entrained to the natural moon cycle. In northern latitudes, the intensity of the moonlight is too low to be used reliably to reset the lunar activity cycle which is therefore entrained by tidal stimulation. Above the Arctic Circle, the moon is very faint and the semi-lunar rhythm disappears. In these populations, the larvae live further up the beach, egg laying sites are therefore available at normal low tide and pupation follows a tidal rhythm (Neumann and Heimbach, 1979).

There are circumstances in which animals need to do more than simply ensure that they do the right thing at a particular time; they need what is in effect a clock which they can consult continuously in order to predict and interpret changes in the environment. Thus bees which visit different types of flower at different times of day really do need a clock, as do birds which use the sun for navigation, and this is provided by their self-sustaining, endogenous rhythms.

A final function of self-sustaining endogenous rhythms which can be entrained to external events is in the measurement of photoperiod and thus, in many species, the timing of reproduction. Pittendrigh has suggested that many species detect the regular changes in day length which mark the passing of the seasons by comparing the phases of two hypothetical circadian oscillators; these are entrained to dawn and dusk respectively in such a way that their phase relationship is a unique consequence of the day length. This is a simplified version of a highly complex model, but it is clear that reliable, endogenous, entrainable rhythms are necessary if it is to work. Computer simulations have shown that the timing of an activity cycle that is the product of an endogenous rhythm entrained to a regularly occurring environmental event is more stable when their periods are not too similar. This counterintuitive result suggests the circadian nature of many endogenous cycles, the fact that they only approximate to the period of the geophysical cycle they track, is not just noise in the system but may be a vital

The adaptive significance of behaviour   165

design feature in the production of regular cycles and reliable clocks. Comparison between species, between individuals within a species and between the same individuals under different conditions shows that the closer the period of a circadian oscillator is to 24 hours, and thus the less stable it is according to this theory, the tighter are its other homeostatic controls (Pittendrigh and Daan, 1976; Kramm, 1980).

In general, however, although rhythmicity of one kind or another is probably a universal feature of animal life, and although an enormous amount of research has gone into the question of what causes it, for the most part, our information about function is at the level of plausible speculation, albeit clever and exciting speculation.

5.5 The adaptive significance of the way animals use space

5.5.1 DISPERSAL PATTERNS

The life history of many species consists of one or several phases of dispersion or migration followed by periods in which the animal remains in a particular area. The migrations of animals are so spectacular that the question of why animals make these journeys, in the sense of how this increases their fitness, has received a great deal of attention (Baker, 1978). Some of the complex issues involved can be illustrated by a consideration of dispersive and non-dispersive phase found in some insects. The planthopper, *Prokelisia marginata*, exists in two forms, one (the winged morph) with well developed and the other (the wingless morph) with poorly developed wings. While it is expensive to produce wings and dangerous to fly about, the winged forms may be better able to survive in variable conditions. As a consequence of this balance of advantage and disadvantage, selection may act to maintain the two forms in the population, in proportions depending on the variability of the environment. This idea was tested by comparing the proportion of winged and wingless forms in two types of habitat; one consisted of high marshes which was more or less constant throughout the year while the other was beside streams which frequently swept away the vegetation in the winter. As predicted, there was a good correlation between the amount of stable, marshy habitat in a given area and the proportion of wingless bugs found there; observation indicated that the winged forms were indeed faster at colonizing previously empty areas. Further studies in the stable habitat showed it to be heterogeneous in the quality of food available. Figure 5.6 shows the number of winged and wingless bugs found on plants whose sap contained different amounts of protein, which is of major importance in determining reproductive output in this species. In both cases, the richer the plant, the more numerous the bugs but this relationship is more marked for the winged form, which is able to respond more quickly to changes in environmental quality. This study therefore supports the

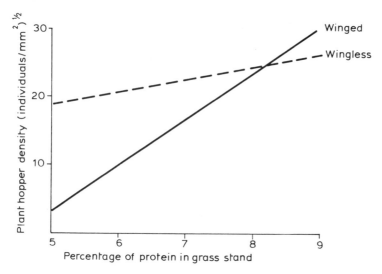

Figure 5.6 The adaptive consequences of different dispersal patterns; the density of winged and wingless *Prokelisia marginata* on plants with different protein contents (after Denno *et al.*, 1980).

idea that dispersal is adaptive where the quality and/or quantity of some important resource is unpredictable in space or time (Denno *et al.*, 1980).

These results do not necessarily imply that an unpredictable environment is the only selective force promoting dispersal. For example, Hamilton and May (1977) have shown theoretically that the need to avoid competition among relatives can maintain a dispersive phase even in a homogeneous environment and with a high cost of dispersion.

5.5.2 DECIDING WHERE TO LIVE

Having dispersed, an animal potentially has a choice of where to settle and the behaviour involved in this process is usually described as habitat selection, although it is not possible to make a clear distinction between habitat selection and other decisions an animal makes about what to do where. This section will discuss habitat selection in the conventional sense of decisions about the geographical area and the ecological niche within it in which an animal concentrates all its activity. However, habitats defined in this way are rarely uniform and therefore this section also discusses the factors determining exactly how an animal exploits its living area when this is locally variable. Most studies about these finer scale decisions concern feeding behaviour, and the discussion therefore concentrates on optimum foraging theory: how does an animal decide where to feed and what detemines how it moves about within and between feeding areas? Questions about choice of diet, while not involving decisions about

The adaptive significance of behaviour   167

the use of space, follow on logically from these, hence their inclusion in this section.

In many cases, the area in which an animal spends its life is determined by where it hatches or is born, which may be the result of decisions made by its parents. A great deal of work has been carried out on choice of oviposition site in insects since so many of these are agricultural pests. To give just one example, aphids of the species *Pemphigus betae* settle and feed on immature oak leaves and form galls in which they produce parthenogenetic offspring; the number of aphids with a single gall thus reflects the reproductive success of the stem female. Eggs laid on larger leaves produce significantly more offspring than those laid on small leaves and, when given a choice, females lay preferentially on such large leaves. In this species, therefore, the choice of oviposition has identified adaptive consequences which probably relate to differences in food availability (Whitham, 1980).

Larvae of the polychaete *Spirorbis borealis* settle on seaweed at the end of the pelagic phase, during which time they are very vulnerable. Since they are less easily dislodged from rough seaweeds such as *Fucus* than on smooth seaweeds such as *Ascophylum,* careful choice of settling site is likely to be important. Larvae collected from exposed sites where the sea is rough showed a marked preference for *Fucus* over *Ascophyllum* as a settling site; in larvae from sheltered sites in which the latter is the only species of seaweed available, this preference was reversed and the larvae settled more rapidly. The behaviour of the larvae thus ensures that they settle quickly when there is no possibility of, and less need for, careful choice of substrate but that they select the most appropriate seaweed when a choice is available. In both these populations, the heritability of settling is lower and dominance effect higher for the preferred than for the less preferred substrate. This suggests that natural selection has acted on choice of settlement site, but in different directions in the two populations (McKay and Doyle, 1978).

Here, choice of habitat is the combined result of the need to bring a vulnerable phase to a quick end and the need to avoid being dislodged by waves. In other cases, choice of habitat may enhance fitness by reducing the likelihood of predation. Thus wood rats (*Neotoma lepida*) build their burrows in areas where there are large numbers of spiky cacti (80% of the variability of wood rat density can be accounted for by the abundance of cacti). This behaviour carries a cost since the rats, especially when young, may get impaled on the spikes. Where there are a lot of cacti, there are few empty burrows and (since these are never abandoned) this indicates that more rats survive. Predation is a common cause of death in this species and the results therefore suggest that by choosing to live among cacti, the rats are gaining protection against predators. However, since the cacti also provide the rats with food and water, this need not be the only, or even the main way in which this particular example of habitat selection enhances fitness (Brown, Leiberman and Dengler, 1972).

Habitats are rarely uniform and it is of interest to find out what determines precisely where an animal concentrates its activities and how this changes with time. In the context of foraging behaviour, this issue concerns the time an animal spends feeding in different parts of the habitat and its pattern of movement within and between feeding sites. There are many cases in which animals concentrate their foraging behaviour in the more profitable parts of their range. For example, wild oven birds searching for insect prey on the forest floor restrict their searching to areas where prey have been found (Zach and Falls, 1979) and this, presumably, enhances their feeding success. However, such results do not tell us whether the observed distribution of feeding represents the best possible solution to the problem of finding patchily distributed food.

In order to answer this question, optimality models are used (see page 153) and, to recapitulate briefly, these involve identifying and defining the courses of action which the animals could follow and choosing the currency which is to be maximized. Optimal foraging theory usually proposes that animals are designed to maximize the net rate of energy intake, which is assumed to correlate with ultimate fitness. The rate at which the animals collect calories when using all the specified feeding strategies is then worked out, so that the one which results in the greatest net intake of energy can be identified; the model is then tested by seeing whether this optimal strategy describes the behaviour of real animals.

(a) *Foraging in patches of different quality*

An optimality model which can be used to study the selective forces determining how foraging animals distribute their time in the different parts of their feeding range has been developed by Parker and Stuart (1976). Assuming initially that the animal's feeding habitat is composed of a series of discrete, identical patches in which searching for food is confined, and that the animal cannot tell the quality of the patch before it arrives there, the model suggests that searching entails a cost (I) in some units which ultimately reflect fitness (such as time and energy spent finding and handling food). While the animal is searching, it extracts gain (G) from the environment, again in fitness related units such as calories. In addition, travelling between patches incurs a cost, in time, energy or risk (S). The net gain from searching in one patch is calculated by $G\text{net} = G - S - I$.

These are the assumptions of the model; the variable to be maximized is the net rate of gain from the system, in this case the net rate of energy intake. The behavioural options open to the animal, or the strategies it can adopt, are the various possible times it could spend feeding in a given patch; development of the model involves working out what length of time spent in a patch would maximize the net energy intake rate. Stated verbally, the animal should clearly remain in the patch as long as the net rate of gain it can expect in that patch in the future is greater than the net gain rate it can expect were it to leave the patch on which it is feeding and start a new search phase; a particular patch should be left as soon as this ceases to be the case. The problem can be analysed graphically to determine the optimum time to spend searching in a given patch and how this depends on the relationship between gain (G) and investment time (I). If G increases linearly with I, the best strategy is to stay in the patch until satiated. However, if as seems more likely, the rate at which gain is extracted is a decreasing function of I (Fig. 5.7(a)), for example, if foraging depletes the food resource, the animal will maximize its net rate of energy gain by leaving the patch after a certain investment time. The maximum rate at which gain can be extracted from such a system can be determined by extending the abscissa beyond the origin by an amount determined by the search time (S) and drawing a tangent from this point to the curve of $G(I)$. The I value at which the tangent contacts the curve (I_{opt}) gives the time in the patch which maximizes the net rate of energy intake. Staying longer means it takes too long to find any more food in the old patch and leaving sooner means that the cost of finding a new patch is paid too early.

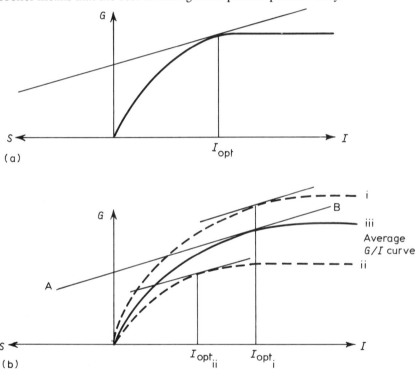

Figure 5.7 Using optimality theory to investigate an animal's use of a patchy feeding habitat; the optimal time to spend in patches of different quality (after Parker and Stuart, 1976). (a) Rate of increase in G falls off with I; patches identical; (b) rate of increase in G falls off with I; patches differ in quality; I_{opt_i} represents the point at which the rate of gain in patch i falls to the average level for the habitat as a whole; $I_{opt_{ii}}$ represents the equivalent point for patch ii.

In real life animals do not feed in patches which are identical, and the model therefore needs to be extended to determine how long animals should spend in various parts of its foraging habitat when these differ in quality. An optimally foraging animal should leave a patch when the rate of intake of calories it can expect in that patch is lower that the average rate of intake from the habitat as a whole. In Fig. 5.7(b) the problem is solved graphically. The environment consists of two types of patches with different $G(I)$ curves (i and ii); curve iii represents the average $G(I)$ curve for the habitat as a whole. The line AB represents the average net gain for the whole habitat and the point at which a line of slope AB touches either $G(I)$ curve gives the I_{opt} for that patch. Thus all patches in the habitat however much food they contained at the start of the foraging period, should be exploited down to one critical level at which the rate of gain of energy is equal to the average rate of gain for the habitat as a whole; this is Charnov's marginal value theorem (Charnov, 1976).

Provided its assumptions are valid, the model can be assessed by investigating the validity of its predictions. The first is that animals behaving so as to maximize their net rate of energy intake should reduce the food levels in all patches down to the same, marginal, value. A number of field observations indicate that animals may forage according to this rule. Thus although flowers differ in the volume of nectar they contain initially, after foraging by bumblebees the volume remaining is very similar (Heinrich, 1979a). However, several bees were almost certainly foraging simultaneously, which complicates interpretation of this result and a number of experiments have therefore been carried out using single foraging animals under controlled laboratory conditions. Krebs, Ryan and Charnov (1974) gave captive chickadees (*Parus atricapillus*) prey in artificial cones in which different numbers of mealworms could be hidden. They set up three different patch types and used the time elapsing between the last prey capture in a patch and the time the bird left that patch, the 'giving up time', as an index of the level to which each patch was depleted. They found that the giving up time was similar for all three patch types; in other words, the birds were leaving each patch when the density of prey had been reduced to the same critical level.

This experimental set up was also used to test the second prediction of the model, namely that the critical resource value at which patches are left is dependent on the average resource level for the habitat as a whole. At lower overall prey densities the giving up time was longer for all patch types. Since giving up time may not be a reliable indicator of depletion level, Cowie (1977) made direct observations of the foraging behaviour of great tits (*Parus major*), again in artificial trees and again using mealworms as prey. The worms were hidden in small cups with lids that took different times to remove so that the time taken to reach food (travel time) varied. Cowie recorded each food item as it was eaten and thus obtained a record of the cumulative food intake with foraging time; this followed an exponential curve which, together with the travel times, was used to predict how long the birds should spend in each patch. Figure 5.8 shows that there was a reasonable fit between observed and predicted times and therefore suggests that the behaviour of foraging tits may have been moulded by natural selection so as to maximize the net rate of energy gain. Cowie was not satisfied by the fit and improved this by adding to his travel time a figure representing the energy costs of travelling between patches.

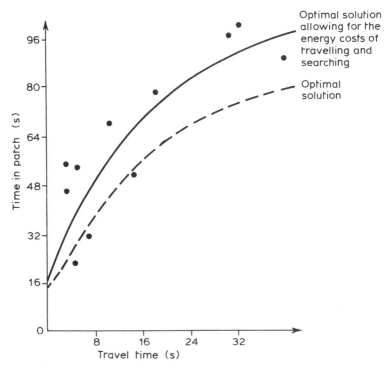

Figure 5.8 Testing the marginal value theorem in the laboratory; the predicted and observed relationship between time spent in each patch and travel time in tits where (•) represents a data point (after Cowie, 1977).

The most detailed test of this theory of optimal patch use in natural conditions concerns hummingbirds (*Selosphorus* spp.) foraging for nectar, a food which is found in discrete flowers rather than continuously distributed (Pyke, 1978a). The flowers (which grow in vertical inflorescences, each of which was considered to be one patch) vary in quality. It is assumed that the birds decide whether to leave a patch after exploiting each flower and the analysis asks when they should leave one inflorescence and start feeding at another if their behaviour is designed to maximize the net rate of energy gain. The energetic costs per unit time of flight between inflorescences is assumed to be the same as that of hovering flight during feeding and concentration of the nectar is assumed to be constant; these two assumptions mean that nectar volume alone determines net energy intake. The

172   *The Study of Animal Behaviour*

marginal value theorem predicts that hummingbirds should remain on an inflorescence when their estimation of the probable rate of nectar intake at the next flower (the expected volume (E) divided by the average time required to remove it (T)) is not less than the gross rate of nectar intake in the foraging area as a whole (G). The expected nectar volume at the next flower for which this inequality will hold is called the expectation threshold and equals GT.

G and T were calculated from field observation of the foraging behaviour of hummingbirds and of the nectar volume of samples of flowers in the field; (the figures are 2.9 microlitres per second and 1.1 seconds respectively giving an expectation threshold of 3.19 microlitres of nectar). E, the amount of nectar which the birds expect of the next flower, is more difficult to work out since it depends on how the birds assess probable nectar content. There are various ways in which they might do this but deductions from their observed foraging behaviour suggest that they probably use the amount of nectar extracted from the last flower (nectar levels of different flowers on the same inflorescence are correlated), the number of flowers in that inflorescence which have already been probed (which correlates positively with the likelihood that the next flower has already been probed and is therefore empty) and the number available (which correlates negatively with the likelihood of a revisit).

Using the observed relationship between nectar levels of neighbouring flowers and observed revisit probabilities and assuming that the birds do estimate the nectar volume expected at the next flower in this way and that they obey the marginal value rule, a series of departure thresholds can be calculated which predict precisely how much nectar the birds require from the present flower in order to keep them in an inflorescence of a certain size when a certain given number of flowers have already been probed. Since it is not possible to measure how much nectar is extracted from a given flower, this set of rules cannot be tested directly but it can be used to predict the probability that hummingbirds will leave an inflorescence of a given size after a particular number of flowers have been probed and thus the frequency distribution of the number of flowers probed per inflorescence. The results of this calculation (for inflorescences of 8 and 12 flowers) and the observed frequency distributions for hummingbirds foraging in the wild on inflorescenses of less than 18 flowers are shown in Fig. 5.9. The observed and expected mean number of flowers for inflorescences of both sizes agree well; in addition, the shape of the observed and theoretical distributions are similar, with peaks at 3 and 6 flowers (the observed peak at 13 flowers could not be predicted from the model as data for inflorescences of this size were not available for the calculations). After all the measuring and calculations, the observed behaviour fits the predictions derived from optimal foraging theory rather well. This means that if the assumptions of the model are correct, then these birds allocate their foraging efforts in such a way as to maximize their net rate of food intake.

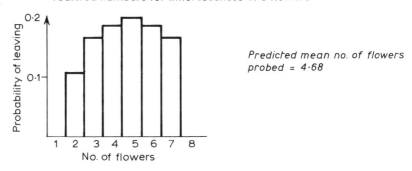

Predicted numbers for inflorescences of 8 flowers

Predicted mean no. of flowers probed = 4·68

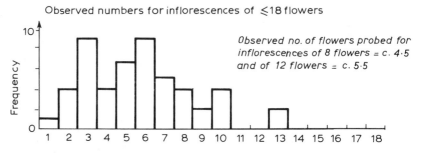

Predicted numbers for inflorescences of 12 flowers

Predicted mean no. of flowers probed = 5·10

Observed numbers for inflorescences of ≤18 flowers

Observed no. of flowers probed for inflorescences of 8 flowers = c. 4·5 and of 12 flowers = c. 5·5

Figure 5.9 Testing the marginal value theorem in the field; observed and predicted frequency distributions of the number of flowers probed by hummingbirds on inflorescences of different sizes (after Pyke, 1978a).

(b) *Patterns of movement between resource points*

The precise search paths animals use are subjected to three possibly conflicting demands, the need to reduce the cost of travelling, the need to avoid revisiting the same point before the resource has been renewed and the need to keep in a generally profitable environment. Honey bees foraging on artificial flowers tend to move to nearby flowers which reduces the time and energy they spend in travelling but increases the chance of their visiting the same flower twice in quick succession. The bees increase the distance flown between flowers after visiting a number of empty flowers and also tend to fly straight ahead between flowers. These two features of the flight path reduce the chance of rapid revisiting of flowers and also ensure that bees leave areas in which food is sparse (Waddington and Heinrich, 1981).

It seems fairly clear that the way bees move while foraging increases the efficiency of this behaviour; however, in order to understand precisely how natural selection has acted on this aspect of behaviour, it is desirable to know whether the solution is an optimal one and, if so, what is being maximized. The foraging paths of another bee species, the bumblebee, have been the subject of a series of increasingly sophisticated models developed by Pyke (1978b) to find out whether their search paths maximize the net rate of energy intake. Just one of these will be outlined, to illustrate the precision with which functional hypotheses about behaviour can be developed and tested when these are supported by accurate field data. The model assumes that a number of bees are foraging for nectar which is found in a large two-dimensional array of highly localized, randomly distributed flowers which once depleted cannot be renewed. The amount of nectar in an unvisited flower is a continuous random value whose condition cannot be assessed from a distance. During one foraging bout, many flowers are visited and the gain from a flower depends on whether it has already

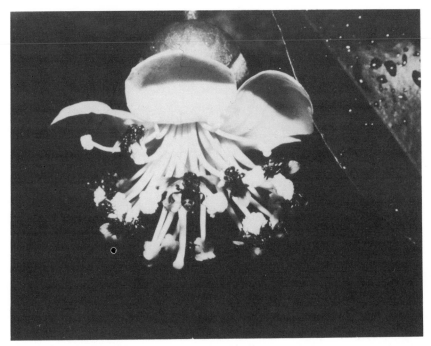

Plate 4 Foraging bees.

been visited; both gains and costs resulting from foraging can be expressed in units of energy. Before leaving the flower on which they have just been feeding, bees point themselves in some specified direction with respect to the path by which they arrived at the flower, scan a sector of a given angle around the aimed direction and move towards the closest flower within this sector. Several models were developed, demanding increasingly sophisticated feats of memory on the part of the bees; in the model to be considered here, which fitted the observed behaviour of bumblebees best, foraging bees base their decisions about flight paths on a memory of the angle from which they arrived at the present flower and the one before that, and modify the scan angle in response to the amount of energy obtained in the present flower. The behavioural options open to the bees are the various values that the scan angle can take. Solution of the model involves working out the energetic consequences of search paths of bees using different strategies, so that the set of rules which maximizes the rate of energy intake can be determined.

The net rate of energy gain is calculated as follows (Pyke, 1978b).

$$G = \bar{e} - \lambda_1 \bar{d}/v - \lambda_2(c_1 + c_2\bar{e})$$

$$T = \bar{d}/v + (c_1 + c_2\bar{e})$$

$$E = G/T = \frac{\bar{e} - \lambda_1\bar{d}/v - \lambda_2(c_1 + c_2\bar{e})}{\bar{d}/v + (c_1 + c_2\bar{e})}$$

where G is net energy gain per flower
$\bar{e}$ is mean energy obtained per flower
λ_1, λ_2 are energetic costs per unit time
$\bar{d}$ is distance
v is speed
$\lambda_1\bar{d}/v$ is the mean cost of moving between flowers
c_1 is time to land
c_2 is rate of energy extraction
$(c_1 + c_2\bar{e})$ is the mean cost of extracting energy from the flower
T is the time taken to extract G
E is the net rate of energy gain

In this model, e and d are variables, the other terms being parameters to which values are ascribed. The net rate of energy gain is determined by the mean energy obtained per resource point and the mean distance between resource points and on how these depend on the rules of movement. Solution for the optimal path is complex, but, in brief, the movement rule which maximizes the net rate of energy gain is to aim departure from the present flower so that the angle between the arrival and departure path is small, with right- and left-handed turns alternating and to increase the scanning angle with the amount of energy gained at the resource point. If the bees are behaving according to this model, the following

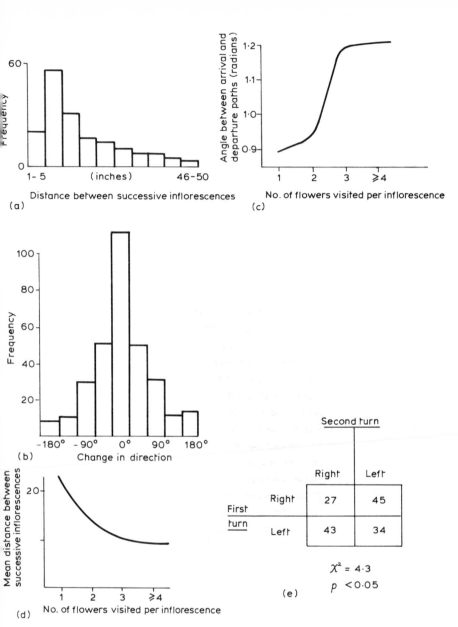

Figure 5.10 Using optimality theory to study the adaptive significance of movements in foraging bumblebees (Pyke, 1978b). Testing the model's predictions: (a) the distribution of distances between successive inflorescences is leptokurtic; (b) the distribution of angles between arrival and departure paths is unimodal, with a peak at 0°; (c) the angle between arrival and departure paths increases to an asymptote with energy obtained (which is proportional to the number of flowers visited per inflorescence); (d) the distance between successive inflorescences decreases to an asymptote with energy obtained; (e) right- and left-handed angles alternate.

predictions should be met: 1. the frequency of very long and very short moves between flowers is greater than that expected from a normal distribution; 2. the frequency distribution of the differences between the directions of arrival and aimed departure should be unimodal, symmetric and have a mean of zero; 3. the size of the deviation from zero should increase to an asymptote as the amount of energy obtained at the present flower (which correlates with the number of flowers visited per inflorescence) increases; 4. the distance moved between flowers should decrease towards an asymptote as energy in the first flower increases, since in the optimal search path, the scanning width increases with energy and the distance to the next flower decreases with sector width; 5. the bees should alternate left- and right-handed turns. Figure 5.10(a–e) shows that all these predictions are upheld.

Thus data collected from observations of undisturbed bees foraging on real flowers support the predictions of the model remarkably well and are compatible with the suggestion that bees use knowledge of the energy obtained at the flower from which they have just fed and the direction of arrival at this and the preceding flower to produce foraging paths which maximize their rate of energy intake.

(c) *Choice of diet*

Questions about whether animals should eat poor prey items when they encounter them, while not concerned with use of space, follow on from the models described above and will be discussed briefly in this section. It is usually assumed that the currency being maximized is energy gain per unit time and that the animal searches for a number of prey items simultaneously; these are instantly recognizable, encountered according to their abundance, consumed one at a time and not dangerous. In addition, each type of food item takes a fixed amount of time to catch and eat (its handling time) and provides a fixed amount of energy.

The strategies available to the animal are the various numbers of types of food that it could include in its diet; development of the model involves determining for each of these diets the net rate of energy gain, the diet for which this value is highest being the optimal one. As long as the ratio of food value to handling time for each potential addition to the diet is greater than the net rate of food intake for the diet without that addition, the diet should be expanded to include the next most profitable prey item; when this ceases to be the case, the optimal diet has been identified. Figure 5.11 shows how this can be done using a graphical solution.

The model produces a number of testable predictions; rather obviously, the animal should prefer food items with the highest food value per handling time ratio and, since the inequality is either true or false, should not show partial preferences, either accepting or rejecting all items of a particular food type. The absolute abundance of a low quality food type should not influence whether or not it is eaten; instead this depends on the abundance of more profitable prey types. When more profitable prey is common, time to find good prey is low and the

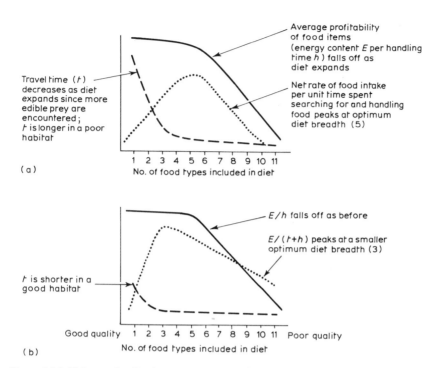

Figure 5.11 Using optimality theory to investigate the adaptive significance of an animal's choice of diet; graphical derivation of optimal diet breadth (after Krebs, 1978). (a) Poor habitat; (b) good habitat.

benefit from food items being easier to find in a broad diet is overridden by the fact that it is less nutritious; the peak in $E/(t+h)$ is pushed towards the left and the animal should become more selective (Fig. 5.11).

The prediction that animals prefer different food types according to their profitability has been found to be true for many species; to give just one example, foraging ants of the species *Pogonomyrmyx rugosus* provided with seeds of three different sizes at different densities harvested first the most profitable seeds (the second largest since the largest ones had a longer handling time). The prediction that inclusion of less profitable food types will depend not on their own abundance but on that of the more profitable items is also supported by this data, in that diet breadth is significantly greater at lower seed densities (Davidson, 1978). This prediction has been tested under more controlled conditions in a number of laboratory experiments; for example, in bluegill sunfish (*Lepomis macrochirus*) feeding on *Daphnia* handling time for prey of different sizes is approximately constant and profitability is determined by size of prey alone. In order to find out whether diet breadth broadens as search time increases, sunfish were presented with prey of different sizes at different overall prey densities. The number of each prey type that would be eaten if these were taken in the

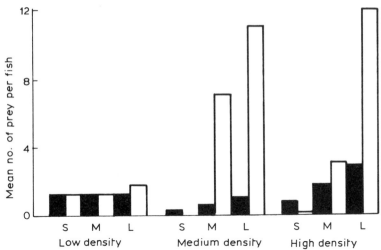

Figure 5.12 Testing the theory of optimal diets; observed (open) and predicted (shaded) proportions of large (L), medium (M) and small (S) prey in the diet of sunfish feeding at different food densities (after Werner and Hall, 1974).

proportions in which they were encountered was calculated, allowing for the fact that larger prey are easier to see. Figure 5.12 shows these proportions together with the number of different prey types which were actually eaten, assessed by stomach analysis. At low prey densities, the different types were taken in the proportions in which they were encountered, corrected for relative visibility. At intermediate densities the two larger size classes were taken, while at high densities prey of the largest size were eaten almost exclusively (Werner and Hall, 1974).

However, there are a number of cases where the predictions of optimal foraging theory are not met. For example, crabs include less profitable prey types in their diet as their abundance increases (Elner and Hughes, 1978); this discrepancy is explained by suggesting that the crabs cannot in fact recognize the type of prey before they start to eat and that rejection is costly (i.e. one assumption of the theory was not met). In addition, partial preferences were shown in all the studies quoted above. This may be because the foraging animal needs to sample the environment in order to assess resource levels and the profitability of different prey types (Krebs, Kacelnik and Taylor, 1978). Thus plausible explanations can be provided for these departures from the predictions of optimal diet theory; however, the possibility remains that diet breadth is not adapted to maximize the net rate of energy intake.

5.5.4 PROBLEMS WITH OPTIMAL FORAGING THEORY

Thus, optimality theory has been applied to the question of how selection acts on various aspects of an animal's foraging behaviour, with some success. However, the optimality approach in general and optimal foraging theory in particular has been criticized in a number of ways and these criticisms will be considered briefly.

(a) *Equating costs and benefits*
As stated earlier, the ultimate currency in which costs and benefits need to be assessed is lifetime reproductive output, yet it is rarely possible to measure the consequences of particular strategies in these terms. Even if the units in which costs and benefits are measured are ultimately related to fitness, unless these units are the same, combining the various beneficial and detrimental consequences in order to arrive at a figure for the net benefit derived is problematic.

The models outlined above assess the costs of different strategies in terms of the time or energy required to perform the behaviour concerned. This ignores more complicated, but realistic, costs such as that of maintaining a large deficit. For example, two different feeding strategies with the same net rate of energy gain may have different effects on fitness if one involves maintaining a large deficit for longer before reducing it by one large injection of energy (Houston, 1980).

There may not be a single dimension of usefulness along which the various strategies can be ranked. Some complicating factors are that different animals may be good at different things; for example, individual bumblebees specialize in particular types of flowers which they are particularly skilful at exploiting (Heinrich, 1979b). This kind of observation presents problems for optimal foraging theory as it is usually applied, since there is clearly no unique ranking of foods which is common to all members of the species and therefore there can be no such thing as an optimal diet for the species as a whole.

(b) *Constraints other than the need to accumulate energy*
Animals are subject to important constraints other than the need to obtain energy. Thus, other components of a balanced diet may be important; redshank (*Tringa totanus*) eat crustacea in preference to worms even though the latter are less profitable, possibly because they contain some special nutrient (Goss-Custard, 1981). In the winter, thermoregulatory constraints force chickadees to forage in sites which are sheltered from the wind, regardless of food distribution (Grubb, 1978) while sparrows trade off predation risk and heat loss against food intake (Grubb and Greenwald, 1982). In the presence of predators, sticklebacks feed from the edge of schools where prey capture is slower but does not require such concentration (Milinski and Heller, 1978). All these examples show that a foraging strategy which maximizes the net rate of energy gain may not be the one which maximizes fitness.

These other requirements can be incorporated into optimality models; thus moose (*Alces alces*) feed on three main types of plant, deciduous and coniferous land plants and aquatic vegetation. Aquatic plants have a low energy content but

The adaptive significance of behaviour   181

contain large quantities of sodium which is essential for the moose. In addition, however, foraging on aquatic plants poses thermoregulatory problems; the moose get cold. Two optimal diets were identified depending on whether moose maximize the rate of energy intake or minimize feeding time, subject to the constraint that the diet must provide a minimum amount of sodium and that moose can only hold a certain volume of food in their stomach. The optimal and the observed diets are shown in Table 5.6; there is a very good fit between the observed proportions of the three food types eaten and those predicted by the energy maximization model (Belovsky and Jordan, 1978).

Table 5.6 The observed diet of moose and optimal diets calculated on the basis of energy maximization and time minimization, given a minimum daily sodium requirement (Belovsky and Jordan, 1978).

	Optimal Diet		*Observed diet*
	Energy max.	*Time min.*	
Percentage of			
Aquatic plants	17.8	21.8	17.7
Deciduous plants	75.0	78.2	74.6
Forbs	7.2	0	8.0
Energy intake (cal)	15 458	14 000	15 861
Time feeding (min)	299	254	307

The impact of conflicting selection pressures on foraging can be incorporated directly into optimality models, rather than as a constraint on the system, providing their effects can be measured in the same units. For example, notonectid bugs (*Notonecta hoffmanni*) are subject to predatory attacks by larger conspecifics when they are foraging, early instars being more vulnerable in this respect than later ones. Sih (1980) developed a model for the allocation of feeding time in areas of different profitability when these also differ in predation risk. Thus the bugs were presented with a choice between an area with abundant prey but which also contained predators and a predator-free but less profitable area. The bugs were rarely actually eaten by conspecific predators but spent time avoiding them; the impact of predation can therefore be included as a factor which reduces the rate of food intake. The model calculates the site at which feeding rate is greatest for bugs at different stages of development and predicts that foragers will spend most time in the site which gives them the highest rate of food intake. Table 5.7 shows a good fit between the results of these calculations and the observed preferences of the different instars.

However, if such conflicting demands cannot be converted into a single currency (as in the notonectid model) or considered as a simple constraint (as in

Table 5.7 Relative feeding success and choice of feeding area of notonectid larvae of different ages given a choice between a high prey density area with predators (H) and a low prey density without predators (L). Correlation between relative advantage in H and strength of preference for H across intars = 0.986 (p < 0.01).

	Feeding rate	*Choice*
First instar larvae	L > H	L >> H
Second instar larvae	L = H	L > H
Third to fifth instar larvae	L < H	L < H

the moose model) optimality models become more difficult to use. An interesting alternative approach is to use models from economic theory in which the interacting impacts on fitness of various consequences of behaviour can be represented simultaneously in multidimensional space and analysed graphically or by matrix algebra (Rapport, 1981).

(c) *Questions about time scale*
Even if it is possible to compare strategies in terms of a single, common currency, the results of optimality models will depend critically on the time scale involved. For example, different optimal copulation times are obtained depending on whether male dungflies maximize the net rate of egg fertilization over the life of one cowpat or over their complete breeding period.

(d) *The assumptions of optimality models*
In developing optimality models, simplifying assumptions have to be made which make the mathematics more tractable but which may not reflect accurately the behaviour of real animals (a criticism which could be applied to any complex model). Two common assumptions of optimal foraging models are that the animal's state and therefore the optimal solution remains constant (models are static rather than dynamic) and that the profitability of all the members of particular food types or patches are constant and can be unambiguously determined (models are deterministic rather than stochastic and information is complete). Once again, the models can be expanded if these assumptions prove invalid. Heller and Milinski (1979) have developed a dynamic optimality model of the behaviour of sticklebacks foraging on swarms of *Daphnia*. They assume that the optimal feeding strategy is influenced by hunger state; the fish trade off needs induced by hunger level against the costs of concentrating on swarming prey and the model is developed to determine the strategy which maximizes fitness under these circumstances. It predicts, among other things,

that since they accept higher risks if they are short of food, the fish should achieve their greatest rate of food intake at high prey density when hungry and at low prey density when less hungry; the rate of prey capture of fish in these two states feeding from swarms maintained artificially at high and low density agree with this prediction. This extension of optimal foraging theory in which fitness consequences are dynamic rather than static therefore successfully predicts the behaviour of sticklebacks suggesting that natural selection has moulded foraging according to these rather complex requirements.

Optimal foraging theory clearly requires that animals are somehow aware of the nutritional consequences of using particular strategies. If food types or food patches are not fixed in this respect but show random variation about a mean level, foraging animals must sample the various food sources in order to estimate their value; many departures from the predictions of deterministic optimality models (for example, the existence of partial preferences and occasional use of unprofitable patches) have been explained in these terms (Krebs, Kacelnik and Taylor, 1978). However, lack of predictability may influence foraging decisions in a more profound way since an additonal risk (of doing very badly) is attached to utilization of a resource and an additional benefit (the chance of doing very well).

This complexity has been incorporated into the study of foraging decisions by Caraco, Martindale and Whittam (1980) who tested the possibility that a predator's preferences might be based not on a deterministic measure of the value of the resource, or even on its average value, but on the whole probability distribution of values. He uses decision theory to investigate the contribution of both the mean and the variability of the value of a resource to the preferences which animals show. The mathematics are complex but the important results of his analysis can be stated fairly simply. Two groups of juncos (birds) were deprived of food either for one hour, in which case they could achieve a positive energy balance under the conditions of the experiment, or for four hours, which necessarily produced a negative energy balance. The birds were placed one at a time in a cage with a food source at each end; one of these contained a fixed number of seeds while the other contained two different numbers of seeds on 50% of the presentations. After an initial period in which the birds learned about the particular food distributions, they were given 20 trials to see whether they fed preferentially at one or other food source. Using various combinations of fixed and constant schedules, the relative importance placed by the birds on overall level as opposed to variability was determined. The prediction is that the birds with a positive energy balance should always avoid the risk imposed by the variable food source. Those with a negative energy budget, which cannot get enough in these tests even at the highest fixed level, are expected to accept the risk of doing badly for the chance of doing very well, this being the only way they escape from serious energetic deprivation. When deprived for the shorter period, the birds avoided the risky foraging site even when this provided a higher average food intake. With longer deprivation periods, the reverse was found, the birds preferring the more variable reward to the certain one even if the latter had a higher average reward rate. Thus the variability of a resource as well as its average value is important in determining foraging preferences, the relative importance of these two aspects depending on the animal's state. Again, optimal foraging models have been expanded to take into account these more realistic assumptions about the real world but with every increase in complexity the calculations become more intricate and the results more difficult to interpret.

(e) *Alternative explanations*

Optimal foraging theory has been criticized on the grounds that much simpler models can often account for the observed results and should therefore be accepted in preference to the optimality models. Thus, the choices made by sunfish when presented with prey of different sizes (Werner and Hall, 1974) could be the result of the fish simply taking whichever prey seems largest, a combined effect of size and distance (O'Brien, Slade and Vinyard, 1976), rather than the result of some complex optimization process. There are two separate questions at issue here; the first, whether either or both models adequately account for the behaviour of the fish can be resolved by testing all their predictions against the real world. The second is whether the optimal foraging model should be rejected if both fit the data. Since the apparent size theory is a causal model while the optimal foraging theory is a functional model, the two are not mutually exclusive; the former could provide the behavioural mechanism whereby sunfish achieve the optimal diet. Sticklebacks select prey according to the apparent size rule where this will result in maximization of food intake rate but not when it would fail to maximize the rate of food intake (Gibson, 1980).

However, there is more to this sort of criticism than a failure to recognize the distinction between causal and functional explanations of behaviour since the causal mechanism controlling feeding has implications for the use of optimality models to study its function. Sensory and motor abilities place detectable limits on the range of behavioural options whose adaptive consequences the models must differentiate. However, perceptual and cognitive constraints may restrict in more subtle ways the extent to which an animal can attain a theoretically optimal solution for which it has the necessary motor equipment. Thus, natural selection may favour the causal mechanism which gives the cheapest approximation to an optimal solution. Departure from the predictions of an optimality model may arise because the animal is using such an adaptive rule of thumb. On the other hand, the model may misrepresent the selective consequences of differences in foraging behaviour and should be rejected.

Thus the optimality approach has stimulated a great deal of research into the function of feeding but its models have had to become increasingly complex to represent accurately the way natural selection acts on foraging behaviour.

5.5.5 CONSTRAINTS ON USE OF SPACE RESULTING FROM THE PRESENCE OF CONSPECIFICS

The presence and activities of other animals have been ignored in the examples discussed so far, although these are likely to influence an animal's use of space. An influential general theory on the way in which animals adapt their use of space to the presence of conspecifics is Fretwell and Lucas's ideal distribution theory (1970). They consider an area in which resources are uniformly distributed within localized habitats which differ in their suitability. The area is occupied by a number of animals which are identical in the fitness they attain in a given habitat, which are capable of moving between habitats and which choose the habitat which offers the best fitness prospects at the time of settling. Their attempts to enter and settle in their chosen habitat are not prevented by the animals already there but the profitability of each habitat decreases with an increase in the number of residents, which settling animals are able to assess. Because the animals select the best habitat and are free to settle where they choose, this predicted distribution is called the Ideal Free Distribution.

Each habitat has a basic suitability or fitness prospect at low densities, depending on food supply, predation levels, nest site availability and so on; the actual suitability of a given habitat is the basic suitability reduced by an amount proportional to the number of animals living in it. According to the model,

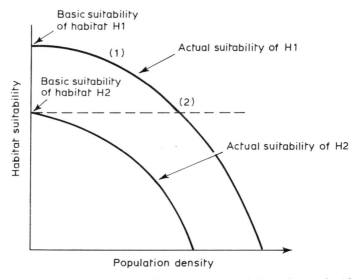

Figure 5.13 The impact of conspecific competitors on habitat choice; the ideal free distribution (after Fretwell and Lucas, 1970). Animals initially colonize habitat H1 which has the highest basic suitability (1) and as a result its actual suitability falls. At point 2 the actual suitabilty of H1 equals the basic suitability of H2, a poorer habitat, and the animals start to colonize the latter.

186   *The Study of Animal Behaviour*

animals looking for a place to settle base their choice on the actual suitability of the available habitats. This means that at low densities they settle preferentially in those habitats which have the highest basic suitability and by doing so reduce their actual suitability (1). There comes a point (2) at which the superior intrinsic qualities of the best habitat are sufficiently offset by the effects of high densities for its actual suitability to be the same as the basic suitability of the next best habitat, which should now be colonized (Fig. 5.13).

The suggestion that animals take into account both intrinsic properties and population density when choosing a place to live, seeking the best that is on offer at the time, can be tested by comparing observed and expected settlement patterns and by measuring the fitness of animals in different habitats. Milinski (1979) offered a number of sticklebacks foraging simultaneously in an aquarium a choice between two feeding areas in which prey were provided at different rates. After a period of variability, during which the sticklebacks were presumably finding out about the food supplies, they distributed themselves according to the ratio of patch profitabilities; all the fish therefore attained the same feeding rate and none could do better by switching.

The ideal free theory can be extended to accommodate situations in which resident animals actively prevent others from settling near them by assuming that resource guarding decreases the actual suitability of the habitat for potential settlers to what is called its apparent suitability. The resulting reduction in fitness is determined by density but not habitat type. In this situation, animals are assumed to settle in the habitat with the highest apparent suitability and again, an equilibrium point is reached in which this is equal for all occupied areas. The distribution of animals at this point is called the ideal despotic distribution and for animals behaving in this way, the fitness of animals settling in habitats of different quality is not the same; instead it is higher in more suitable habitats.

Stem mother aphids of the species *Pemphigus betae* produce parthenogenetic offspring in galls on immature leaves. Those which have already settled actively deter others from colonizing the leaf; they thus behave like despotic animals. The position of the gall provides a record of habitat choice, the number of galls per leaf shows the population density and the number of aphids per gall provides one measure of the fitness of aphids settling in different sites. It is therefore reasonably easy to collect the information necessary to see whether these aphids settle according to the ideal free or despotic rules. Stem mothers preferentially colonize large leaves and as Fig. 5.14 shows, the number of aphids per gall decreases with leaf size. Large leaves are therefore more suitable than small ones and are colonized first. However, as the number of galls per leaf (competitor density) increases, the number of aphids per gall (fitness) decreases. Thus the way the aphids influence each other's fitness is in accordance with the model. However, the average fitness of aphids settling on leaves with different numbers of galls per leaf is equal. Thus the stem mothers seem to be adjusting their densities in different quality habitats such that the average fitness is the same in

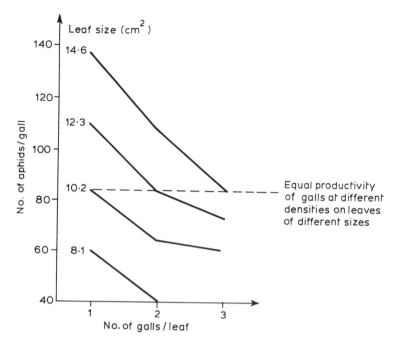

Figure 5.14 The impact of conspecifics on habitat choice; settlement patterns in gall aphids (after Whitham, 1980).

leaves of different size; in other words, although they behave as despots, their fitness in different habitats is as predicted by the ideal free model. This discrepancy arises because the system does not conform with the assumptions of these two models in one important respect; although each leaf represents a single habitat in behavioural terms, being the area within which an aphid can wander around once it has landed, leaves do not actually provide a uniform environment. Since these animals suck sap, galls at the base of the leaves do better than those at the edge and on heavily populated (larger) leaves the unfavourable distal areas are used; larger leaves therefore house both the most productive galls (at the base) and the least productive (at the edges). The average fitness of stem mothers on large leaves is therefore the same as those on small leaves, but the variability is greater (Whitham, 1980).

5.5.6 TERRITORIAL BEHAVIOUR

The behaviour of despotic animals, maintaining an exclusive area by aggressive means, results in the phenomenon of territoriality. Several functional questions are of interest: Why do some animals show territorial behaviour while others do not? Why do some territorial animals defend larger areas than others? and Why are territories of a particular shape?

Development of a satisfactory theory with any degree of generality has been hampered by the fact that territoriality serves different functions in different species, serves many functions within a single species and has a number of disadvantages. Given these complications the most fruitful way to approach the question of the adaptive significance of territoriality in all its manifestations is to identify the various fitness-related consequences and to determine the circumstances under which a particular pattern of territorial behaviour results in a net increase in fitness, in other words to carry out a cost benefit analysis.

(a) *Why defend a territory?*

The kinds of benefit which can accrue from territoriality are an improved food supply (sunbirds, Gill and Wolf, 1975), improved ability to acquire mates (lark buntings, Plesczynska, 1978), to rear young (gulls, Hunt and Hunt, 1976) or to avoid predators (great tits, Dunn, 1977). The kinds of costs which may be incurred are the time and energy which are spent in territorial defence, the risk of predation and the risk of injury from intruders. The problem of choosing a common currency in which to equate these is not easily resolved, except in the case of feeding territories maintained by nonbreeding animals when risk of predation is low and defence mainly involves advertisement rather than overt fighting. In such cases, it is possible to express cost and benefits in terms of energetic losses and gains, assuming that these do have implications for fitness; thus most quantitative analyses have concentrated on feeding territories. Considering first the conditions under which it is adaptive to defend a territory, the general principle is that if the cost of doing so equals or exceeds the resultant increase in energy availability, territorial behaviour should not occur.

The goldenwing sunbird (*Nectarina reichenowi*) is a nectar feeder which, when not breeding or migrating, resides in localized areas containing nectar producing flowers. Gill and Wolf (1975) recorded for freely foraging birds: the size of territory defended, the number of flowers in the territory, the amount of nectar in the flowers, the time spent by the birds feeding at each flower, the total time spent on the territory and how this was apportioned into the various activities in which the birds engaged. In general, the number of flowers per territory was remarkably constant regardless of territory area which decreased as new flowers emerged. Nectar levels are significantly higher in defended flowers; while it could be that better flowers are defended, it may be that the key beneficial consequence of territoriality is to allow sunbirds to feed from flowers with more nectar. If the birds can meet their energetic requirements more quickly from nectar rich flowers and if when they are not foraging they are sitting (which requires less energy), the benefits from territorial defence can be expressed in terms of the energy saved by having time to sit rather than feed; costs can be expressed in terms of energy used up in defence and the two can therefore be compared directly.

The percentage of the daylight hours required to meet the daily energy

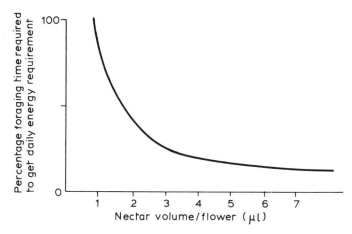

Figure 5.15 The economics of territorial defence in goldenwing sunbirds (after Gill and Wolf, 1975). The percentage of daylight hours required for foraging at different nectar levels.

requirement was calculated for a range of nectar levels (Fig. 5.15); the curve falls off very rapidly as nectar volume increases. From these values, the net savings resulting from territorial defence (the gain in energy by sitting rather than foraging – the loss in energy due to chasing) can be calculated for various defence levels and different levels of nectar productivity. These are shown in Table 5.8 and indicate that at nectar levels above 2 microlitres per flower the costs of defence soon outweigh the energy saved by sitting; if selection does act on sunbirds in this way, territorial defence should not occur when the flowers have a nectar level above this critical value. It was observed that on one particular day, in the morning when nectar levels were high, sunbirds did not defend territories, but as the levels dropped during the course of the day to about 2 microlitres per flower, territorial defence started up. In addition, when high levels of defence are

Table 5.8 The net saving in energy resulting from territorial behaviour at various defence and nectar levels.

		Net energy in cal / day saved at different defence levels measured in percentage of daily time budget				
		1%	*2%*	*3%*	*4%*	*5%*
Average nectar level						
Undefended flowers	*Defended flowers*					
1	2	2066	1706	1346	986	626
2	3	449	89	−271	−631	−991
3	4	48	−312	−672	−1032	−1392
4	6	41	−319	−679	−1039	−1399

required to maintain exclusive use of a territory, and therefore the costs are high, defence is again uneconomic; when sunbirds are abundant and therefore intrusions into the territory frequent, sunbirds cease defending their territories. Thus the predictions derived from the general proposition that territories will be defended when energetic gains exceed energetic costs are met quite accurately in these birds, indicating that the selective forces acting on the birds have been identified correctly.

(b) *Why defend a territory of a particular size?*
The fact that territorial defence has costs as well as benefits also determines the size of territory which an animal defends. The benefits of defending a territory probably increase with territory size, but so also do the costs. Assuming that the critical requirement is to maximize gain rather than to minimize costs; the optimum size of territory is that for which the difference between costs and benefits is greatest. This depends on the precise relationship between costs or benefits and territory size; in Fig. 5.16, costs increase exponentially with area while two different benefit functions are shown. In Fig. 5.16(a), benefits increase with area up to a certain point and then level off; this might be the case if the territory contains a resource which the animals need but which they cannot store. The benefit functions are shown for two different resource levels. Beyond the points max. and min. (shown in the figure for high resource levels only) costs are greater than benefits and territorial defence is uneconomical. At O benefits exceed costs by the largest amount and this is the optimal size of territory for animals designed to maximize net gains. The optimal territory size is smaller when resource levels are high than when they are low (OL > OH).

In Fig. 5.16(b), on the other hand, the benefits of territoriality increase linearly with territory area, with a slope dependent on resource levels; this situation might occur if, for example, the animal can store energy over and above its needs or can convert it to some other form such as eggs. Again, beyond min. and max. territorial defence is uneconomical and again an optimum territory size exists for each resource level. However in this case the optimum size is larger at high resource levels (OL < OH). If the curves for costs and benefits against area do not intersect, then there is no optimal territory size. If costs always exceed benefits, territorial defence should never occur; if the converse is the case, the bigger the territory, the better.

To give some examples of the application of these models, breeding adult females of the territorial fish *Eupomacentrus leucostrictus* convert excess food into eggs and can therefore continue to benefit from an increase in territory size and conform to the pattern of Fig. 5.16(b); breeding males, on the other hand cannot use extra food and conform to the pattern of benefits shown in Fig. 5.16(a). Thus the prediction is that while females should increase the size of their territories as food density increases, males should do the opposite. Artificial manipulation of food supplies produced an increase in territory size in all the females tested while

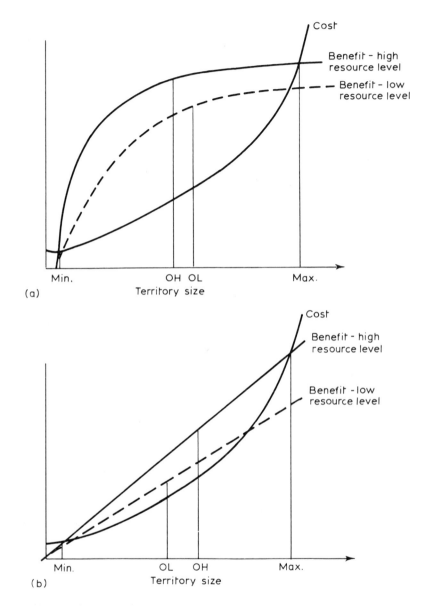

Figure 5.16 The economics of defending territories of different sizes; maximum (max.), minimum (min.) and optimal territory size for various hypothetical cost and benefit functions. (a) Cost of defence increases geometrically and benefit of ownership increases to an asymptote with territory size; (b) cost of defence increases geometrically and benefit of ownership increases linearly with territory size. OH and OL represent the optimum territory size at high and low resource levels respectively.

among the males half showed a decrease in territory size and half showed no change (Ebersole, 1980).

Weaver ants of the species *Oecophylla longinoda* are strongly predacious and defend territories vigorously against conspecifics and other competitors. The territory can be considered as a circle of radius *r* containing a uniform and stable food source. Since the nests contain many hungry larvae, large quantities of food can be put to good use; benefits therefore increase as a linear function of area (or a squared function of radius). Since the nests are diffuse, transport costs are low; so also are defence costs (there is an ample supply of sterile workers) which increase as the perimeter of the territory increases (i.e. linearly with *r*). Thus benefits increase more rapidly with area than do costs; territorial defence is always economical and as long as the egg-laying capacities of the queen are not exceeded there is no optimal territory size. According to the model, colonies should defend as large an area as possible. The ants are indeed very ferocious, using a complex recruitment system in defence of their territories which may measure as much as 1600 square metres. It is believed that other factors not incorporated in the model, such as the need to maintain coordination between nest members, ultimately limit territory size (Hölldobler and Lumsden, 1980).

(c) *Why defend a territory of a particular shape?*

On the question of optimal territory shape, Hölldobler and Lumsden have developed a model for the territorial system of harvester ants (*Pogonomyrmex barbatus* and *rugosus*). Workers of these species travel along long and semi-permanent trails and if the trails of neighbouring colonies are made to cross artificially fierce fighting ensues; the trails can therefore be considered as part of a territory. These ants exploit spatially patchy but long-lived resources and the question of optimal territory shape relates to the distribution of these resources. The area which could potentially be included in a territory is envisaged as a system of sectors of angle *a* and radius *r*. The cost per unit time required to defend each sector is an increasing function of both *a* and *r*. The net profit derived from the whole territory is the difference between the sum of the net benefits of all sectors containing food and the sum of the costs of exploiting all sectors; this is maximized if only those sectors with the smallest values of *r* and *a* consistent with getting sufficient food are defended. The predictions are, rather obviously, that the colony should shut down empty sectors and those which are too expensive to exploit economically, because they are too small, because the food in them is too far away or because they are already owned by another colony. Recruitment activity by scouts which have encountered a new food source is indeed dependent on such factors.

5.6 The adaptive significance of an animal's aggressive responses

The existence of aggression has already been discussed in the context of territorial defence; at issue here is the adaptive significance of an animal's repertoire of aggressive actions and how it is deployed. At one level, the answer to the question is simple; animals fight in order to gain access to resources which are in short supply, whether these be food, mates or nest sites. While the precise benefits gained in any particular case can only be determined by empirical research, in general, individuals which fight readily and effectively would appear to have a competitive edge over their rivals. In fact, the converse question of why animals do not always engage in all-out fights presents a greater problem. It is a common observation that while animals can and do inflict serious injury on each other (Geist 1971, 1974), they rarely make full use of their weapons during the course of a fight. Instead, as Lorenz in particular has stressed (1966), fights tend to be decided by threat displays and ritualized trials of strength. Given the obvious advantage to the animals concerned of gaining limiting resources, why do they show this self-restraint? In the past, a commonly invoked, though by no means universally accepted, explanation was that the species as a whole gains if fights take a conventional rather than a dangerous form since fewer of its members will be injured. In effect this argument is based on the assumption that selection can occur at the level of groups as well as individuals, a concept which is discussed in more detail below (see page 257).

5.6.1 GAMES THEORY AND THE HAWK–DOVE MODEL

However, given the fact that fighting has costs as well as benefits, selection will not necessarily favour the most aggressive animals. This point has been recognized for a long time but its implications were not investigated formally until Maynard Smith applied the techniques of games theory to the problem. This has been described above (p. 156) but as it has revolutionized the study of the adaptive significance of fighting it will be discussed more fully here.

Briefly, the analysis involves specifying a set of proposed patterns of aggressive behaviour, or strategies, which animals might use in a fight, and determining the various deleterious and beneficial consequences associated with the performance of each strategy against opponents playing the same set of strategies, to generate a pay-off matrix. The overall pay-off for animals using a particular strategy is the sum of its pay-offs against all possible strategies, corrected for their frequency in the population. Assuming that the frequency of a given strategy in one generation is dependent simply on its average pay-off in the preceding one (i.e. that reproduction is effectively asexual), the changes in frequency of the different strategies can be determined. From this it is possible to work out whether there is any strategy which cannot be outcompeted by any other strategy when it is common in the population; such a strategy, if it exists, is an evolutionary stable strategy (ESS); if the model accurately depicts the consequences of contests among real animals, an ESS describes the fighting behaviour which should be seen in the real world.

The first games theoretical analysis of animal fights developed the famous hawk–dove model (see page 157), briefly, hawks always fight fiercely until one or other opponent is seriously injured or until the opponent retreats. Doves, on the other hand, while equal in all other respects, display rather than fight and retreat if attacked. Animals using these two strategies meet at random, and therefore the different kinds of encounter occur in proportion to the frequencies of the two strategies. When two hawks fight, they have an equal chance of winning or being injured; when two doves meet they also have an equal chance of winning but both winners and losers pay the cost of a long display session. Hawks always beat doves without any risk of injury; doves never win such encounters but flee before being seriously injured and do not waste any time about it; these relationships are summarized in Table 5.5. Where the value of winning is greater than the risk of injury, hawks always do better than doves, hawk is therefore an ESS. However, when the reverse is the case, doves do better than hawks in a population consisting predominantly of hawks, since they do not pay the price of injury; in a population of doves, a rare hawk will always win with no risk of injury. Thus under these conditions neither hawk nor dove is an ESS and the population will tend towards that proportion of hawks and doves (the evolutionarily stable mixture) for which the average pay-offs of the two strategies are equal.

In the original model, hawk and dove participated in a game involving three other strategies, bullies, which fight fiercely until their opponent fights back, retaliators which fight conventionally until attacked in which case they fight fiercely and prober–retaliators which mostly behave like retaliators but occasionally sample their opponents's behaviour with a short bout of fierce fighting. When all five games are played against each other, retaliator is the only pure ESS, although for some starting frequencies, a mixture of hawks and bullies is evolutionarily stable (Gale and Eaves, 1975). Thus which strategy, if any, is evolutionarily stable depends on the other strategies against which it is played and on the parameters of the game and on the conditions prevailing at its start.

This pioneering analysis has generated great interest in the technique of games theory and the development of many other models and it is worth considering exactly what this approach has contributed to our understanding of the selective forces acting on animal aggression.

5.6.2 WEAKNESSES OF THE HAWK–DOVE MODEL

The assumptions on which the hawk–dove model is based are quite unrealistic and this reduces its value as a functional explanation of aggression in real animals. The main oversimplifications of the model are:

1. The implicit assumption that like reproduces like in proportions dependent on pay-offs implies that the strategies are inherited in a simple manner and that reproduction is asexual.

2. The strategies proposed do not resemble the behaviour shown by real

animals; for example, by only allowing animals to escalate or display the model ignores the fact that animals often start off a fight with conventional displays but subsequently show a series of increasingly aggressive and dangerous behaviour.

3. Several of the assumptions about the outcome of fights are unrealistic. Thus injury does not always bring an escalated (hawk-like) fight to an end and escalated fights may end without injury. In addition, where animals cannot inflict serious injury on each other (doves meeting doves), the fight does not last for a fixed period of time with each contestant having a 50% chance of winning, as the hawk–dove model assumes; in the real world, such ritualized contests last for varying lengths of time.

4. The model assumes that the animals whose fighting is under investigation are equal in all respects other than the strategy they use. However, this is very rarely the case; opponents may differ in their fighting ability, in what they stand to gain from winning and in a number of other ways.

5. On a related point, the model assumes that the behaviour a fighting animal shows is not influenced by any information that it has about its opponent; in fact it is extremely likely that animals are able to collect and use information gained about opponents both before and during the course of an aggressive encounter.

6. The model assumes that hawks and doves meet at random, which may not be the case; animals which show site attachment are likely to encounter the same opponent on different occasions and their behaviour may be influenced by the memory of previous fights. In addition, if animals tend to live near their relatives, since the strategies are inherited, they are likely to encounter other animals playing the same strategy more often than expected and this will influence the overall frequency of the different kinds of interaction. It also means that in determining the (inclusive) fitness consequences of a given strategy, the fact that the animals against which a given strategy wins or loses are relatives has to be taken into account (see page 259).

In an attempt to make the results of games theoretical analysis more relevant to the behaviour of real animals, these unreal assumptions have been altered in a series of models, mostly developed by Maynard Smith and his collaborators.

5.6.3 GAMES THEORY MODELS IN SEXUALLY REPRODUCING SPECIES

Phrases such as 'a mutant dove' imply that substitution of one allele for another at a single locus can bring about a major change in behaviour. From what is known of the genetics of behaviour (Chapter 8) this is possible but rather unlikely. In addition, parents will only produce offspring which all play the same strategy if reproduction is asexual or if the strategies represent homozygous conditions and mating is positively assortative. In sexually reproducing species, the mechanisms of inheritance constrain the ability of a population to evolve towards a theoretically predicted ESS. Where the ESS is a pure strategy, and in the absence of assortative mating, mixing of genes in zygotes will merely slow down the rate of evolution towards the ESS. Where a mixed strategy is predicted, sexual reproduction may make it impossible to reach the evolutionarily stable proportions of phenotypes; evolution will tend to take the population as near to these proportions as the genetic mechanism will allow (Maynard Smith, 1981).

5.6.4 CONFLICTS BETWEEN DOVES; THE WAR OF ATTRITION MODEL

Maynard Smith's War of Attrition model examines in more detail encounters between doves, which are resolved by the exchange of ritualized signals alone, by assuming that the animal which displays for longest will win the fight (hence the name). The strategies are the different times for which animals are prepared to display when this carries a cost (for example energy or time) proportional to the duration of the display. Intuitively, no single display time will be an ESS since a mutant displaying for just a little longer will always win. On the other hand, a very long display time is not stable since the value of winning is dissipated by the cost of displaying and mutants with shorter display times will actually have higher overall pay-offs even though they never win. It can be shown that the evolutionary stable strategy is to display for an unpredictably variable period of time chosen from a negative exponential distribution of display times defined by the following equation:

$$p(x) = (1/V)e^{-x/V}$$

where p is the probability of displaying for a time x and V is the pay-off for winning. It would not pay the combatants in such a war of attrition to give their opponent any information about how long they intend to display.

Thus the two main predictions of the model are that fights should last for varying lengths of time, with a negative exponential distribution and that displays should be of a constant intensity which is unrelated to what behaviour the animal concerned is going to show next. Although there is disagreement on this point (Hinde, 1981; Caryl, 1981a), these predictions are in broad contrast to the classical ethological picture of the evolution of displays as a series of improvements in their ability to transmit information about the animals' intentions. Reanalysis of published data (Caryl, 1979, see Fig. 5.17) shows that these conform reasonably well with the predictions of the model: display lengths fit a negative exponential distribution and the probability of the fight ending as a function of how long it has lasted is a constant in iguanas (Rand and Rand, 1976) and none of the displays used by great tits is a good predictor of attack (Stokes, 1962). There is thus surprisingly good agreement between the predictions of the model and the behaviour of these animals, indicating that the picture of the selective forces acting on aggression embodied in the War of Attrition model is broadly correct.

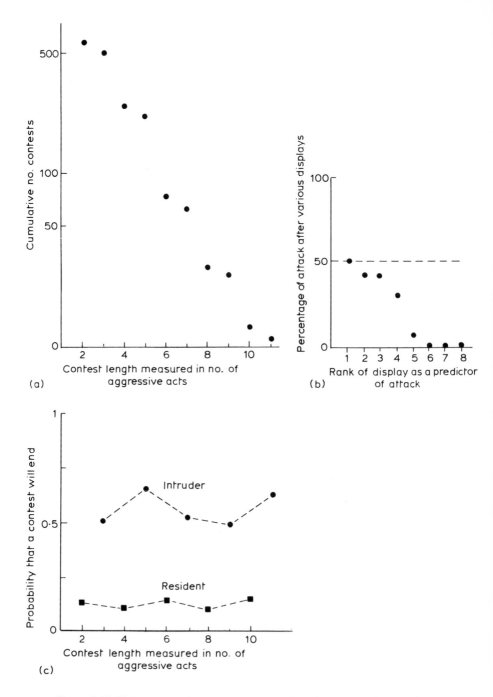

Figure 5.17 Using games theory to investigate the adaptive significance of aggressive behaviour: testing the predictions of the War of Attrition model (after Caryl, 1979); (a) fighting female iguanas show an exponential distribution of fight lengths; (b) displays used by fighting great tits are not good predictors of attack; (c) the probability of a fight ending is independent of how long it has lasted in female iguanas.

The fact that fights between real animals generally start with harmless displays with more dangerous tactics being shown as the fight progresses can be accommodated by a modified version of the War of Attrition model in which display time is replaced by the risk of injury which the combatants are prepared to run (Maynard-Smith and Price, 1973). The level of escalation reached in a fight is determined by that to which the least adventurous of a pair of contestants is prepared to go. The two opponents are equally likely to be injured during the fight (and therefore to lose) but if neither is injured, the animal which is prepared to escalate to the lower level gives up when that point is reached, leaving its rival to enjoy the fruits of victory. If the cost of damage is greater than the gain from winning, the ESS is to escalate up to an unpredictable level with a probability distribution determined by the relative sizes of reward and risk; the greater the risk compared to the benefit, the lower the escalation levels. This analysis confirms the commonsense conclusion that the more serious the injury that is being risked, the smaller the chance the animals will allow themselves to incur it.

5.6.6 GAMES WITH ASYMMETRIES BETWEEN OPPONENTS

(a) *Uncorrelated asymmetries*
The hawk–dove model has been expanded to accommodate the fact that animals differ (Maynard Smith and Parker, 1976). Firstly, the possibility is considered that animals might use some trivial difference between them to settle contests with the minimum of costs. Thus animals can be in one of two states A and B (for example, the initial discoverer of the resource or a newcomer) which have no direct influence on the outcome of a fight. Hawks fight and doves display regardless of their state but animals using the so-called 'bourgoise' strategy play hawk when the initial discoverer and dove when the newcomer. The pay-off matrix for this game is shown in Table 5.9(a); since it is in each state for half of its fights, bourgoise behaves like a hawk half the time and like a dove the other half. In encounters with hawks and doves, it does no better than animals showing these simple strategies; however, when playing against another bourgoise it wins half the contests and never incurs any costs, an additional pay-off which makes bourgoise an ESS.

In order to prove that an uncorrelated asymmetry is used to settle contests conventionally, it is necessary to show that animals in one of two states always win contests, that for any given pair of opponents, changing states changes the outcome and that if both animals are in state A, escalated contests will occur. Female zebra spiders (*Salticus scenicus*) feeding on an artificial substrate can be in one of two states when foraging, wandering or stationary and switch rapidly between these. Stationary spiders were found to win 92.5% of the fights in which they were involved; the equivalent figure for wanderers is 37.5% and these

The adaptive significance of behaviour   199

mostly involve encounters with other wanderers. These spiders may therefore use the uncorrelated asymmetry of prior residence to settle contests; they can probably afford to do so because the pay-offs for remaining on a particular bit of wall are low (Jaques and Dill, 1980).

Table 5.9 Making games theory models of animal fights more realistic (from Maynard Smith and Parker, 1976).
(a) Pay-off matrix for the hawk–dove game with an uncorrelated asymmetry, where V is the pay-off for winning, D is the cost of serious injury, T is the cost of wasting time; the cost of minor injury is omitted in this game.

	Playing against		
	Hawk	*Dove*	*Bourgoise**
Pay-off to			
Hawk	$1/2(V-D)$	V	$1/2(1/2(V-D))+V/2$
Dove	0	$V/2-T$	$1/2(V/2-T)$
Bourgoise*	$1/2(1/2(V-D))$	$V/2+1/2(V/2-T)$	$V/2$

*Opponent acts like a hawk half the time and like a dove the other half.

(b) Pay-off matrix for the hawk–dove game with an asymmetry in Resource Holding Potential (RHP), where x is the probability of a type A winning a fight against a type B.

		Animal B (RHP = $1-x$)	
		Escalates	Displays
	Escalates	B gets: $V(1-x)-Dx$	0
Animal A		A gets: $Vx-D(1-x)$	V
RHP = $x(>0.5)$			
	Displays	B gets: V	$V/2$
		A gets: 0	$V/2$

(b) *Asymmetries in the benefits acquired by winning*
Real opponents are rarely equivalent in their ability to win or benefit from fights and models have been developed to see what effect this kind of asymmetry might have on the outcome of fights. The War of Attrition could be expanded to accommodate a situation in which the value of the resource is different for the two combatants by assuming that there are two kinds of animal, A and B, with the value of the resource to A (V_a) greater than that to B (V_b). If the asymmetry is ignored, the ESS is to show the usual distribution of display times, based on the average pay-offs for the two states. The fate of a mutant which takes account of the asymmetry, displaying for a time m when in state A and not displaying at all when in state B, is considered when the cost of display is less than the value of the

resource. Calculation of the pay-offs for the original strategists and the mutants is complicated, but as might be expected, the result is that the mutant is an ESS, being able to invade a population of original strategies when rare and resist invasion when common. Intuitively, this is because ignoring the asymmetry means that the cost of displaying is paid in all encounters rather than only half and that if these are won, the benefit is small. Thus here again, individuals which use some asymmetry to settle disputes without escalated conflicts will enhance their fitness. During the rut, red deer stags without hinds, which have more to gain from winning than a harem holder, initiatiate more fights, a result which is consistent with the prediction that the opponent with the most to gain should fight longer and more fiercely (Clutton-Brock *et al.*, 1979).

(c) *Asymmetries in fighting ability*
The possibility that one opponent may be more likely to win a fight than the other due to a difference in fighting ability or Resource Holding Potential (RHP) is included in a modified hawk–dove model by introducing a variable x which represents the probability of an animal with the highest RHP (type A) winning a fight against an animal of type B, x being greater than 0.5. Four possible strategies exist: play dove in both states, play hawk in both states, play hawk when in A and dove when in B and the converse. The pay-off matrix for this game is shown in Table 5.9(b); the outcome depends as usual on the values of the risk of injury (D) and the reward for winning (V) but also on the value of x, the extent of A's advantage over B. Briefly, if the risk of injury is serious and/or the advantage to A is large, then escalation only when in state A is an ESS. If the risk of injury and/or the advantage to A is small, the ESS is to escalate in both states. Finally, and unexpectedly, if the risk of injury is large but the relative advantage of A is small, then the strategy of escalation if in state B can be evolutionarily stable. Thus provided that the animals can assess their relative RHP accurately, this cue can be used as a conventional means of settling contests; this is usually in the common sense direction that the animal most likely to win escalates but certain conditions favour escalation by the animal which is most likely to lose.

If, as these models suggest, animals are likely to settle fights on the basis of their relative RHP, bluffing is possible; where features which give the impression of enhanced RHP are cheaper to evolve that a genuine increase in RHP, an individual possessing such a feature (for example, large apparent size) would win cheap victories over competitors in a population using the largest-wins convention. Suppose a population initially consists of non-bluffers, playing the ESS 'escalate if larger, never escalate if smaller and escalate with a probability D/V if the opponent is of equal size'. A bluffer mutant arises which appears to be one size class bigger than it really is; the bluffer may be optimistic, in which case it behaves like an animal of its apparent size or pessimistic, in which case it behaves according to its real size. The outcome of the model is slightly different in the two cases although the overall conclusion is the same. Taking the case of the pessimistic bluffer, an animal playing this strategy rarely gets into an escalated fight since when it is ready to do so (i.e. when its opponent is the same as its actual size or smaller) the opponent is not (having assessed it as larger or of equal size respectively). The mutant will therefore enjoy a higher average pay-off than an animal playing the original strategy and will invade the population; the analysis also shows that the pessimistic bluffer strategy is stable against invasion when it is frequent and is therefore an ESS (provided $D/V > 1$).

It seems intuitively likely that with the passage of time, the ability to distinguish the bluff from the real thing would evolve. Again, a games theoretical model has been developed to investigate the fate of an animal with this ability in a population of bluffers. Taking the apparent size of an animal as its real size plus a bluff component, a mutant which can estimate real size directly and makes its strategic decisions on this basis appears in a population of animals which base their decisions on apparent size. Animals playing the original strategy will give way in a number of encounters which they would have won if it came to a fight, whereas the mutant escalates and wins in such situations and, given sufficiently high D/V levels, it will invade the population. Thus these analyses suggest that animals should settle fights conventionally on the basis of relative fighting ability and that escalated contests should occur only when opponents are evenly matched; in addition, animals should be able to distinguish bluff from reality and decisions about whether or not to escalate should therefore be made on the basis of indicators of RHP which are difficult to bluff.

To continue with the example of fights between rutting male red deer, many attempted take-overs are successful and stags aged less than five years, which have very little chances of winning against older harem holders, tend to avoid fights except with animals of the same age. In addition, while stags of different fighting ability often approach each other, fights generally occur only between evenly matched animals, suggesting that deer can assess the RHP of potential rivals and only fight if they have a chance of winning. Male stags are notorious for the loud roars they give during the rutting season, especially when they are challenged for possession of a harem of females. Most fights are preceded by a period of roaring, especially if opponents are similar in fighting ability and fights ensue more often when it is the challenger that is roaring most. Individual stags have a characteristic rate of producing sounds during a bout of roaring and this is positively correlated with their ability to win fights. There is thus considerable circumstantial evidence to suggest that stags use roaring rate to predict fighting ability and thus settle aggressive encounters without overt fighting. Roaring requires a great deal of energy and only stags which are in good condition can maintain a high rate of roaring; it therefore provides an accurate indicator of how likely an opponent is to fight fiercely and would be difficult to bluff (Clutton-Brock et al., 1979).

Real animals almost certainly gain information about the fighting ability of their opponent during the course of a conflict and use this to determine their future actions. The various possible consequences of such behaviour, how these may interact and the circumstances under which the information gained might be valuable, were investigated in yet another of Maynard Smith's models. Fights are seen as a series of rounds between two opponents which differ in RHP; at the end of each round the two animals decide whether or not to continue and they do so on the basis of the outcome of the immediately preceding round. The animals know how much RHP influences the chances of winning but at the start of the fight they do not know their relative RHPs. Each round can potentially be won by either opponent and the loser incurs a cost (which becomes greater as the fight progresses) presumably in the form of injury or exhaustion. The outcome of each round gives some information about the relative RHP of the two opponents but how reliable this is will depend on just how strictly relative RHP dictates success. If these are very closely linked, an animal which had lost one round is likely to lose the rest; if a high relative RHP only gives a slight advantage, the loser of one round may still turn out to be the winner. The strategies in this game are the number of rounds an individual will lose before retreating; development of the model involves formalizing the trade off between acquiring information about RHP and risking injury.

The calculations are complex, but the evolutionarily stable number of rounds (or the stable mixture) can be determined for various values of the reward, of the cost of injury and of the extent to which RHP determines the outcome. Where success is strongly determined by RHP and provided that the costs of injury are not too high, there is a pure ESS and the more the outcome is determined by RHP the fewer rounds the animals should play; the greater the value of the reward, the more likely animals are to ignore defeats during the early stages of a fight.

5.6.8 GAMES WITH NON-RANDOM ENCOUNTERS

As mentioned earlier, all the models discussed so far calculate the frequencies of the different kinds of encounter (which must be known in order to work out overall pay-offs) from the frequencies of each different strategy in the population. In other words, they assume that animals meet at random in large populations and thus make no allowance for the fact that real animals probably encounter the same individuals on different occasions. Van Rhijn and Vodegal (1980) have developed a games theoretical model which accommodates this realistic possibility. The strategies they define are a far cry from the simple behavioural options of the hawk–dove model. For example, their threat–right strategy is defined as follows: the animal behaves like a Maynard Smith dove if making the first move against an unknown animal or one it has previously defeated. It then behaves like a hawk if the opponent does not retreat and retreats itself if injured. It never takes the initiative against an animal by which it has previously been beaten and retreats if such a dominant animal initiates any kind of aggressive interaction.

They ran a series of simulations in which this threat–right strategy was played against three other strategies, for animals which differed in RHP. For a whole range of different conditions, the threat–right strategy was an ESS, intuitively because by never challenging a previous victor and by giving a warning before attacking previously defeated opponents it avoids damaging fights. The model therefore predicts that animals will make use of information of previous fights.

Another source of non-randomness in encounters arises because most animals do not live in truly mixed populations; instead they tend to be more or less closely related to their neighbours. This means that encounters will tend to be between animals using the same strategies, assuming these to be inherited; calculations of the frequency of types of encounter should be corrected to allow for this if the average pay-offs for the different strategies are to be determined correctly. An additional complication of fights between relatives, is that the pay-offs need to be reduced for winners by the fact that the defeated rival is a relative and increased for losers for the same reason (Grafen, 1979).

5.6.9 THE CONTRIBUTION OF GAMES THEORY TO OUR UNDERSTANDING OF THE ADAPTIVE SIGNIFICANCE OF THE WAY ANIMALS FIGHT

Even this brief review makes it clear that games theory models of animal fights have received a great deal of attention from both theoretical and practical biologists. If, as has been suggested, this approach represents a major breakthrough in the analysis of the evolutionary process, it should have enhanced our understanding of the way selection acts on fighting animals.

The models start by making their assumptions explicit and by defining precisely the costs and benefits of different fighting patterns; by doing this, they clarify the issue of what animals which fight in a particular way gain from a single fight and how frequency dependent risk of injury detracts from the overall fitness of very fierce animals. Many of the models show that under certain not-too-rigorous conditions fights may be settled conventionally; it is therefore unnecessary to invoke selection acting at the level of groups to account for the existence of ritualized aggression, although the models cannot prove that group selection has not been involved. These are useful contributions and there are some who believe that this is all that can legitimately be expected of games theory (Caryl, 1981b).

In principle, the predictions of a games theory model can be compared with those of real animals to see whether it accurately describes the selective consequences of fighting in any particular case. For example, the hawk–dove model makes the qualitative but counter-intuitive prediction that, under certain circumstances, populations consisting of a mixture of hawks and doves are to be expected, with the two forms having the same fitness. There are a number of reports of species whose members show aggressive and non-aggressive modes; for example, male tree frogs (*Hyla cinerea*) either defend calling sites to which they attract females or remain silent and intercept females as they approach calling males (Perrill, Gerhardt and Daniel, 1978). The frogs switch readily from one behavioural mode to another and the success of the two strategies in getting mates appears to be fairly similar; this may represent a mixed strategy.

However, the situations in which most real fights occur are much more complex than that envisaged by the hawk–dove model and more sophisticated models might be more applicable. As discussed above, games theory models of animal conflict have moved from simple two-strategy games to those in which the behavioural options are complex conditional strategies which may involve a change of behaviour during a fight depending on how the (possibly related) opponent behaves and how likely it is to win. These more sophisticated models are much more satisfactory to those familiar with the behaviour of real animals and could potentially provide quantitative predictions to identify the precise selective consequences of different patterns of aggressive behaviour in particular animals. However, the predictions of these later models are critically dependent on the value of a number of parameters for which accurate estimates are not yet available; in the present state of knowledge, they cannot therefore be used in this way.

Thus the new way of looking at the adaptive significance of aggression which games theory provides has clarified a number of complex theoretical issues and has stimulated empirical research. However, realization of its full potential requires careful studies of the determinants, outcomes and fitness-related consequences of fighting in real animals as well as, and possibly instead of, more theorizing.

5.7 The adaptive significance of an animal's breeding habits; mating systems

Animals reproduce themselves in an enormous variety of ways and it is important to establish whether this diversity is the product of natural selection and, if so, in what ways the performance of one rather than another breeding habit enhances fitness. Several aspects of an animal's breeding habits can be questioned and are summarized briefly below.

1. The reproductive effort at different stages in the life span; age at maturity.
2. The number of offspring produced; few large or many small young.
3. The way the young are distributed in time; one large or many small broods.
4. Method of reproduction; sexual or asexual.

5. Relative size of gametes; isogamy or anisogamy.
6. Whether male and female gametes are produced by a single individual; hermaphrodites or males and females.
7. The proportion of reproductive investment in male and female entities; the sex ratio.
8. The mating system; monogamy, polygamy or promiscuity.
9. The behaviour surrounding mating; simple or elaborate courtship.
10. The nature of parental care; absent, biparental or uniparental (and in the latter case, by male or female parent).

Although most of these are morphological and physiological rather than behavioural characteristics, these different aspects of the way animals breed are all interrelated. For example, age at maturity may be related to the need to compete for mates, the sex ratio of a species may dictate its mating system and a difference in size between male and female gametes has important implications for the extent of parental care shown by the two sexes.

5.7.1 LIFE HISTORY PARAMETERS

Variation in a number of life history parameters is known to depend, in part at least, on genetic differences; for example, substitution of one allele for another at a single locus changes the age of maturity in platyfish (Kallman and Schreibman, 1973). These characteristics are therefore potentially responsive to natural selection and it is reasonable to ask whether different life history patterns are of adaptive significance. This is a complex issue in which traits such as fecundity, brood size and longevity are traded off one against the other. Such a situation lends itself to optimality modelling and this exercise has had some success (Sibly and Calow, 1983), although the assumption that all variation in life history parameters must necessarily have an adaptive explanation has been criticized (Stearns, 1980).

5.7.2 QUESTIONS ABOUT SEX

The existence of sex and the precise form it takes have profound influences on behaviour. Although sexual reproduction with anisogamy and separate male and female individuals is common, there are a number of complex reasons for not reproducing sexually. Because a sexually reproducing population must include male as well as female entities, and since only females produce the eggs which give rise to young, if sexual and asexual females are equally fecund, the requirement that approximately half of the former's offspring must be males gives sexual reproduction what Maynard Smith calls its two-fold disadvantage. This advantage is reduced if males contribute to the care of the young, a male and a female together producing more surviving offspring than one asexual female.

Even when this is the case, sexual reproduction carries an additional cost in the form of the time and energy spent and risks incurred in finding a mate and ensuring fertilization.

The essence of the sexual cycle is the generation of genetic variability and the obvious place to look for compensating advantages of sexual reproduction is therefore its power to produce new combinations of alleles already present in the gene pool. To oversimplify, an animal which is well adapted to a constant environment should reproduce asexually and thus produce many offspring, each equally well adapted. However, if the environment is variable and particularly if this variability is unpredictable, an animal which produces diverse offspring stands a better chance that at least some will survive. A number of theoretical models (Maynard Smith 1978a; Hamilton, Henderson and Moran, 1981), show that under certain, surprisingly restrictive circumstances, individuals increase their fitness by reproducing sexually as a consequence of producing more variable young. The most critical condition is a variable environment, but this advantage is amplified if competition between siblings is significant; in this case, production of offspring sufficiently different to be optimally adapted to different microconditions reduces competition between them.

The generally accepted theory about why there should be large and small gametes assumes that dimorphic gametes evolved from ones which were approximately the same size. Slightly larger gametes make fitter zygotes and are therefore favoured by selection even though individuals producing these produce fewer. There is very strong selection pressure on the smaller gametes to seek out and fuse with larger ones; since smaller gametes can be produced in larger numbers, the latter can outcompete the larger gametes in any attempt they might make to resist them. Eventually, two distinct types of gamete will result, large immobile eggs and small, mobile sperm, middle sized ones having fallen between two evolutionary stools (Parker, Baker and Smith, 1972). In contrast, Alexander and Borgia (1979) suggest that the primitive gametes were in fact of different size (as in some conjugating protozoa) and that production of equally sized gametes is the derived condition. Whatever its evolutionary origin, differentiation of gametes into energetically expensive, sessile eggs and cheap, motile sperm introduces an asymmetry into sexual relations which influences many aspects of behaviour.

In many animal species, the sex ratio is close to unity. Fisher provided a satisfactory explanation of why this should be the case; because only one sperm can fertilize one egg, when either sex is rare individuals of that sex will do well and parents which produce more offspring of that sex will leave more grandchildren. Selection will therefore favour production of the sex which is rare at any given time and a balanced sex ratio, or more precisely, an equal ratio of investment in the two sexes will result. The model does not apply if, for example, females are fertilized by their brothers; the sex ratio should then be strongly biassed in favour of females since only one or a few males could fertilize all the females and any more males would represent wasted offspring. In fig wasps (*Idarnes* spp.) in which the males have no wings and mate with neighbouring females which are usually their sisters, the ratio of males to females is 22 to 235 (Hamilton, 1967).

5.7.3 MATING SYSTEMS

Given a certain proportion of adult males and females in a population, what selective forces influence the pattern of mating that they show? More specifically, what determines how many times an animal mates and whether or not it restricts its attentions to a single partner? These are questions about mating systems.

A mating system describes the social and sexual context in which mating occurs. Animals display great diversity in the patterns of association between breeding males and females and it is helpful to impose some sort of order on this diversity by classifying mating systems into types. Traditionally, the primary criterion is the number of members of the opposite sex with which males and females mate. Thus, according to one commonly used scheme, a mating system in which both male and female mate with just one partner is called monogamy; this type of mating system is found in swans, rock ptarmigans, foxes and some crustacea. If an individual of one sex has exclusive access for mating to several members of the opposite sex, the mating system is said to be polygamous. This is polygyny if a male is shared between several females as in the case of elephant seals, zebras and honeyguides and polyandry if a female is shared between several males; the latter mating system is found in jacanas and sandpipers. Where both males and females mate more than once the system is called promiscuous as in the case of sticklebacks and great tailed grackles.

These broad categories can be further subdivided according to a number of other criteria. Thus the mechanism by which the mating system is maintained is used to produce subdivisions of polygamy. Resource based polygamy describes a situation in which individuals monopolize resources necessary to members of the opposite sex, those which control most resources getting many mates. The mating system of honeyguides is an example of resource based polygyny; the males defend territories containing varying numbers of bees' nests on which the females feed and while they are feeding, they mate with the resident male (Cronin and Sherman, 1977). Female jacanas defend large territories on marshes within which a number of males, their mates, defend smaller territories. The larger the territory a female can defend, the more mates she gets (Jenni and Collier, 1972). Harem defence polygamy describes a situation in which individuals of one sex directly control access to potential mates by aggressively deterring rivals. Elephant seals show this pattern of mating, with the large harem holding bulls defending a group of adult females against all comers (Le Bouef, 1972). Finally, mating priority may be determined by dominance status without reference to resources and without coersion, the highest status animals attracting many mates. This type of mating system is called dominance polygyny when the females are choosing, as in the case of a number of lekking species such as the kob, the ruff and certain species of Hawaiian *Drosophila*, and dominance polyandry, if males are choosing, as in the case of the phalarope (Emlen and Oring, 1977).

Temporal relationships have also been used to distinguish mating systems within a broad category; long-lived species which pair monogamously for just one breeding season are said to show short-term monogamy. In contrast, long term monogamy is shown by kittiwakes which normally pair for life. In polygamous species, an animal may mate with several individuals of the same sex at the same time, in which case they are said to show simultaneous polygamy (e.g. elephant seals). Alternatively, they may have several mates in succession; this type of mating system is called serial polygamy.

The aspects of mating systems so far discussed are intimately connected with the question of whether parental care is shown and if so, which partner provides it. Thus shared rearing of offspring is sometimes included in the definition of monogamy, while a version of resource defence polygamy is sometimes distinguished in which males differ in the quality of parental care that they offer; this quality is used by females when choosing males, some of which therefore acquire several mates. Zebras, in which the stallion defends the young against predatory attack, may come into this category (Alcock, 1979).

Like all classifications of biological phenomena, this scheme is not perfect and there are many examples which do not fit neatly into the pigeon holes described above. For example, female elephant seals mate preferentially with high ranking males and their mating system therefore combines elements of both dominance and harem defence polygyny. Male impala defend food supplies as well as the females themselves; should this be classified as harem or resource defence polygyny? It is perhaps better to think of mating systems as points in a space defined by a number of axes (number of mates, length of pair bond, extent of care of young by male or female etc). Most mating systems fall into clusters in this space but some mating systems lie outside the clusters. In addition, two mating systems which clearly come into the same category may still represent rather different phenomena. For example, the mating system of red-winged black birds and the lark bunting are accurately described as resource based polygyny. However, in the former case the male defends a depleting resource (food) and in the latter a nondepleting resource (shade); the effect of polygyny on the females concerned and therefore the selective forces which act on the mating system are very different in these two cases. Mating systems can also vary considerably within a single species. For example, where food is sparse, yellow bellied marmots mate monogamously, but when food is abundant mating is polygamous (Downhower and Armitage, 1971).

An additional complication in attempting to understand the diversity of mating systems is that for the vast majority of animal species the context within which mating occurs is simply not known. This is particularly the case for small, inconspicuous animals which are difficult to observe, but even in well studied cases, the precise distribution of matings is not known. The red-ringed blackbird has been the subject of intensive study and it has already been quoted as an example of resource based polygyny. However when territory owning males were vasectomized before mating had occurred, significant proportions of the females on their territory produced fertile eggs (Bray, Kennelly and Guarino, 1975). While this may be an artefact (the males may have been disturbed by the operation and their territories thus made artificially vulnerable to intrusion) it may mean that the mating system is more promiscuous than is generally believed.

Thus, mating systems represent complex constellations of characters which may vary greatly within and between species. There is evidence that in some cases this variability in mating system has a genetic basis and is therefore potentially responsive to natural selection; for example, in *Drosophila melanogaster*, artificial selection is effective in altering female remating times in both directions, producing promiscuous females which mate several times in quick succession and monogamous females which effectively mate just once (Pyle and Gromko, 1981). It is legitimate to ask whether these differences are the product of natural selection. Many attempts have been made to explain this variability in terms of adaptation to different features of the environment and general life style. This exercise is complicated by the fact that the same mating system may have evolved from a different starting point under different selective forces in the various groups in which it occurs. For example, resource based polygyny is found in fish, in birds and in mammals but the primitive condition from which this state arose seems to have been promiscuous mating with no parental care in fish, monogamy with shared parental care in birds and polygyny with maternal care in mammals. The selective regime producing a shift towards resource based polygyny is likely to have been quite distinct in these different groups.

Generally applicable theories about the adaptive significance of mating systems have therefore been hard to produce but there have been some attempts, the most influential of which are the Verner–Orians Polygyny Threshold Model and the Emlen–Oring Polygamy Potential Model; most other models embody similar principles. Both these models concentrate on the evolution of polygyny from a monogamous origin, because a fundamental asymmetry exists between the sexes in their ability to benefit from multiple matings. This point was first made by Bateman (1948) and developed in more detail by Trivers (1972). In brief, because females produce larger gametes, they necessarily produce fewer; this means a male can potentially fertilize more eggs than a single female can produce. While males can therefore substantially increase the number of offspring they produce by mating with many females, a female will not normally produce more young if she mates with several males. As a result, polyandry and promiscuity are likely to be rarer than polygyny and monogamy.

There are a number of circumstances in which this principle does not hold and females do benefit from mating with a number of males. Thus, it may be in the female's interest to allow multiple matings in order to avoid the cost of resistance (see page 236). Multiple mating may also have a number of more direct advantages for females; for example, if a single male cannot provide enough sperm to fertilize a female's full complement of eggs, then she will benefit from multiple matings. In field crickets, females which mate twice produce significantly more fertilized eggs than those mating once (Sakaluk and Cade, 1980) and female *Drosophila melanogaster* remate as their existing sperm supplies begin to run out (Pyle and Gromko, 1978). Where genetic diversity is important, females which mate with several males may produce more surviving offspring. Electrophoretic studies show that female lobsters (*Homarus americanus*) mate with more than one male, producing litters with progeny differing from mendelian ratios; production of genetically diverse offspring may increase the fitness of the females concerned (Nelson and Hedgecock, 1977). If males provide females with some resource other than sperm at mating, as in the case of hanging flies (*Mecoptera*) where males provide females with food as part of the courtship ritual, it may pay females to mate several times to gain more resources (Thornhill, 1981).

There are also circumstances under which males cannot increase their fitness by multiple matings; this is most commonly the case when males invest heavily in their offspring, in which case multiple matings may not result in more surviving offspring, but may also happen if the cost of acquiring additional females is high. For example, Knowlton (1980) describes a species of snapping shrimp (*Alpheus armatus*) in which the males move between the anemones in which they live in order to mate with several females; where predators are abundant such movement is too costly and the males remain with a single female.

(a) *The Verner–Orians polygyny threshold model* (the VO model, Orians, 1969)
This model assumes that polygyny is always beneficial to males, and therefore that its occurrence depends on the consequences of polygynous matings for females. It also assumes that males offer something to potential mates (genetic quality, ability and willingness to care for young or a resource such as food or nest sites) and that males differ in quality or quantity of what they offer. Reproductive success of females depends on the quality of their mate and the presence of more than one female sharing whatever one male has to offer reduces their breeding success. Males make no distinction between females, accepting all that come their way; however, females are able to detect both the quality of potential mates and their marital status and pair with the male which offers the best prospects at the time of settlement. Taking the case where males occupy territories of differing quality (Fig. 5.18(a)), the higher the quality of territory on which a female settles, the greater her fitness. The curve relating fitness to territory is lowered (by the same amount for territories of different quality) by the presence of another female. As territories of lower quality are gradually colonized, there comes a point (PT) at which the disadvantage of nesting in a low quality territory outweighs the disadvantage resulting from the presence of competing females. The fitness of a female who is about to settle under these circumstances will be

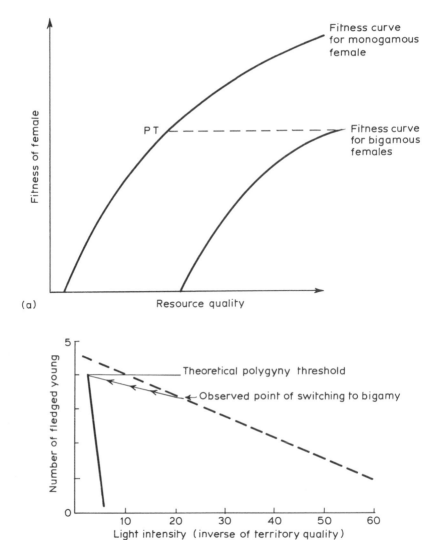

Figure 5.18 The Verner–Orians polygyny threshold model of mating systems (a) diagrammatic representation of the model; the fitness of a female increases with the quality of resources held by her mate, but fitness is decreased if the resource is shared by other females. Above the polygyny threshold (PT), whose level depends on the magnitude of the difference in resource quality and of the deterimental effects of sharing, a female does better to mate monogamously with a low quality male; below the threshold, polygamous mating with a high quality male is more advantageous. (b) A test of the model using lark buntings; the fitness of females nesting monogamously and bigamously on territories of different quality (after Pleszczynska and Hansell, 1980).

greater if she shares the highest quality territory than if she settles mono-gamously on the next best unoccupied territory. The point beyond which it pays a female to share a good mate is called the polygyny threshold and in species for which this point is fequently reached, polygyny will be the predominant mating system.

This model can be assessed by examining the assumptions on which it is based and testing the various predictions derived from it. If the properties of a given polygynous system meet the assumptions and the situations in which polygyny occurs as predicted, the model does provide an adequate description of the selective processes determining whether animals are monogamous or polygynous.

An elegant example in which these assumptions and predictions have been tested (Pleszczynska, 1978) concerns lark buntings (*Calamospiza melanocorys*). Males of this species establish territories which vary in quality, particularly in the amount of cover provided, and this difference influences the fitness of females nesting on their territories (Fig. 5.18(b)). The presence of a resident female on a territory reduces the expected success of a second female since the males only help the primary female. Males appear not to reject any females but females can recognize differences in territory quality and choose their mates accordingly; the assumptions of the model are therefore met. The direct predictions of the model are: that males will get different numbers of mates, that the number of mates will relate to territory quality, that females will begin to settle polygynously on good quality territories before all the available territories are filled and that the fitness of females nesting monogamously and those settling at the same time which choose to nest polygynously are the same. These predictions are met, although the switch to polygyny occurs at a slightly lower territory quality than expected; the females are therefore behaving conservatively about the point at which they abandon monogamy. Pleszczynska argues that by doing this the females are increasing their chances of surviving the winter and are thus maximizing their lifetime reproductive success (Pleszczynska and Hansell, 1980). By manipulating the amount of cover on different territories it was possible to alter the number of mates each male obtained exactly as predicted and even to produce trigamous males which do not occur naturally. The Verner–Orians model does seem to depict accurately the selective forces moulding mating systems in lark buntings.

Such detailed information is not available for the majority of species and in order to provide more general predictions, the model can be developed further by investigating the kinds of factors which influence its main parameters and thus the general situations in which polygyny is to be expected.

1. Variability in territory quality will be influenced by the patchiness of the environment (in a variable environment some territories will be of very good quality and others of very poor quality) and by population density (at high densities, males may be forced to occupy poor sites). Under these conditions, the

polygyny threshold will often be crossed.

2. The extent to which the females can benefit from what the males have to offer is usually discussed in terms of some resource which is necessary for successful rearing of young. In this case, the increase in fitness resulting from improved resources will be large if the requirements of the young are great and if the extent to which they can benefit from it does not level off; in such cases, the polygyny threshold will often be crossed. Thus if the resources concerned are scarce, if the young are highly dependent on them and if they do very much better with very much more of it, then polygyny is the predicted breeding system.

3. Similar factors influence the third parameter of the model, namely the extent to which females suffer from sharing a mate. A high degree of dependence of the young on the resource concerned, whether this be food or the attentions of the male, will increase the costs to females and the polygyny threshold will be raised. The extent to which sharing reduces fitness also depends on the way in which the male distributes parental care among his various clutches. If he concentrates on that of the first female only, as is the case for lark buntings, then the second female can expect a very much reduced share of the resources. Alternatively, if there is a long gap between the arrival of different females, the detrimental effects of polygynous mating may be reduced. Finally, the behaviour of the females themselves is important; if they avoid each other, competition may be minimized but if they fight, costs of polygynous mating may be increased.

These various derived predictions of the VO model have been tested and, in some cases, have been supported. Thus, the prediction that polygyny is to be expected in patchy habitats is supported by the observation that while marsh nesting species constitute a very small fraction of all passerines, four of these are polygynous, although since nine of them all belong to the same family, this figure is suspect (see page 140). Equally, the model predicts that polygyny will occur when the cost of sharing is low; in mammals, where males do not contribute much parental care, and thus the cost of sharing is small, polygyny is common.

However, there are many cases in which its rather precise assumptions are not valid: where males cannot benefit from polygyny, for example, if the attentions of both parents are essential for survival of the young, the model does not apply. Equally, where females do better in larger breeding groups (as in lions, Bertram, 1976), the VO model is neither applicable nor necessary since there is no conflict of interest between the sexes; in such situations the picture it presents of females putting up with disadvantageous competition for the privilege of mating with high quality males is not an accurate one.

The model is intended to accommodate cases where males vary in genetic quality as well as in resources for mates and/or young. Since genetic quality is not depleted by polygynous matings, the required disadvantage to the females of polgynous mating must come from indirect competition for other resources or increased risk of injury or predation; this could well be the case but it makes the model more complex. In addition, since we do not really know what genetic quality means, it is hard to measure it.

The model does not apply if females are unable to assess either the quality of the territory or the marital status of potential mates. Male fly catchers, (*Ficedula hypoleuca*) often have two mates; the male only rears the young of the first female and, contrary to the prediction of the model, the second of two polygamously mated females raises fewer young than monogamous females laying at the same time. Alatalno *et al.* (1981) suggest that females are unable to tell whether males are already mated since they defend what amounts to two distinct territories, keeping the primary female in one while attracting a secondary female to the other. Similarly, because it assumes that females are free to choose their mate, the Verner–Orians model does not apply in cases where the female's choice is restricted as a consequence of guarding by males or aggression by resident females.

In general, therefore, the direct predictions of the VO model have been met very precisely for a number of species in which the assumptions apply and for which the parameters are known; it thus tells us a great deal about the selective forces acting on mating systems in these specific cases. However, it is less useful as a hypothesis from which broad generalizations can be made partly because there are so many cases for which the assumptions are not met and partly because mate quality is such a complex concept.

(b)*The Emlen–Oring model of polygamy potential* (the EO model, Emlen and Oring, 1977)

Another influential model which attempts to provide general rules for predicting the occurrence of different mating systems is phrased in rather less precise terms than the VO model and depends on the following parameters:

1. The polygamy potential, or the ability of a portion of the population to control access to potential mates or to resources essential to them. The higher the potential for control, the greater the variance in mating success.

2. The ability of animals to realize this potential, which depends mainly on the degree of parental care required for successful rearing of young. Exclusive access to a number of mates will not increase fitness if all the offspring die through lack of adequate care.

The state of these two parameters is determined by ecological variables (such as food distribution) and physiological ones (such as the rate of development of the young). Polygamy potential is high when potential mates or resources they need are clumped in space or time. Female seals come ashore in large numbers on the limited parturition sites while female marmots probably group to avoid predation; both are therefore economically defensible and harem polygyny is possible. In sandpipers and phalaropes, males arrive at the breeding areas in large numbers and females are able to establish exclusive access to small groups of mates. In the bee *Xylocopa virginia* eggs are clumped; the males are able to detect those which contain females and to defend areas in which potential males are likely to emerge. In other species (e.g. *Xylocopa torrida*), the sites of emerging females are unpredictable but the flowers on which they feed are clumped; males defend flowers and mate with females as they forage (Marshall and Alcock, 1981). Jacanas live in marshes in which suitable nest sites are patchily distributed and therefore defensible; females can therefore potentially monopolize the resources needed by the males for successful breeding.

When can this polygamy potential be realized? In general, males are more often able to exploit it than are females (for the reasons outlined above) and therefore polygyny is expected to be more common than polyandry. Polygyny is expected to give way to monogamy when young depend on paternal care either because they need a lot of resources (species with altricial young are more likely to be monogamous than those with precocial young), or because they need things that can only be provided by two cooperating individuals (monogamy is common in birds because incubation is so demanding) or because the male provides something the female cannot (species in which vulnerability to predation is high and males have weapons should be monogamous).

Most examples of the generally rare phenomenon of polyandry come from the shorebirds. While there is no reason to expect a single explanation to account for all of these, in this group the young are precocial and food is abundant; therefore one parent can rear a brood alone. The polyandrous species tend to live in harsh environments in which efficient incubation is essential; clutches are often lost and replacement eggs required. Emlen and Oring (1977) suggest that male incubation, a necessary preadaptation for female emancipation, has evolved in shorebirds to allow the females to make up the energetic costs of clutch replacement. The actual cost of producing the rather small clutches may not be that large; however, it may suffice to reduce slightly the females' incubation efficiency and thus to predispose the system towards female desertion and polyandry rather than male desertion and polygyny (Erckmann, 1983 and see p. 241).

Lek mating systems (dominance polygyny) are expected when the polygamy potential is low but males are unnecessary for rearing young. In carpenter bees (*Xylocopa varipunctata*), emerging females are hard to find and once their cuticle has dried, females are large and strong and resist attempts at guarding them. The polygamy potential is low but the young receive rather little care of any sort. The males defend territories in the crowns of trees for several hours in the late afternoon, actively repelling other males and displaying to females which may land on the foliage and mate. Territories contain no food and the highly mobile females visit many territories before mating. The females apparently assess the quality of the males in some way and although the territories are not congregated, they appear to constitute a dispersed lek system (Marshall and Alcock, 1981).

Various attempts have been made to explain why males congregate into one area in classic leks; for example, the display sites may be places which females reliably visit. Alternatively, Bradbury (1981) proposed that clumping is actually disadvantageous to the males, reducing their prospect of survival and increasing competition. He suggests that it has evolved as a result of benefits to females, comparing males being easier when the latter are in one place. Selection has therefore favoured females which gravitate towards clusters of males and this in turn has favoured males which use communal display areas.

In general, the EO model highlights the kinds of selective forces acting on mating systems in general, providing broad principles which require more detailed development before they can usefully be applied in any specific case. In contrast, the VO model explains the occurrence of polygyny quite well in a few well studied cases. Between them, and their many descendants, while they do not allow us to derive firm predictions from first principles about the mating system to be expected in any given set of conditions, they do allow us to shorten the odds.

5.8 Adaptive significance of behaviour accompanying mating

The activities of both sexes in the period before and after mating occurs are extremely variable. In some externally fertilizing species there is no direct contact between the partners, the eggs and sperm being released into the external medium where fertilization occurs in a soup of gametes; behavioural adaptations are restricted to choice of breeding sites and rhythms which ensure that the two sexes release gametes at the same place and time. In other species, males and females go through a more or less complicated sequence of actions before and sometimes after mating. This behaviour can be a brief and business-like affair but is usually more elaborate and may consist of long sequences of spectacular, costly and often bizarre actions. Thus, the birds of paradise get their name and reputation from the exquisitely coloured plumage which the males display in elaborate dances, apparently as a prelude to mating. Differences in courtship, both between and within species, are likely to have implications for breeding success and are potentially subject to strong selection pressures. Traditionally, the adaptive consequences of courtship have been interpreted in the context of the obvious common interests of the two participants.

5.8.1 IDENTIFYING THE CORRECT SPECIES

Since hybrids are often inviable and almost always infertile, it will pay both sexes to ensure that their gametes fuse with those of a conspecific and many features of courtship can be understood in terms of this requirement. The broad pattern of courtship that an animal shows tends to be typical of the species concerned. For example, males of the cricket species *Teleogryllus oceanicus* and *T. commodus* both sing songs to attract females but these are quite distinct (see Fig. 8.1(c)) involving different patterns of wing movements and controlled by different alleles at a single locus. Females of both species are attracted to the songs of conspecific males, while hybrids between them prefer the songs of hybrid males. It seems that song production and the response to it are controlled by the same, or very closely linked, genetic mechanism (Hoy and Paul, 1973). This is one of a number of examples supporting the idea that differences in courtship are at least partly the result of selection to avoid heterospecific mating (see page 299).

5.8.2 PREVENTING MATING WITH CONSPECIFICS OF THE WRONG SEX

The sounds, sights and smells of courtship are often produced by one sex only and the presence or absence of the appropriate cue, besides indicating the species of the signaller, therefore also provides information about its sex, another important aspect of mutually successful courtship. However, the sexes must also be in the correct state; in many mammalian species, the scents which the females produce change with oestrus state and only those produced during oestrus are attractive to males (Keverne, 1976). They thus provide accurate information about the sex and physiological state of the female concerned and prevent waste of time and effort in courtship which would be fruitless for both sexes.

5.8.3 SYNCHRONIZING THE BEHAVIOUR OF POTENTIAL MATES

Courtship signals therefore act to bring together animals which could potentially mate successfully. At a finer level, the behaviour of the two partners must be coordinated and synchronized so that inappropriate tendencies such as aggression, fear or hunger are suppressed, sexual motivation aroused and the often complex manoeuvres necessary for successful sperm transfer efficiently carried out. Detailed analysis of the sequences of interacting responses shown by male and female during courtship can often identify the ways in which courtship by one partner influences the behavioural state of the other; information analysis of the courtship of salamander species identified and measured the precise extent to which the various activities on the part of the two sexes influence their partner's behaviour (Arnold, 1972 and see page 41). The best documented example of the effects of courtship on the behaviour and physiology of the partner is provided by Lehrman's work on ring doves (1965). For example, exposure to a courting male raises the oestrogen levels of an adult female ring dove and increases her readiness to mate; at the same time the experience of courting a responsive female raises the testosterone level of the male birds. Courtship therefore serves to bring both partners into a hormonal state appropriate for carrying out the complex breeding cycle.

5.8.4 THE IMPACT OF INTRA-SEXUAL COMPETITION FOR MATES

These studies, and many more like them, show that courtship can indeed serve the interests of both sexes by allowing species and sex recognition and fine scale synchronization of mating responses. However, if animals behave in such a way as to maximize their fitness, courtship and mating may have competitive as well as cooperative aspects, with conflicts of interests both between members of the same sex and between males and females.

As discussed above, (see page 210), sperm are smaller and cheaper than eggs and the breeding success of males is therefore usually limited not by how many gametes they can produce but by the number of females they can acquire. In contrast, females cannot usually increase the number of young they produce by mating many times. They can, however, increase the quality of their young by careful choice of mates. Thus reproductive competition is a major feature of the life of most male animals (and of some females) and this may well act as a strong selective agent making them highly efficient at all aspects of mating.

Male animals in general show a number of characteristics which can reasonably be interpreted as adaptations to increase their chances of getting into the vicinity of potential mates. Knowlton (1980) studied the snapping shrimp (*Alpheus armatus*) in two different environments; these animals live in close association with anemones and the adults associate in male–female pairs. In one study site, a large expanse of uniform, rubbly sea bed with rather few predatory fish, a number of differences between male and female shrimps were observed. The males showed striking black coloration on their spines and larger claws but also differed from the females in their patterns of movements, making frequent forays away from their own anemone. Knowlton suggests that these characteristics of males increase the number of fertilizations they attain; for example, one wandering male fertilized approximately 2100 eggs in 31 days by shuttling between two females which is considerably higher than the number fertilized by the most successful sedentary male. In the second study site, the males do not wander in this way, probably because they risk attack by the abundant predators in this area; the other differences between the sexes are also absent.

In some circumstances, selection may favour females which actively seek mates; for example, male mormon crickets (*Anabrus simplex*) produce spermatophores, comprising up to 30% of their body weight, which provide the females with nourishment as well as sperm. This considerable investment by the male in each mating makes them a limiting resource for females; they remain in one place and females seek them out, finding them by means of the low frequency vibrations they produce (Gwynne, 1981).

Some of the most spectacular features of the behaviour associated with mating are the result of direct competition between individuals for mates. Male elephant seals fight long, hard and viciously for priority of access to females, male tree frogs compete for the best sites from which to call for females while female jacanas compete for territories with many potential nesting sites for their mates. Thus animals fight for access to potential mating partners, to resources they need to attract partners or for resources that members of the opposite sex need for breeding.

In all these cases, any characteristic which enhances competitive ability will augment fitness. Possession of weapons is an obvious example, and Knowlton's data on shrimps indicate that larger claws in males may have evolved as a result of selection for effectiveness in competition for mates. Size is a significant determinant of fighting ability (see page 201) and where competition for mates is severe, members of the limited sex tend to be larger than those of the limiting sex. Thus in the amphibia, males are larger than females in species in which fighting for mates occurs (Shine, 1979) while in jacanas, females are larger than males and territorial females are larger than nonterritorial females. This is not to imply that any example of sexual dimorphism in size is necessarily the result of competion for mates.

Other aspects of courting and mating behaviour can be seen as adaptations which enhance the number of eggs fertilized once mating has occurred. Primates such as the chimpanzee (in which oestrus females mate promiscuously and sperm from different males are in competition) have larger and more productive testes relative to their body size than those such as the gorilla (in which oestrus females are mated by one male only). This correlation holds across a range of primate species; production of large quantities of sperm may enhance an individual's chance of fertilizing the eggs (Harcourt *et al.*, 1981; see Fig. 9.4).

Where internal fertilization occurs, the form of the intromittant organ may be the result of selection to outcompete rivals. In hanging flies the last male to copulate with a female is most likely to fertilize her eggs; in other words, sperm displacement occurs. The length of the aedaegus in 4 species of *Bittacus* corresponds exactly to the length of the spermothecal ducts of the females suggesting that sperm is transferred directly into the spermotheca, possibly replacing any stored sperm (Thornhill, 1981). Where such sperm displacement does occur, there is strong selection in favour of being the last and therefore favoured male. Males of many species (dungflies, Parker, 1978; fruitflies, Gromko and Pyle, 1978; bank swallows, Beecher and Beecher, 1979) guard females up to the time of oviposition, to prevent other males mating subsequently and displacing their sperm. Alternatively, mating plugs may be produced which physically prevent further mating for a certain period of time. Male heliconid butterflies transfer a scent to the females at mating which appears to reduce the attractiveness of the females to other males (Gilbert, 1976), while in *Bittacus apicalis* during long copulations a substance produced by the male is passed into the female's body where it inhibits receptivity and promotes ovulation (Thornhill, 1981).

On the other hand, where sperm precedence occurs or if females mate just once, there is a selective premium on behaviour which increases an individual's chances of mating first. Female two-spotted spider mites (*Tetranychus urticae*) mate soon after their final moult and sperm from the first mating precludes later insemination. Mating success therefore depends critically on getting access to the females as soon as they emerge, and the males use the female's moulting hormone to locate the pupae which they subsequently defend; the closer the female is to eclosion and therefore to mating, the fiercer the fights (Potter, 1981).

Thus many details of courtship and mating behaviour can be seen as adaptations to increase mating success at the expense of rivals of the same sex.

5.8.5 THE IMPACT OF SELECTIVENESS IN POTENTIAL MATES

Given two potential mates in the same place at the same time, it will not always be in the best interests of both partners if mating occurs; courtship may therefore be moulded by the need to induce a potential mate to copulate as well as by the need to compete with other members of the same sex.

(a) *Does mate choice occur?*

Proving that active choice of mates occurs is a difficult task; in the first place, it is necessary to establish that the opportunity for choice actually exists. Female carpenter bees are large and mobile and have been observed flying around a number of males before settling and mating; in this species, females have the opportunity to select mates and appear to take advantage of this (Marshall and Alcock, 1981). Similarly, male mormon crickets, which invest up to 30% of their body weight in a single spermatophore, have been observed to reject 29 out of 40 females which presented themselves for mating (Gwynne, 1981).

Having established that choice of mates is possible, it is necessary to identify departures from random mating. This is usually done by comparing animals which are observed to be successful at acquiring mates with those that are unsuccessful to identify ways in which they differ. Thus large toads of the species *Bufo americanus* were overrepresented among those found in amplexus (Gatz, 1981). However, such results do not necessarily mean that females are actually choosing to mate with particular types of male; a number of other possibilities need to be ruled out before this conclusion can be accepted. Non-random mating would result if some males were better at restraining females (female soldier beetles (*Chauliognathus pennsylvanicus*) try to dislodge males and larger males are better able to resist these attempts; McCauley and Wade, 1978) or at preventing other males from taking over (in the toad *Bufo Bufo* larger males are more effective than small ones at deterring take-over attempts, Davies and Halliday, 1978). In these cases, there is no need to invoke choice by females to explain non-random mating.

In the case of *Bufo americanus*, displacement of males in amplexus either by rival males or by the females was very rarely observed. It is possible that larger males are more efficient at locating females in some way but no differences in movement patterns were observed between larger and small males. Reproductive success in this species is closely associated with calling and females were frequently observed moving towards calling males, but calling sites are not defended. The possibility that larger males are more successful at obtaining calling sites can therefore be ruled out. The deeper calls of larger males probably travel further and may therefore be more conspicuous; however, females do not

Plate 5 Sexual advertisement? A male frog calling at a breeding pond.

always make for the nearest calling male. Active choice by females of larger males is therefore a possibility (Gatz, 1981).

Laboratory observations and experiments on hanging flies show that females mate with males which offer insects in preference to those which offer saliva bundles, which are in turn accepted in preference to males with no nuptial offering (Thornhill, 1981).

(b) *Is mate choice adaptive?*
Theory suggests that careful choice of mates by members of the limiting sex will enhance their fitness; however, there is little direct evidence on this point. Comparison of two species of hanging flies shows that predation by spiders, an important source of adult mortality in these insects, is male biassed in *Hylobittacus bittacus* but not in *Bittacus strigosus*, a species which does not practise nuptial feeding. This suggests that the preference by *Hylobittacus* females for mates with large food items may reduce their vulnerability to predation (Thornhill, 1980), although other differences between females of these two species might be responsible. Direct observation of the consequences of selecting different mates in bullfrogs (*Rana catesbeiana*) shows that the eggs of females which choose to mate with larger males, with better quality territories, have a greater chance of surviving (Howard, 1978). Experimental manipulation indicates that this behaviour is indeed of adaptive significance. For example, offspring of female *Drosophila melanogaster* given the opportunity to mate non-randomly survive better than those of females which were denied this opportunity but which experience an equivalent amount of courtship (Partridge, 1980b).

The adaptive significance of mate choice has been intensively studied in the mottled sculpin (*Cottus bairdi*). Males of this species defend nest sites and subsequently care for the eggs; females lay a single clutch of eggs. Some degree of selectivity is therefore expected in both sexes. Gravid females arrive at the spawning sites more or less synchronously, so that choice by males is potentially possible; when presented simultaneously with two gravid females, the males court the larger, which will produce more eggs. Females also mate selectively on the basis of size and a female which chooses a mate in the top 5% size class increases her reproductive success by 22% over those spawning with average sized males. However, the situation is complicated by the fact that the first clutch in a nest has a much higher chance of surviving than the last clutch. For females, choosiness about size of mates therefore carries a cost because by increasing the time to lay it reduces the chance that the eggs will be a favoured first batch. The decrease in fitness which results from being the last batch of a clutch is greater than the increase from mating with a very large male and choice with respect to size should therefore be relatively crude.

To discover just how selective the females are, a number of models were developed in which males were chosen on the basis of increasingly stringent criteria (such as random mating, mating with the larger of two males or mating on the basis of both quality of spawning site and size of male). Only the second model gave an accurate prediction of the number of spawnings per male in a natural population, which indicates that the females only invest a small amount in their choice of a mate (Downhower and Brown, 1980).

The fact that being choosy about mates may have costs as well as benefits makes it a suitable subject for an optimality study. Parker (1979) developed a purely theoretical model of optimal selectivity in which the cost is paid in terms of increased search time, with its attendant risks. The model assumes that offspring fitness increases with selectivity up to a certain point beyond which the law of diminishing returns applies; the hypothetical curve of gain (in offspring fitness) against the proportion of potential mates that are rejected is shown in Fig. 5.19 for a given time taken to produce a single brood (search time plus the time necessary to replenish resources). The optimal selectivity (or the optimum number of search costs which the animal should be prepared to pay) is that which maximizes the rate of gain in fitness per unit time and can be found graphically by taking the tangent from the origin to the curve. This model shows that choosiness about mates is amenable to optimality analysis, but since there is no species for which the relevant parameters are known, the model does not provide predictions about search times for any given species.

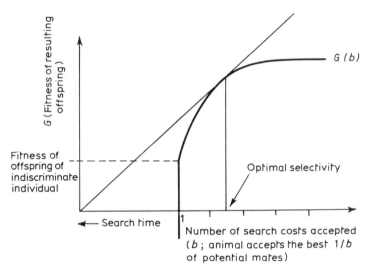

Figure 5.19 Using optimality theory to study the adaptive significance of being selective about mates (after Parker, 1979).

(c) *What characteristics determine mate choice?*
The suggestion that one or both sexes exert active choice of mating partners and that this may have adaptive consequences has therefore received a certain amount of support. Considerable effort has also gone into identifying the ways in

224   *The Study of Animal Behaviour*

which mate choice enhance fitness. In general, selective mating may pay off in terms of some phenotypic characteristic which has direct beneficial consequences for the animal or its offspring; alternatively, the supposed advantage may lie in an advantageous genotype for the resulting offspring. These various criteria are listed below.

Potential mates may be assessed on the basis of phenotypic qualities:

As a provider of gametes
As a provider of care and protection for partner
As a provider of care and protection for offspring
As a provider of resources for partner or for young

Potential mates may be assessed on the basis of genotypic qualities:

As a provider of genes determining overall viability
As a provider of compatible genes
As a provider of genes for traits which enhance sexual attractiveness

(d) *Beneficial consequences of mate choice arising from the partner's phenotype*
Size in females of many species correlates directly with egg production and therefore provides a good indicator of their quality as a provider of gametes, or fecundity. As mentioned above, male mottled sculpins mate selectively with larger females and get more eggs as a result. In woodfrogs (*Rana sylvatica*), larger (older) males produce more sperm and can therefore provide more fertile matings than can smaller males. Since females cannot tell how many times before a male has mated, choosing larger males will give a better chance of fertile matings (Smith-Gill and Berven, 1980).

Male ring doves perform various actions associated with mating, including courting, nest building and copulation itself. Various endocrinological manipulations have shown that the actions earlier in this sequence are dependent for their expression on higher levels of testosterone than those later on (Erickson and Martnez-Vargas, 1975). It is suggested that this state of affairs allows the female to determine at an early stage that the male has sufficiently high testosterone levels for mating to occur successfully, although the predictive value is by no means perfect. It is also not quite clear how this proposed selection pressure acting on females could have brought about the change in male physiology, unless the males also benefit from making their intentions clear.

A number of examples have been described in which severe fighting takes place over mates, usually by males for females; the females involved quite often get injured or killed during these fights. Thus female *Bufo bufo* may be asphyxiated (Davies and Halliday, 1978) and female dung flies dismembered or drowned (Borgia, 1981) during fights among males for their favours. In both cases, pairing with larger males which are better able to deter competitors may protect females from such damaging fights.

Kittiwakes (*Rissa tridactyla*) pair preferentially with former mates, especially if previous breeding attempts were successful; they may in effect be selecting mates of proven breeding potential (Coulson, 1966).

While mates may be selected on the basis of their intrinsic phenotypic qualities, it is also possible that choice is based on the quality of the resources they offer. Thus, the number of song phrases produced in a ten minute period by male stonechats (*Saxicola torquata*) correlates significantly with the readiness with which they subsequently feed and defend young. There are some indications that females use the information contained in the song in assessing potential mates (Greig-Smith, 1982). Male bullfrogs defend territories on which the females lay their eggs and these differ in their suitability as places for the eggs to develop; females mate selectively with the larger males, which defend the best oviposition sites (Howard, 1978). Mate choice by female hanging flies has been intensively studied (Thornhill, 1981). Males in these species provide no parental care but collect insects which they offer to females in exchange for copulation. In *Panorpa latipennis*, the males, whether caught in the wild or reared in the laboratory, offer prey of between 19–30 mm to females and the females, again whether wild-caught or lab-reared, mate preferentially with males which have high quality insects. Females mating with males whose insects fall into this size range spend longer *in copula*, receive more sperm and also show increased survival and fecundity. In other words, the males' reproductive success depends on the quality of the insects they offer and the females' fitness is enhanced by their preference for males with good quality insects.

(e) *Beneficial consequences of mate choice arising from the partner's genotype*

If an animal can determine the overall strength and viability of prospective mates, and is free to mate as it chooses, and if differences in strength and viability have some heritable basis, then selective mating in favour of the most viable mate will increase the overall genetic quality of their offspring. Therefore animals are expected to choose mates on the basis of characters which reflect viability, especially where offspring quality rather than number of fertilized eggs determines reproductive success (i.e. usually for females). The kind of cues an animal might use as indicators of viability are large size (which might reflect heritable differences in foraging skill), age (which might reflect heritable differences in general efficiency) or status (a correlate of competitive ability). In *Bufo quercicus*, larger males, which are either faster growing or older, are chosen as mates by females (Wilbur, Rubenstien and Fairchild, 1978). Female lemmings in oestrus associate with the scent of a dominant male, or a socially naive male which will subsequently become dominant, in preference to the scent of a subordinate male. This preference is reversed in dioestrus females (Huck, Banks and Wang, 1981). It is therefore possible that females of these species do select mates on the basis of characteristics which could reflect their general viability.

A more controversial suggestion (Zahavi, 1975), is that since the ability to survive to maturity with a handicap provides an unfakable indicator of general viability, animals of the limiting sex should select mates which bear such a handicap. On this theory, the peacock's tail is a handicap which the males endure because peahens use it as an unbluffable index of quality and select mates accordingly. Theoretical analysis of this suggestion has shown that the ability to survive some non-inherited handicap such as a broken limb could act in this way (Maynard Smith, 1978b). Where the handicap is inherited, the situation is less favourable for Zahavi's model; while the offspring of females selecting mates on the basis of a handicap are likely to be more attractive than average, they are also likely to have the handicap.

The possibility that animals may select mates whose genes mix well with their own, which would result in the production of better quality young, has also been discussed. In a number of species, courtship and mate choice appear to be arranged so as to produce a degree of outbreeding. There are many reports of animals rejecting very close relatives as mates. Given a choice between females which are genetically identical to each other except in the possession of different alleles at the locus controlling histocompatibility, male mice show a preference for females bearing the allele which differs from their own (Yamazaki *et al.*, 1976); this behaviour probably prevents inbreeding but may also improve the immune response (Howard, 1977).

However, in other cases, mating patterns are such as to promote inbreeding. For example, snow geese (*Anser caerulescens*) come in two types, blue and white; birds of different morphs mate preferentially with individuals of the same colour as those with which they were reared. Under natural conditions, this will usually mean that they mate with birds of a feather (Cooke, 1978). Male Japanese quail direct their sexual behaviour towards females which look like, but not too like, the individuals with which they were reared; in normal circumstances and given the hereditary nature of looks in this species (Truax and Siegal, 1981), this means that they mate with reasonably close relatives (Bateson, 1979). Similar effects have also been observed in the wild; thus, female great tits tend to mate with males showing song types which are similar but not identical to those sung by their fathers (McGregor and Krebs, 1982). It has been suggested that such intermediate levels of inbreeding as a consequence of mate selection may represent an adaptive optimum (Bateson, 1979).

There are many striking features of the courtship of animals, and of male animals in particular, which are apparently so much more complex than would appear to be necessary for simply attracting from a distance mates of the appropriate species that the various selective forces described above have been considered inadequate to account for their evolution. The elaborate tail of long-tailed widow birds (*Euplectes progne*) and the complex song of sedge warblers are two examples. It has therefore been suggested, initially by Darwin (1871), that these traits have evolved purely as a consequence of females choosing mates on the basis of some arbitrary, inherited, characteristic. Male sedge warblers which naturally sing complex songs mate earlier than those which produce simpler songs (Cathpole, 1980 and see page 141). Experimental manipulation of tail length in male widow birds increases the number of active nests on their territories. Although this may be because males with long tails are more conspicuous, there are indications that females actively discriminate in favour of males with long tails when selecting a mate (Anderson, 1980). The advantage that males gain from possessing such favoured traits is obvious; the females benefit not because it is of direct value to themselves or their offspring, nor because it is an unbluffable indicator of fitness, but because the sons of males with this trait are likely to inherit it and thus to be successful in attracting mates in their turn. Females mating preferentially with males bearing the trait in question may have less viable offspring but, because of the success of their attractive sons, they leave more grandchildren than those which mate indiscriminately. This process will continue, with females preferring and males displaying increasingly exaggerated versions of the trait until some counter selective process, such as seriously increased chances of mortality or excessive time needed to find a suitable mate, comes into play. Thus breeding male frogs of the species *Physalaemus pustulosus* produce simple whines when calling alone, even though females prefer more complex songs. The counter balancing selection in this instance seems to be predation by bats, which are also attracted to more complex songs. When males are singing in groups and, presumably, competition for females occurs, they increase the complexity of their calls (Ryan, Tuttle and Rand, 1982).

The possibility that such bizarre and otherwise disadvantageous characteristics have indeed evolved because they tempt females to mate has been tested by means of models. O'Donald (1980) considered a polygamous mating system with an equal sex ratio in which the presence or absence of the proposed attractive trait in males depends on alternative alleles at a single locus; female choice of mates is also determined by two alleles segregating at a single locus. Individuals with the attractive trait are assumed to suffer a certain decrease in viability. Computer simulations using this model with various values for the initial frequency of the different alleles produce the rather obvious conclusions that the allele for the, initially rare, attractive characteristic will increase in frequency at the expense of its alternative only if discriminating females are present in sufficient numbers. When this is the case, there is an accelerating increase in frequency up to a point beyond which further increase is slow. Less obviously, the process is speeded up if the two loci are linked and slowed down if either is dominant or sex linked.

The model therefore shows that reproductive benefits arising from female choice could outweigh disadvantageous consequences of a character for viability provided that females exist which exert such a choice of mates. There are several ways in which such a preference might arise. In the first place, it may simply be that males with the trait are easier to find and that, initially, this enhances mating success without any active female choice. Alternatively, preference by females for an extreme version of some trait used in courtship might exist because it ensures reproductive isolation in areas where closely related species exist (Trivers, 1972). On the other hand, the existence of females which prefer the trait might be a biproduct of the genetic mechanism controlling it. In crickets, male song and female preference do indeed seem to be controlled by the same genetic mechanism, although it is not clear why this is the case. Fisher took a different approach to the problem by suggesting that, initially, female choice was based on some characteristic which directly enhanced fitness and was favoured because this resulted in the production of generally fitter offspring; however, once this preference had evolved, what Fisher called a 'runaway' process along the lines suggested above would favour exaggerated versions of the character, even if this resulted in the loss of its previous beneficial effect on fitness.

Even if the existence of females preferring the trait can be explained, the idea still presents problems; given the intensity of selecting during the runaway phase, it is not clear how sufficient genetic variation could be maintained to allow the process to continue. If the preference exerted by the females is an absolute one, the selection pressure disappears when all males around are at or above this value; if the preference is relative, the selection pressure is still potentially active, but cannot be expressed if sources of heritable variation in the trait disappear. Although the theory can be rescued by proposing mutations in a polygenic system, temporal fluctuations in selection or high rates of migration, the final drawback is an almost complete lack of hard data with which it could be tested.

The examples discussed in previous sections show that females of some species do make an active choice of mates which may be genetically determined. In some cases, this choice does not seem to be of direct advantage to the female, although this may simply reflect our ignorance (warblers which can sing complex songs may be fitter in the body building sense). The assumptions on which the idea that male ornaments have evolved as a consequence of female choice is based are therefore not unreasonable but the only unique predictions arising from it which could possibly be tested given our present knowledge are those about the effect of the genetic mechanism on the process. Given the techniques of behavioural genetics (Chapter 8), it would be possible to collect the necessary information about the mechanism of inheritance both of characteristics on which mate choice is based and of the preference for it, but this has yet to be done.

5.8.6 ALTERNATIVE MATING STRATEGIES

It is clear, therefore, that reproductive behaviour is subject to strong selective forces arising from the activities both of competitors and of prospective mates and that success is not attained without incurring costs. Within a single species, individuals may differ in the cost they are willing or able to incur, even to the extent that entirely different methods are used to acquire mates by individuals within a single population. A few of the many species in which this has been descibed are listed below; it is clearly not a rare and insignificant occurrence but a common pattern of behaviour which requires explanation.

Some species in which males use more than one method of obtaining mates

- *Centris pallida* (Alcock, Eickwort and Eickwort, 1977): some males patrol a large home range over the sites in which females are pupating, fiercely guarding them when they emerge, successful guards copulating with them. Other males hover near shrubs and capture unmated females as they come to feed.
- Fig wasps (Hamilton, 1979): in a number of species of wasp which develop within the fruit of the fig (e.g. *Idarnes* spp.) some males are winged, emerge from the fig and mate with females outside, but do not fight. Other males are wingless, have large heads and mandibles and are extremely aggressive; they stay inside the fig and mate with the available females.
- Hanging flies (Thornhill, 1981): most males capture insects with which they attract females; others offer saliva or attempt forcibly to copulate with passing females.
- Crickets (Cade, 1979): most males attract mates by calling from territories which they defend aggressively. In addition, a number of males stay quietly in the territories of calling males and intercept females arriving there in response to the territory holder's calls.
- Bluegill sunfish (Gross and Charnov, 1980): this species nests in dense spawning colonies, in which some males (parental males) are large and brightly coloured, defend territories, construct nests and provide parental care for the young. Small, light coloured and non-aggressive males are also found, which remain close to the substrate and make rapid dashes into the nests where they deposit sperm (sneaker males).
- Treefrogs (Perrill, Gerhardt and Daniel, 1978): in this species some males defend territories to which they actively attract females, in this case by singing, while others remain quietly on these territories intercepting females as they arrive.
- Iguanas (Trivers, 1976): once more, most males defend territories where they display and mate. Others exist as satellites within these territories and try to mate with spare females. Yet others remain at the edges of territories, displaying to females as they enter or leave.
- Ruffs (Van Rhijn, 1973): resident males, which have dark ruffs, defend territories in leks and display actively to females. Satellite males have pale or white ruffs, do not defend territories and are tolerated by territory owners. They display to females and mate with those which are successfully attracted onto the territory.
- Elephant seals (Le Boeuf, 1972): most males compete for control of groups of females but some have no harems and 'sneak' copulations and mate unobtrusively with females of those which have.

It is necessary to know how these behavioural differences originate; individual male tree frogs show the various patterns of mating behaviour on different occasions, but male *Centris* bees stick to a particular method of mate acquisition, those which defend female emergence sites being consistently larger than those which search for females at feeding sites. Similarly, in the hanging fly *Panorpa*, the males which present insects to potential mates tend to be large ones (Table 5.11). In iguanas the territory holders are older, larger males as is the case for harem holders among elephant seals. In these species, the different ways of getting mates seem to be a response to circumstances such as size or age. However, there are cases in which the different patterns of behaviour are fixed properties of individual males determined by genetic differences. In the case of the ruff, the indications are that the dark aggressive–light unaggressive difference is inherited; in the sunfish, although sneakers are younger than parental males, a single male does not perform both patterns during his lifetime. Studies of the growth history of the two types, as reflected in the rings on the scales, indicate that sneakers start producing sperm at about two years while parental males only start to do so at 6 years old. There therefore appear to be two different life history patterns, parentals delaying maturity until they reach a large size at about 7 years and sneakers maturing early, at a small size, and probably also dying early. Since the fish which eventually become parentals tend to be the largest members of their cohort at 0 and 1 years, this may represent a conditional strategy based on size at an early stage but Gross and Charnov believe the difference is inherited.

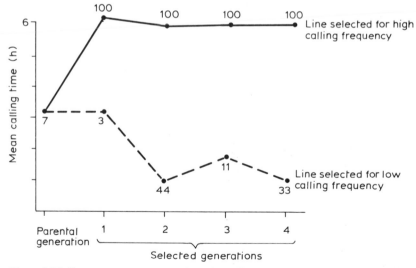

Figure 5.20 Demonstrating a genetic basis for differences in mating strategy; the effects of selective breeding for calling frequency in male crickets (after Cade, 1981). The figures indicate the percentage in each generation which called (upper line) or remained silent (lower line).

The one species in which differences in mate acquisition are known to be under genetic control is the cricket, *Gryllus integer* (Cade, 1981). Laboratory males of this species were monitored for calling frequency and 2–4 males at the two extremes of the distribution were mated to stock females. This process of selective breeding was continued for four generations; Fig. 5.20 shows the mean calling time and the number of males which called or remained silent in the two lines in each generation. There is a strong and rapid response to selection, indicating that at least some of the original variation in calling frequency had a genetic basis.

In order to compare the overall fitness of males which acquire mates in different ways, it is necessary to know the costs and benefits of each strategy. The evidence on this point is scanty; assessment of benefits is largely based on monitoring mating frequency, assuming that this leads to successful sperm transfer. In crickets for example, Table 5.10, all observed matings involved calling males and the number of females attracted was very much higher for calling than for silent males. In hanging flies (Table 5.11), matings are more frequent for males offering insects and also last long enough for maximum sperm transfer and for induction of a nonreceptive phase in the female.

Table 5.10 The number of males, females and parasites attracted to male crickets with different calling patterns (Cade, 1979).

| | *Number attracted of:* | | | |
	♀ *Crickets*	♂ *Crickets*	*Parasitic flies*	*% Parasitized in nature*
Callers	21	16	18	78.6
Non callers	0	0	0	16

As far as costs are concerned, Cade has shown that calling crickets attract rival males and are more heavily parasitized by the larvae of parasitic flies (Table 5.10); these home in on the calling songs when looking for prey on which to lay their eggs. Thus the reproductively successful calling males have reduced chances of survival due to heavy parasite infestations. In contrast, the large male hanging flies with insects which are more likely to attract females are less likely to be killed by spiders than are smaller males (Table 5.11).

In fig wasps, winged males must find females but wingless males run a high risk of injury and death during fierce fights over females. The advantages and disadvantages have been incorporated into a model to explain why these two forms exist (Hamilton, 1979). Females are assumed to suffer no disadvantage from mating with a wingless male. They lay one egg at a time in figs selected at random; if male, the egg develops into the winged or wingless form in proportions

Table 5.11 Relationships between size, mating strategy, reproductive success and spider predation in *Panorpa latipennis* (from Thornhill, 1981).

Male size	Percentage of matings (2 crickets / enclosure) involving:			Mean number of matings	Number killed by spiders (3 crickets / enclosure)
	Cricket	Saliva	Force		
Large	71	27	3	5.8	0
Medium	22	60	18	1.9	5
Small	4	54	42	1.2	20

(S and s) determined by the genetic constitution of the mother or of the male itself. Wingless males mate with all the females inside their fig while winged males mate outside. The number of females available to winged males therefore depends on the proportion of figs which do not contain any wingless males. Assuming random oviposition and random determination of male type this follows a Poisson distribution:

$$e^{-sM}$$

where M is the mean number of males reared per fig.

The reproductive value of winged males

$$= V^1 = e^{-sM}/1-s$$

The reproductive value of wingless males

$$= V = (1-e^{-sM})/s$$

When there are few males per fig, winged males are at an advantage since they find females easily and do not pay the cost of fighting. At high male densities, few figs are free from winged males, unmated females are rare and the proportion of winged males drops. Figure 5.21 shows the stable proportions (i.e. the proportion at which the two forms have equal fitness) of winged and wingless males calculated from the model for various numbers of males per fig, together with the observed frequencies. 'The fit is far from impressive but is good enough to suggest that this is the right general kind of idea.' (Hamilton, 1979).

5.8.7 DARWIN, NATURAL SELECTION AND SEXUAL SELECTION

Thus, many aspects of courtship and related behaviour in animals can be seen as the product of natural selection acting on animals to maximize their reproductive

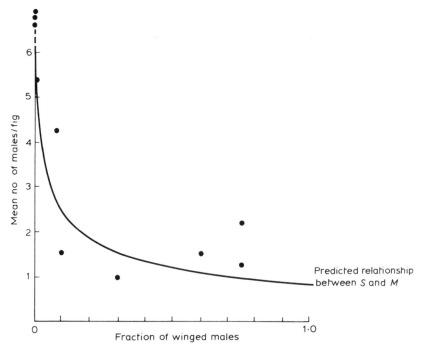

Figure 5.21. The equilibrium values of the proportion of winged males, *S*, at which $V = V^1$, for various values of the average number of males reared per fig, M; the observed values for ten species of fig wasp are shown.

output, through the medium of competition with members of the same sex and of choosiness on the part of prospective mates. The combined effect of these two processes may be the evolution of alternative reproductive strategies. Darwin (1871) made a distinction between natural selection, acting to increase an animal's chances of surviving and of coming into contact with potential mates and sexual selection acting on its chances of mating once potential mates have come together. The latter process allowed the evolution of characteristics which are disadvantageous in everyday life but which give their owners a competitive edge during reproduction. Darwin recognized two main forces at work in producing the striking morphological and behaviour differences between the sexes in many species; competition between members of the same sex for mates and the struggle to persuade members of the opposite sex to mate.

These two processes of competition and persuasion do clearly represent very strong selective forces acting on courtship and related behaviour. However, characteristics which are adaptive in one context often have adverse consequences on others; feeding adaptations may interfere with anti-predator defences and the need to keep warm may conflict with the need to find food. Such extreme characteristics as the tail of the peacock, which may function purely to impress females but which seriously reduce chances of survival, are not absolutely distinct from the perfect camouflage of many species which provides protection against predation but impairs mobility. In both cases one of the many selection pressures acting on an animal is particularly strong and adaptation to this pressure interferes with the animal's ability to respond to others. A separate category of sexual selection is probably not necessary, however spectacular the results of the pressure to acquire mates.

5.8.8 CONFLICTS OF INTEREST BETWEEN THE SEXES

Whether or not we need to recognize a separate category of selection to account for some features of courtship, there is clearly pressure on the limiting sex to select mates carefully and on the limited sex to compete for many matings. It will often be the case that when a male and female encounter one another, the optimum outcome for the two sexes does not coincide. A number of sources of such conflicts of interests between the sexes have been recognized;

1. Characteristics which give the male (usually the limited sex) a mating advantage over other males may impose a cost on the female. Thus male dungflies often damage or even kill females in the course of fights with rivals, male lions sometimes kill cubs fathered by other males while female marmots whose partners mate polygamously have to compete for resources.

2. Given the unequal investment of males and females in production of single gametes, it will often be the case that it is not in the female's interest to mate with a poor quality male when it is in his interest that she do so.

3. Finally, in cases where selection favours parental care by one parent, there is a conflict of interest between the sexes as to which should provide it; both could potentially increase their fitness by deserting and remating, provided the other stays behind and rears the young successfully.

It is one thing to recognize that fitness of males and females may be maximized by different outcomes; it is quite another matter to determine how this conflict of interests is resolved. In the case of the marmots, females have lower reproductive success on the territories of polygamous males. As a result of their aggressiveness towards other females attempting to settle, the actual number of females a male has on his territory is a compromise between his optimum (as many as possible) and hers (one). In the case of the pied flycatcher, a similar conflict of interests may have led to 'deceit' of the female by the male; in this species, the male defends what are in effect two separate territories. He displays and attracts a mate to one of these and eventually confines his parental attentions to this first brood. While the primary female is incubating, the male behaves like a batchelor on the other territory. A female which arrives subsequently cannot tell until it is too late that the male already has a brood of young which will monopolize all his paternal care (Alatalno *et al.*, 1981).

The clearest theoretical treatment of conflicts between the sexes about mating decisions is provided by Parker's games theoretical analysis (1979). The analysis, which is complex because the costs and benefits are strongly asymmetric, will be outlined very briefly. The simplest game allows just two strategies for males and females, assuming that the male is ready to mate and the female is not. The female may passively accept a suboptimum male (incurring a cost $-R$) or she may reject him with a probability q, incurring a cost of $-S$ fitness units against a persistent male. The male's strategies are to withdraw if rejected, which brings neither costs nor benefits, or to persist with a probability p, a likelihood r of succeeding and a cost of $-U$. Half of the encounters between passive females and non-persistent males end in mating; the pay-off for mating is M. Table 5.12 shows the pay-off matrix for the various combinations of strategies.

Table 5.12 Games theoretical analysis of sexual conflict; the pay-off matrix for a game played between passive and rejecting females and non-persistent and persistent males (after Parker, 1979).

		Female is	
		passive	rejecting
Male is		$(1-q)$	(q)
non-persistent $(1-p)$	Female gets	$-R/2$	0
	Male gets	$M/2$	0
persistent (p)	Female gets	$-R$	$-S-rR$
	Male gets	M	$rM-U$

Where M is the pay-off for mating, R is the cost of accepting a poor-quality male, S is the cost of resisting, U is the cost of overcoming resistance and r is the probability that the female fails to defer the male. Persistence will spread if: $(1-q)M/2 < (1-q)M+q(rM-U)$; resistance will spread if: $-R/2\ (1-p)-Rp < p(-S-rR)$.

In populations of passive females and non-persistent males both q and p will increase to fixation if the cost of rejection relative to the cost of accepting a suboptimal male (S/R) and the cost of persistence relative to the benefit of mating (U/M) are both less than 1. For a given, presumably fixed, probability that persistence will succeed in overcoming the females' resistance, males will win the conflict ($p = 1$, $q = 0$) if the cost of rejection is high and the cost of persistence low; females will win the evolutionary race ($q = 1$, $p = 0$) if the opposite is true. If costs are high for both sexes the outcome is difficult to predict and will depend on which sex first reaches a critical threshold. While it is illuminating to regard courtship as a situation in which the interests of the two parties concerned are not in perfect accord, theory has clearly far outstripped data in this area. Models such as Parker's are of value in highlighting the complexity of the conflict and identifying the factors which might influence its outcome, but need to be followed up by the collection of data which will allow parameters to be estimated and predictions to be made and tested in specific cases.

5.9 The adaptive significance of parental care

The third source of conflict between the sexes needs to be seen in the broader context of the selection pressures favouring parental care. Animals differ in the degree and kind of care they expend on their young; at one extreme are self-sacrificing distraction displays in which a parent risks its own life to lure a predator away from its young. On the other hand, female kangaroos, when closely pursued by a predator, eject the joey from their pouch, providing a diversion during which they can escape (Low, 1978). Such conspicuous variation begs some sort of evolutionary explanation and it is reasonable to ask whether the pattern of parental care that a given animal shows enhances its life time reproductive output.

That parental care is adaptive when it does occur seems rather obvious, but it is useful to know how and how much it increases the production of viable offspring. Female salamanders of the species *Desmognathus ocrophaeus* remain with their eggs for several days after laying, manipulating them and defending them against predation. Egg batches were reared under a variety of conditions, and their survival monitored. Two sets were reared from laying with the female as normal, either protected against or exposed to predators, one set was reared from hatching with artificial manipulation and rinsing while the last set were left alone. Figure 5.22 shows the survival of the eggs reared under these conditions. The difference in survival between motherless eggs left alone or artificially manipulated indicates that protection from fungi and parasites represents one beneficial consequence of parental care in this species. The difference in survival between the eggs reared normally in the presence and absence of predators indicates that parental care does improve breeding success via reduced predation, but that this is not totally effective in preventing eggs being eaten (Forester, 1979).

The precision with which selection can shape parental care in animals is demonstrated by a games theoretical analysis of nest provisioning in the digger wasp (*Sphex ichneumoneus*). Some wasps expend energy in digging their own nests; others enter nests which have already been dug by another wasp and which may

Plate 6 Parental investment by the female; a mother spider monkey carrying her infant.

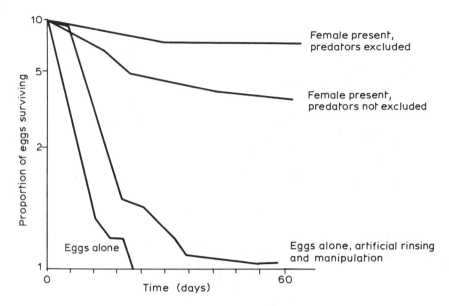

Figure 5.22 The adaptive significance of parental care; survival rates of broods of salamander eggs reared under different conditions (after Forester, 1979).

already contain a larva. If these two forms of behaviour represent a genuine balanced polymorphism, the pay-offs from both should be equal. The number of eggs successfully hatched is not significantly different for the two forms; '... enterers do well when they are rare because they are unlikely to be joined, but poorly when common for the converse reason.' (Brockmann, Grafen and Dawkins, 1979).

Neither of these studies helps to answer the questions of why parental care is shown by some species and not by others and, when it is shown, which sex does it. The main source of evidence on this point has traditionally been correlations between ecological conditions or biological features and particular forms of parental care. The presence or absence of any sort of care depends largely on the environment in which the young develop. Briefly, in harsh, variable environments parental care in the form of selection and provision of nest sites and protection of the developing young is likely to occur. Thus 57.4% of fish species found in freshwater, a rather variable habitat, guard their eggs; the equivalent figure for the more constant marine habitat is 15.4% (Bayliss, 1981). This line of reasoning can be extended to explain why in some species one parent cares for the young while in others both do so. Thus, in fish, where guarding is relatively easy to do alone and feeding is not usually necessary (or possible, since the young are so small), such care as occurs is usually performed by just one parent; in birds where the eggs require a great deal of costly care in the form of incubation, the two parents usually cooperate in rearing the young. Within mammals there is a strong correlation between the stage of development of the young and the presence of uni- or bi-parental care. Thus, altricial, low birth weight young tend to be cared for by both parents and precocial, high birth weight young by just one (Zeveloff and Boyce, 1980).

Where a single parent can provide the care needed by developing young, what determines whether this is performed by the male or the female? There is a broad correlation between the form of fertilization and type of parental care. For example, among fish species where one parent is involved in care of the young, 86% of internally fertilizing species show maternal care while 70% of externally fertilizing forms show paternal care. It has been suggested that this correlation between external fertilization and paternal care arises because reliability of paternity is higher when this form of fertilization is used; however, a male which deserts one brood because they may be the offspring of another individual is no more certain that any subsequent broods will be his own (Gross and Shine, 1981).

Thus, while there are a number of empirically demonstrated correlations between the form of parental care and the ecology and physiology of the species concerned, none of these are universal and no single selective force has been unambiguously identified as determining which sex deserts. Given this complexity, theoretical models could potentially play a role in making sense of conflicting data. Arguing from the general principle that animals will behave in such a way as to maximize their fitness, Trivers (1972) proposed that the key factor in determining which sex deserts is the amount of parental investment that each has made in the brood. Parental investment is defined as any investment made by an animal in one of its offspring which increases the latter's chances of survival at the cost of the parent's ability to invest in other offspring; the sex whose past parental investment is highest is expected to care for its young, while the other leaves after fertilization to attempt more matings. Although this idea is intuitively attractive, economic theory suggests that animals should make decisions about future behaviour alternatives on the basis of their expected future pay-offs and ignore past investment unless this directly influences future results (Dawkins and Carlisle, 1976).

The predictions of these two theories were put to an empirical test by manipulating brood size in red-winged blackbirds to give values ranging from 1–5 rather than the normal clutch of 3–4. Past investment was the same in all cases, but expected future pay-offs varied, the larger clutches representing a higher future pay-off (if the birds recognize the difference and if the cost of incubating a large clutch is not higher than normal). The level of aggression shown by the blackbirds to a simulated predator was used to measure how much the birds were prepared to invest in their broods. A significant positive relationship exists between the size of clutch and the amount of attacking shown (Robertson and Biermann, 1979). In this context, therefore, parental investment seems to depend not on past investment as suggested by Trivers but on expected future pay-offs as proposed by

Dawkins and Carlisle. In contrast, the readiness with which parental savannah sparrows (*Passerculus sandwichensis*) give alarm calls on the approach of a human observer depends on the age of the brood (or past investment) and is independent of the number of days available for renesting (or future pay-off). It may be that renesting potential is difficult to assess accurately and that since in general this correlates with the age of the brood, the latter may provide the easiest way of assessing future pay-off (Weatherhead, 1979).

Maynard Smith (1977) has drawn these ecological and physiological correlates of parental care together into a single, coherent theoretical framework with the help of a series of games theory models. These make explicit the fact that the different patterns of parental care have costs as well as benefits and that the magnitude of these depends on the behaviour of the partner. The simplest model assumes a discrete breeding season and allows just two strategies for both sexes, deserting or guarding. These decisions are made independently for the two sexes; thus whether or not one partner deserts depends entirely on its own pay-offs and cannot be directly influenced by the behaviour of the other partner. The model is developed to find paris of strategies for males and females such that it will not pay either sex to diverge from their strategy so long as most of the opposite sex stick to theirs. The model also assumes that the female which deserts does not remate but can lay more eggs (W as opposed to w where $W > w$, see Table 5.13 for a definition of parameters) and that since sperm are cheap to produce there is no equivalent traed-off between male fecundity and male parental care. A male which deserts has a certain probability (m) of finding a new mate whom he will also desert. The probability of survival of the young is

Table 5.13 Applying games theory to the question of parental care; the pay-off matrix for a game played between males and females which guard or desert (after Maynard-Smith, 1977).

		The female	
		guards	*deserts*
The male			
guards	Female gets	wP_2	WP_1
	Male gets	wP_2	WP_1
deserts	Female gets	wP_1	WP_0
	Male gets	$wP_1 + mwP_1$ = $wP_1(1+m)$	$WP_0(1+m)$

Where w is the number of eggs produced by a female which subsequently has to guard; W is the number of eggs produced by a female which does not guard; P_0, P_1 and P_2 are the number of young raised by 0, 1 or 2 parents respectively and m is the probability that a deserting male will acquire another mate.

influenced by the postcopulatory investment of both sexes such that $P_2 > P_1 > P_0$, where P_0 represents the survival chances of unguarded young, P_1 that of young guarded by a single parent and P_2 that of young guarded by both parents. It is assumed that males and females are interchangeable as single parents.

The matrix of net pay-offs gained by the two sexes when each strategy is played against every other strategy together with the conditions under which the various combinations are evolutionarily stable are shown in Table 5.13. Any of the four combinations could be evolutionarily stable. Thus if $wP_2 > WP_1$ and $P_2 > P_1(1+m)$ both sexes will guard. If $WP_0 > wP_1$ and $P_0(1+m) > P_1$, both will desert. When selection favours uniparental care, the female will guard and the male desert if $wP_1 > WP_0$ and $P_1(1+m) > P_2$. If $WP_1 > wP_2$ and $P_1 > P_0(1+m)$ the converse applies.

This model accommodates the various empirical correlations between parental care and ecology or physiology as factors which alter the value of its parameters. Thus, in a stable environment where young are precocial, P_0 will not be much less than P_2 or P_1. Equally, in fish, since the fry are so small that their parents cannot easily feed them, for example, and P_1 and P_2 are not much greater than P_0. In both cases, desertion by both sexes is likely to be an ESS. On the other hand, since predators of fish fry are likely to be small, one parent is as effective as two at protection and P_2 is not likely to be much more than P_1. Hence when parental care does occur, it is likely to be uniparental. In birds, where incubation is expensive and predators large relative to the parents, P_2 will often be greater than P_1 and thus biparental care is likely to be an ESS. Once it pays both parents to guard, further evolution will favour the division of labour, which will increase the size of P_2 relative to P_1 and make deviation from this strategy less likely. A weakness of the model in this respect is that it excludes the possibility that one sex may be better at doing something for the young than the other (larger males may be better at defence and only females can lactate); where this is the case, P_1 can have different values depending on whether the male or the female is involved. This will influence the likelihood of deserting in the two sexes.

If eggs are expensive to produce ($w << W$), female desertion is likely, as in the polyandrous birds (see page 216). Finally, the probability of remating by a male will depend on the population size, the sex ratio, the relative quality of the male concerned and various aspects of the social system. For example, if males compete aggressively for space or resources necessary for breeding, the chances of remating are reduced; this will also be the case if the females mate more or less simultaneously, of if they require a prolonged courtship before mating can occur.

Although this model is simple, its assumptions are reasonably realistic and it allows prediction of which type of parental care is to be expected in different circumstances. It represents a sophisticated and quite accurate picture of the way selection might act on the interactions between parents and their offspring.

5.10 The adaptive significance of living in groups

Animals of some species are regularly found in association with adult conspecifics; this may be a consequence of high population densities and concentrated resources or of lack of selection for dispersal. However, social life involves a number of manifest disadvantages and the question of what, if any, counterbalancing advantages animals gain by living in groups has been the subject of much discussion. Some of Tinbergen's comments on this subject are quoted below.

'The benefits which individuals derive from grouping together can be of various kinds. Among these, the defence against predation is the most obvious one. Members of a flock of higher animals can warn each other in case of danger, and the flock as a whole is therefore as alert as the most observant of its individuals. Moreover, many animals join each other in communal attack. . . We find numerous other functions of flocks . . . goldfish, for example, eat more in a group than when isolated. They also grow more rapidly. . . The marine flatworm *Procerodes* withstands fluctuations in salinity better when living in a group than when isolated. The achievements of cockroaches in orientation tanks are better when they are living in groups of two or three than when they are kept in isolation. The advantages of crowding in *Daphnia* . . . lie in reduced vulnerability to predation. This is due to a 'confusion effect' on the predator. . . Crowding in *Vanessa io* caterpillars protects them from songbirds such as redstarts; the latter were consistently observed leaving groups of caterpillars alone but pecked up every one that crawled away from the group'. (From Tinbergen, 1953).

5.10.1 STUDIES OF THE ADAPTIVE SIGNIFICANCE OF GROUP LIFE

Systematic application of objective research techniques to the question of whether, how and how much group life contributes to fitness was stimulated by Tinbergen's observations but started in earnest with the publication of Crook's study of social organization in weaver birds (1964). Cross-species comparisons revealed a correlation between group size and ecological conditions; large group size predominates in open country species while forest living species tend to live alone or in pairs. Of the many possible explanations for this association, Crook favoured the idea that group size is an adaptive response to the interacting effects of predation pressure and food distribution. Thus, in forests where food is thinly but evenly distributed, and crypsis is the most effective form of defence against predators, selection favours small group size. In the savannah, where food is unpredictable but abundant, and secure nest sites are available, the birds do better to forage and nest in large groups; they are more efficient at locating food, there is plenty to go round when it is found and the invulnerable nest sites protect the noisy groups from predation.

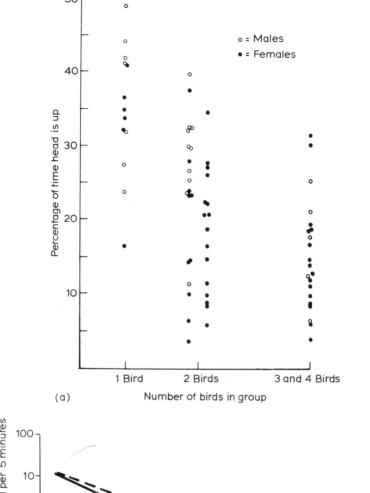

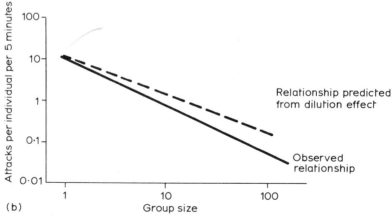

Figure 5.23 Group life as an adaptation to predation. (a) Time spent scanning the environment in ostriches feeding in groups of different sizes (from Bertram, 1970); (b) the number of attacks directed by fish towards ocean skaters in groups of different sizes (after Foster and Treherne, 1981), the correlation between the number of captures/unit time and group size = -0.66 ($P < 0.01$).

This is a fairly sophisticated hypothesis (both abundance and distribution of food and both vulnerability to and type of defence against predators determine group size) and it has held up well as an explanation of the presence or absence of group life in these birds. The use of cross species comparisons to generate and test hypotheses about the adaptive significance of group size has been extended to a number of taxa. For example, black and white colobus monkeys (*Colobus guereza*) live in groups of about eleven adults while red colobus monkeys (*C. badius*) live in much larger troops. Both species are vulnerable to predation and this is probably the main reason for their social habits; however, food distribution sets an upper limit on group size which is different for the two species. Red colobus monkeys feed preferentially on young shoots; this means that their food supply is highly clumped in time and space, hard to find but, once located, sufficiently abundant to feed a large group. The black and white colobus monkey eats leaves of all ages from a few species of tree; sufficient food for a small group only can be found within a localized (Clutton-Brock, 1975).

Within species comparison can be used to answer the same question; guppies collected from sites with abundant predators have an inherited tendency to school more strongly than those collected from streams where predators are rare. Thus a possible adaptive consequence of group size in this species is reduced vulnerability to predation (Seghers, 1974).

Direct measurement of the consequences of living in groups has also provided information about the survival value of this behaviour; Fig. 5.23(a) shows the amount of time spent looking around with the head raised in ostriches (*Struthio camelius*) feeding in groups of different sizes (Bertram, 1980). Birds foraging in groups spend less time with their heads raised than do those foraging alone; living in groups may allow ostriches to spend less time looking out for predators and therefore more time feeding.

A number of experiments have been carried out to investigate the adaptive significance of living in groups. Thus, the success rate of predators of various types was lower when larger artificial groups of small fish were being hunted (Neill and Cullen, 1974). This type of experiment has been repeated in the wild using natural pigeon flocks and a trained gos hawk (*Accipiter gentilis*) as a predator, with similar results (Kenward, 1978). Thus animals living in groups gain a very real advantage in terms of reduced vulnerability to predation. Captive great tits foraging in groups for mealworms hidden in artificial trees acquired significantly more food than those foraging alone, indicating that selection for improved feeding ability may be responsible for the social tendencies of this species (Krebs, MacRoberts and Cullen, 1972).

In parallel with all this empirical research, the use of theoretical models has played an important role in the development of our current understanding of the selective advantages of living in groups. The classic example of this approach is Hamilton's model of the selfish herd, described on page 149. Hamilton invented a population of hypothetical frogs each behaving according to a set of very simple

Plate 7 Group living and vigilance; a flock of grazing pink-footed geese.

rules designed to reduce its own chances of being eaten by an equally hypothetical snake. Computer simulations indicated that frogs which are initially distributed at random will end up in clumps if they obey these rules. This simple and
elegant model does not pretend to provide an accurate picture of what goes on in
the real world (although there are reports of animals behaving like Hamilton's
frogs) and makes no predictions about the size of group in which frogs should live.
What it does show is that there is no need to postulate the action of group
selection to explain why animals live in groups.

5.10.2 THE BENEFITS RESULTING FROM GROUP LIFE

Thus group life does appear to have the various beneficial consequences proposed by Tinbergen and there is now an enormous literature on this question. To
summarize briefly what has already been reviewed in many places (Bertram,
1978).

(a) *Group membership protects animals against predation*
Animals living in groups may benefit as a result of increased vigilance (pigeons in
larger flocks react to an approaching predator at a greater distance, Kenward,
1978); they may also be less easy to detect (grasshopper mice searching for meal
worms have a lower success rate when searching for clumped than dispersed
prey, Taylor, 1977). Group living prey may also benefit by the dilution effect
(swamping their predators) and by the confusion effect (predators switch
between prey and thus have reduced success). Both these effects have been
demonstrated for ocean skaters (*Halobates robustus*). The skaters live in groups on
the water surface attacked from below by fish predators and since they cannot see
the approaching fish, improved predator detection is not a complicating factor.
Figure 5.23(b) shows the number of attacks made by small fish on groups of
different sizes. The attack rate declines rapidly with group size but slightly more
sharply than predicted if the benefit derives from a simple dilution effect. This
discrepancy is ascribed to the confusion effect. Putting a figure on the strength of
these two effects 'an individual living in a group of 15–17 is about 16 times less
likely to be attacked but the probability of success is only 3 times less' (Foster and
Teherne, 1981). Finally, many group living animals benefit from the greater
effectiveness of communal attack against predators. Colonial nesting in fieldfares
(*Turdus pilaris*) increases the effectiveness of mobbing potential predators and
thus enhances the chances of successfully rearing young both of the fieldfares
themselves and of other small birds nesting nearby (Wicklund and Andersson,
1980).

(b) *Group living improves food supply*
Group life can enhance feeding success by increasing the efficiency of prey
detection; thus, the enhanced feeding rates of great tits foraging in groups is the

Plate 8 Living in groups can improve feeding efficiency; social facilitation in pink-footed geese.

result of the birds searching in the same or a similar place on noticing that one of their companions had found food. In the laboratory, weaverbirds (*Quelea quelea*) pick up subtle cues about which of their companions have recently found food and copy the behaviour of these successful birds on subsequent foraging episodes (De Groot, 1980). Social life can also enhance the efficiency with which food is exploited once it has been detected; hyenas (*Crocuta crocuta*) hunt in larger groups when going after zebra (which can counterattack effectively) than when going after the less dangerous wildebeeste, while cape hunting dogs (*Lycaon pictus*) use complex hunting strategies, sharing the lead and cutting corners. Finally, nectar feeding bats of the species *Leptonycteris sanborni* forage in groups, moving from flower to flower in a coordinated manner, taking it in turns to feed and leaving for the roost at the same time. This feeding pattern reduces the chances of bats visiting flowers which have recently been exploited and which therefore have low nectar levels making foraging more efficient for all the bats.

(c) *Other advantageous consequences of group life*
These bats are also more efficient at conserving heat and at assimilating their food when they roost in groups and thus illustrate several other beneficial consequences of social life (Howell, 1979). Finally, enhanced breeding success must added to the list of potential benefits; for example, groups of two or three male lions are much more likely to take over prides of females than are solitary individuals and thus enjoy greater breeding success (Bygott, Bertram and Hanby, 1979).

5.10.3 THE COMPLEX COSTS AND BENEFITS OF GROUP LIFE; CARACO'S MODEL (1979)

Thus living in groups of various sizes may well be the result of natural selection. For some species the various beneficial consequences of group life have been identified and it is occasionally possible to put a figure on their size. However, social life is a complex phenomenon and raises in an acute form the problems of finding out the adaptive significance of behaviour. In the first place, as the previous section makes clear, group life often has a number of different beneficial effects on fitness. Once social life has evolved, for whatever reason, selection will probably favour animals which make maximum use of its various advantageous biproducts. For example, the primary selection pressure leading to group life in herons was probably the need to reduce predation but individuals which used cues from the behaviour of other herons in the search for food would subsequently enjoy enhanced fitness; to understand the adaptive consequences of social life in modern herons we need to know about both these effects (Krebs, 1974). Equally, living in groups can have harmful as well as beneficial consequences. For example, group foraging in redshank reduces vulnerability to predation and when these birds are feeding on snails (which live under the sand and are detected by tactile cues), this behaviour does not depress feeding success. However, during the day, redshank also feed on crustacea (which they hunt by sight) and the movements of large numbers of birds disturb these animals, causing them to retreat into their burrows where they are more difficult to find. In these circumstances, therefore, group foraging has the deleterious effect of reducing foraging success as well as the beneficial one of reducing vulnerability to predation and the relative importance of the effects depends on conditions in which the birds are feeding (Goss-Custard, 1970). Finally, individuals in a group are not all equivalent in what they gain and lose from sociality; for example, Baker (1978) has reanalysed data from the experiments of Krebs, MacRoberts and Cullen (1972) on group foraging in great tits. Of 18 birds finding food, 9 were prevented from eating it by other birds and 8 of these were subordinates. Thus in calculating the increase in food intake resulting from social foraging, the number of prey items found needs to be reduced by the probability that the finder may not actually be able to eat it. In fact, given the flock size and prey distribution used in the experiment, only the dominant birds achieved enhanced feeding rates as a result of group foraging.

Given these complications, theoretical models have been of great importance in working out the interacting effects of the various fitness-related consequences of group life. Perhaps the most successful and sophisticated of these, though not by any means the most complicated and difficult to follow, is that of Caraco and his collaborators. The model is designed to investigate the adaptive significance of group size in winter flocks of small birds. It makes a number of precise assumptions about the birds and how they are influenced by living in groups and from these it deduces the optimal group size for birds of different rank and in different conditions. The assumptions are that the birds are designed to maximize their chances of surviving the winter, and that they are vulnerable to predation but can take effective action if the predator is seen soon enough. The birds need to take in a certain minimum amount of energy per day if they are to avoid starvation and whether or not they manage this depends, in part at least, on how much time they can spend foraging. It is also assumed that the birds squabble over individual food items and over good feeding sites, from which dominant birds are able to exclude subordinates. All these assumptions are quite reasonable in the light of the observed behaviour of small birds in winter.

The model proposes that if a bird decides to join a flock it can afford to spend less time scanning its environment for predators, since many pairs of eyes are better than one; it therefore has more time available for feeding. In addition, provided that living in groups does not make the birds more conspicuous and all individuals are equally susceptible to predation, group life also reduces vulnerability to attack through the dilution effect. However, living in groups exposes the birds to interference from the aggressive behaviour of their companions; this interference, which has a more marked effect on subordinate birds, reduces the time available for foraging and increases with group size.

The aim of the model is to work out how the birds should behave in order to maximize winter survival, which depends mainly on how much of the birds' crowded day can be devoted to foraging. This can be determined by specifying precisely how scanning time and interference time change with group size for dominant and subordinate birds. From these relationships, the group size which maximizes daily foraging time can be identified. The optimal group size is smaller for dominant birds than for subordinates. However, it is likely that as well as maximizing feeding time, the birds also seek to minimize their chances of predation. In other words both birds and scientists are faced with a multivariate optimization problem. Caraco uses the mathematics of decision theory to investigate possible trade-offs between increased predator avoidance and decreased foraging time and thus to find the group size which maximizes survival. The main components of the complex decision criterion are shown below.

Joining a group feeding in a habitat of quality λy rather than feeding alone in a habitat of quality λx enhances survival if:

$$\frac{\omega_1 \times h(n+1) \times \ln p \ (A|n+1)}{\omega_1 \times \ln p \ (A|n=1)} \quad + \quad \frac{\omega_2 \times \ln(1/T_T) \ (T_F|n+1)_i \times \lambda y}{\omega_2 \times \ln(1/T_T) \ (T_F|n=1)_i \times \lambda x} \ > 1$$

$\qquad\qquad$ concerns predation $\qquad\qquad\qquad\qquad\qquad\qquad$ concerns food

where ω_1 and ω_2 are factors reflecting the weighting given to the demands of avoiding predators and obtaining food, respectively; $h(n)$ is the rate at which predators attack a group of n birds; $h(1) \times 1$; $p(A|n)$ is the probability of avoiding predation in a group of size n for a single attack. This depends on the probability of any member of the group detecting a predator and the probability that an individual bird will escape to cover, given a predator has been detected. The value is logged because the model assumes that the birds base their decision on the product rather than the sum of realizable levels of predator avoidance and food intake; T_T is the total time available for foraging; $(T_F|n)_i$ is the foraging time available to individual i, while foraging in a group of size n. This is T_T reduced by interference time (which increases with group size and depends on status) and by scanning time (which decreases with group size); λx and λy are the rates of energy intake per unit time in the two habitats ($\lambda 1$ is the maximum). The group size for which this inequality is maximal is the optimum group size and depends on the precise relationship between group size and attack rate, avoidance probability, scanning time and interference time.

A final complexity which is recognized but not actually incorporated into the model is that dominant birds may be using a longer term energy maximization strategy than subordinate birds, since they can defend reliable feeding sites. Thus the model takes into account several different consequences of group size which interact in complex ways, allows for the possibility that the birds are simultaneously maximizing two different currencies and accommodates the fact that birds of different status, besides having different fitness–group size curves, may optimize on different time scales. A number of predictions, which depend mainly on the first part of the model, can be generated:

1. If the risk of predation is high, either because predators are abundant or because cover is scarce, scanning time increases and interference time is reduced; in addition, the probability of attack will be high and the dilution effect is important. Both group size and scanning time should therefore increase and interference decrease. Such an impact of predators on group size is expected on other models but the predicted effect on scanning and interference are special to this one.

2. At high temperatures or high food densities, less time is needed for foraging, the time which can be spent fighting increases, interference is increased and subordinate birds in particular should leave the group. These are strong predictions in the sense that they are counterintuitive and not too dependent on parameter values.

3. Because interference time for subordinates is greater than that for dominants, the latter are expected to forage more efficiently.

A number of field studies were carried out to test the validity of the original assumptions and to see whether these predictions are met. A dominance structure exists within winter flocks of juncos, and scanning decreases while both pecking and interference increase with group size. The latter effect is mainly the result of increased aggression on the part of the dominant birds which forage more efficiently and defend high quality feeding sites; thus the assumptions of the model are valued for this species.

The impact of predation was studied by flying a trained hawk over a group of feeding juncos and noting the effect on group size and time budgets. The results are shown in Table 5.14; just as the model predicts, group size increases, and the birds spend more time scanning and less fighting (Caraco, Martindale and Pulliam, 1980). Observations of group size and behaviour at different temperatures showed that as the temperature rises from 9 to 19 degrees, one fifth of the

Table 5.14 Test of the model's prediction; the effect of the presence of a predator on group size and time budgets (from Caraco, Martindale and Pulliam, 1980).

Flock size	1	3–4	6–7
Sample size	159 (79)	162 (52)	149 (162)
Proportion of time spent:			
Scanning	0.3 (0.57)	0.13 (0.27)	0.07 (0.33)
Feeding	0.7 (0.43)	0.77 (0.69)	0.85 (0.60)
Interference	0.0 (0.0)	0.1 (0.04)	0.08 (0.07)

( ) Denotes figures after the birds were exposed to a predator.

time which the birds previously devoted to feeding is spent in other activities; there is a 5-fold increase in aerial chases by the dominant birds with the predicted decrease in group size. Increasing the food supply had similar effects (Caraco, 1979). Altogether, the predictions of the model are met very closely indicating that it correctly embodies the ways in which group life influences fitness.

This model is successful because it refers to animals whose biology and behaviour are well known and therefore makes realistic assumptions and because it uses mathematical techniques which can accommodate the many and complex consequences of group life. It therefore produces precise, strong, and counter-intuitive predictions which were tested against accurate field data. As a result the selective forces which determine size of foraging group in small birds during the winter are now quite well understood.

5.11 Behaviour which cannot be explained by classic natural selection theory

5.11.1 AN OUTLINE OF THE PROBLEM

Since natural selection favours those characteristics which increase repro-ductive success, the behaviour of animals is expected to contribute to and perhaps even maximize fitness. The preceding survey of various aspects of animal behaviour has indicated that at least the first of these expectations is commonly fulfilled; in many cases behaviour is of adaptive significance to the animals concerned. However, in equally many other cases it is by no means obvious that this is so. Although this may simply reflect our ignorance of the animals con-cerned, there are many well studied examples of regularly occurring behaviour which reduces the animal's chances of surviving or breeding or both and there-fore cannot be explained even in the sophisticated framework of optimality models and game theory.

Most examples of such behaviour can be accommodated in one of three broad categories:

(a) *Protecting others from predation*
In many group living animals an individual which sees a predator gives an alarm call or display which alerts its neighbours but renders the caller itself more conspicuous and therefore more vulnerable. For example, ground squirrels (*Spermophilus beldingi*) on sighting a predator give a chattering call which causes neighbouring animals to take cover, while the predators often home in on the calling animal (Sherman, 1977). In similar circumstances, herd living ungulates such as Thomson's gazelles, alert their companions by displaying a conspicuous tail patch ('stotting'); others such as the eland mount cooperative attacks on predators which threaten one of their number (Kruuk, 1972).

(b) *Sharing food*

Cape hunting dogs hunt communally and regurgitate food for their companions. Communal hunting is extremely efficient and presents no problems for the theory of natural selection, but giving up hard earned food to other adults is not so easy to explain.

(c) *Increasing the reproductive output of other animals*

Individuals of many species help each other in the various requisites for successful breeding. Male bush turkeys (*Meleagris gallopavo*) form groups whose members cooperate in competition for access to females. Should the group be successful, the dominant male mates with the female with no attempts at interference by his subordinates (Watts and Stokes, 1971). Similarly, in troops of olive baboons a male competing with another for a female may solicit help from a third animal; if the two together are successful in driving off the rival, only the initiator of the attack mates with the female, the helper protecting the couple from interference (Packer, 1977).

Lions suckle young which are not their own (Bertram, 1976), while group living breeding birds such as the famous groove-billed ani take turns at incubating mixed broods of eggs in a communal nest. There is a great deal of competition during egg laying, each female pushing existing eggs out of the nest

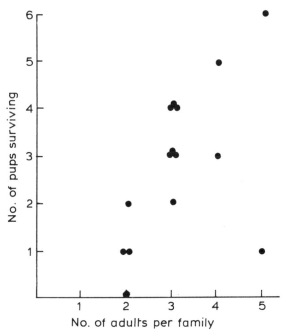

Figure 5.24 The number of young reared by jackals with different numbers of helpers (from Moehlman, 1979).

as she lays. In the end, most, but not all, of the surviving eggs belong to the dominant female and, because of their position in the nest, these hatch first and are better able to compete for food than are the young of the subordinate females. The dominant pair rears more young as a result of the communal breeding system, but the subordinate pairs rear fewer (Vehrencamp, 1978).

In these examples, all the animals concerned have contributed to the communally-reared brood; however, in a surprising number of species, mature animals have been observed caring for young which are not their own, rather than breeding themselves. Blackbacked jackals (*Canis mesomelas*) form long-term monogamous pair bonds; the male and female hunt cooperatively and share in the care of their offspring. They may be aided in this by up to five adult jackals which help in provisioning and guarding the young; Fig. 5.24 shows a significant positive correlation between the number of helpers and the survival of the pups indicating that the fitness of the breeding pair is increased dramatically by the activity of the helpers (Moehlman, 1979). In many species of birds adult helpers cooperate with a mated pair in the rearing of young. To give just one example, the splendid wren (*Malurus splendens*) normally lives in territorial groups consisting of a mated pair and several non-breeding adult birds which participate in territorial

Table 5.15
(a) The number of young reared per nesting attempt by groups of splendid wrens with different numbers of helpers.

Number of helpers	Number of young reared / nesting attempt	
0	1.69	
1	1.95	
2	2.05	no significant differences
3	2.20	
4–7	2.25	

(b) The number of young reared per nesting attempt by naive females with and without helpers and the lifetime reproductive success of females with and without helpers (after Rowley, 1981).

Condition	Number of young fledged per nesting attempt by naive females	Mean number of seasons survived	Lifetime number of young surviving to breeding age
Without helpers	0.78	1.35	0.65
With helpers	2.25	1.88	1.50
	$p < 0.01$		$p \approx 0.05$

defence and in feeding and protecting the young of the breeding pair. While the presence of helpers has only a weak influence on the survival of young when all groups are considered, it does significantly increase the number of young fledged by naive females (Table 5.15). In addition, the activities of helpers reduce the energy burden on the breeding female and marginally increase her survival and lifetime reproductive output (Rowley, 1981). Both jackal and wren helpers have retained the capability of breeding; however, in the most advanced social insects (termed *eusocial*) workers which provision or guard the young of another individual (the queen) have often lost the capacity to reproduce (Wilson, 1971).

In all these cases, animals apparently behave in a way which is of benefit to some other individual but detrimental to their own prospects of surviving and reproducing. Such behaviour is often referred to as altruistic behaviour, though there is no suggestion that the animals concerned necessarily have disinterested motives. It is hard to see how such behaviour could have evolved by the process of natural selection as traditionally conceived and considerable effort has been put into the search for other explanations.

5.11.2 ANIMALS MAY ULTIMATELY BENEFIT FROM THEIR 'ALTRUISTIC' BEHAVIOUR

In many of these examples, the sacrifice may be more apparent than real. For example, alarm calls and stotting displays could actually increase the survival of the animals concerned. As an illustration, Charnov and Krebs (1974) have suggested that by galvanizing its companions into activity, a bird producing an alarm call provides a large crowd in which it can take cover; since it alone knows the direction from which the predator is approaching, it can make sure that there are many other birds between it and danger. To give some rare data on this subject, when pairs of klipspringer (an antelope, *Oreotragus oreotragus*) are being hunted by jackals, they frequently detect the predator when it is outside its attack distance. In these cases, duetting alarm calls are given and the animals flee to safer, high ground from which they continue to call. 'In all cases, the jackal showed no interest in pursuing the group once they reached safety; in fact it left the area as soon as duetting started.' This suggests that the calls may be signals to the predator that the animal is alert and therefore unlikely to be caught (Tilson and Norton, 1981).

Animals caring for young other than their own may actually benefit in the long run. In some habitats at least, subordinate groove-billed ani benefit from communal brood rearing in terms of a reduced risk of predation even though their short term breeding success is low (Vehrencamp, 1978). Non-breeding helpers may also potentially benefit in a number of ways. In the splendid wren, breeding territories are in very short supply and a young bird has little chance of finding an empty one; in contrast, older helpers have a 41% chance in any given breeding season of taking over the territory on which they live or neighbouring ones as existing pairs die. This may well explain why they stay, although it does not account for the fact that they help (Rowley, 1981).

It has also been suggested that one animal may incur a cost in order to benefit another if the act is likely to be reciprocated in the future. In this case the cost is only a short term one and in the long term, the animal actually benefits (Trivers, 1971). For this idea to work, the costs incurred must be small compared to the benefits and the likelihood of reciprocation strong, as it may be if the animals concerned have long lives, low dispersal rates and some mechanism for discriminating against cheats. There is at least one case in which something along these lines does seem to be happening; in a troop of olive baboons, not all the males help one another in fights and there is a strong correlation between the frequency with which a male goes to the aid of others and the frequency with which it is successful in enlisting aid. In other words, individuals which do not readily give help are less likely to get it (Packer, 1977). Given the relatively low cost of the act, the great benefits derived from it, the long life of baboons, the cohesiveness of their troop and this apparent sanction against cheats, Triver's theory may provide an explanation of this altruistic behaviour. However, this theory of reciprocal altruism makes heavy demands on the cognitive capacities of animals and is unlikely to provide an explanation for many of the examples above.

5.11.3 GROUP SELECTION

It has been suggested that altruistic traits have evolved as the result of selection working at the level of groups or populations rather than individuals. The disadvantageous consequences for the individual are outweighed by the advantageous consequences for the group in which it lives, which is therefore more likely to persist while other groups die out. As a result, animals showing the altruistic trait will become the predominant type in the species as a whole. This process could augment the action of natural selection at the individual level but may also work in opposition to it.

Many species do exist in relatively distinct populations or groups and these may differ in the behaviour of their members. In addition, some groups die out while others survive and their fate probably depends in part on this behaviour. Conditions for selection at this level would therefore appear to exist and Wynne-Edwards (1962) has suggested that this process is responsible for the evolution of many altruistic characteristics, such as refraining from breeding in order to avoid over exploiting food supplies. The main criticism of this idea is that group selection could not work when opposed to individual selection. It is hard to see how a disadvantageous trait could become sufficiently common within a group for its members to benefit in the first place and, even if such a trait did become common, how replacement by cheats would be avoided. For example, animals which failed to limit their reproductive rate would leave more offspring (also selfish), thus reversing the effect of group selection.

In order to clarify this point, a number of models have been constructed to establish whether it is theoretically possible for survival and extinction at the group level to effect evolutionary change when it is counteracted by the effects of similar processes at the individual level and, if so, under what circumstances. The question of how frequently such conditions prevail in nature and thus how important the process might be in real life can then be settled by empirical observation. Taking Maynard Smith's classic model (1964) as an example, a species consists of altruists (which incur costs themselves as a result of which all the members of their group enjoy an enhanced fitness) and non-altruists, which behave selfishly. The species is established in a series of local populations occupying a transient resource for a limited number of generations; during this time they are subjected to the process of natural selection. When the resource is used up, the populations disperse and small groups of individuals then establish new colonies, whose composition will depend on the proportion of altruistic and non-altruistic types in the whole population. By chance, some of these new groups will contain only altruistic animals, which gets round the first theoretical objection to group selection. In mixed populations, non-altruists will always increase in frequency at the expense of altruists but since such populations are deprived of the beneficial effects of altruism, they will contribute fewer animals to the next phase of dispersal. Maynard Smith concluded that while an altruistic characteristic could spread through a population as a result of group selection, conditions under which this could occur (very small group sizes, very little migration and very high extinction rates) are rarely met in real life and therefore that group selection has not played a significant role in the evolution of altruistic traits.

However, there is disagreement about just how unlikely these required conditions are; for example, effective population size may be very small in many species (Baker and Marler, 1980) and structured migration, which is quite common, will decrease the gene swamping effect of movement between populations (Oosterhoff, 1977). Recently, Boorman and Levitt (1980) have developed a variation of Maynard-Smith's model which implies that group selection may have had a more important role in the evolution of altruistic traits than is generally accepted. The model envisages a series of habitable sites which are colonized by one male and one female taken at random from a population of altruistic and non-altruistic animals. At this stage, extinction is common and depends on the proportion of altruists in the propagule, this being the point at which group selection acts. Surviving propagules then increase in size with altruists and non-altruists changing in frequency under the influence of natural selection until the carrying capacity of the environment is reached. The genetic constitution of each propagule is then fixed, with those founded by selfish parents containing only selfish animals, those founded by altruists consisting only of altruists; the probability that those founded by a mixed pair end up consisting of only selfish animals depends on the size of the relative disadvantage suffered by altruists and on whether the hypothetical allele for altruism is dominant or recessive. In this model the problem of how groups consisting mainly of altruists could ever arise is solved by assuming that group selection acts on very small units established by a single pair, whose constitution is determined by random matings within the gene pool. The fact that non-altruists will generally outstrip altruists in mixed groups is accommodated by allowing natural selection the major role in determining gene frequencies in the propagules during the expansion phase.

Development of the model involves determining the frequency of the various group types in successive time periods, given various values for the relative fitness of altruistic and selfish animals and for the effect of altruists on the likelihood of extinction faced by propagules. As in the case of the models discussed above, the conclusion is that an allele for altruism can evolve to fixation under certain conditions; however, these conditions are much less restrictive. The model also predicts that under a wide range of circumstances stable polymorphic populations are likely to evolve. Boorman and Levitt believe that colonization of empty habitats by a single breeding pair is likely in a number of species, particularly in arthropods, and therefore that the high rate of extinction assumed by the model is not unreasonable. In short they conclude that 'the . . . model is quite strikingly favourable to polymorphic equilibria in which a high proportion of altruistic genes are represented' and advocate 'a tempering of the now widely held view that group selection is usually a weak evolutionary force'.

5.11.4 KIN SELECTION

(a) *The theory*
According to classical evolutionary theory, any inherited characteristic which causes its bearer to leave more offspring will increase in frequency, because in subsequent generations there will be more individuals in the population which have inherited from their parents the genes controlling its development. More broadly, any inherited trait which causes more copies of the genes controlling its development to be present in the next generation will be favoured by selection, regardless of where these genes come from. The overall genetic contribution an animal makes to subsequent generations (its inclusive fitness) is a consequence of its own breeding success and of the effect of its behaviour on that of animals carrying the same genes (Hamilton, 1964). It is therefore possible for an altruistic trait to evolve provided that the beneficiaries also carry the gene which makes animals like this.

There are a number of behavioural mechanisms which would ensure that an altruistic action primarily benefits individuals which carry genetic material coding for the same characteristic. For example, animals might behave altruistically only towards those individuals which have been observed to behave altruistically themselves or which have some recognizable characteristic which is pleiotropically controlled by the genes determining the development of the altruistic trait. However, perhaps the simplest way to achieve this is to direct altruism towards relatives. The mechanism of heredity is such that two animals are likely to have the same allele at a particular locus if they are related to each other and the closer the relationship the higher this probability is. Inherited altruistic behaviour directed at relatives could therefore increase in frequency in a population even though it reduced the individual fitness of the altruistic animal; Maynard Smith (1964) has called this process 'kin selection'.

Hamilton's creative contribution in this area was to recognize the potential importance of kin selection and to formulate precisely the conditions under which this could lead to the evolution of altruism. Briefly, genes controlling such a characteristic could increase in frequency provided:

$$b/c > 1/r$$

where b represents the benefit to the recipient, c represents the cost to the altruist and r is the probability that they share the allele coding for altruism. The arithmetic by which this probability can be calculated has been outlined many times (Dawkins, 1977; Krebs and Davies, 1981); briefly, since each meiotic division which occurs in the pedigree of two related individuals decreases by 50% the chance that they have inherited the same allele at a given locus, the probability of shared genes is usually estimated by Wright's Coefficient of Relatedness r, which is defined as follows:

$$r = (1/2)^n$$

where n represents the number of generation links between the individuals concerned, summed over all possible pathways between them. The value of r is 0.5 for parents and their offspring and for full sibs, 0.25 for grandparents and their grandchildren and for half sibs, 0.125 for cousins and so on. These figures give a reliable estimate of the probability of shared genes, provided that there is no history of inbreeding in the population, that there is no assortative mating and that the frequency of the allele is not changing rapidly under the influence of selection.

While the concept of kin selection requires that altruistic behaviour be directed towards related individuals, this need not involve actual recognition of kin; if animals do not disperse far from their natal region, or if they migrate as groups of relatives, altruistic behaviour directed towards neighbours will of necessity be directed towards kin. However, some animals do have the capacity to recognize kin even when they are unfamiliar; tadpoles of *Rana cascada* reared individually associate preferentially with sibs rather than non-sibs (Blaustein and O'Hara, 1981) while a similar ability has been documented in pigtailed monkeys (*Macaca nemestrina*) (Wu *et al.*, 1980). In a precise demonstration of this ability, inbred strains of the bee *Lasioglossum zephyrum* were interbred to give a range of degrees of relatedness. A positive linear relationship was found between the readiness of guard bees to allow a strange individual into the nest entrance and the closeness of its relationship to the bees in the nest; it is suggested that they use smells to make this discrimination (Greenberg, 1979).

(b) *Testing the predictions of the theory*

The theory of kin selection is attractive in its simplicity and in the elegance with which, on paper at least, it solves the problem of the evolution of altruism. The likelihood that such behaviour really has evolved in this way can be determined by testing predictions from Hamilton's formulation against the behaviour of real animals.

Thus, Hamilton predicts that the more closely two animals are related, the more likely they are to behave altruistically towards each other. This does not mean that a particular animal should necessarily dole out altruism to its companions in different amounts according to the degree to which they are related; if the recipient can continue to gain from any altruism on offer, this should all be given to the closest relative. However, if the law of diminishing returns applies, there will come a point at which the closest relative cannot gain much more from additional altruism and the donor should switch its attentions to its next closest relative and so on (Weigel, 1981); in this case altruism should be distributed precisely according to relatedness.

Ground squirrels, whose alarm calls enhance their risk of predation, live in colonies from which the males migrate when they approach maturity; females remain in their natal area. This means that females are more closely related to their neighbours than are males and Hamilton's rule predicts that they should be more prepared to incur the risk of giving an alarm call. This prediction is met, with females giving alarm calls more readily than males (Sherman, 1977); the male round tailed ground squirrels (*S. tereticaudus*) call before they leave their mother's home range but even then they do so less than females (Dunford, 1977). However, the first of these observations is also compatible with the suggestion that alarm calling is a component of parental care (Shields, 1980).

The elands, which defend their companions against predators, live in small cohesive groups whose members are likely to be related to each other, unlike the Thomson's gazelle, for example, which live in large, diffuse herds and do not show such behaviour (Kruuk, 1972). Members of groups of bush turkeys which cooperate in gaining females are thought to be brothers (Watts and Stokes, 1971), though this has been questioned (Balph, Innis and Balph, 1980); kin selection therefore provides a possible explanation for such behaviour. While the chances of a subordinate male mating are very small, the likelihood that copies of his genes will be present in the next generation in the bodies of his nephews is quite high. In groups of pigtail macaques, the monkeys discriminate between relatives and non-relatives in giving help during fights, aiding those animals with whom they have a closer degree of relatedness more readily than those which are more distantly related (Massey, 1977). Female lions in the same pride tend to be related, and this may explain why they suckle each other's young. In the superb blue (*Malurus cyaneus*) and in the splendid wren (Rowley, 1965, 1981), in jackals (Moehlman, 1979) and many other species in which non-breeding adults help a breeding pair to raise young, the helpers are the offspring of previous broods and therefore related to both parents and young. They may therefore be enhancing their inclusive fitness by increasing the number of siblings their parents can produce. Jackal pairs breeding alone have very low reproductive success, sometimes rearing no young at all; on the other hand, each additional helper adds an average of 1.5 successfully reared pups to the litter. Thus staying to help causes a greater increase in inclusive fitness than breeding as a lone pair.

Thus many of the examples of altruistic behaviour described above could be explained in terms of kin selection. However, perhaps the most compelling piece of evidence that kin selection may be a powerful force in the evolution of altruism comes from consideration of the unusual sex determining mechanism of the hymenoptera. In this group, during the production of eggs, the number of chromosomes is halved as it is for any other sexually reproducing species. If the egg is fertilized, it normally develops into a female with the usual diploid number of sex chromosomes and the normal 50% chance of sharing genes with its mother. If, on the other hand, it remains unfertilized, the egg becomes a male with a haploid set of chromosomes. There is no need for a reduction division in the production of sperm which are therefore of uniform genetic constitution. This means that sisters produced as a result of a single mating have a 75% chance of inheriting the same allele at a given locus; on the other hand, the average relatedness between females and their haploid brothers is only 25%. Female hymenoptera are therefore more closely related to their sisters than they are to their offspring but less closely related to their brothers.

A number of predictions follow from this unusual situation if Hamilton's rule applies. In the first place, altruism is likely to evolve in this group; highly developed social life with cooperative brood care and sterile castes have probably evolved as many as eleven times among the hymenoptera but only once in all other insect groups, in the termites (Wilson, 1971). Secondly, the altruistic animals are likely to be female in hymenoptera; this is in fact the case, the sterile workers being female in all eusocial hymenoptera, while termite workers come in two sexes. However, since female hymenoptera are especially unrelated to their brothers and provided that the workers are free to behave as they choose, they are expected to devote three times as much care to sisters as to brothers. The actual weight of adult flesh produced in the form of reproductive males and females has been measured in a number of ant species. In all but two species, which were slave makers and therefore subject to rather different selective forces, the ratio of male to female weight was about 1:3 as predicted (Trivers and Hare, 1976).

Hamilton's law predicts when animals should be selfish; for example, conflicts between parents and offspring over distribution of parental care can be interpreted in the light of differential degrees of relatedness. An individual's relationship with itself is 1 and with its sibs is 0.5. Its inclusive fitness will be enhanced only by allowing its parents to care for its siblings, if the benefit derived by these siblings is greater by a factor of at least 2 than that which the animal itself would gain if it received the parental care; where the benefit is less than this, the animal should attempt to monopolize the care (Trivers, 1974).

The size of the costs and benefits are also expected to influence the evolution of altruism by kin selection, although similar predictions follow from all the candidate theories. However, once it has been shown that kin selection could apply, in that the donor and the recipient are related, the relative size of the costs and benefits can indicate what the dynamics of this process are likely to be. Many of the species in which adult young of previous broods help their parents to rear more recently produced young live in ecological conditions in which suitable breeding territories are hard to come by; in such a case, the chances of a young animal breeding successfully are small and therefore the cost of staying to help is lower than it might otherwise be (Brown, 1978). This possibility has been put to a quantitative test in the case of the acorn woodpecker (*Melanerpes formivorus*); the probability that an individual will stay and help rear younger siblings is greater in saturated environments where the chances of successful breeding are very low than in less dense conditions where some unoccupied breeding territories exist (Stacey, 1979).

In a few cases, sufficient data are available to work out precisely the arithmetic of altruism. In the superb blue wren (Rowley, 1965), pairs with helpers rear an average of 2.83 young compared to 1.5 young for those without; thus the effect of the presence of helpers is 1.33 more surviving babies. If all individuals which left their parents managed to breed, helping would never pay. However, observation shows that while 100% of the females obtain mates, only 70% of the males do so. Thus the figure for expected breeding success for males which leave (1.5 young, since they will have no helpers) has to be reduced by 30% to 1.05. Thus for females, inclusive fitness is enhanced by leaving while for males the converse is the case. Hamilton's law predicts that males should help and females should not and this is exactly what is observed.

(c) *Problems with kin selection theory*
Altogether, there is an impressive array of evidence supporting the idea that kin selection is an important evolutionary force and that Hamilton's rule accurately describes its effects. However, questions have been raised about its value, both as a general theory for the evolution of altruism and as an explanation for the details of such behaviour in specific cases.

1. By definition, the theory of kin selection relies on the fact that relatives tend to have genes in common; however, immediately following the critical mutation of a proposed selfish allele to an altruistic one, relatives may not also possess the mutant, altruistic allele. The theory therefore has problems in explaining the initial spread of such an allele. To put the problem in its most extreme form, if the allele stops its carrier breeding, it is hard to see how the gene could get itself into

the bodies of other animals so that kin selection has an opportunity to work.

2. There are a number of problems involved in calculating (as opposed to measuring directly) the probability that two animals will have the same allele at a given locus. Wright's coefficient of relatedness only provides a reliable estimate of this probability if there is no inbreeding or assortative mating and if the gene is not subject to strong selection. If there is a history of inbreeding in the population, parents are likely to be genetically similar and r will underestimate the probability of shared genes. Hamilton's formula can be expanded to take account of inbreeding, but information about the breeding history of wild populations is rarely available.

Hamilton's formula can also be modified to accommodate the possibility of non-random mating; the appropriate comparison is not between the recipient and the donor but between the offspring of these animals and an altruistic trait will spread if:

$$b/c > \mathrm{Ray}/\mathrm{Rby}$$

where Ray is the relationship between the altruist and its own young and Rby is that between the altruist and the beneficiary's young (West-Eberhard, 1975). If mating is random, both these coeficients decline by a half for each generation transfer and this formula simplifies to the more familiar form. However, if mating is non-random, the predictions will differ from Hamilton's, in a direction dependent on the nature of the non-randomness, altruism being more likely if positive assortative mating occurs and less likely if the reverse is the case.

The effect of selection will depend on the direction of the change in gene frequency; if it is decreasing, r will overestimate the probability of shared genes and if it is increasing the probability will be underestimated. The importance of this effect will depend on the rate of chance and on how many generations separate the individuals for whom the calculation is being made.

All these complications have been incorporated into the formula for calculating the probability of shared genes, but its subsequent application in specific cases depends on information about population structure and behaviour which is rarely, if ever, available.

3. Hamilton's development of the theory of kin selection was based on what has been called 'the arithmetic of inclusive fitness' (Charlesworth, 1980). In this approach, the behavioural possibilities are taken as given and the conditions under which inclusive fitness will be maximized are worked out by logical deduction from natural selection theory, constraints imposed by the mechanism of inheritance of the trait being ignored. In contrast, models using the methods of population genetics condense the ecological forces of selection into single, usually fixed, fitness parameters which express the relative advantages of each genotype and determine how the frequency of different alleles will change in successive generations, given certain assumptions about the genetic system involved. These two approaches to the problem of the evolution of altruism by kin

selection make quite different sets of simplifying assumptions and may well produce different predictions.

Many population genetic models of altruism have been developed and with one exception (Yokoyama and Felsenstein, 1978) these are all single gene models; the difference between an altruistic and a selfish animal depends deterministically on substitution of alleles at a single locus. In one example, a large, randomly mating population is considered with discrete generations in which the allele for selfishness (a) is fixed and a mutant (A) arises. Being rare, this initially occurs only in heterozygotes and enhances the probability that the animal will behave altruistically towards selfish siblings to a variable extent dependent on the degree of dominance, chance events and environmental features. Altruism reduces the fitness of the carrier but increases that of the recipient in inverse proportion to the number of selfish sibs among which the benefit is distributed. Since the allele is rare initially it is only found in the offspring of selfish (aa) individuals paired to heterozygote altruists (Aa). The frequencies of selfish and altruistic offspring in such a family can then be determined from the laws of inheritance and their relative fitnesses calculated from the assumptions outlined above. Assuming that mating is random, the frequency of the two alleles in subsequent generations can be derived from the same laws of inheritance. Using different values for the model's parameters (for example, the degree of dominance and the costs and benefits of altruism), the conditions, if any, under which the allele controlling altruistic behaviour will increase in frequency can be determined (Charlesworth, 1978a).

This model like several others (including the polygenic one) shows that conditions exist in which an altruistic gene could spread because of its beneficial effect on relatives and that, over a certain range of parameter values, Hamilton's rule accurately reflects the impact of costs and benefits on this process. However, given other, equally realistic parameter values, these effects are not as predicted by the inclusive fitness approach. For example, where costs and benefits are both high or where these combine in a multiplicative rather than an additive way (Cavalli-Sforza and Feldman, 1978), their absolute values as well as their relative ones are important determinants of whether the allele will spread. At present, so little is known about the precise costs and benefits of altruism, that this quantitative difference in prediction is not too serious. However, some of the predictions of population genetics models also differ qualitatively from those of the inclusive fitness. For example, Boorman and Levitt (1980), among others, conclude that '. . . the comparative advantage of haplodiploidy is at most a qualified advantage and there are quite plausible axiom sets . . . where the balance of advantages and disadvantages is different from the predictions of Hamilton.' If this conclusion is correct, and not all population genetics models agree here, the widespread occurrence of altruism in the haplodiploid hymenopterans argues against the importance of kin selection in its evolution, rather than providing the strongest single piece of evidence in its favour.

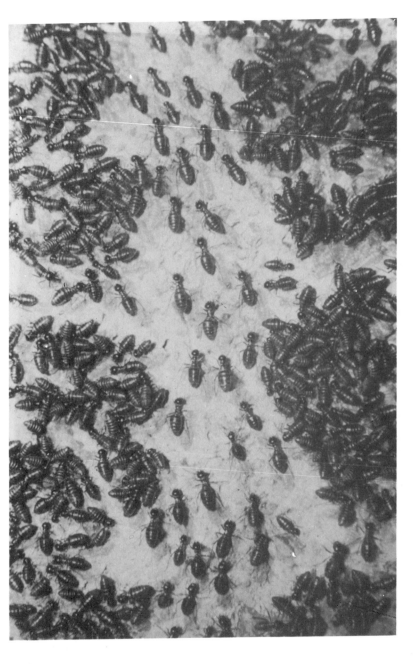

Plate 9 Sterile castes (of termites), a problem for the conventional theory of natural selection.

Where the predictions differ, the tendency is to assume that inclusive fitness arguments, as epitomized by Hamilton's law, are less exact and therefore more likely to be wrong. However, there are no grounds for believing the simplifying assumptions of this approach to be more unrealistic than those of the population geneticist. The population genetics approach allows for the complex behaviour of genes but oversimplifies that of animals while the inclusive fitness approach ignores constraints due to the mechanism of inheritance but makes realistic assumptions about the consequences of behaviour.

4. In addition to these problems with kin selection as a general theory, there are a number of examples in which the predictions of Hamilton's rule are not met. If haplodiploidy is such a strong preadaptation to sociality, why are the majority of hymenoptera not eusocial and why do other haplodiploid forms not show altruistic behaviour? Equally, altruism can be shown between animals which are not particularly closely related to each other. The most widely quoted case in point is the termites; these insects have a conventional sex determining mechanism and thus apparently no especially close relationship between siblings but have a highly developed cooperative social system with a number of sterile castes. It has been suggested that termites as a group are likely to be sufficiently inbred for siblings to be more closely related than parents and offspring and also that the necessity to reingest vital gut symbionts from other termites after each moult preadapts these insects to social life (Bartz, 1979). However, recently a peculiar rearrangement of the chromosomes has been reported in a number of termite species (technically a series of translocations including the sex chromosomes which form a ring during gamete formation and preclude crossing over, Syren and Luykx, 1977) which means that a large fraction of the genome is functionally sex linked; as a result, termites of these species have a significantly greater than 50% chance of sharing a particular gene with their like sexed sibs (Lacy, 1980). Thus both sexes could potentially increase their inclusive fitness by devoting themselves to their like-sexed sibs rather than to their offspring. If this chromosomal peculiarity is widespread among termites, the fact that they all show such well developed altruistic behaviour would actually provide strong evidence in favour of the importance of kin selection especially if it were shown that workers direct their care towards animals of the same sex.

A number of other examples in which altruism and relatedness do not go hand in hand could be quoted. Thus in both dwarf mongeese (*Helogale parvula*) and Mexican jays (*Phelocoma ultramarina*) breeding pairs have several helpers but these are not necessarily related to the breeding pair (Rood, 1978; Brown and Brown, 1981); even the supposedly high degree of relatedness within a pride of lions has been questioned (Packer and Pusey, 1982). In all these studies, estimates of relationships are based on lineages worked out by field observation; the use of enzyme polymorphisms is a more reliable way of estimating the probability that two individuals share a particular gene. Females of many wasps lay and rear their eggs in cells either alone or in pairs; in the latter case, one of the females lays most of the eggs while the other helps to look after them. The suggestion that the two females might be sisters and thus that the helper may be increasing her inclusive fitness has been tested by use of enzyme polymorphisms. Thus, Metcalf and Whitt (1977) showed that in *Polistes metricus*, the degree of relatedness between the females sharing a nest is 0.63 which supports the suggestion that kin selection is responsible for the altruistic behaviour of the second female. However, in other *Polistes* species the relationship is less close (0.39 and 0.43 respectively for *P. exclamus* and *P. apachus bellicus*). In these species, females must often rear broods which are much less closely related than their own offspring would be (Lester and Selander, 1981).

These problems do not prove that kin selection does not work; however, they do indicate that it may not be sufficient in itself as an explanation for the evolution of altruism in all cases and that at least some other factor(s) must be postulated. In the case of *Polistes* wasps, such an additional force seems to be the reduced vulnerability to predators and parasitoids of nests with more than one female; this is decreased by 38% which more than balances out the reduced relatedness of the second female and the objects of her care. Although Hamilton never claimed that kin selection could provide a universal and complete explanation for the evolution of altruism, others have done so. Thus '. . . how can altruism, which by definition reduces a personal fitness, possibly evolve by natural selection? *The* answer is kinship . . .' (Wilson, 1975, the emphasis is mine).

5.11.5 PARENTAL MANIPULATION

In the light of these and other problems with kin selection, Alexander (1974) suggested that altruism between siblings may have evolved as a consequence of manipulation by parents of their offspring. On this theory, the inclusive fitness of the offspring is reduced but that of their mother is increased; this can be seen as a version of kin selection in which parents prefer to produce children ($r = 0.5$) rather than grandchildren ($r = 0.25$) and are in a position to get their own way. This process more easily explains the spread of an altruistic mutant from very low levels and for the existence of altruism where there is no specially close relationship between sibs.

In support of this theory, Alexander points out that 'no parental insects are known to tend their offspring to adulthood and to overlap with them without developing sterile castes.' In other words, whenever the possibility for parental manipulation exists, sterile castes occur. A number of population genetics models have been developed to investigate the evolution of altruism by parental manipulation. Charlesworth (1978a) showed that a gene coding for altruism could spread through a population as a result of such a process and that the critical cost–benefit ratio at which an altruistic gene will spread is always lower for parental manipulation than for kin selection.

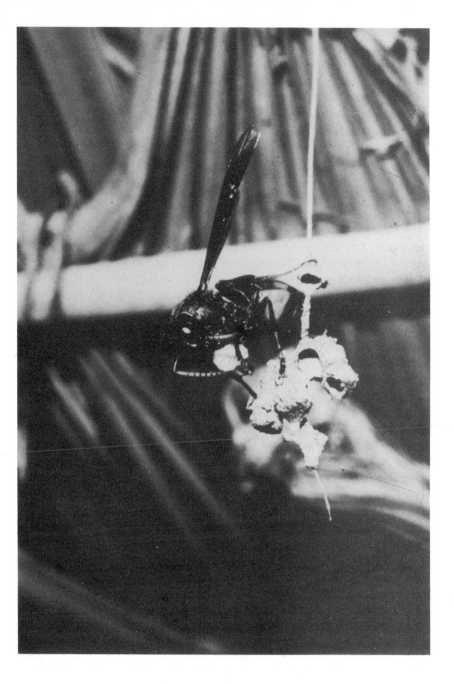

Plate 10 Factors other than kinship may favour communal nesting in hymenoptera; a hornet (*Vespa tropica*) destroying a larva of the wasp *Parischnogaster mellyi*.

The processes of natural selection, kin selection, parental manipulation and group selection are not mutually exclusive; different examples of apparently altruistic behaviour may well come about through the action of different types of selection and a particular case may have evolved through the combined effects of several of them. While we are far from having a complete understanding of the selective forces moulding altruistic behaviour, we have a list of processes which, acting alone or together, provide plausible hypotheses about its evolution in many cases.

5.12 Overview; sociobiology and behavioural ecology

The previous sections describe how the comparative and experimental approaches of classical ethology have been complemented and extended by cost–benefit analyses, optimality theory and by the frequency dependent optimality models of games theory. Application of these techniques has indicated that many aspects of behaviour enhance and possibly maximize fitness and (following recognition of the impact of an animal's actions on the fitness of its relatives) inclusive fitness. While the modern approach to the function of behaviour developed in part out of Tinbergen's formulations in *The Study of Instinct*, its methodology, terminology and the battery of candidate explanations are sufficiently different to justify two new names. Behavioural ecology is the most general term for modern attempts to interpret behaviour as an adaptation to the environment while sociobiology is that part of behavioural ecology which refers to social life (Wilson, 1975).

The approach epitomized by these two new disciplines has enhanced our understanding of the adaptive significance of behaviour by giving a new slant on old facts and has provided explanations for some previously inexplicable behaviour patterns. For example, alternative reproductive strategies, which were previously dismissed as abnormal (Morris, 1952), are now seen as the result of selection acting to maximize an individual's reproductive output in a highly competitive situation; the apparent coyness towards prospective mates of females of many species, traditionally interpreted as a failure in the efficiency of court-ship, is readily understood once the fact that different outcomes maximize fitness for males and females is recognized. A range of different behavioural phenomena which previously defied functional explanation at the individual level (from ritualized fighting to reproductive sacrifice) can be interpreted as the result of kin selection. The theoretical deliberations of behavioural ecologists and socio-biologists have also stimulated research in various directions. To give one example, games theory models of fighting predict the existence of mixed strategies. The search for such behavioural phenomena has increased our knowledge of animal combat. Where mixed strategies have been observed, testing the prediction that animals using them have equal fitness has stimulated the development of techniques for measuring the various beneficial and harmful consequences of aggression.

5.12.1 WEAKNESSES IN THE SOCIOBIOLOGICAL APPROACH
TO BEHAVIOUR

Thus this change in the way the function of behaviour is studied has been broadly beneficial. However, there are a number of weaknesses in the general approach, which will be designated sociobiology in what follows:

(a) *Oversimplified treatment of the development of complex behavioural traits*
Most sociobiological models refer to broad, global categories of behaviour such as altruism and selfishness and do not specify the precise behavioural differences between animals of these two types. These complex differences in behaviour are then assumed to depend in a deterministic way on substitution of one allele for another at a single locus; all animals with the 'gene for altruism' are perfectly altruistic while all those without it are completely selfish. Genes certainly do influence behaviour and it is possible that a single gene substitution could influence some key process in a complex behavioural system and thus bring about a major behavioural change. However, research into the genetics of behaviour (Chapter 8) has shown that, in many cases, the inheritance of differences in complex behavioural traits depends on the combined effects of a number of genes and that these interact with the environment in highly complex ways during the course of behavioural development. Thus by concentrating on global behavioural traits and postulating a single gene deterministically converting one form to another, the subtlety of the behavioural effects of single genes, the complexity of interactions between genes and the pervasive influence of the environment on the development of behaviour are all ignored.

In defence of the sociobiological approach, it has to be pointed out that when such realistic complexities are incorporated into models of behavioural evolution, these become so complex that depending on choice of parameter values, a whole range of different outcomes can be obtained; thus while single gene models are unrealistic, polygenic models are unmanageable.

There are two ways out of this dilemma; the first is to use single gene models of the evolution of behaviour, but to be absolutely clear about precisely what these can and cannot do and to put limited weight on any quantitative predictions derived from them. The second is to use ethological techniques to find out precisely what behavioural differences distinguish altruistic animals from selfish ones (or whatever major behavioural trait is at issue). The techniques of behavioural genetics can then be used to determine whether and how these carefully defined behavioural differences are inherited. The finer the level of a behavioural difference, the more likely it is to be inherited by a simple genetic mechanism and therefore to be a good candidate for a model which is at once realistic and tractable.

(b) *Overemphasis on complex theoretical models rather than hard data*
At present, sociobiological understanding is heavily dependent on the use of theoretical models and suffers from a dearth of accurate data on real animals. The models can clarify our assumptions and reasoning about the adaptive significance of behaviour and tell us what might have happened but unless the parameters, and in particular the consequences of behaviour, are accurately measured, they cannot be used to identify the selective forces acting on behaviour in any given case. There are a few intensively studied systems, such as social life in lions and mating systems in dungflies, for which much of the necessary information is available, but even here new and often contradictory facts are always emerging. This is not an insuperable problem, since the techniques for collecting the necessary information are available; however, it is one which needs to be solved rather than merely acknowledged.

(c) *A naive adaptationist attitude*
In *The Study of Instinct*, Tinbergen (1951) wrote 'It is no use denying that there are behavioural elements that may be non-adaptive . . .'. However, this warning has been largely ignored and basic to much sociobiological theory is an underlying assumption that the process of selection has moulded and optimized all aspects of animal behaviour. Even when attempts are made to put the assumption to the test, if observed behaviour does not correspond to predictions, another variable is often introduced into the fitness equation or kin selection, reciporcal altruism and parental manipulation invoked. The problem lies not in the fact that these different explanations exist but in the common assumption that they provide a complete inventory of the sources of evolutionary change. Other reasons can and have been suggested for the existence of behavioural differences and these do not necessarily lead to adaptation.

5.12.2 REASONS WHY BEHAVIOURAL DIFFERENCES MAY NOT
BE ADAPTIVE

1. A difference in behaviour may be the result of selection for some other characteristic. For example, body size, litter size and tameness are pleiotropically linked in mice; a difference in tameness may therefore be a biproduct of selection for body size or litter size.

2. A group of animals whose behaviour differs from others of the same species may be living in an unsuitable environment; mosquito fish (*Gambusia affinis*) living in freshwater lay fewer, larger eggs than those living in brackish water. This is not an adaptive response to the freshwater environment but a result of physiological stress (Stearns, 1980).

3. Differences in behaviour which persist over generations may not be genetically controlled; Caspian terns (*Hydroprogre caspia*) nesting singly are more aggressive towards conspecifics than those nesting in colonies. Young birds reared in colonies habituate to the presence of conspecifics and become less aggressive, which increases their chances of settling in colonial nest sites and producing young which have the same experience. The converse is true for solitary breeders (Bergman, 1980).

4. The evolutionary origin of behavioural differences may lie in random events of various kinds. Much persistent variation in, for example, the size and sex composition of groups of *Propithecus verreauxi* appears to be random in origin, perhaps the result of genetic drift and of no adaptive significance (Richards, 1974). In the case of courtship displays, while the evolution of a conspicuous signalling device may be explicable in terms of enhanced inclusive fitness, the evolution of one particular signal rather than another may depend on a random event.

5. On a similar point, a trait can only evolve if it shows heritable variability; thus evolution of one trait (such as production of many eggs) rather than another (such as extensive parental care) in a given situation may depend on initial inherited variability in these two traits rather than on their different adaptive consequences. Voles of the species *Microtus townsendii* do not show the regular four yearly population cycles that are found in many other species. It is possible to look for an adaptive explanation for this difference but the reason for the absence of cycles seems to lie in the fact that in this species there is little heritable variation in the aggressive behaviour on which the population cycles depend (Krebs, 1979).

6. Behavioural differences may be the result of phylogenetic constraints rather than adaptation to the environment. Feeding fox sparrows (*Passerella iliaca*) scratch at leaves with their feet while brown thrashers (*Toxostoma rufum*), a rather similar passerine feeding on the same sort of food in the same places, turn the leaves over with their beaks. This difference in feeding technique could be explained in terms of adaptations to slightly different diets, but its evolutionary origin seems to lie in a structural difference between the birds. Ancestral thrashers were long and thin and had to keep their feet well back in order to reach food without falling over; this precluded the use of the feet to scratch for food. Both feeding techniques may be efficient methods of finding food but the difference between them can only be understood in the light of this phylogenetic constraint (Hailman, 1976).

The combined result of such genetic and structural constraints and of random events is that animals are likely to use different solutions to the same problem, or to show 'multiple adaptive peaks', to use Lewontin's term (1978). The great blue heron and the great egret (*Casmerodius albus*) are closely related and are both large, hunt in groups, and nest monogamously in open habitats, the male making considerable parental investment. They therefore have very similar life styles and in particular, the goals of courtship for the male would appear to be the same,

Table 5.16 Aspects of the courtship ritual of the great blue heron and the great egret (from Mock, 1980).

	Heron	Egret
Plumage colour	Polychromatic	Monochromatic
No. of plumage tracts	3	1
Total no. of displays	14	16
Display rates/min in unpaired males	2.5–2.6	5.4–6.5
No. of contexts in which 'stretch' is shown	3	1
No. of 'more variable' homologous displays	8	0
Regular sequential relationships among displays	Absent	Present

namely to form a close pair bond with the best available conspecific female while defending a suitable nest site. As might be expected for such closely related birds, their behavioural repertoires share a number of homologous actions; however, there are a number of differences between the species in the details of their courtship. These are summarized in Table 5.16; it seems that herons have enriched particular displays by adding colour and introducing minor variations while the egrets combine existing, simple displays into variable sequences which are performed at a rapid rate. It is suggested that rather than being an adaptive response to different needs, these represent two equally efficient ways of solving the same problem (Mock, 1980).

All this is not to deny that natural selection acts on behaviour to produce adaptation or that many inherited behavioural differences both within and between species are the result of this process. However, the adaptationist paradigm ignores the possibility of other sources of evolutionary change either by failing to report negative results or by providing plausible but untested (*not* untestable) functional explanations for what may be non-adaptive behavioural differences. Notwithstanding the spectacular success of inclusive fitness theory and optimality modelling in suggesting adaptive explanations of behaviour, it is worth remembering that there are many examples of behaviour which obstinately resist explanation even after considerable study. To end this chapter on a salutary note, if a female antarctic plunderfish (*Harpagifer bispinis*) which is guarding her eggs disappears naturally or is removed, another fish, usually a male takes over. If he is removed another fish takes over and so on. The fish which assume guard duty do not eat the eggs, are not the parents or siblings of the eggs and do not gain any long term advantage such as access to suitable nesting sites. Nor are the animals concerned likely to be related or to belong to discrete, isolated groups, since these fish are widely dispersed during their planctonic stage (Daniels, 1979). Classical natural selection, kin selection, parental manipulation and group selection all fail to provide convincing functional explanations for this behaviour; in short, we simply have no idea why these animals behave in this way.

CHAPTER 6

The phylogeny of behaviour

To understand the evolution of a particular behaviour pattern we need to know what selective forces act on it and the evolutionary changes that these have produced. The nature of the selective forces acting on behaviour formed the subject of Chapter 5; in this chapter the question of the phylogenetic history of behaviour will be considered.

6.1 Sources of evidence about the phylogeny of behaviour

6.1.1 THE FOSSIL RECORD

The most direct evidence about phylogeny is provided by the fossils which, for all their inadequacies, represent the only genuinely historical record of the course of evolution. However, since actions normally leave no permanent trace to be fossilized, this is not a very fruitful source of information about the evolution of behaviour. There are some exceptional cases where the consequences of behaviour have survived as fossils. Figure 6.1 shows a series of fossil tracks left by feeding organisms from the Cambrian to the lower Carboniferous. From their form and position in the fossil series, the following sequence of events in the evolution of foraging behaviour in this group can be proposed; the animals originally fed in loosely meandering paths just below the surface but gradually showed a greater tendency to move sideways and to burrow deeper until the tracks finally took the form of extremely regular spirals. This series of changes probably increased the efficiency of foraging by reducing the chances of covering the same ground (Seilacher, 1967).

The frequency and type of bone fractures observed in excavated human skeletons can be used to provide information about their way of life (Table 6.1); the incidence of post cranial bone fractures in American indians of different periods correlates with their mode of life, deduced from other evidence; post-cranial fractures become less common with the transition from a nomadic, hunting lifestyle to life in more or less modern towns. This correlation can be used to assess the lifestyle of populations for which only skeletons are available (Steinbock, 1976).

Even when the consequences of behaviour are not preserved in this way, we can get some information about the behaviour of fossilized animals from structures which regularly correlate with a particular behaviour in similar forms alive today. For example, fossil ants resembling modern worker ants have been found in the eocene; it is reasonable to conclude that these animals showed at least some of the worker-like behaviour of their modern counterparts and

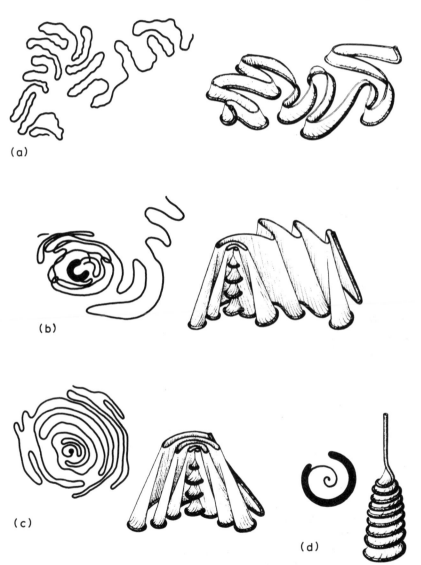

Figure 6.1 Tracing the course of behavioural phylogeny from fossils; fossilized tracks left by an unknown sediment feeder (*Dictyodora*) in deposits from the Cambrian (a) to the lower Carboniferous (d) (from Seilacher, 1967).

Table 6.1 Making deductions about behaviour from fossilized remains: the incidence of postcranial fractures in amerindian populations differing in age and way of life (from Steinbock, 1976).

Date	Way of life	% of skeletons with postcranial fractures
4000–1000 BC	Nomadic hunters	10.7
1000 BC–1000 AD	Permanent villages	5.4
1000–1600 AD	Agriculture/towns	3.9

therefore that they lived in complex social groups with division of labour (Lin and Michener, 1972). The information obtained in this way can be very precise; for example, study of the vocal tract and the way muscles are attached to bones in modern humans has demonstrated that these place constraints on the phonetic repertoire. Given this information, measurements of the fossilized hominid skulls can be used to make deductions about exactly what sounds these people could and could not produce. For example, neither *Australopithecus* nor primitive Neanderthals were able to pronounce the vowels i,u and a or the constanants g and k; more advanced Neanderthals did not have these structural restrictions on speech (Lieberman, 1977).

6.1.2 ONTOGENY

There are a number of classic examples of the temporary appearance in ontogeny of behaviour typical of forms which are apparently phylogenetically older; these have been used as the basis for evolutionary speculation. For example, unlike other songbirds, adult larks and pippets walk rather than hop, but young of both species go through a stage of hopping. It is therefore suggested that walking replaced hopping in the phylogeny of locomotion in these species; however, hopping might well be the most efficient method of locomotion in young of both larks and pippets. Such examples are rare and can only really be used as supporting evidence for existing hypotheses about phylogeny.

6.1.3 THE BEHAVIOUR OF INTERSPECIFIC HYBRIDS

There are some grounds for believing that when behaviour displayed by inter-specific hybrids differs from that of one or both of their parents, the hybrid behaviour may represent reversion to an ancestral form. Briefly, the genetic mechanisms whereby a particular behaviour pattern shown by a common ancestor is suppressed or altered during evolution are unlikely to be identical in the two parental species; suppression therefore breaks down in the hybrid and the ancestral behaviour is unmasked. For example, neither pintails nor yellow-billed teals give the down–up display during courtship; however, this behaviour pattern is observed in pintail–teal hybrids and, according to the argument outlined above; was therefore present in their common ancestor (Lorenz, 1941). Similarly, shelduck feed by dabbling and goosanders by diving; hybrids between these species dabble, which is therefore assumed to be the more primitive pattern (Lind and Poulsen, 1963). However, the behaviour of hybrids could be disrupted rather than ancestral and on its own this sort of evidence about the phylogeny of behaviour is inconclusive.

6.1.4 COMPARATIVE STUDIES

The remaining source of information about the course of evolution, and therefore the one which is of most importance in unravelling the evolutionary history of behaviour, is the comparison between living animals. It is a matter of empirical observation, as well as a logical deduction from the mechanism of heredity, that the distribution of similarity and differences in groups of species tends to correlate with phylogenetic relationships. This fact can be applied to behaviour patterns in two ways; in the first place, the distribution of behavioural characteristics can be used to identify natural groups of animals on the basis of probable descent from a common ancestor. To give just one example, when structural characteristics alone are used, there is uncertainty about the precise taxonomic relationship between *Hymenoptera* belonging to the groups *Aculeata* and *Parasitica*. Detailed studies of the grooming movements used by members of these two groups indicate that they are more closely related than was generally believed (Farish, 1972).

More important in the present context is the use of the comparative method to work out the phylogenetic history of behaviour. Put at its simplest, given reliable, independent evidence about the phylogenetic relationships between a number of taxonomic groups, the distribution of a behavioural trait among their members can be used to make deductions about the behaviour of a hypothetical common ancestor, the pattern which is most widely distributed in the group being the archetypal form. For example, Table 6.2(a) shows the number of grasshopper species which have various different components in their courtship displays. Tipping and ordinary stridulation are widespread and therefore assumed to be primitive, although tipping is commonly lost and both may be supplemented or replaced by vibratory stridulation, shaking and ticking (Otte, 1974). By comparing minor differences in the form of broadly similar behaviour patterns in increasingly related groups, this process can be used to reconstruct the behaviour of more and more recent common ancestors and thus to produce a possible evolutionary history of the modern forms of the trait in question.

In the absence of independent and precise information about the phylogenetic relationships of the animals concerned, this exercise is more difficult. However, if we assume that evolution occurs in a similar direction at different speeds in different lines within the same group, behaviour resembling that of close and

Table 6.2 Making deductions about the phylogeny of behaviour from comparative studies (from Otte, 1974).

(a) The number of oedipodine grasshopper species with various components in their courtship song.

Behavioural component	Number of species	Number of genera
T+OS	22	16
OS	22	12
T	1	1
T+OS+VS	8	5
T+OS+S	5	3
T+S	6	6
T+VS+TK	1	1
T+TK	1	1

(b) The form of courtship song and its possible phylogeny in two groups of grasshoppers.

Species	Courtship song	Proposed course of evolution
Encoptolophus subgracilis	T-OS	
E. costalis (Colorado)	T-VS-OS	
E. costalis (Texas)	T-TK-VS-OS	
E. sordidus	T-TK-VS-OS-VS′	
Trimerotropis pallidipennis	T-OS	
T. maritima	T-OS-S	
T. californica (California)	T-S	
T. califonica (Arizona)	S	

Where T is tipping, OS is ordinary stridulation, VS is vibratory stridulation, VS′ is a variant of VS, S is shaking and TK is ticking.

distant common ancestors will be found among living forms. Behavioural phylogenies can therefore be reconstructed by arranging existing forms in a plausible sequence. Table 6.2(b) shows a possible phylogeny of courtship singing in two groups of grasshoppers using this method. Tipping and ordinary stridulation are the primitive form in both cases; in the *Encoptolophus* group ticking and vibratory stridulation have been added to the song while in the *Trimerotropis* group ordinary stridulation and tipping have been replaced by shaking.

To give a classic example, courtship behaviour in males of a number of species of balloon fly (*Empididae*) related to an uncertain event, can be arranged in a plausible series, with the most distinct forms at either end and those sharing some properties with both extremes placed in the middle (Kessel, 1955). Such a series is illustrated in Table 6.3; initially, males offer prospective mates a large bundle of silk; the amount of silk in the bundle is gradually reduced, and replaced by small fragments of insects. Finally the silk disappears altogether, with the males offering females a complete insect.

In the absence of any precise information about the phylogenetic relationships of the species concerned, it is not easy to decide on the direction of such a series of changes. In fact, Kessel envisaged the sequence going the other way, with insect gifts as the primitive form, on the grounds that evolution usually produces complex forms and that all the flies in this taxonomic group catch insects but not all make silk. However, this ability may have been secondarily lost and there are cases where this rule of thumb (evolution produces complexity) does not apply; for example, primitive hymenopterans show more varied grooming sequences than advanced ones (Farish, 1972). If the function of the behaviour concerned is known, this can help in deciding the direction in which the proposed behavioural changes have occurred, given that evolution is expected to increase efficiency. Courtship feeding in balloon flies reduces the chances that females will eat courting males but it is not obvious that a ball of silk suppresses the females' predatory inclinations more effectively than an insect would do. Since independent evidence about the direction of evolution is not available in most cases, deciding about the order in which a proposed series of changes occurred presents a real problem in unravelling behavioural phylogenies.

Table 6.3 Making deductions about the phylogeny of behaviour from comparative studies; a possible sequence for the evolution of courtship feeding in balloon flies (after Kessel, 1955).

Species	Courtship behaviour
Hilaria sartor	Male presents female with complex ball of silk
Empimorpha geneatis and Empis aerobatica	Male presents female with complex ball of silk containing small prey fragments
Empis bullifera	Male presents female with prey item in small silk balloon
Other Hilaria species	Male presents female with intact prey animal entangled in a few silk threads
Empimorpha comata and other Empis species	Male presents female with prey animal without silk

Another problem raised by this kind of application of the comparative approach concerns the difficulty of identifying which behaviour patterns shown by animals in the different groups are homologous (alike as a result of descent from a common ancestor) rather than analogous (alike because they are independent adaptations to the same problem). There is some agreement in the copious literature on this subject that to be considered homologous, behaviour patterns must be inherited (otherwise they would not evolve and could have no phylogenetic history) and preferably by the same or similar genetic mechanisms, must occur in closely related species, must involve similar movements of the same structures and perhaps appear at the same point in a behavioural sequence and in the same context. In addition, the idea that behaviour patterns used by different species are homologous is supported if the movements involved are distinctive in some way which is not obviously related to their function. Convincing information on these points is easier to obtain if the behaviour concerned is a precise, simple movement rather than a more complex characteristic, and if comparisons are made between closely related species rather than across broader groupings. For example, during courtship male ducks of several related species give a distinctive display described as the head-up–tail-up to attract the attention of nearby females; this usually occurs in a sequence with other movements (grunt–whistles, head-up–tail-up, turn-back-of-head). In this case, therefore, the evidence indicates that the head-up–tail-up display is a homologous behaviour which has been inherited from a common ancestor by a number of species (McKinney, 1978). Behaviour patterns which are not so similar in form may still be taken as homologous if intermediate versions are found within a group of related species. In the case of courtship feeding in empidid flies, presenting whole insects and presenting a ball of silk are not obviously homologous but given the existence of species which present a mixture of silk and insect material, the proposal that one represents an ancestral form of the other becomes more plausible.

However, in the absence of independent information about phylogenies, the possibility of convergence is very real. In several duck species, wing preening is used as a display during courtship; this is a distinctive movement whose form is not obviously related to the function it serves and which might therefore represent homologous movements, inherited from a common ancestor. On the other hand, it may equally well have evolved from displacement preening independently on several occasions, behaviour shown in a motivational conflict being a common evolutionary source of displays (McKinney, 1978).

In spite of these problems, many attempts have been made to reconstruct the course of behavioural evolution from comparative data; these are most successful if accurate phylogenies of the animals concerned are available, in which case it is possible to make quite strong deductions about the way behaviour has evolved. Where such information is not available, comparative data can only suggest possible phylogenetic sequences which may bear little resemblance to actual evolutionary events.

6.2 Some representative behavioural phylogenies

6.2.1 TONGUE MOVEMENTS IN REPTILES

At one extreme these techniques and, in particular, the comparative approach have been used to elucidate the phylogenetic history of simple, precisely measured, small-scale movements. For example, Gove (1979) filmed the tongue movements of 25 species of lizard and 30 species of snake. On the basis of the known phylogenetic relationships within this group, she proposed that this behaviour evolved from the simple downwards extension of the tongue to lap water (as in present day lizards), through single oscillations to the complex, multiple oscillations that advanced snakes show while sampling the air for chemical cues.

6.2.2 PREDATORY BEHAVIOUR IN GASTROPODS

Many predatory gastropods feed by boring through the shells of other molluscs, leaving a hole of characteristic shape. Table 6.4 gives a measure of the variability in position of the bore hole in a series of fossilized gastropods of similar shape killed by the predatory gastropod *Lunatia heros* over a period of 20 million years from Miocene to recent. There is little change in the mean position of the bore hole along the long axis of the shells but a significant decrease in its variability. As evolution progressed, the predatory behaviour of these animals therefore became more stereotyped and, if shells are more vulnerable at particular points along their length, perhaps more efficient (Berg, 1978).

Table 6.4 The variability in the position of boreholes made by *Lunatia heros* feeding on gastropod prey fossilized at three different geological periods (from Berg, 1978).

Age	Mean position on long axis of shell relative to short axis	Coefficient of variability
Miocene	0.49	15.7
Pleistocene	0.50	12.3
Recent	0.54	9.1

6.2.3 AGGRESSIVE INTERACTIONS IN FISH

If behaviour is analysed by sufficiently sophisticated methods, and provided reasonably precise information about phylogenetic relationships is available, the evolution of more complex behaviour including social interactions can usefully be studied. For example, in Old World rivulin fish, whose phylogeny is well known from morphological and chromosomal evidence, the males use a complex series of movements during aggressive encounters. Eight movements were recorded during observations of fights between conspecific males in 18 species from 6 genera. The sequence in which these actions were shown by individual fish was analysed (see page 71); this was similar for all members of the same species, but differed significantly between species. A number of the more commonly occurring transitions were found in all 6 genera and in most species, especially those which on other evidence are more primitive. These widespread transitions were used to construct a hypothetical archetypal fight sequence which is shown in Fig. 6.2 part a. All the other sequences could be derived from this supposedly primitive pattern and comparison between them shows the kinds of changes in aggressive behaviour that have occurred in this group of fish. Thus, the relative frequency of the different elements have been altered; for example, fin clamping predominates over full display in *Epiplatys* species but is relatively rare in *Nothobranchius* species. In some cases, this process has resulted in the complete loss of certain acts; for example, in *Roloffia liberiensis* (Fig. 6.2 part b) jaw lock is never observed while quiver has dropped out of the repertoire of aggressive behaviour in *Nothobranchius palmquisti* (Fig. 6.2 part c). These lost elements are never replaced by entirely new actions even in the most advanced species. However, the movements may vary in form; thus, in species in which quiver has been lost, tail beating is often directed towards the head rather than the flank of the opponent. In addition, in some more advanced species higher level sequential interactions are found between the individual elements. For example, in *R.*

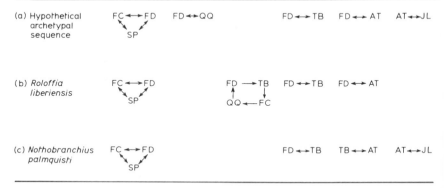

Figure 6.2 Sequential relationships between behaviour patterns used by Old World rivulin fish during fights (after Ewing, 1975), where FC = fin clamp, FD = full display, SP = sigmoid posture, QQ = quiver, TB = tail beat, AT = attack, JL = jaw lock, ⟷ represents two-way transitions between actions and → represents one-way transitions. Actions are arranged from left to right in order of their maximum expression during an encounter.

liberiensis, asymmetrical transitions between 4 elements indicate a cycle in which full display gives way to tail beating, then fin clamping and then quivering, which then switches back to full display. Thus, with detailed behavioural records, sophisticated techniques of analysis and a precise knowledge of the phylogenetic relationships of the species concerned, strong hypotheses about the phylogeny of the organization of behaviour can be constructed (Ewing, 1975).

6.2.4 HYMENOPTERAN SOCIAL SYSTEMS

Just because it is so complex, many attempts have been made to unravel the phylogenetic history of the evolution of the social system of the hymenoptera and the communication on which it is based. Within the bees, individuals of some species such as the poppy bee (*Osmia papaveris*), lead solitary lives, feeding themselves and digging burrows in which they place a single ball of pollen before laying eggs. In contrast, honey bee females (*Apis mellifera*) come in two castes, queens which reproduce and workers which care continuously for the young, construct cells, defend and clean the hive and forage; caste determination is based on food supply during development, with queen larvae being given the protein-rich royal jelly. These two species of bee therefore differ profoundly in a whole range of interacting behavioural characteristics. The selective forces which might have favoured complex social life have been discussed above (see page 262); the question here is whether and how one of these forms could possibly have given rise to the other. Comparative studies show that a number of modern forms exist whose behaviour may well represent intermediates between these two extremes. For example, in *Lasioglossum marginatum* increased longevity of the mother and extension of the period of maternal care means that the mother is present when the first eggs hatch. Emerging females could therefore remain at the nest and lay their eggs alongside their mother. In other species this has led to a division of labour between adult females; in *Augochloropsis sparsilis* there are two kinds of females, similar in structure but with some specializing in pollen gathering and others in egg laying. In bumblebees (*Bombus* spp.), large, overwintering queens lay eggs which hatch into smaller females which care for the queen's successive broods, being thus born with a predisposition to work rather than lay; this may represent a primitive version of the food-based caste determining system of the honey bees. *Osmia, Lasioglossum, Augochloropsis, Bombus* and *Apis* do not represent an evolutionary series; they are living species belonging to different taxonomic groups each with a distinct phylogenetic history. However, they show us social systems which represent possible intermediate forms between solitary and highly social life. The phylogenetic sequence leading to the social system of the honey bee which they imply is plausible and accommodates the known behaviour of a range of species, including many not mentioned here, in a single, reasonably economical, scheme (from Brown, 1975).

The phylogeny of behaviour   285

(b)

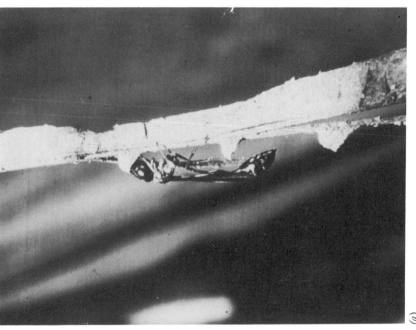

(a)

Plate 11 Possible stages in the evolution of complex social organization in the hymenoptera. (a) A single female *Parischnogaster jacobsoni* at her nest; (b) a small group of *Liostenogaster varipicta* at a communal nest.

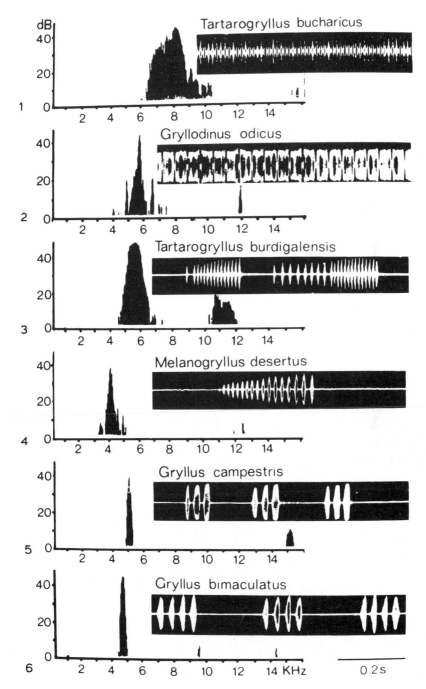

Figure 6.3 Frequency spectra and oscilloscope traces (inset) of the calling songs of six sympatric cricket species (from Elsner and Popov, 1978).

6.3 Deriving general principles of behavioural evolution

A quite plausible reconstruction of the evolution of a particular behaviour may be derived from the application of studies such as those described above. Broad surveys of complex behaviour in a wide range of contemporary species can suggest the intermediate forms through which a modern behaviour may have evolved. If the animals compared are closely related and if the behaviour concerned is fine grained, the plausible becomes the probable; it also becomes possible to discover general principles about how behaviour changes during evolution.

6.3.1 SOUND PRODUCTION IN CRICKETS

Sound production and reception in crickets have been intensively studied and the neurophysiological mechanisms and their genetic bases are well known. Crickets produce sounds by rubbing their elyta together, and behavioural observation and experiment show that temporal patterning is a significant aspect of the song. Analysis of wing movements and spike patterns in motor neurons shows that wing beat frequency during flight is the same as that used during stridulation and that the same muscles and motorneurons are used in the same ways during these two activities. It seems likely that stridulation movements evolved from flight movements, with minor alterations in auxiliary muscles changing the up-and-down movements of flight to the to-and-fro movements of stridulation. Figure 6.3 summarizes the song patterns of six sympatric species of cricket; a likely sequence of changes in the production of the song is that the continuous trill of the primitive forms (traces 1 and 2) was gradually broken up into chirps by amplitude modulations. Initially these varied irregularly in duration and in the number that occurred in a single pulse of sound (3) but in more advanced forms, these parameters were fixed (5 and 6) and systematic variation of amplitude within chirps occurred (4). These changes are presumably brought about by alteration of the properties of the identified inter-neurons, motor neurons and neuromuscular junctions which bring about this behaviour.

There is much less information about the evolution of sound reception in females; sense organs which detect airborne vibration appear to have evolved from proprioceptors monitoring body movement. Further evolution took the form of increasingly complex higher order sensory processing in parallel with the production of more sophisticated songs by males. This comparative study has identified a possible phylogenetic sequence of the song types, demonstrating the kind of changes which have taken place in the overt behaviour and suggesting possible physiological bases for these (Elsner and Popov, 1978).

6.3.2 COURTSHIP IN PEACOCKS

A constellation of similar evolutionary changes are believed to have occurred in many cases where related species show homologous display movements. These are well illustrated in a classic study of the evolution of courtship displays in the peacock. The proposed course of evolutionary events is as follows; in the ancestors of the peacock (presumed to resemble the modern domestic fowl *Gallus domesticus*), during courtship the male gave a call like that used to attract companions to a new food source, while scratching the ground, stepping back and picking up pebbles, which served to attract females. The movements became exaggerated as in the Impayan pheasant (*Lophophorus impejanus*) in which the male bows rhythmically before the hen with wings and tail expanded and in the peacock pheasant (Polyplectron bicalcaratum) which scratches the ground and bows with spreading wings and tail, offering any available food to the female. Finally, feeding disappears altogether in the peacock itself, which erects its elaborately coloured tail feathers and shakes these in front of the female, taking several backwards steps and bowing (Schenkel, 1956).

In such proposed phylogenies a series of changes in the signal tends to occur, accompanied by appropriate changes in the sensory systems of the receiver. The movements may change in form, often becoming more stereotyped; thus the irregular pecking of the cock and stridulation of primitive crickets give way to the regular movements of the Impayan pheasant and the repetitive calls of more advanced crickets. Many such changes in form and temporal patterning can be interpreted as the result of an alteration in some threshold for performance of different components of behaviour. The functional context in which the action is shown may change; thus, movements of flight become movements of calling and behaviour which accompanies feeding is used in a sexual context. This is associated with a change in the causal relationships of the behaviour patterns. As discussed above, displays often have their evolutionary origins in the behaviour shown by animals in motivational conflicts; in peacocks, displacement feeding movements have been incorporated into the courtship ritual, and performance of the display in adults is no longer dependent on the original motivational conflict. The fact that juvenile male peacocks have been observed pecking at food and scratching while showing the courtship movements supports this idea. Finally, morphological alterations evolve which enhance the conspicuousness of the movements. The peacock's tail and the movements by which it is displayed represent a celebrated example of the ritualization of display movements. Classically, this process was seen as the consequence of a mutually beneficial improvement in the efficiency of information transfer. In the modern view, it results from successive attempts to manipulate and avoid manipulation as both participants seek to maximize their inclusive fitness.

Thus, notwithstanding the limitations of the techniques for studying the phylogenty of behaviour, these have suggested possible intermediate stages in the evolution of highly complex behaviour, have allowed deductions to be drawn about the probable phylogenetic history of simpler actions among closely related species and have identified some of the kinds of evolutionary change to which behaviour is subject.

CHAPTER 7

The role of behaviour in the evolutionary process

As indicated in Chapter 5, there are many cases in which inherited behavioural variation results in differential fitness for the animals concerned. Behaviour is therefore expected to evolve under the influence of natural selection and it has been argued that this process is particularly rapid because behaviour has such complex causes and consequences (Wilson, 1975). However, behaviour has a role in the evolutionary process which goes beyond its direct impact on fitness. This involves three distinct but interrelated effects: in the first place, the behaviour of other animals represents a major selective force acting on an individual, secondly, by its behaviour an animal can dictate the selection pressures to which it is exposed and lastly, the behavioural repertoire of a species influences the structure of the gene pool and thus the rate and direction of evolutionary change.

7.1 The behaviour of other animals as a major selective force

7.1.1 THE BEHAVIOUR OF CONSPECIFICS

The success of games theory, in which pay-offs depend on the behaviour of other animals, in depicting the adaptive consequences of behaviour bears witness to the importance of the actions of conspecifics as a selective force. To give just a few examples, intrasexual rivalry over mates has led to a whole range of adaptations enhancing an animal's chances of mating successfully. These adaptations may be behavioural (the aggressive behaviour of parental male bluegill sunfish results in priority of access to females, while the inconspicuous behaviour of sneaking males enables them to obtain some fertilizations; Gross and Charnov, 1980 and see page 230), physiological (the testes of primates are more productive in species such as the chimpanzee in which competition for females is intense; Harcourt *et al.*, 1981 and see page 220) or morphological (the large claws of shrimps enhance their chances of acquiring mates; Knowlton, 1980 and see page 219). Choosiness by potential mates also provides a powerful selective force moulding the structures and behaviour used during courtship; for example, the peacock's elaborate tail and the sedge warbler's complex song are thought to have evolved because females mate preferentially with males in which these characteristics are well developed (see page 227). Both these processes can lead to a series of adaptations and counter adaptations on the part of the animals concerned, and result in rapid evolutionary change.

For group living species, the behaviour of social companions is a dominant feature of the environment in which the animals live; group living animals are exposed to strong social selection, just as courting animals are exposed to strong sexual selection. They have evolved mechanisms that reduce the impact of, or enhance effectiveness in, competition and make the most of the various beneficial side effects of group life, for example, by division of labour and the ability to form alliances. As a result 'Individuals of social species having these specialized characteristics are in a sense trapped into group life' (West-Eberhard, 1979). In highly social animals such as many Old-World primates, an individual spends its entire life in intimate proximity to a number of conspecifics and social events probably have more impact on fitness than any other aspects of its environment. Selective forces such as these, imposed by the behaviour of social companions may have been responsible for the evolution of human speech and the enormous increase in size in the human brain (Humphrey, 1976).

7.1.2 THE BEHAVIOUR OF HETEROSPECIFICS

The importance of the behaviour of predators as a selective force impinging on prey species and vice versa has long been recognized, as has the fact that these are likely to result in the evolution of a series of adaptations and counter adaptations. The perfect camouflage of prey such as the hawkmoth caterpillar and of predators such as the devil flower mantis illustrates the power of these processes in bringing about evolutionary change. To show how the impact of predator and prey as selective agents can be modified by the details of their behaviour, both clumping of prey and the concentration of predators in the most profitable patches increase the readiness with which the density of both species will return to equilibrium levels following perturbation (Hassell and May, 1974; Hassell, 1979).

The behaviour of heterospecific competitors can alter an animal's fitness in and choice of habitat. For example, Werner and Hall (1979) have studied the relationship between fitness, population density and habitat choice in three species of sunfish distributing themselves between open water, vegetation and exposed sediment in artificial ponds. Each habitat type has its own unique prey community requiring different feeding tactics. The efficiency with which each species exploits the three habitats was determined by monitoring growth. All three do better in vegetation, but this is particularly the case for the green sunfish (*Lepomis cyanellus*); pumpkinseed sunfish (*L. gibbosus*) do better than the others on sediment. If the fish select the habitat which offers the best fitness prospects taking into account their efficiency at exploiting it and the number of competitors, when all three species are present and both habitats have plenty of food, initially all three species should feed in vegetation. As resources decline, there will come a point for each species at which they would do better feeding at lower densities on sediment. However, this point comes sooner for the pumpkinseed than the bluegill and last of all for the green sunfish. This is therefore the sequence in which the fish are expected to switch to the sediment and Fig. 7.1 shows that this is what happens. Even in the absence of direct behavioural interaction, the presence of heterospecific competitors can therefore change the profitability of a given habitat and thus influence the places animals choose to live in.

Kangaroo rats of the species *Dipodomys ordii* and *D. merii* overlap widely in their broad habitat and eat similar sized seeds. However, manipulating the density of one species had no effect on the distribution of the other, indicating that, in spite

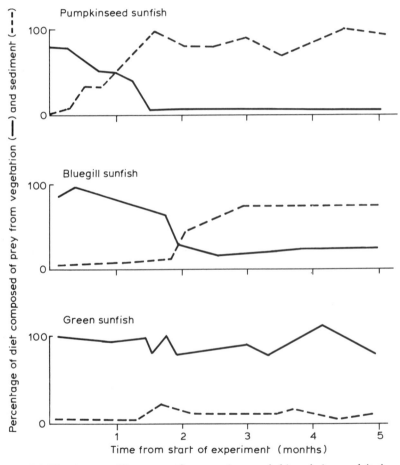

Figure 7.1 The impact of heterospecific competitors on habitat choice; exploitation of vegetation and sediment habitat (assessed by stomach analysis) by sunfish of three species in the five month period after stocking artificial ponds (after Werner and Hall, 1979).

The Study of Animal Behaviour

of the similarity of their diet, the distribution of these mice is not immediately determined by the density of the heterospecific competitor. The two species have evolved differences in habitat preference within the same broad category of open country, with *D. ordii* tending to occupy grassy areas and *D. merii* found where the vegetation is more sparse, probably in response to the potentially high degree of competition between the two species (Rosenzweig, 1979).

Behavioural interaction between species can result in evolutionary change even when the organisms concerned have mutually beneficial effects. For example, bees foraging for nectar obey the marginal value theorem, leaving each inflorescence when the nectar volume falls below a critical threshold (see page 171). In the flower *Delphinius*, efficient pollination requires that bees bring pollen to the female flowers at the bottom of each inflorescence and leave the inflorescence having collected pollen from the male flowers at the top. The flowers have evolved under the impact of the foraging behaviour of the bees so that the amount of nectar in each flower decreases from bottom to top. The bees therefore feed from the richer, lower flowers first, pollinating them in the process, and leave the flower when they reach the less profitable male flowers at the top (Pyke, 1978c).

7.2 Behaviour dictates the selection pressures to which an animal is exposed

In a very general way, behaviour dictates the activity of selection since it is by behaviour that structures are presented to the environment; wings of different sizes cannot alter the efficiency of flight and thus fitness until they are spread. In addition, by its influences on population structure (see below) the way an animal behaves dictates the broad kind of selection pressure to which it is exposed. Thus animals which live in small, isolated groups could, potentially, be exposed to the action of group selection. If these groups are long-lived and stable, the potential for reciprocal altruism exists. Finally, if animals tend to associate with related individuals, kin selection becomes important, ameliorating the effect of competition and possibly leading to the evolution of altruistic traits.

Within the general paradigm of natural selection at the individual level, a change in behaviour, for example in its temporal or spatial patterning, can protect the animal concerned against adverse environmental conditions, including those imposed by other animals. For example, the 24 hour eclosion rhythm of *Drosophila melanogaster* ensures that flies emerge into air of the appropriate humidity (Pittendrigh, 1956) and see page 162), differences in the time at which closely related *Dacus* species court reduces the risk of infertile cross species mating (Tychsen and Fletcher, 1971 and see page 164) and by nesting among spiny cacti, wood rats reduce their vulnerability to predation (Brown, Lieberman and Dengler, 1972 and see page 168).

In species which are able to modify their habitat, this process may be taken further so that the animals in effect manufacture their own environment; the carefully prepared display areas of bower birds, the dammed ponds of beavers, the nests and burrows of social insects and finally the whole complex culture of *Homo sapiens* provide examples. When such habitat modification is accompanied by some sort of understanding and anticipation of the action of the major selective agents, as it is in humans and, perhaps, in a few other primate species (Boehm, 1978), the evolutionary role of conventional natural selection is greatly reduced.

Even in species with less sophisticated behavioural capacities, a change in behaviour can place the animal concerned in a new environment and set in train a series of evolutionary changes. Although morphological changes, for example an enlarged gape, and physiological changes, for example improved oxygen transport, may also have a catalytic effect, Mayr (1978) writes '. . . behaviour often – perhaps invariably – serves as a pace-maker in evolution. A change in behaviour, such as the selection of a new habitat or food source, sets up new selective pressures and may lead to important adaptive shifts. There is little doubt that some of the most important events in the history of life, such as the conquest of land or of the air, were initiated by shifts in behaviour'. To give just one example, *Anopheles bambusicolus* differs from closely related mosquito species in its choice of sites in which to lay eggs, being prepared to enter restricted apertures and lay on small water surfaces; this has apparently opened up an entirely new and poorly exploited adaptive zone (Pittendrigh, 1956).

Such a behavioural shift may have its origins in a genetic change, whereby an inherited preference is modified by mutation and passed on to subsequent generations. For example, a single gene substitution in the butterfly *Colias eurythine* changes the choice of light and temperature conditions, and thus also the time of day at which the females are active, from noon to around dawn and dusk. On the other hand, the initial alteration in behaviour may be the result of an environmental change rather than a genetically determined behavioural switch. Animals of some species settle preferentially in areas in which they were raised; for example, ants reared from a young age in environments which smell different (the presence or absence of thyme) when given a choice of environment settled preferentially in that smelling like the one in which they had been reared (Jaisson, 1980). In such species, following an enforced or accidental change in environment, the new habitat will become the preferred one for subsequent generations.

Whatever the origin of the behavioural change, the descendants of the animals concerned are exposed to a different selective regime from the rest of the species. If this segregation persists, the animals are likely to evolve characteristics which adapt them to their new environment. Such evolution may result in micro-geographically differentiated sub-populations and eventually, perhaps, in distinct species. In several *Drosophila* species, flies collected from different places differ significantly both in their chromosomal arrangements and in their allozyme frequencies. In addition displaced flies return to their area of origin or an ecologically similar one. Differences in habitat preferences are thus associated with (and may have initiated the evolution of) inherited within-species variation (Taylor and Powell, 1977). Such developmental flexibility of behavioural preferences (whether for habitats, diets or mates) coupled with an imprinting process whereby new preferences persist in successive generations gives behaviour a potentially important role in the initiation of evolutionary change.

7.3 The impact of behaviour on population structure

The direction and speed of evolutionary change depend on the structure of the population concerned. All models of evolutionary processes make critical assumptions about the extent to which the population is subdivided, the size of such subdivisions, how genetically distinct these are and whether mating is panmictic. Whether or not such assumptions are valid in particular instances depends, in part at least, on the behaviour of the animals concerned. For example, genetic polymorphisms are readily maintained in a population if individuals differing in their fitness in different habitats practise habitat selection accordingly (Taylor, 1976) and under certain circumstances such a situation can lead to sympatric speciation (Maynard Smith, 1966).

7.3.1 BEHAVIOURAL INFLUENCES ON GENE FLOW BETWEEN POPULATIONS

Social behaviour can determine whether a species exists in reproductively isolated populations. For example, many animals live in groups from which strange conspecifics are aggressively excluded. The existence of such groups and their impact on the breeding structure of the population are usually studied at the same time by looking for local differences in gene frequency within a species. For example, pocket gophers (*Thomomys bottae*) live in groups of 12–26 individuals within an aggressively defended territory. Electrophoretic analysis of allozyme frequencies identified considerable variability in the genetic constituton of these groups, indicating that they may well represent partially isolated subpopulations (Patton and Feder, 1981).

The mouse is a classic example of a species in which the population is apparently subdivided in this way as a result of aggressive behaviour. On the basis of studies of home ranges of wild mice, observations of their behaviour in artificial enclosures and description of naturally occurring gene distributions, this species is thought to live in small semi-isolated groups consisting of one male, several females and their offspring, in territories from which intruders are fiercely excluded (Rowe and Redfern, 1969; Selander, 1970). Such a behaviourally imposed population structure would seem likely to have profound influence on the evolutionary processes to which this species is subject. However, when female mice with a genetic marker were introduced into discrete populations of wild mice, the marker gene spread rapidly suggesting that, at least for female mice in relatively large populations and with plenty of hiding places, gene flow is not in fact hindered by social interactions (Baker, 1981).

How much animals disperse or migrate and how this process is organized clearly has important consequences for population structure. Movement between local groups will reduce genetic differentiation provided that dispersal is random. The gene mixing effect of dispersal will be reduced if different kinds of animals show different movement patterns (large, unbanded landsnails (*Cepea nemoralis*) disperse more readily than other types; Oosterhoff, 1977), if related animals tend to move together (sibling voles tend to have similar dispersal patterns; Hilborn, 1975), or tend to settle near animals which are similar to themselves. White-crowned sparrows living in different areas have local song-dialects and gene frequencies differ between dialect groups (Baker *et al.*, 1982). Newly fledged sparrows were marked at or near their place of hatching in a large area through which a boundary between two dialects passed; the site at which they were subsequently recaptured as adults was then recorded. Figure 7.2 shows the number of birds caught in different parts of the study area which moved towards the boundary between hatching and nesting; fewer birds moved towards the boundary than predicted by a model of random dispersion and those which did tended to move parallel to the boundary once they reached it. 'There is a small but real trickle of cross-dialect exchange that is roughly five times less than expected.' Clearly, song type and the bird's response to it are restricting recruitment to existing populations (Baker and Medwaldt, 1978).

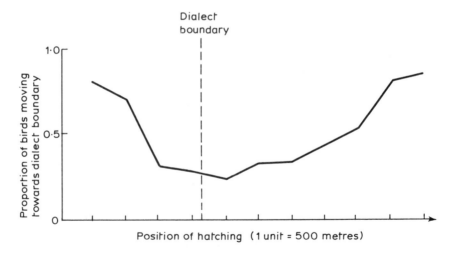

Figure 7.2 Behavioural restrictions on gene mixing; the effect of a song dialect boundary on the direction of pre-breeding movements in song sparrows (after Baker and Medwaldt, 1978).

The Study of Animal Behaviour

(a)

(b)

Plate 12 Differential choice of habitat by closely related species; the voles *Clethrionomys brittanicus* (a) and *Microtus agrestis* (b) in their natural environments.

Behavioural characteristics can influence the actual size of local breeding populations; for example, in the vole *Microtus townsendii* density dependent aggression by females interferes with settling by juveniles and keeps the population size below that which would be found if the latter settled freely (Krebs, 1979). Behaviour can also influence the effective population size, or the number of animals which actually contribute genes to subsequent generations. For example, in highly polygamous mating systems, only a small number of individuals of the sex which monopolizes mates (usually the male) actually breeds, thus reducing the effective population size. In order to assess the impact of such a social system on effective population size, it is necessary to know which individuals father which offspring under natural conditions, since subordinate males may sneak matings. In the bat *Phyllostomus hastatus,* males defend groups of females with whom they mate; analysis of three polymorphic loci showed that on average 90% of the young in a harem could be the offspring of the dominant male and thus that relatively few males father most of the next generation (McCracken and Bradbury, 1977). In contrast, while behavioural observation indicates that dominant males do almost all the copulating in rabbit (*Oryctolagus cuniculus*) groups, studies of allozyme frequencies showed that they are only slightly more successful at breeding than are subordinates and that 'social structure in rabbit populations does not have major genetic consequences' (Daly, 1981).

Table 7.1 The role of behaviour in maintaining species distinctness; various features of the mating calls of two closely related species of cricket frogs in areas where they do and do not coexist (from Blair, 1958).

Species / location	Dominant frequency	Nature of song
		From different localities
Acris gryllus (separate)	*ca* 3900 (read from figure)	Series of simple notes at regular intervals of *ca* 0.25 secs.
Acris crepitans (separate)	*ca* 3800	Series of simple notes at slightly less regular intervals of *ca* 0.25 secs.
		From the same locality
Acris gryllus (coexisting)	3480	Series of simple notes, initially at intervals of *ca* 0.65 secs, then at intervals of *ca* 0.22 secs.
Acris crepitans (coexisting)	4043	Series of trilled notes of increasing length at very regular intervals of *ca* 0.21 secs.

The extent to which mating is random within local populations also depends on the behaviour of the animals concerned. A breeding system in which mating is promiscuous will have a different effect on the gene combinations which occur in subsequent generations than one in which a male and a female pair for life, even if the initial choice of mate is random. However, animals are often selective in their choice of mates (see page 221). Mates may be chosen on the basis of how closely related they are to the animal in question. Females of the parasitoid wasp (*Nasonia vitripennis*) choose males which have been reared on host plants different from their own in preference to those males which have been reared on the same host plant. The latter are likely to be related to the females and it is suggested that this mechanism promotes outbreeding (Grant *et al.*, 1980). Laboratory studies on quail (Bateson, 1979 and see page 227) and field studies of snow geese (Cooke, 1978 and see page 227) and great tits (McGregor and Krebs, 1982 and see page 227) all demonstrate the existence of mechanisms of mate choice which promote a certain amount of inbreeding. In such cases, non-random mating will influence genotype frequency in the population increasing the proportion of heterozygotes where outbreeding is favoured and increasing the proportion of homozygotes where inbreeding is favoured to an extent dependent on population size, but the frequency of different alleles in the population will not be affected. In contrast, if mates are chosen on the basis of some specific, inherited characteristic, allele frequencies in the population as well as genotype frequencies will change; as mentioned above, the behaviour of conspecifics thus acts as a selective agent bringing about evolutionary change.

If differential mating is based on a characteristic which differs between locally adapted populations, these become effectively isolated from each other and speciation may result. The importance of such behavioural mechanisms in maintaining a distinction between closely related, sympatric species has been demonstrated on many occasions. For example, many male cricket frogs produce courtship songs to attract females and maximum auditory sensitivity of the female corresponds very closely to the properties of the song produced by conspecific males (Caprianica, Frishkopf and Nevo, 1973). Table 7.1 summarizes various aspects of the mating calls of two closely related species of cricket frogs, at various points of their range. In areas where the two species do not coexist the songs are very similar but where they overlap 'their calls differ in every measurable characteristic. . . . Thus selection against hybridization in the overlap zone has sharpened the differences between calls in the two species and thus increased the effectiveness of the isolating mechanism.' (Blair, 1958.). This represents convincing evidence for the importance of behavioural differences in maintaining species identity and stresses the fact that a knowledge of how animals behave is important for an understanding of how they evolve.

The role of behaviour in the evolutionary process   299

CHAPTER 8

Behavioural genetics

8.1 The objectives of research into the inheritance of behaviour

Scientific study of the inheritance of behaviour, or behavioural genetics, is a multi-disciplinary exercise and although the immediate task of all behavioural geneticists is to describe the relationship between what animals do and the genes they possess, this may be the means to two broadly distinct ends.

Much research in behavioural genetics is aimed at characterizing the genetic mechanisms underlying naturally occurring behavioural differences. This information is necessary if the developmental origin and evolutionary significance of such differences are to be understood. A quite distinct objective in behavioural genetics is to work out whether and how the activities of genes (during development and in adult animals) influence the behaviour of whole animals and, ultimately, to formulate general principles of how functional nervous sytems are put together (Brenner, 1973).

A complete investigation into the genetics of behaviour would involve a number of steps, the first being identification of a behavioural difference. It is then necessary to determine whether this behavioural difference owes anything to genetic variation among the animals concerned, rather than to the environmental conditions in which they developed. If it turns out that the genotype is a variable to contend with, the success of any subsequent genetic analysis depends on identification of the precise behavioural nature of the effect. For example, a change in mating speed could be the result of lowered general activity, reduced responsiveness to social stimuli or an impairment of the muscles necessary for mating; careful behavioural study can distinguish between these different effects. Next the genetic mechanism by which the difference is inherited must be elucidated. How much of the variation in mating speed can be accounted for by genetic effects? How many genes are involved? On what chromosomes are they situated? What is the relationship between different alleles at the same locus and between alleles at different loci influencing the same character? The biochemical, physiological or structural means whereby the various components of the genetic mechanism exert their influence must then be identified. Knowing the pattern of inheritance of a naturally occurring behavioural difference (and its impact on fitness) the dynamics of its transmission from one generation to the next and thus the probable evolutionary fate of the behavioural trait can be investigated. Once this procedure has been carried out for a range of different behavioural patterns, whether these occur naturally or are generated artificially, it may be possible to derive general principles about the nature of genetic influences on behaviour.

8.2 Potential contributions of genetics to the study of animal behaviour

The deliberations of geneticists help us to understand animal behaviour in a number of ways.

8.2.1 AS AN ADDITIONAL RESEARCH TOOL IN THE ANALYSIS OF BEHAVIOUR

By relating genetically produced differences in structure or physiology to alterations in behaviour it is possible to identify the mechanisms which control behaviour traits in adult animals. This is especially valuable in species which are too small for physiological manipulation. For example, genetic mosaics are being used to pinpoint the neural structures which control courtship in *Drosophila melanogaster* which could not easily be investigated using more conventional techniques (Hall and Greenspan, 1979; Tomkins and Hall, 1983 and see page 331).

Genetically produced differences may also be used to assess the adaptive significance of behaviour. The use of genetic markers to determine reproductive output in animals showing different behaviour patterns has been of enormous value in behavioural research. In addition, genetically produced behavioural variation can be used to investigate the impact of behaviour on fitness. For example, it has been suggested that in species with sperm displacement males enhance their fitness by delaying remating in females with whom they have copulated (see page 220). Experimental manipulation of remating time is possible but this is likely to have complex consequences. Variation in the remating time in *Drosophila melanogaster* (in which sperm displacement does occur) was produced by using male flies with different alleles at the esterase locus; this is a naturally occurring polymorphism and the presence of esterase-6 in the seminal fluid reduces remating time from *circa* 3.9 to 2.9 days. This is associated with a reduction in the number of offspring produced by the mating from 7.9 to 6.5. Thus genetic variation can be used to demonstrate and measure the benefit to the male resulting from increased remating time in the female (Gilbert, Richmond and Sheehan, 1981). The genetic architecture of a trait can also provide evidence about the selective forces which acted on it in the past (Broadhurst, 1979), although the evidence is ambiguous (see page 146). Briefly, directional selection favouring extreme phenotypes is likely to produce low heritability (see page 305) and strong dominance relationships in the direction of the favoured form. For example, mating speed in *Drosophila melanogaster* males has a low heritability and strong directional dominance in favour of fast mating, indicating that these flies have been the subject of strong directional selection for this trait in males (Fulker, 1966).

Finally, the behaviour of interspecific hybrids has been used to identify behaviour patterns which are possible candidates for evolutionary precursors of modern forms (see page 278), although here again the results are not always easy to interpret (Franck, 1974). For example, parrots of the species *Agapornis fischeri* and *A. roseicolis* tuck nest material into their rumps; hybrids between these species often tuck it in the feathers of other parts of the body as do some more primitive species in this genus. It was therefore concluded that rump tucking evolved from tucking elsewhere in these birds (Dilger, 1962).

8.2.2 AS A SOURCE OF ESSENTIAL INFORMATION ABOUT BEHAVIOUR

In the examples listed above, genetic manipulation is used as just one of a number of techniques in studies with conventional ethological aims. However, there are areas of research into animal behaviour in which further progress depends on a knowledge of the genetics of the behaviour patterns concerned; the two prime examples are unravelling the ontogeny of behaviour and working out the probable course of behavioural evolution under the impact of natural selection.

An understanding of the development of behaviour requires identification of all the factors which influence this process and of the ways in which they exert their effects. Since the genome is a major source of input to the developing system, behavioural ontogeny will not be completely understood until we know which genes influence behaviour and how they do so.

The ultimate aim of much research into the adaptive significance of behaviour is to produce estimates of the inclusive fitness of animals with different behavioural traits. However, accurate measurements of inclusive fitness cannot be obtained without detailed knowledge of the genome and breeding structure of the species concerned (see page 264). In addition, the way in which behavioural variants with particular inclusive fitnesses will change in frequency under the influence of natural selection depends on how these are inherited. Most theoretical models assume that the difference depends on an allele substitution at a single locus. Such models can provide information about what might have happened; for example, this approach has demonstrated that, under certain circumstances, altruism could evolve by kin selection and has thus produced sociobiology's main contribution to our understanding of behaviour. However, realistic models and precise predictions about changes in frequency of specific behaviour patterns cannot be derived until we understand the actual mechanisms by which these are inherited.

8.3 Quantitative genetics

The technique of classical genetics can be applied to behavioural differences just as it can to morphological ones, as demonstrated by Rothenbuhler's classic studies of brood care in honey bees (1964). When developing larvae die within their cells, most bees remove the cap from the cell and carry the corpse out of the nest; however, in some strains the bees do not show this hygienic behaviour with the result that infections spread quickly through the hive. Having developed methods of artificial insemination of queen bees and obtained pure breeding strains of hygienic and unhygienic bees, Rothenbuhler carried out crosses between males and females from these two strains to produce an F1 and beween male offspring and females of the hygienic strain to produce an F1-parental backcross. For each resulting hive he recorded whether the bees uncapped the cells and whether they removed dead larvae from artificially uncapped cells. The progeny of the initial cross (the F1 generation) all showed both unhygienic traits, neither uncapping the cells nor removing the largae from open cells. In the backcross, all four possible kinds of bees were found (those which both uncapped and removed, those which uncapped but did not remove, those which removed but did not uncap and those which did neither) in equal proportions. These results suggest that the difference between hygienic and unhygienic behaviour in bees depends on two pairs of alleles, one influencing uncapping and the other removing; these alleles are situated at loci on different chromosomes, with the unhygienic traits dominant over the hygenic traits in each case. It is worth stressing that it is not the whole complex response that depends on only two genes but the difference between the hygienic and unhygienic conditions.

Unfortunately, few breeding studies in which the animals concerned are chosen for their behavioural traits produce such elegant results, the reason being that much behavioural variation is continuous. It is possible to classify bee hives unambiguously into those whose workers are hygienic and those whose workers are unhygienic; however, for traits such as mating time in fruitflies, which spans a range of values from less than one minute to more than three hours, simple, unambiguous classification into clearcut categories is impossible.

Such continuous variation may be the result of a number of independently segregating genes acting on the trait in question, of an environmental factor which can take on a range of values or of a combination of both. Breeding between extremes of such a continuum throws up a range of phenotypes in the progeny whose distribution cannot easily be accounted for by segregation of alleles at one or two loci; analysis of the genetic basis of such continuous variation requires the techniques of quantitative genetics (Falconer, 1980).

Briefly and very simply, it is assumed that the phenotype of an individual is jointly determined by an environmental influence (E) and a genetic influence (G) which combine together additively to bring about a deviation (P) from the mean population value for the trait in question. In the population as a whole, the total variance in a continuously varying trait (VP) is seen as the arithmetic sum of the variance due to the effects of these two influences. Thus:

$$VP = VG + VE$$

The assumption that the genotype and environment combine additively to determine the phenotype depends on these two sources of influence being independent. However, it is known that a given genetic difference may not have the same impact on phenotype in different environments (the genotype which under normal circumstances causes the intellectual impairment typical of the syndrome of phenylketonuria does so to a much lesser extent in individuals with access only to food low in phenylalanine and high in tyrosine) and that the effect of a particular environmental manipulation may influence different genotypes differentially (exposure to the same stimulus at the same age produces stronger filial imprinting in domesticated than in wild mallard; Cheng, Shoffner and Phillips, 1979). There are thus interactions between genotype and environment which have their own effect on variance and make the determination of phenotypic variance more complex than depicted above; these can be accommodated by introducing an interaction term into the equation representing the components of phenotypic variance.

In addition, there may be a correlation between an animal's genotype and the environment it experiences. To give an incompletely documented example, male sticklebacks show inherited differences in their level of aggression (Sevenster and Goyens, 1975) and, as an indirect consequence, their young differ in the number of attacks they receive from other fish; young sticklebacks with aggressive fathers thus inherit a tendency to be aggressive themselves and also experience to a different degree environmental features which may also determine how much they fight (Cullen, in Huntingford, 1976). Equally, genetically distinct animals may choose different habitats in which to live (see page 167). There is obviously tremendous scope for such genotype–environment correlations where behavioural traits are concerned and these will produce over- or underestimation of the variance due to genetic effects depending on whether genotypes are associated with environments whose influence on the trait is in the same or in an opposite direction. Here again, a correlation term can be incorporated into the variance equation, but in practice this is very difficult to measure.

The proportion of the total phenotypic variance which depends on genetic differences between individuals (VG/VP) is called the degree of genetic determination (or heritability in the broad sense). This is not a very useful statistic for predicting resemblances between relatives or response to selection in a sexually reproducing species, since it depends on the genotype as a whole and this is disrupted at each meiotic division. Some of the effects of genes on the level of a continuously varying trait are due to dominant alleles suppressing recessive alleles at the same locus and to interactions between alleles at different loci. These relationships may be lost when the genotype is reconstructed; their effects must therefore be distinguished from the average effects of the presence of particular genes regardless of the genetic background in which they are expressed, if the condition of the trait in successive generations is to be predicted. Statistically, this involves separating the variance due to dominance relationships (VD) and epistasis (VI, for interaction effects) from that due to the average or additive effects of genes (VA). Once again, the model can be expanded to include these different effects of genotype on variance as follows:

$$VP = VA+VD+VI+VE+\text{interaction and covariance terms.}$$

The much publicized statistic of heritability (in the narrow sense) measures the proportion of the total phenotypic variance which can be ascribed to the additive effects of genes (VA/VP); while this provides no information about the genetic mechanism whereby these additive effects come about (how many genes are involved, and where they are situated), it summarizes their consequences concisely and much research in quantitative genetics has been directed towards estimating this ratio.

The relative importance of additive genetic effects will depend on the environment in which these are expressed (to take an extreme position, in a completely uniform environment, VE will be zero and heritability correspondingly high) and on the genetic structure of the population concerned (if many alleles with dominant effects are present in the gene pool, VD will be high and heritability low). Since these both vary from time to time and from place to place, heritability is not an immutable measure of the extent to which genes influence a particular trait but a reflection of the manner in which additive genetic effects alter its expression in one particular breeding population, in one particular environment and at one particular time; extrapolation between populations is only possible if all relevant genetic and environmental conditions are constant. Although evolutionary biologists need to know the extent to which the level of continuously varying traits can be predicted across generations, measures of their heritability may therefore not be very helpful; this statistic is difficult to determine in the field and estimates made in the laboratory may not be relevant to wild populations.

Heritability concerns variance in characteristics of adult animals not how these develop; it therefore provides no information about the probable effects on a (behavioural) trait of environmental manipulation, whether this is deprivation of paternal care in sticklebacks or an educational programme for children. The relative importance of additive effects of genes in determining phenotypic differences in one environment tells us nothing about the effects of changing that environment; the mean level of a characteristic whose heritability is 100% in one environment could be changed out of all recognition by an appropriate alteration in the environment.

A number of characteristics are discontinuous in the sense that they come in two (or more) discrete forms, but do not segregate in a simple mendelian manner; the difference between the forms therefore appears not to depend on single gene effects. Such a trait can be accommodated within the framework of quantitative genetics by postulating a continuously variable factor controlling the expression of such traits by means of a threshold (or series of thresholds; Falconer, 1980). Individuals whose levels of the continuous, underlying variable fall below the threshold have one phenotype and those with a level above it take the alternative form. Assuming a normal distribution of this underlying variable, the position of the threshold and the average distance from it of a population of individuals can be estimated from the proportion of the two discontinuous traits. Assuming equal variance and the same threshold, the state of the underlying variable in two groups can be compared and, eventually, an estimate of heritability obtained. Inherited variation in the trait may come about by alteration in the position of the threshold, a change which might well involve a single allele substitution, or by a shift in level of the underlying variable, which probably involves genes with small effects in a polygenic system.

There is reason to believe that much behavioural variation is a consequence of alteration in such a system (Manning, 1979). For example, since unhygienic bees occasionally remove dead larvae, Rothenbuhler believed that the discrete behavioural difference between these and their hygienic counterparts represented a shift in the threshold for performing hygienic responses rather than complete loss of the machinery for producing them. In contrast, in hybrids between sword-tail fish (*Xiphophorus helleri* × *X. montezumae*), courtship behaviour of one parental species is shown at low levels of sexual motivation and of the other at high levels; this suggests that the two pure species differ in overall level of sexual motivation rather than in the threshold at which different acts are performed (Franck, 1974).

8.4 Techniques for identifying the genetic origin of a known behavioural difference

8.4.1 CROSSES BETWEEN BEHAVIOURAL VARIANTS

(a) *Crosses between closely related species*
Since closely related species often show substantial behavioural differences while being sufficiently similar in other respects for breeding between them to be successful, studying the behaviour of interspecific hybrids is a useful source of information on the inheritance of behaviour. A few selected examples will be discussed here to illustrate the kinds of information about behaviour which they can provide.

Larvae of the cricket species *Gryllus campestris* and *G. bimaculatus* differ markedly in aggressiveness, the former fighting much more readily than the latter. The behaviour of the two parental species and of the progeny of crosses between them through to the F2 and backcross generations are summarized in Fig. 8.1(a). The difference in larval aggression between these two species appears to be inherited under the influence of a single genetic unit with the aggressive form dominant over the peaceful one (Hörman-Heck, 1957).

Such clearcut results are rare, a more common sort of finding being illustrated in Fig. 8.1(b). Juvenile brook char (*Salvelinus fontinalis*) are very aggressive while lake char (*S. namaycush*) do not fight readily. These differences are summarized in a compound score which varies continuously within each pure species, low scores indicating high aggression. Hybrids between the two species have inter-mediate aggressive scores, indicating that there is a genetic basis to the be-havioural difference between the species. The fact that variation in the F1 generation is continuous probably means that it depends on alleles segregating at a number of loci. The mean score for all the hybrids is closer to the low level of the brook char than the high scores of the lake char which suggests that directional dominance may exist in favour of the more aggressive phenotype. The distri-bution of the scores in the reciprocal hybrids is significantly different, each being more similar to their maternal than their paternal parent. Since neither species shows any kind of parental care, and given that the similarity exists in both sexes, this may mean that some kind of cytoplasmic inheritance is involved (Ferguson and Noakes, 1982).

Such differences between reciprocal hybrids are easier to interpret when crosses involve species with a small number of chromosomes. The calling songs of male crickets of *Teleogryllus oceanicus* and *T. commodus* are shown in Fig. 8.1(c). These species differ in a number of features; the calling song of *T. oceanicus* consists of a chirp of 5 pulses and a series of trills of 2 pulses each while that of *T. commodus* consists of 1–4 long trills. The songs of reciprocal hybrids between these species are intermediate between the parental species in most parameters; the system of inheritance is therefore a polygenic one. For parameters such as the number of pulses per chirp, there are no differences between the reciprocal hybrids, which indicates that the genes responsible for the behavioural dif-ferences must be the autosomes; however, the number of trills resembles that of the maternal species in both cases. Since male crickets are XO, all hybrid males receive their single X chromosome from their mother; thus the number of trills in the calling song of the hybrids is influenced by some X linked factor. Variation in different components of the calling song in these crickets thus depends on dif-ferent genetic mechanisms, at least one being polygenic (Bentley and Hoy, 1972).

The response of hybrid female crickets to different calls was also investigated (Hoy, Hahn and Paul, 1977); while females of both pure species move towards the song of conspecific males, hybrid females of both types respond preferentially to the song of males of their own group. This correspondence between the form of the song produced by male crickets and the behavioural preference of genetic-ally similar females indicates that these parameters are coupled in some way.

The extent to which cross species hybrids can be used to identify the precise genetic mechanism underlying behavioural differences can be illustrated by two of the many examples in which the behaviour of hybrids between *Drosophila* species

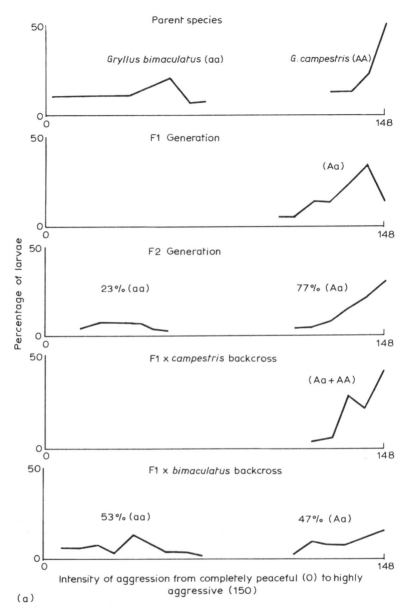

Figure 8.1 Studying the behaviour of interspecific hybrids. (a, *above*) Aggressive behaviour of hybrids between the cricket species *Gryllus campestris* and *G. bimaculatus* and a possible genetic model (after Hörmann-Heck, 1957); (b, *opposite*) aggressive behaviour (summarized in a multivariate score) of hybrids between brook char and lake char (from Ferguson and Noakes, 1982); (c, *opposite*) the calling song of *Teleogryllus oceanicus* (A) and *T. commodus* (D) and reciprocal hybrids between them (B represents *T. oceanicus* ♀ ×*T. commodus* ♂, C represents *T. commodus* ♀ ×*T. oceanicus* ♂). Arrows indicate the beginning of the subsequent phase. Time bar = 0.5s (from Bentley and Hoy, 1972).

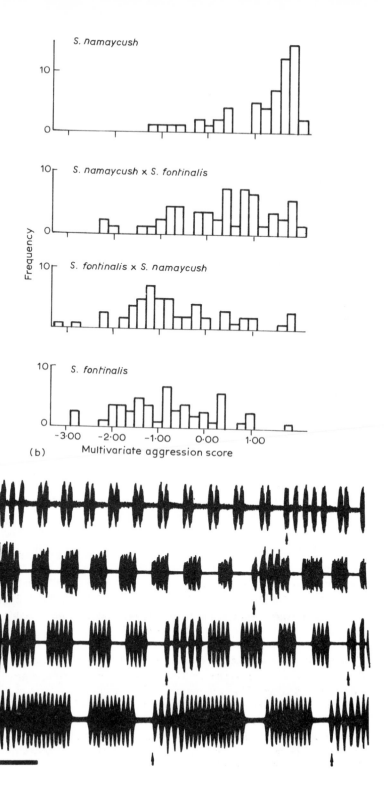

S. namaycush

S. namaycush x S. fontinalis

S. fontinalis x S. namaycush

S. fontinalis

(b) Multivariate aggression score

A

B

C

D

(c)

has been studied. *Drosophila* males produce songs during courtship which are thought to be critically involved in species recognition. The inheritance of inter-specific differences in these songs has been intensively studied. For example, *D. pseudobscura* produces two types of song, type 1 in which pulses are repeated at a high rate and type 2 in which they are repeated at a low rate, while *D. persimilis* sings only the latter song; in addition, repetition rate of pulses in type 2 songs is higher in *D. simulans* than in *D. pseudobscura*. F1 hybrids closely resemble their maternal parent in the presence or absence of the two song types and in the actual pitch of the sound produced, indicating that this is controlled by sex linked genetic factors. Offspring of the F1-parental backcross fall into two discrete categories for song type and pitch in a ratio of 1:1, indicating that the interspecific differences in these characters depend either on a single segregating factor or on several closely linked factors. On the other hand, all the hybrids showed inter-mediate levels for the repetition rate within pulses of the type 2 song and the distribution of this feature in the backcross is continuous; this quantitative difference between the parental species therefore seems to be inherited by a polygenic system, situated on the autosomal chromosomes (Ewing, 1969).

Where the different autosomes can be identified with genetic markers, their role in production of behavioural differences between species can also be identi-fied. When presented simultaneously with conspecific males and males of the closely related *D. mojavensis*, females of the species *D. arizona* discriminate positively in favour of conspecifics. A series of crosses between these species and their hybrids produce flies with a range of known combinations of the chromo-somes of the two species (identified by allozyme markers). The response of *D. arizona* females exposed simultaneously to a conspecific male and a male of one of these variants can be used to identify the influence of each chromosome on the ability of the males to elicit courtship from these females. To summarize some of the results, the presence of a Y chromosome from *D. arizona* on an otherwise *D. mojavensis* genotype markedly increased the probability that the male concerned would be accepted; the presence of chromosome II had a similar effect, while chromosome III produced a small reduction in the probability of acceptance. Thus the Y chromosome and chromosome II have to alter something about these males which determines their success in mating with *D. arizona* females. Interestingly, in the *D. pseudobscura* complex, the part of the genome which is on chromosome II in *D. arizona* and *mojavensis* has been translocated onto the X chromosome; these results are therefore comparable with Ewing's (Zouros, 1981).

(b) *Crosses between local strains*
Behavioural differences within a single species are the raw material of natural selection and therefore of most interest to evolutionary biologists and there is no reason to assume that these are controlled by the same genetic mechanisms as those responsible for differences between species. Crosses between naturally

occurring strains or geographic races of the same species can provide information on this point.

Populations of blackcaps (*Sylvia atricapilla*) from different regions show marked differences in migratory behaviour, the percentage of birds from populations of blackcaps in Finland, Germany, France and Africa showing migratory restlessness in captivity being 100, 100, 80 and 23 respectively; thus the further south the birds live the weaker is their tendency to migrate. When birds from the German and African races were crossed, 56% of the resulting offspring showed migratory restlessness in captivity and for the birds which did so, the proportion of each day spent in this behaviour and the number of days for which it lasted was intermediate between the levels for the two parental strains. These results suggest that the naturally occurring differences in migratory patterns between populations have a genetic basis (Berthold and Querner, 1981).

The characid fish *Astyanax mexicanus* normally lives in schools in river systems in central America but also forms a number of blind, cave dwelling populations. The cave fish assume a body angle of 45 degrees when feeding while the river

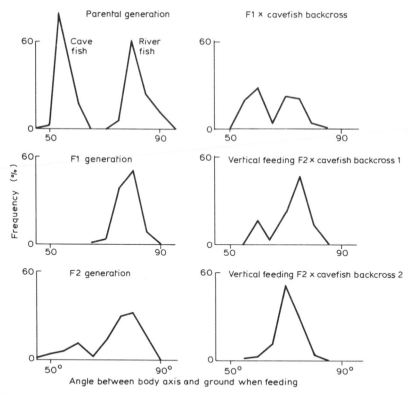

Figure 8.2 Crosses between naturally occurring behavioural variants of the same species; feeding angles of hybrids between river- and cave-dwelling forms of the fish *Astyanax mexicanus* (after Schemmel, 1980).

form feeds in a vertical position even when deprived of visual cues. Feeding angles in the F1 progeny from crosses between the normal fish and the cave dwelling variant and from the F2 generation and backcrosses are shown in Fig. 8.2. The distribution of feeding angles in the F1 generation is almost identical to that of the river fish, although the mean body position is not quite so steep. In the F2 the phenotypes segregate, with fish feeding at high and low angles in an approximately 3:1 ratio. Thus the trait may be controlled by a single factor with the vertical feeding angle dominant over the alternative position, a suggestion which is supported by the 1:1 ratio of feeding types in the F1 backcross to the cave fish. The offspring from one of the F2 backcrosses to the cave dwelling form all feed vertically, as expected if the F2 parent was homozygous for a dominant factor at a single locus. In another backcross between a vertical feeder from the F2 generation and the cave dwelling form two forms appeared, as expected if the F2 parent was a heterozygote but these occurred in a ratio of 3:1 rather than the expected 1:1. These results indicate that the distinct differences in behaviour between the river and cave forms of this fish are a result of genetic variation and most of the crosses suggest a single factor with nearly complete dominance for the vertical feeding typical of the river form. However, the 3:1 ratio of the two forms in one F2 backcross and the slight downward shift in mean angle in the progeny of all crosses indicates that some other factors must also be involved; a model in which alleles at 3 loci segregate independently fits the data very well (Schemmel, 1980).

(c) *Crosses between behavioural variants within a population*
In both these studies, considerable variation in behaviour was found within populations as well as between them and the inheritance of these differences needs to be understood. In Rothenbuhler's classic experiments, the inheritance of naturally occurring behavioural differences within freely interbreeding forms was studied by means of crosses between individuals differing in the behavioural trait in question; many other experiments along these lines have been performed, though not all have such clearcut results. Examples of naturally occurring behavioural differences which have been traced to the presence of mutant alleles at single autosomal loci in mice are *waltzer*, which behaves as its name suggests and *nervous* which shows a variety of abnormalities in coordination. The behavioural variant *cacophany* in *Drosophila melanogaster* suffers reduced mating success because it produces a song with an abnormal waveform and interpulse intervals; this difference from the normal song depends on the presence of a sex-linked, recessive mutant allele (Schilcher, 1977).

While such naturally occurring inherited behavioural differences are of importance in understanding the evolution of behaviour under the influence of selection, their effects are often quite complex. The completely different aim of working out how genes influence development of the nervous system requires identification of large numbers of simple behavioural differences whose inheritance depends on alleles at a single locus, since their underlying biochemical or physiological bases can be determined more easily. With this end in view, Benzer and his collaborators (Benzer, 1973) exposed fruit flies to mutagens and screened their progeny for behavioural differences. They then used crossing experiments to identify those which depend on sex linked alleles at a single locus; these were then used in subsequent analysis of the nature of the genetic influence. Table 8.1 lists a few of the behavioural mutants which have been identified in this way, selected for their possible relevance to the naturally occurring behavioural variants discussed in Chapter 5.

Table 8.1 Some behavioural mutants of *Drosophila melanogaster*.

Mutant	Behaviour
Non-phototactic	Flies fail to show normal movement towards light
Hyperkinetic	Flies walk oddly and when etherized twitch their legs violently
Fruitless	Male flies court females but never initiate copulation and are themselves courted by normal males
Coitus interruptus	Males court and mount females but terminate copulation after about 60% of the normal duration
Period mutants:	
arhythmic	Circadian periodicity of eclosion lost
short period	Period of eclosion cycle reduced
long period	Period of eclosion cycle extended

Mass screening for mutagen induced behavioural variation has been performed with the same broad objective for the nematode *Caenorhabditis elegans* by Brenner and his collaborators. Many deviants from normal behaviour dependent on mutation at a single locus have been identified, ranging from complete paralysis to continuous spiralling, abnormal responses to chemostimulation and impaired mating efficiency (Brenner, 1973; Ward, 1977; Hodgekin, 1983). Both these studies are discussed further below.

8.4.2 SELECTIVE BREEDING FROM EXTREMES OF A BEHAVIOURAL CONTINUUM

It is possible to determine whether genetic differences are responsible for continuous variation in a behavioural trait by selective breeding between similar individuals at one or other extreme of the continuum. If all the original variation depends on differences in the environment and if this is held constant across generations, there will be no response to selective breeding however long it is continued. On the other hand, if any of the original variation is due to additive genetic effects, selection will pick out extreme genotypes and, since these will be passed on to subsequent generations, the mean value of the trait in the two selected lines will change. The rate at which this occurs depends on how selective the breeding regime is (the selective differential) and on how much of the original variation depended on additive genetic effects. Thus, if a behavioural trait responds to selection, the original variation had some genetic basis and the rate of the response can be used to estimate the heritability of the trait. For example, male crickets do not all call equally readily; the amount of singing responds to a regime of selective breeding, indicating that the behavioural variation depends on genetic differences (Cade, 1981 and see page 231).

A classic example of the use of selective breeding to investigate the genetic architecture of a behavioural trait concerns mating speed in *Drosophila melanogaster*. 50 male and 50 female flies were placed in communal mating chambers and the ten pairs which mated first removed to set up a fast mating line; the ten slowest flies were used for a slow mating line. The average mating speed for each line in 25 generations of selection is shown in Fig. 8.3; the response to selection was rapid and marked in both directions and the heritability of the trait was estimated at 0.3. Crossing between the two high and between the two low lines produced offspring with mating speeds similar to those of their parents, indicating that the genetic basis of the changes produced by selection was the same in each group. Crosses between the high and low lines produced flies with intermediate mating times and there were no differences between the reciprocal crosses. Thus mating speed in this species seems to depend on polygenic systems without sex linkage (Manning, 1961).

To give a more recent example using the same species, the speed of remating by female flies following a successful copulation is variable; selection among wild type flies for the first 10 of 75 females to remate produced a rapid and strong response (the mean interval dropped from *circa* 5 to less than 3 days in 5 generations) and a heritability estimate of 0.3 was obtained (Pyle and Gromko, 1981).

The responses of continuously varying traits to artificial selection usually depend on reassortment of alleles at many loci whose effects are hard to disentangle. However, it is possible to find out where these are located by carrying out a series of crosses between the selected strains and a tester strain in which the different chromosomes carry genetic markers. For example, by using a series of interlocking vertical mazes, large numbers of fruit flies were identified which differed in the strength of their geotactic response. Selection for geotaxis produced significant response in both directions but particularly in the direction of stronger negative response (Hirsch, 1967). In order to identify the effect on geotaxis of the three main chromosomes, males of a particular strain (the unknown strain which may be an unselected control, the high selected line or the low selected line) are crossed to females of a tester strain in which chromosomes II, III and X carry genetic markers and in which crossing over is prevented by

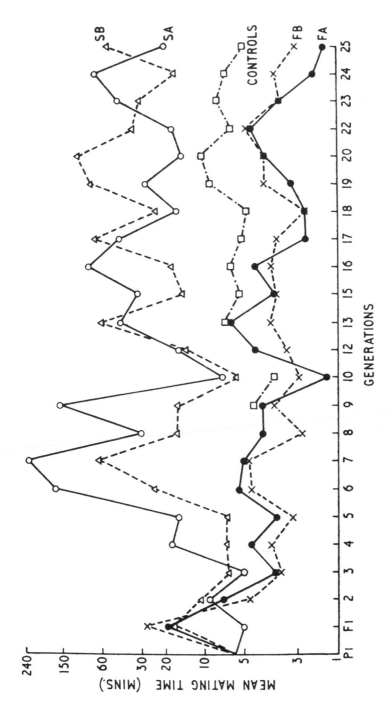

Figure 8.3 Selective breeding for extremes of a behaviour continuum; mating time in lives of *Drosophila melanogaster* selected for fast (FA and FB) and slow (SA and SB) mating speed (from Manning, 1961).

inversions. The female progeny of this cross are backcrossed to males of the unknown strain to produce flies which have a range of different combinations of chromosome types. Comparison of geotaxis in flies which are homozygous for the unknown strain in particular chromosome pairs and in those which are heterozygous allows the effect of recessive genes on that chromosome to be detected. Thus Table 8.2 shows that, when the unknown strain is the unselected group, chromosomes X and II strengthen positive geotaxis while chromosome III enhances negative geotaxis. When the unknown strain is the selected high line, the positive effects of chromosome X are enhanced and the negative effects of chromosome III reduced. When the unknown strain is the selected low line the negative effect of chromosome III is enhanced and the positive effects of the other two chromosomes are reduced. Thus there are genes distributed on all three major chromosomes of *D. melanogaster* which affect the flies' response to gravity and which can be changed by selective breeding (Hirsch, 1967).

Table 8.2 Discovering the chromosomal location of genetic changes produced by artificial selection; effect on geotaxis score of the presence of chromosomes X, II and III from 3 strains of *Drosophila melanogaster* (from Hirsch, 1967).

	Chromosome		
Unknown strain	X	II	III
Unselected	1.03	1.74	−0.29
Selected for positive geotaxis	1.39	1.81	0.12
Selected for negative geotaxis	0.47	0.33	−1.08

Using a tester strain with marker genes at a number of known sites along all the major chromosomes, it is possible to obtain flies with combinations of identified sections of each chromosome. By comparing their scores on a continuous trait it is possible to identify regions of the genome which have a detectable effect on that characteristic. This technique has been applied to fruit flies selected for copulation duration; the main effect of selection for low copulation duration depends on genetic factors on the right arm of chromosome II, although the X chromosome also makes some contribution (MacBean, 1970).

8.5 Screening known genetic variants for behavioural differences

Because so much is now known about the general rules of inheritance and about the genome of particular species, an additional source of information about the inheritance of behaviour exists which can be used where general principles about the way genes influence behaviour rather than the inheritance of naturally occurring behavioural differences are concerned. By screening the behaviour of individuals which are known to differ in genetic makeup, behavioural effects of genetic variants can be identified.

A large number of mutant alleles with recognizable effects on morphology or physiology have been identified and their pattern of inheritance established in a number of species. The behaviour of such mutant forms can provide information about whether and how genes influence behaviour. There are a number of mutants in mice which have recognizable morphological effects but which also produce behavioural differences; for example the autosomal recessive *albino* was identified by its effect on morphology but it also produces mice which nibble less, are less active and more successful at mating.

However, as usual, *Drosophila melanogaster* provides the classic example of a mutant originally identified by its morphological effects and subsequently found to influence behaviour. The *yellow* mutant in this species is a sex linked recessive which alters the colour of the cuticle but has a number of other, pleitropic, effects. Male flies differing from a wild stock only in the presence of the yellow allele at this locus are less successful at mating and also produce abnormal courtship with more orientation but less vibration and licking. Since vibration produces song it is possible that the reduced success of yellow males at gaining copulations depends on their abnormal courtship (Bastock, 1956). Male *D. melanogaster* homozygous for the autosomal allele *ebony*, which also alters body colour and which is found as a polymorphism in several natural populations, show reduced success in competition for females in the light; however, in the dark this situation is reversed (Rendel, 1951).

8.5.2 VISIBLE DIFFERENCES IN CHROMOSOME STRUCTURE WITH BEHAVIOURAL EFFECTS

Natural populations of many *Drosophila* species are polymorphic for sections of chromosome which have been inverted and thus are effectively single gene complexes. These inversion polymorphisms have been intensively studied and a number of behavioural differences between flies with different inversion sequences have been described. For example, in *D. persimilis* different karyotypes show different habitat preferences (Taylor and Powell, 1977) while in *D. pseudobscura* males with certain inversions enjoy enhanced mating success with all categories of female (Anderson and McGuire, 1978).

8.5.3 COMPARING NATURALLY OCCURRING, ISOLATED POPULATIONS

Many species exist naturally in discrete populations which are known or believed to be genetically distinct. If members of such species differ in their behaviour when reared under identical conditions in the laboratory, especially if they show no parental care or if cross-fostering has been arranged, then the behavioural difference may well be due to genetic effects. There are many examples of behavioural differences between naturally occurring strains of *Drosophila* which persist when the flies are maintained in the laboratory. For example male *D. pseudobscura* derived from flies collected in different regions differ in mating speed, in geotaxis and in phototaxis. In the other classical subject of behavioural genetic research, offspring of wild mice trapped in different parts of the United States and raised under standard conditions differed in a variety of behavioural traits such as open field activity and defaecation and nest building (Plomin and Manosevitz, 1974). To give some less conventional examples, geographically isolated subspecies of deermice (*Peromyscus maniculatus borealis* and *blandis*) differ in the breadth of their diet (Gray, 1979), strains of the platyfish *Xiphophorus maculatus* differ in the age at which they reach maturity (Kallman and Schreibman, 1973), while sticklebacks from different localities in Holland differ in the enthusiasm with which they creep through their nests during courtship (Sevenster and T'hart, 1974). These results indicate that naturally occurring differences in behaviour may well be genetically determined, although since the extent of the genetic difference between populations is usually unknown, nothing more specific can be concluded about the genetic mechanisms without further study.

8.5.4 CORRELATING DEGREE OF RELATEDNESS AND BEHAVIOURAL SIMILARITY

Where controlled breeding programmes are not feasible, a knowledge of the laws of inheritance and the consequent degree of similarity to be expected between relatives can be used to detect behavioural differences of genetic origin. There is a significant correlation between parent and offspring and between full sibs in open field activity in mice, just as there is for aggressiveness in sticklebacks (Sevenster and Goyens, 1975) and for age at maturity and dispersal tendency in voles (Krebs, 1979); differences in these aspects of behaviour are therefore likely to depend on underlying genetic variation.

In addition, the more closely related two individuals are, the more likely they are to be genetically similar; therefore if a correlation exists between the degree of relatedness of pairs of individuals and the extent to which they resemble each other in some behaviour, this indicates that the variation in the behaviour is at least partly determined by genetic differences. Estimating additive genetic effects on variance from such data is complex but this kind of evidence has been used to identify genetic influences on personality traits in humans.

8.5.5 INBRED STRAINS

One of the most useful sources of information in the search for genetically determined behaviour in animals is the inbred strain. If in a breeding line matings are arranged between closely related animals, the number of heterozygous loci decreases with each generation until the members of a given strain are effectively identical in genotype. In any given programme of inbreeding it is a matter of chance which allele becomes fixed at a particular locus; therefore while members of the same inbred strain are genetically identical, different strains derived from the same population are likely to differ genetically. Any behavioural difference between members of a single strain must be the result of environmental influences but differences between strains depend on both genetic and environmental effects. There are an enormous number of inbred strains of mice which have been produced for medical purposes and differences between these in open field activity, in aggression, in susceptibility to audiogenic seizures, in learning ability, in mating speed and in the period and phases relationships of their circadian rhythmicity, to name but a few, have been identified (see Plomin, De Fries and McClearn, 1980 for a review). Inbred strains are also available for *Drosophila* species and these have been found to differ in general activity, in mating speed, in duration of copulation, in pheromone production and in grooming, again to give just a few examples (see Ehrman and Parsons, 1981 for a review). The fact that so many behavioural differences between inbred strains have been identified in mice and fruit flies indicates that a large amount of genetically determined behavioural variation existed in the natural populations from which the strains were derived.

By observing the range of variation of a trait in the offspring of crosses between strains more detailed information about the nature of the genetic system involved can be obtained. For example, two inbred strains of bees differing in the intensity of their response to sting alarm pheromone were crossed to give F1 and backcross generations; the former all resembled the strain with the most intense response and the latter showed the two forms of response in equal numbers indicating that the difference in question depends on segregation at a single locus with the more intense response dominant (Collins, 1976).

The complete set of matings between all possible combinations of males and females for a number of strains is called a diallel cross. Analysis of the variance of the progeny of all these crosses for a trait in which the parental strains differ allows identification of the proportion of this variation which is the result of additive genetic effects, of dominance interactions and of epistasis; in addition, maternal effects and, if the crosses are repeated in different environments, genotype–environment interactions can be identified. For example, Table 8.3 shows the results of a diallel cross between six strains of *Drosophila melanogaster* which differ in mating speed (Fulker, 1966). They give a low heritability estimate and a high degree of dominance in the direction of rapid mating speed. A similar analysis between four different strains of the same species which differ in the inter-pulse interval of their courtship song produced the opposite result, this characteristic showing high heritability and low dominance (Cowling, 1980). It

Table 8.3 Using diallel crosses between inbred strains to discover the genetic architecture of a continuously varying behavioural trait; mating speed in male offspring of all possible crosses between six strains of *Drosophila melanogaster* measured on two separate occasions. Briefly, variance within rows and columns gives a measure of additive genetic variance (D), variance of rows within columns and vice versa reflects the effects of dominance (H), variance between reciprocal crosses measures maternal influences (M) and variance between replicates indicates environmental effects (E); $D = 0.69$, $H = 1.31$, $E = 0.26$, heritability $= 0.5D/(0.5D+0.25H+E) = 0.36$ (from Fulker, 1966).

Strain of father of males tested	Strain of mother of males tested						Statistics	
	6CL	Ed	Or	W	S	F	$V_r{}^*$	$W_r{}^*$
6CL	*1.4*	3.6	2.2	3.2	2.6	3.0	0.759	0.547
	1.2	2.6	2.6	3.8	3.4	3.2		
Ed	4.0	*3.0*	3.7	3.4	3.2	3.2	0.172	0.001
	3.2	*3.8*	4.6	4.0	2.8	4.2		
Or	2.3	3.4	*1.8*	3.4	2.4	2.8	1.120	0.903
	1.6	4.6	*0.8*	4.0	1.6	3.8		
W	3.2	4.4	3.8	*3.0*	2.4	3.6	0.218	0.020
	3.4	3.0	3.2	*2.2*	3.6	4.2		
S	2.4	3.6	2.0	2.4	*1.2*	2.4	0.707	0.585
	3.2	4.0	2.2	4.6	*1.2*	3.8		
F	3.3	4.0	3.2	4.6	2.0	*2.8*	0.524	0.382
	3.8	4.2	2.8	3.4	3.6	*1.8*		

$^*V_r$ is the variance within an array, and W_r is the covariance of the members of an array with the nonrecurrent inbred line. W_r and V_r were calculated from the diallel table averaged over both reciprocals (above and below the inbred lines, shown in *italics* in the diagonal) and replicates.

would appear that natural selection has favoured faster mating speed but not an increase in inter-pulse interval in this species.

By a series of judicious crosses, it is possible to produce different combinations of chromosomes from the original strains and thus to identify the contribution of each of these to the original behavioural difference. For example, larvae of two strains of *Drosophila melanogaster* both homologous for chromosomes II and III were found to differ significantly in their foraging behaviour; the white strain showed more crawling, a higher rate of feeding movements and longer feeding tracks than the ebony strain. Progeny of crosses between these strains were intermediate in behaviour and there were no differences between reciprocal crosses; therefore the difference must be polygenically determined by genes located on the autosomes. A series of crosses in and out of a tester strain with markers on chromosomes II and III and with recombination suppressed by an inversion, produced flies with all possible combinations of these two main autosomes from the two original strains, each pair always being homozygous. Table 8.4 summarizes the behaviour of the larvae with these different chromosome arrangements. Flies whose homozygous chromosome II was from the ebony stock showed low crawling rates while those with chromosome II from the white stock showed high crawling levels, both regardless of the origin of chromosome III. Differences in crawling behaviour would therefore seem to be attributable to genetic factors on the second chromosome. On the other hand, feeding rate differed in all the four chromosome combinations and thus the genetic factors which determine the original difference in feeding rate in the two strains cannot be located on a single chromosome (Sokolowski, 1980).

Table 8.4 Identifying the chromosomal location of genetic factors responsible for behavioural differences between inbred strains; the frequency of performance of crawling and feeding movements in larvae of fruit flies with chromosomes II and III (homologous) coming from one or other of two parental strains (after Sokolowski, 1980).

Origin of chromosome II	Origin of chromosome III	
	Ebony strain	White strain
	Crawling rate	
Ebony	27.7	58.2
White	137.1	137.2
	Feeding rate	
Ebony	112.9	301.7
White	50.7	157.2

8.5.6 RECOMBINANT STRAINS

A powerful technique which can indicate the number of segregating genetic factors responsible for differences between inbred strains even where these are continuous and which, if genetic markers are available, can also identify their location, is the production of recombinant strains. Two inbred strains are crossed to give an F1 generation whose members are genetically identical but heterozygous for any loci in which the two original strains differed; crosses among the F1 generation produce F2 progeny in which the genes of the original strains have undergone recombination. A large number of breeding lines are set up from this F2 generation and inbreeding enforced for up to 20 generations. Homozygosity will increase in each of these lines but the alleles at any particular locus which become fixed will differ in the different lines. If a sufficient number of inbred lines, or recombinant strains, have been established, all the recombinant forms in the F2 will be sampled; the distribution of their phenotypes will therefore reflect the number of segregating factors underlying the difference between the original strains. At the most extreme, if this was the result of a pair of alleles at a single locus, recombinant strains will come in the form of just one of two distinct phenotypes in equal numbers.

For example, male mice of the inbred strain C57 BL/6 By are more aggressive (in a neutral arena towards a non-aggressive opponent) than males of the inbred strain BALB/cBy. Of 7 recombinant strains established from F2 crosses between these two stocks, 2 showed levels of aggression similar to those of the BALB/cBy strain, 3 showed levels similar to the C57 BL/6 By strain, one showed higher levels and one lower levels than either parental strain. These results, together with some other evidence, indicated that the differences in aggression between the two original strains depended on alleles segregating at two loci with high tendency to fight dominant (Eleftheriou, Bailey and Denenberg, 1974). Recombinant strains have mainly been used to study the inheritance of behaviour patterns of interest to psychologists rather than ethologists. To give some more examples, 5 recombinant strains were established from the grandchildren of mice of 2 inbred strains with marked differences in level of inter-cranial self stimulation; the behaviour of the recombinant strains fell into one of two categories, with 3 resembling the behaviour of the high line and 2 that of the low line. This indicates that the different threshold for self stimulation shown by the two original strains depended on a single allele substitution (Cazala and Guenet, 1980).

In contrast, recombinant strains from parental strains of mice with high and low susceptibility to audiogenic seizures showed a range of phenotypes for this trait; not only did the overall susceptibility vary continuously but the response itself took a number of different forms with respect to latency, duration and severity. The original difference in susceptibility cannot be ascribed to a single factor with a major effect and the trait must therefore be subject to multifactorial control. In this study, the original strains carried genetic markers for a number of chromosomes; there was a significant association between susceptibility to seizures and a genetic marker (inductability of aryl hydrocarbon hydroxylase) which depends on loci on one or more of chromosomes 8, 9, 17 and 19 (Seyfried, Yu and Glaser, 1980).

8.6 Characterizing the precise behavioural effects of genetic differences

Thus although it is more difficult to work out the pattern of inheritance of what animals do as opposed to what they look like, in some cases it has been possible to go a long way towards achieving this objective. The next step is to identify the mechanism whereby the genes concerned produce their behavioural effects; progress in this direction will be slow unless the latter are very precisely characterized. The problem is that the behavioural difference which is initially identified will reflect the interest of the experimenter and may be a consequence of some other inherited behavioural change. This does not mean that the original effect is not subject to genetic influence but that the route by which this is exerted is an indirect one. For example, a difference in mating speed may be the result of an alteration in the behaviour of the male, the female or of both. Even if it depends entirely on one or other partner it may result from a change in sensitivity to a particular stimulus, an alteration in capacity or readiness to perform particular movements or to a difference in overall activity. Genetically determined behavioural changes of these various kinds probably involve quite distinct mechanisms which will be detected by different techniques.

Identifying primary inherited behavioural effects involves screening variant animals for as many behavioural differences as possible. Suggestions as to which of these represents the key alteration can be made from a knowledge of the organization of behaviour in the species concerned; subsequent experimental manipulation may allow it to be determined with certainty. To illustrate the complexity of this exercise as well as its importance, some behavioural comparisons of *Drosophila* differing in mating speed and mating success will be outlined.

Manning (1961) showed that mating speed in *D. melanogaster* responds to selection in both directions and that selection influences the behaviour of both sexes. Selection on the basis of the behaviour of one sex only produced no response in the direction of fast mating males or slow mating females but slow mating in males did respond to selection (a fast female line was not available). This indicates that some complex interaction between the sexes was altered in the initial experiment; it also suggests that natural selection has favoured fast mating males and slow mating females, which concurs with the modern picture of courtship as a conflict between ardent males and choosy females (see page 235).

The flies in the slow lines showed enhanced levels of activity in an open field test compared to those of the fast lines and also had a longer latency before initiating courtship. Manning therefore suggested that the difference in mating speed may be an indirect consequence of selection for different levels of activity. The obvious test is to select flies on the basis of activity and, if there is a response to selection, to see whether the active and inactive flies show slow and fast mating. Flies selected for high and low activity levels showed no difference in mating speed when sexual behaviour was observed in large populations; however, when mating speed was measured by observation of single pairs of flies, the active strain did take longer to mate. This difference is not a result of changes in the effectiveness of courtship in active males, who mate at normal speeds with unselected females, but appears to depend on a change in receptivity and increased frequency of rejection movements in active females (Burnet and Connolly, 1974).

A quite different relationship between mating success and general activity was found in the *ebony* mutant, in which males have severely reduced mating success in the light but are more successful than wild type males in the dark. They are more active than wild type males in the dark and it is possible that this may explain their enhanced success under these conditions. A significant positive correlation exists between success of a fly in attracting females in a competitive situation and the extent to which its activity level is greater than that of its rival (Kyriacou, 1981). An additional complication is that males heterozygote at the *ebony* locus sing more effective courtship songs when young than either homozygote (Kyriacou, Burnet and Connolly, 1978). These two factors may well account for the existence of this otherwise deleterious mutant as a polymorphic form in natural populations.

Male *Drosophila melanogaster* which are homozygous for the sex linked recessive mutant *yellow* on a genetic background obtained by crossing into wild strains showed reduced mating success and low intensity courtship (Bastock, 1956); it seems reasonable to suggest that the former may be the result of the latter. When the same mutant allele is placed on different genetic backgrounds (into the Novosibirsk (N) and Oregon (O) strains), the deficiency in mating success is still found in both cases, but courtship is normal in the N strain. Thus the effect of the *yellow* mutant on courtship depends on the genetic background in which it is expressed and cannot be responsible for the reduced mating success. In both strains *yellow* males are less active than wild type males but since they are unsuccessful at mating even with highly receptive females with whom they make frequent copulation attempts, the lowered mating success is probably not the result of this reduced activity. It may be that the *yellow* allele impairs the cuticle in such a way that copulation is impossible (Wilson *et al.*, 1976).

These examples illustrate that inherited differences in sexual behaviour in *Drosophila melanogaster* may depend on complex interactions between the male and female which may be influenced adversely by both high and low activity levels, which act at different points in the mating sequence and which depend critically on testing conditions. Thus where behaviour in general and social behaviour in particular are concerned the nature of any genetic influence is likely to be subtle and complex. It is possible to classify these effects into different kinds.

In the first place, some inherited behavioural differences involve altered responsiveness to stimuli. Thus in *D. melanogaster* the mutant *orange* impairs the optomotor response as well as other visually evoked behaviour patterns such as the upward response in flight to vertical stripes and the landing response to moving horizontal stripes (Heisenberg and Buchner, 1977). In contrast, some genetic changes alter the response to stimuli only under certain circumstances. For example, selection for a tendency to approach red or blue stimuli in Japanese quail produced a marked response in both directions (Kovach and Wilson, 1980). Quails in both lines were capable of distinguishing blue from red under a range of light conditions and therefore selection produced a change in preference for colours which were both seen clearly rather than an alteration in general sensitivity to different colours (Kovach, Yeatman and Wilson, 1980).

Another type of relatively simple effect of genes on behaviour is via an alteration in the form of motor patterns. Thus the mutant *cacophany* alters the form of wing vibration during *Drosophila* courtship so that abnormal sound waves are produced (Schilcher, 1977). Similarly in crickets and grasshoppers, genetically controlled differences in calling song between closely related species depend on changes in the wing and leg movements that generate the sound (Bentley and Hoy, 1972).

Genes which alter production of olfactory cues can also have a profound effect on social interaction. The mutant *fruitless* produces male flies which fail to copulate with females and also elicits courtship from males which are courted in return; it may be that the mutant males produce female scents which attract other males but also stimulate the mutant flies to court them (Hall, 1978).

The mutant *nervous* in mice produces irregular strokes during overhand grooming of the face. In addition, the relationships between the various stroke types used in face grooming are disrupted, being more variable and without the regularly occurring sequences described for normal mice. Nervous mice sometimes show simultaneous face and body grooming which is never normally observed. The mutant therefore disrupts the relationships between face grooming and other activities and higher order relationships between different face grooming movements as well as the form of the movements themselves. In other words, it is exerting an effect on the organization of the animal's motivational system (Northup, 1977). In hybrids between the sword tail species *Xiphophoros helleri* and *montezumae*, whose complex courtship sequences differ in several respects, males show courtship elements of the paternal species at low levels of sexual motivation but switch to the movements of the maternal species at high levels of sexual motivation. It could be that the capacity to show all the courtship movements is present in both species and that the normal behavioural difference between them depends on a difference in the level of sexual motivation required to elicit them (Franck, 1974).

The various mutants which alter the periodicity of eclosion in *Drosophila melanogaster* also affect the period (normally 70–80 seconds) of the much shorter term rhythm of frequency modulation during the production of courtship song by males. This song frequency rhythm disappears altogether in flies which are arhythmic in eclosion time, has a period of 50–60 seconds in flies with a short period eclosion rhythm and of 90–110 seconds in long eclosion period flies (Hall, 1979; Kyriacou and Hall, 1980). Thus genes may influence a number of quite different behaviour patterns via a rather general effect.

It has been suggested that the inherited differences in the songs of male crickets of the species *Telogryllus oceanicus* and *T. campestrus* and in the response of females to the songs are the result of genetic alteration in a neuronal model of the calling song. This is used by males in generating stridulatory movements and by females in identifying sounds to approach (Bentley and Hoy, 1972). This model was put to a test by observing the response of *T. oceanicus* females to the normal song of their species and to an artificial song with the normal distribution of inter-pulse intervals jumbled together in an abnormal sequence. If the single template explanation for the behaviour of hybrids is correct, the females should only respond to the normal song; however they made no distinction between the two songs (Pollack and Hoy, 1979).

Finally, many of the examples quoted above show that differences in behaviour in one animal may be due to a genetic change in its social partners. Thus, remating time in female *D. melanogaster* can be reduced by artificial selection (see page 314). This is the result of an increase in the proportion of males with active esterase-6 in their seminal fluid; this enzyme is transferred to the female at copulation, promotes loss of sperm from the seminal vesicles and consequently accelerates remating in the female (Gilbert, Richmond and Sheehan, 1981).

8.7 The mechanisms whereby genes influence behaviour

The usual approach to this problem is to screen animals which show inherited behavioural variations for consistently occurring differences in morphology or physiology. If a correlation between a behavioural variant and a morphological/physiological difference is found, it may be that the latter causes the former; this possibility can be tested by experimentally altering the underlying trait in normal animals to see whether this produces a behavioural change. For example, two strains of mice which differ in susceptibility to audiogenic seizures may also vary in other characteristics such as size, coat colour and in the level of any number of biochemical compounds. While most of these differences will not occur consistently in all such comparisons, a regular association exists between low levels of brain neurotransmitters and susceptibility to seizures; artificially raising the level of these substances reduces the occurrence of seizures in susceptible animals. The difference in behaviour may therefore be the result of an alteration in genetic material coding for an enzyme in the metabolic pathway by which serotonin and/or noradrenaline are synthesized. The resulting lowered neurotransmitter levels make the brain more excitable and this makes the animal concerned more likely to have a seizure when exposed to sound.

8.7.1 EFFECTS ON THE STRUCTURES NECESSARY FOR PERFORMING THE BEHAVIOUR

As a rather obvious example, the spontaneously occurring mutant *vestigial* of *D. melanogaster* is wingless and males with this genetic defect, besides being unable to fly, are unable to perform effective wing vibrations during courtship (Lindsley and Grell, 1968). This impairs their mating success, but not as much as might be expected since *vestigial* males are active and remain close to receptive females, mating whenever the opportunity presents itself.

8.7.2 EFFECTS ON MUSCLES OR NEUROMUSCULAR JUNCTIONS

The mutant *unc 54* in *Caenorhabditis elegans*, detected because it produces uncoordinated movement, alters the chemical structure of the myosin filaments in certain body regions (Ward, 1977). The *wings up* mutant of *D. melanogaster* produces degeneration of the indirect wing muscles at pupation (Hotta and Benzer, 1972). In the same species the reversible temperature sensitive mutant *shibire* causes paralysis above 29 degrees, a temperature at which it also blocks neuromuscular transmission. Presumptive muscle and nerve cells from embryo flies homozygous for this condition develop abnormally in tissue culture, indicating that this mutant disrupts the process whereby nerve and muscle cells normally make functional contact (Buzin, Dewhurst and Seekof, 1978).

8.7.3 EFFECTS ON THE SENSE ORGANS

The difference in body angle during feeding in cave and river dwelling forms of the fish *Astyanax mexicanus* could be the result of an alteration in the position of the sense organs on the head. In the river form these are restricted to the mouth and lips but they spread over the lower jaw and underside of the head in the cave form. The behavioural difference between the two forms may thus be an indirect result of the need to bring these differently situated receptors into contact with the substrate (Schemmel, 1980).

Some mutants produce marked and obvious defects in the sense organs and their subsequent effect on behaviour is not hard to understand. Thus, many mutants which influence the response of the nematode *Caenorhabditis elegans* to chemical cues produce defects in the neurons of the sensory structures in the head. For example, Fig. 8.4 shows that worms with a mutation which impairs chemotaxis have alterations in the structure of sensory endings in the head which may be the site of at least part of the behavioural effect (Lewis and Hodgkin, 1977).

8.7.4 EFFECTS ON THE CNS

The *nervous* mutant which produces a variety of motor defects in mice, including abnormalities in grooming (see page 325), causes loss of most of the cerebellar Purkinje cells which play a key role in the feedback loop by which coordination of skilled movement is achieved (Northup, 1972). The possible neuropharmacological basis of audiogenic seizure susceptibility in mice has already been mentioned and similar alterations in neurotransmitter level have been implicated in many other inherited differences in complex behavioural traits.

Figure 8.4 Genes which influence behaviour by altering sense organs, lateral view of the tip of a sensory cell from the head of a normal *Caenorhabditis elegans* (left) and of a worm with a mutation (E 1034) which impairs chemotaxis (right) (from Lewis and Hodgkin, 1977).

The aim of the intensive research programme on *Caenorhabditis elegans* is to identify precisely the effects of specific behavioural mutants on the wiring of 300 or so neurons and ultimately to produce general rules about how genes effect the development of the nervous system. Some progress has been made in this direction although the behaviour patterns concerned are of limited interest to the field ethologist. For example, the mutant *unc 5* makes worms which are able to flex their bodies but, since the contractions are not propagated along the body, are unable to move effectively. In these animals the processes from the ventral nerve cord which normally join to form the dorsal nerve cord wander off erratically during development and therefore the dorsal muscles do not receive an organized nerve supply (Brenner, 1973; Ward, 1977). Other mutants which produce uncoordinated movements influence neurotransmitter synthesis; for example, alteration of a single allele results in loss of coordination and paralysis following stimulation; this is probably a result of the 98% drop in the activity of one form of the enzyme acetyl cholinesterase that the mutant also causes (Culotti *et al.*, 1981).

8.7.5 EFFECTS ON THE ENDOCRINE SYSTEM

An enormous number of inherited differences in the endocrine system have been identified (Shire, 1979) and many of these have behavioural effects. Mice with the mutant *obese* suffer from reduced synthesis of and sensitivity to insulin and as a consequence are obese, inactive and overeat (references quoted in Shire, 1979). Injection of juvenile hormone into some *D. melanogaster* females with a genetically produced inability to lay eggs stimulates ovulation, indicating that these flies may have impaired *corpora allata* (Szabad and Fajszi, 1982). It has been suggested that the reduced receptivity in *D. simulans* females selected for slow mating is due to an alteration in the production or use of juvenile hormone; the flies concerned have normally functioning *corpora allata*, and therefore if the idea is correct, the behavioural difference must be due to an alteration in sensitivity of some target organ (Manning, 1968).

8.7.6 EFFECTS ON SOME TOTALLY UNKNOWN MECHANISM

Notwithstanding all these examples, for the most part, the mechanism whereby an alteration in the genetic material brings about a change in behaviour is completely unknown. There are so many ways and places in which genes could potentially influence behaviour that deciding where to look for altered tissue is by no means easy. Even if a correlation has been established between such behavioural variation and the state of some morphological/physiological feature, this could be the cause or the effect of the behavioural change and both could be independent consequences of the same gene substitution. Again, even if it is the case that an inherited morphological/physiological change does cause the behavioural difference, this does not rule out the possibility that the gene concerned has other kinds of effects on the same behaviour, nor does it tell us how and when a change in the protein coded for by a single gene brings about the morphological change.

8.8 Genetic mosaics

Investigating the behaviour of genetic mosaics can help to solve some of these problems. If animals exist or can be produced which are a mixture of tissues of different genotypes, if the difference includes some genetic factor which influences behaviour and if it is possible to identify which tissue has which genotype, then we can discover the parts of the body which must be of a given genotype for a particular behavioural variant to be expressed. Such body regions are likely to be the primary sites of the behavioural effect of the differences in the genetic material.

Mosaics can be created by combining embryonic cells from animals of different genotypes; the zygote then develops into an individual which is a mixture of tissues of different genotypes (Breakefield, 1979). For example, mosaics were constructed from tissue of mice from two strains with inherited differences in various behaviour patterns including the tendency to kill crickets. The behaviour of the mosaic mice was recorded and their tissues were then assigned to the genotype of one or other strain. The sample sizes were small but there was an indication that cricket attack occurred in mosaics whose olfactory lobe and brainstem had the genotype of the killing strain (Nesbitt, 1978).

However, most work along these lines has been carried out on sex mosaics in *Drosophila melanogaster*. In this species, XX tissue is female and XO tissue is male; zygotes in which one X chromosome is lost during development survive to develop into flies with some XX tissue and some XO tissue. If the zygote was originally heterozygous for a sex linked recessive allele, this will be suppressed in the XX tissue and active in the XO tissue when the dominant allele is lost. Loss of an X chromosome is particularly likely in flies with an abnormal, ring X chromosome and the mechanics of this process are such that the progeny of flies with this aberrant X chromosome include animals which are mosaic for various different parts of their body. If the normal X chromosome carries recessive genes with detectable effects, such as the *yellow* allele which alters the colour of the cuticle, it is possible to identify which tissue is XX and which XO. Observation of a large number of animals with a range of different mosaic patterns allows identification of those parts of the body which must be mutant for abnormal behaviour controlled by a sex linked recessive allele to be displayed. For example, in mosaics with the *hyperkinetic* mutant (which causes the legs to twitch when the flies are anaesthetized) if a given leg shakes, it almost always, but not inevitably, has mutant cuticle; legs with mutant cuticle usually shake but do not always do so.

This indicates that tissue near but not quite at the surface of the leg is involved in production of the abnormal movements.

If it were possible to identify XO tissue in the internal organs, the altered tissue could be identified directly. In the absence of such internal markers, location of the affected tissue depends on a procedure called fate mapping. The blastoderm in *Drosophila* is a two dimensional layer of cells, defined areas of which give rise to specific adult structures. The closer two such sites are on the blastoderm, the less likely the line dividing normal from mutant tissue in a mosaic fly is to pass between them and the more likely the adult structures to which they give rise are to have the same genotype. If information about concordance of genotype is available for a number of pairs of adult structures, it is possible to map the relative positions of their primordia on the blastoderm to produce a fate map. The focus of a behavioural trait controlled by a recessive mutant can then be determined by working out how often it is associated with the XO condition at any two previously mapped structures. The adult tissues whose primordia are known to lie near the focus of the abnormal behaviour are likely to be those through which the mutant exerts its behavioural effects. Because location of the focus depends on bearings taken from any two structures which have already been mapped rather than on identification of abnormal tissue, the cause of the defect is unambiguously separated from its effects.

By this line of reasoning, the *hyperkinetic* mutant is found to have three foci, one for each pair of legs, lying near the primordia of that leg but slightly below it, in the area which gives rise to the ventral nervous system; this suggests that the thoracic ganglia may be the site at which the behavioural effects of this mutant are exerted. In contrast, the focus of the mutant *wings-up*, in which the wings are held in an abnormal position, lies in the region of the blastoderm which gives rise to muscle tissue, indicating that this mutant produces its behavioural effects by altering the muscles which determine wing position rather than the nerves which activate them. Subsequent histological analysis showed that this is indeed the case.

Theoretically, fate maps have one great advantage over the use of non-mosaic mutants or of mosaics without mapping, in that they can distinguish between cause and effect. However, computing the position of the focus of a behavioural mutant is very complex and may be too inaccurate for it to be unambiguously associated with the precursors of a particular adult tissue (Hall, 1979). Where internal markers are available, association of mutant tissue with behavioural phenotype without fate mapping may give more useful results. For example, studies of the distribution of a recessive allozyme marker in mosaic flies indicates that the lamina and the photoreceptors of the ommatidia come from different blastoderm regions and that the lamina is mutant in mosaics with an impaired optomotor response (Benzer, 1973; Hall, 1979).

The main use to which genetic mosaics have been put in conjunction with internal markers depends on the fact that mosaics produced as a result of loss of the ring X in *Drosophila* are also gynandromorphs; these are used to identify those parts of the body which must be of a particular sex if the fly is to show female or male sexual behaviour. The procedure involves creating a large number of mosaic flies with external and, in some cases, internal markers and giving them three main kinds of test: mosaic flies are placed with normal males and performance of the various components of female sexual behaviour recorded, mosaic flies are placed with normal males to determine whether they elicit courtship from the

Table 8.5 Using genetic mosaics to unravel the mechanisms controlling complex behaviour sequences; a summary of the results of mosaic analysis of the control of sexual behaviour in the male and female *Drosophila*. (After Hall, 1979; Hotta and Benzer, 1976; Nissani, 1977; von Schilcher and Hall, 1979; Szabad and Fajszi, 1980; Tomkins and Hall, 1983.)

Behaviour	Focus
Female	
Receptivity to male courtship	Head; dorsal anterior brain Female tissue on both sides is necessary and sufficient for receptivity
Detection of insemination Location of oviposition site Rate of oviposition	Head; probably the brain; behaviour normal if head cuticle is female
Transfer of eggs to uterus Egg deposition movements	Thorax; behaviour normal if thoracic cuticle is female
Attractiveness to male	Abdomen, probably subcuticular; attract courtship if female proportion of abdomen is above a critical value
Release of sperm from spermatheca	Location of focus uncertain; not in head
Male	
Follow Tap Extend wing	Head; dorsal posterior brain Male tissue is one side only sufficient for normal behaviour
Licking	Head; dorsal posterior brain Male tissue on both sides necessary
Song production	Thorax; localized focus in nervous system
Attempted copulation	Thorax; diffuse focus

males and finally mosaic flies are placed with normal females and performance of the various components of male courtship recorded. The results of several such studies are summarized in Table 8.5.

These complex and extensive investigations have provided a great deal of information about the control and integration of sexual behaviour in *Drosophila melanogaster* in a degree of detail which would be hard to match using conventional techniques. In addition, they suggest possible sites of action for a number of mutants which are known to influence sexual behaviour in fruit flies; for example, *fruitless* may alter the abdominal, subcuticular tissue which makes female flies attractive while *cacophany* may alter the neural tissue in the thorax which determines song production in males.

8.9 Animal behaviour and behavioural genetics

At the start of this chapter, a number of ways were outlined in which a knowledge of the genetics of behaviour could contribute to our understanding of animal behaviour; the examples have been chosen to illustrate these. Thus, genetic mosaics have been used to unravel the physiological bases of courtship sequences in *Drosophila melanogaster* and, in the same species, heritability studies have shown that natural selection has acted on mating speed and courtship song in different ways. However, these are questions which could have been answered by other techniques and the impact of genetics on our understanding of animal behaviour must be assessed by considering those areas of research for which information about the inheritance of behaviour is essential.

Brenner's hope (1973) that studies of genetically determined behavioural variants would allow identification of general principles about the construction of nervous systems has not yet been realized. Certainly, many of the inherited behavioural mutants discussed in this chapter do interfere with neurogenesis but broadly applicable rules have yet to be drawn from such results. However, the number of cases in which the physiological and/or morphological basis of genetic effects on behaviour are known is increasing rapidly; given time, these results may be put together to produce general principles about the way genes and environment interact to determine the course of behavioural development.

As far as our understanding of the evolution of behaviour is concerned, the results of laboratory based studies on the behavioural effects of artificially generated mutants at single loci are of little direct relevance. However, since so many theoretical models on this subject assume that substitution of one allele for another at a single locus can bring about a major behavioural change, it is useful to demonstrate the range of behavioural differences which can potentially be produced by this sort of small-scale genetic change. Thus information about the kinds of things that happen to *Caenorhabditis elegans* when its parent eats mutagenic food might be of value to sociobiologists and behavioural ecologists.

However, the main contribution of behavioural genetics in this area lies in its identification of the mechanisms of inheritance underlying naturally occurring differences in behaviour. Differences in schooling tendencies between isolated populations of guppies persist when the fish are reared in identical conditions (Seghers, 1974), the social structure of hybrids between olive and hamadryas baboons (*Papio hamadryas*) is intermediate between those of the parent species (Nagel, 1971) and small groups of mice from different inbred strains show different social systems when housed in large, complex cages (Hahn, 1971). Such studies of the inheritance of complex patterns of social organization are rare but even so, the examples discussed in this chapter include a wide range of behaviour patterns of a kind which have been studied by behavioural ecologists and socio-biologists (Chapter 5). Thus genetic differences have been shown to influence the age at which platyfish breed (Kallman and Schreibman, 1973), patterns of migration and dispersal in voles and warblers (Krebs, 1979; Berthold and Querner, 1981), choice of habitat in fruit flies (Taylor and Powell, 1977), behavioural rhythmicity in flies (Konopka and Benzer, 1971; Kyriacou and Hall, 1980), diet breadth in deer mice (Gray, 1979), foraging patterns in fruit flies (Sokolowski, 1980), territoriality and aggressiveness in crickets and char (Hörmann-Heck, 1957; Ferguson and Noakes, 1982) and parental behaviour in mice (Plomin and Manosevitz, 1974). Inherited differences have also been identified in a whole range of sexual behaviour (mostly in *Drosophila*) including number of mating partners (Gromko and Pyle, 1978; Gilbert, Richmond and Sheehan, 1981), competition between males for females (Kyriacou, 1981), selection of mates by females (Zouros, 1981) and the use of alternative strategies for reproductive competition (Cade, 1981). Finally, genetic influences on altruistic behaviour, the central issue of sociobiology, in the form of care and defence of siblings have been discovered (Rothenbuhler, 1964; Collins, 1979).

Thus genetic analysis is underway, and in some cases at an advanced stage, on all the main subject areas of behavioural ecology and sociobiology. There are some general lessons to be learned from these results: in the first place, as most sociobiologists assume, there is indeed an inherited component to much naturally occurring behavioural variation and in a few cases fairly simple genetic differences can produce marked alteration in behaviour. However, the precise genetic mechanism varies considerably from case to case and polygenic inheritance is the rule rather than the exception where behavioural traits are concerned. The assumption of most sociobiological models that a marked behavioural difference is the result of substitution of one allele for another at a single locus is only likely to prove realistic in a few cases. In addition, environmental factors have been shown to be a significant source of variation for many of the traits discussed above. This fact should be given weight when considering the likely effect of natural selection on identified behavioural differences.

In spite of their obvious relevance, the results of genetic analysis of specific behavioural patterns have not often been linked to sociobiological studies of the same subject. There are two main reasons for this; in the first place, geneticists have been deterred by the naïve picture of inheritance presented by much sociobiological theorizing. Secondly, the traditional subjects of genetic analysis and therefore the animals for which facts and techniques are readily available, are not those of sociobiological research; in fact there is almost a negative correlation between the amount of behavioural genetic and sociobiological interest that different species have attracted. Thus while an enormous amount of research has been carried out on the ecology and behaviour of *Drosophila*, the archetypal subject for genetic research, this is not usually viewed in a sociobiological framework. Equally, while a great deal is known about the behavioural genetics of mice, these animals have also received little attention from sociobiologists. On the other hand, our ignorance about the inheritance of the behaviour of the famous sociobiological species (the red-winged blackbird, the lion, the dung fly) is almost complete. Honey bees present something of an exception to this rule in that while their social systems are of central importance in sociobiological theory, they have been the subject of some behavioural genetic analyses; even here, few attempts have been made to combine these areas of interest. Two solutions suggest themselves; in the first place, sociobiologists might apply their ideas and techniques to species such as mice and fruit flies whose genetics are well known and whose behaviour in the wild is complex and interesting. Secondly, they might make efforts to interest behavioural geneticists in the kinds of behavioural differences which form the subject of sociobiological research, once these have been precisely defined. Cade's (1981) investigation of the genetic basis of different mating strategies in crickets is an example of what can be achieved when the ideas and techniques of these two different approaches to behaviour are combined.

CHAPTER 9

Applied ethology

9.1 Clarification of terms; what is applied ethology?

The characteristics of ethology which distinguish it from other approaches to the study of animal behaviour are the emphasis placed on detailed observation of the movements of unconstrained animals, preferably in their natural habitat, and the application of Darwinian evolutionary theory to behaviour. Research by ethologists has addressed questions about the causes, development, function and evolution of behaviour and has provided part of the body of knowledge and theory which is now labelled behavioural ecology or sociobiology.

The aim of this chapter is to discuss the extent to which ethology can be applied outside its primary area of concern, namely the understanding of behaviour in non-human animals. In what follows, a piece of research is designated as applied if it is used in an attempt to solve one of a number of kinds of problem. Some are of obvious economic or medical importance; thus, ethological research can be used in pest control and in enhancing the productivity of commercially important animals. Other problems, such as devising rational conservation programmes and ensuring the wellbeing of the animals we exploit are aesthetic or moral ones, although their solution may have economically important consequences. Finally, for the present purposes, ethological research which helps us understand our own behaviour is considered as applied whether or not its results have any direct medical, sociological or economic benefit.

To demonstrate a practical application of ethology, it is not sufficient to show that it is sometimes useful to know how animals behave. For example, in order to assess the effectiveness of a new insecticide, it is clearly necessary to know whether insects will come in contact with it. An obvious test is to place a surface treated with the substance in places where the potential victims live and see whether they land on it, yet such an experiment would have been devised and carried out if ethology did not exist; while this would be a piece of practical research involving behaviour it would not represent a triumph of applied ethology. On the other hand, following the development of the ethological concept of the sign stimulus and subsequent efforts to identify and catalogue these, chemical sex attractants with spectacular effects on the behaviour of insects were discovered. The use of such chemicals in the field of pest control is an example of a practical application of ethological research.

This chapter is called 'Applied Ethology' in the interests of brevity rather than because all the work discussed was carried out by people who would describe themselves as ethologists. To be more precise, the subject matter is the practical contribution made by the modern approach to the study of animal behaviour which has at least some of its roots in classical ethology. For example, in order to determine the potential effects of competing species or predators on commercial fish stocks, a question of obvious economic importance, stomach analyses are often carried out; this is an ecological technique, being used to answer a classical ecological question. However, if the theory of optimal foraging is used in interpreting the results, the concepts of behavioural ecology are influencing an attempt to solve a practical problem and the work therefore qualifies for inclusion in this chapter.

9.2 Ways in which ethological research can be applied to practical problems

In all these fields, scientific research in the ethological tradition can contribute in practical matters in three broadly distinct but, inevitably, overlapping ways.

9.2.1 DIRECT APPLICATION OF THE RESULTS OF ETHOLOGICAL RESEARCH

In the most direct application, the actual facts that ethologists discover can be put to work. For example, ethological observations on starlings (*Sternus vulgaris*) showed that these birds give a particular call when disturbed by a predator with the result that the flock takes off and moves to a new feeding area. Taking advantage of this fact, tape recordings of alarm calls have been played to flocks of starlings to prevent their feeding where they are not wanted (Albright, 1976).

Here, the facts are applied to the species on which the original observation was made. In other cases, facts derived from ethological studies of one species have been used to suggest solutions to practical problems involving different species. To give a famous example, Lorenz's observations on territorial fish led him to suggest (probably incorrectly) that their aggression is an instinctive drive which inevitably builds up in animals deprived of the opportunity to fight and which finally finds outlet in attack on some suboptimal stimulus (see page 6). Applying this interpretation of the facts to human behaviour, he suggested that attempts to control human aggression by avoiding situations which elicit it are doomed to failure and that harmless discharge of the aggressive drive, for example in sport, is the only way to control violence (Lorenz, 1966). Even supposing that his original interpretation of the behaviour of fish was correct, such use of ethological facts is problematic since it makes assumptions about the identity of important processes in the groups concerned; these assumptions need to be, but seldom are, tested.

9.2.2 USING THE IDEAS AND CONCEPTS OF ETHOLOGY

Less controversially, the ideas and principles resulting from ethological research can be used to suggest possible solutions to practical problems, although there is no simple distinction between extrapolating facts and using ideas. For example, as already mentioned, the complex models of optimal foraging theory can be used to find effective ways of managing fish stocks. Similarly, the idea that strong and lasting social bonds can form during a sensitive period with no conventional rewards (i.e. imprinting) has been used by Bowlby (1980) in an attempt to understand the effects in humans of early disruption of parent–child relationships.

9.2.3 USING ETHOLOGICAL TECHNIQUES

Lastly, the techniques of observing and analysing the movements of un-constrained animals have been deliberately applied to practical problems. Descriptions of simple movements and the sequential relationships between them in mothers and their babies have been used to pinpoint differences in behavioural development between normal and retarded children (Vietze *et al.*, 1978). Ethograms describing the proportion of time spent in the various components of the behavioural repertoire have been used to detect distress in domestic animals (Wood-Gush, Duncan and Fraser, 1975).

There are many cases in which ethological research has been applied to practical problems and it is not possible to describe them all here. The examples used in this chapter could have been organized in a number of different ways, none of which is entirely satisfactory; they could be classified according to whether facts, principles or techniques are used, whether the contribution is of medical, economic or sociological importance or according to the nature of the problem to be solved. The last of these methods of classification is used here; thus examples are chosen to illustrate the application of ethological research to pest control, to productivity of commercially important animals, to animal welfare, to conservation and to our knowledge and understanding of human behaviour.

9.3 Pest control

There are many examples in which behavioural studies have been used to control the abundance and distribution of animals which have been designated as pests, whether their harmful nature lies in a threat to our domestic plants and animals, to our health or to our comfort. The most famous case in which results obtained by pure ethological research have been applied to pest control is the use of pheromones to eliminate harmful insects. The term pheromone was coined by Karlson and Lüscher (1959) to refer to smells produced by one animal which alter the behaviour of others. Such scents and the reaction to them provide prime examples of the release of behaviour by highly specific features of the environment; the sex attractant of the silk moth (*Bombyx mori*) is the classic example. Extraordinarily low concentrations of this chemical are sufficient to activate mate searching and courtship in the male moths and the sensory basis of this specificity is now well understood (Kasang and Kaissling, 1972). Such sex attractants can be used in a number of ways. For example, they can be artificially disseminated in order to interfere with location of females in the wild or used as bait to trap insect pests.

Because of the great fecundity of insects and because a single male can fertilize a large number of females, trapping and killing is only successful if such pests are in fairly low numbers. In species in which the female is known to mate only once, a much more effective technique of control is to release sterilized males into the environment. Each female mated by such a male is effectively removed from the breeding population while still using up food and egg sites. This technique has been used in an extensive programme aimed at control of the screwworm, the larva of the dipteran fly (*Cochliomyia hominivorax*) which lives in open wounds on domestic livestock and wild mammals, eating its way through their flesh. Since females are known to mate only once, enormous numbers of commercially produced male flies sterilized by X-irradiation were released in the United States in 1962. As a result, the number of infestations reported annually dropped from over fifty thousand to a few hundred in two years; this represented a spectacular success for a control programme based on a knowledge of the breeding behaviour of the pest species (Novy, 1978). However, from 1972 onwards the number of reported cases of screwworms increased; this was partly due to reduced vigilance on the part of the farmers but also partly due to an apparent loss of effectiveness of the biological control. In spite of occasional introduction of wild flies into the breeding programme, the commercial stocks have apparently become genetically distinct from their wild counterparts; in particular, they differ in the form of one enzyme involved in energy metabolism. As a result, energy production is optimal at a different temperature and the flies' activity rhythm is altered. Instead of being active throughout the day, commercially produced flies do not become active until the afternoon, by which time the wild females have all been mated by fertile males. The sterile males are probably less effective in competition for females, partly because of the side-effects of radiation and partly as a result of the alteration in their energy metabolism. It is also possible that wild female flies have responded to the selection pressure imposed by the control programme and mate preferentially with non-irradiated males. More research on the reproductive behaviour of these flies is necessary if these possibilities are to be tested and dealt with (Bush, 1978).

The statement that more information is needed about the biology of the species concerned if control is to be effective is a cliché, but it is still true, although it is easy to be wise after the event. An example of a simple and very successful method of pest control which is based on a broad knowledge of the behaviour of a pest species concerns the herring gull. Outwith the breeding season, these birds forage in loose flocks and roost gregariously at night in safe places. They give two distinct calls which concern danger of predation; the alarm call is emitted by a bird in response to a perceived threat and causes its neighbours to take wing and return when the danger disappears. The distress call is given by a herring gull which has actually been seized by a predator and is therefore in extreme danger; a proportion of nearby birds approach and watch and then depart.

Gull populations have increased dramatically over the course of this century; the birds have taken to breeding in towns and may present a health hazard by feeding on rubbish tips and roosting on reservoirs (Benton et al., 1983). Since the population of gulls at a particular roost is constantly changing, there is little prospect of frightening the birds away permanently with a single, nasty experience. However, by playing taped distress calls (normally a sign that a predator has just caught a gull) at a roost, when and only when the gulls attempt to land, they can be made to leave the site to roost elsewhere. Since the sound is played as infrequently as possible and in accordance with the behaviour of the gulls, their response does not habituate. Using this procedure at a large reservoir near Glasgow caused the gulls to abandon it and settle on a nearby estuary; as a result, the numbers of microorganisms in the water supply has dropped dramatically. Thus, given a broad background knowledge of the behaviour of herring gulls and detailed information about the context, causes, immediate consequences and ultimate functions of the calls they give to predators, effective pest control programmes can be developed.

In this case, most of the information on which the programme was based was collected during purely theoretical studies, but a great deal of research in the ethological tradition is now being carried out with control of specific pests urgently in mind. For example, the fox is one of several wild mammals which can catch and spread rabies and in some areas it is the most important vector. A great deal of information has been collected about the incidence of this disease in relation to factors such as fox density, but in order to understand the way rabies spreads through a previously uninfested area and to devise effective controls, detailed knowledge of the feeding habits, dispersion patterns and social interactions of these animals is necessry. To this end, several intensive studies of these aspects of fox behaviour are being carried out using, among other things, the techniques and principles which ethologists have developed. The results of this research, which are summarized in MacDonald (1980), also have implications for animal welfare and conservation since the disease is horrible and the control methods used have drastic effects on the foxes and on other wildlife.

Studies of the feeding patterns of foxes indicate that they distribute their feeding effort in different areas as predicted by optimal foraging theory and that they cache food. This has implications for fox control, whether by poisons or oral vaccines, since these are put out in bait (MacDonald, 1980). Studies of the movement of foxes with tags and radiotransmitters indicate that part of the fox population remains in a relatively fixed area while the rest disperse. These itinerant foxes are mostly sub-adult dogs and in both these groups males move more than females; their movement patterns depend on the topography of the area and on fox density. Simultaneous radiotracking of several foxes and direct observation show that groups ranging from one pair with young to one male, several females and their offspring live in a single territory the size of which varies in response to food supply. Where several females coexist, one dominant female suppresses reproduction in the others. Thus, fox behaviour is variable in a way which can be related to environmental conditions according to the theories of behavioural ecology. This variability, together with the fact that a floating population of males and a reservoir of non-breeding females are present, needs to be taken into account when devising fox control programmes for a particular area.

A number of computer models have been constructed which simulate the movements and social interactions of foxes, on the basis of realistic assumptions about their behaviour. These are then used to identify the factors which determine the rate of contact between animals in a given area and thus the probability and pattern of spread of rabies through it; altering the level of these key variables will be the most fruitful way of controlling the disease. The parameters of the models cannot yet be assessed with sufficient accuracy to allow them to be used in this way. With more behavioural and ecological data, however, such computer simulations would allow rational decisions to be made about the size of killing zone around a rabies focus which is necessary to prevent the disease spreading should it reach Britain. They may therefore allow the disease to be controlled with minimum cost, in terms of both money and ecological damage.

9.4 Increasing the productivity of commercially important species

There is increasing pressure to maximize profits in all areas where other organisms are exploited commercially, such as fisheries and agriculture; in some cases the methods by which this is achieved depend on research into animal behaviour. For example, in spite of the enormous sums of money spent on stocking rivers and lakes with hatchery reared trout and salmon, these contribute rather little to catches. One possible reason why stocking programmes have been so unsuccessful is that hatchery reared fish often behave abnormally; a major concern has therefore been to identify and, if possible, to find ways of rectifying, behavioural deficits in hatchery reared fish.

A number of behavioural features characterize the species which have been successfully domesticated in the past; they tend to be herbivorous or omnivorous, to live in social groups with the capacity to form stable dominance relationships, to mate promiscuously and to have precocial young which form a close social bond with their mother. In addition, they appear to be especially flexible in the range of environments (physical and social) in which they will remain healthy and breed successfully (Craig, 1981). In an attempt to find suitable candidates for domestication among the large social ungulates of the African savannah, the behaviour of a number of species was observed as the animals roamed about large enclosures. The oryx has a suitable carcass, a desirable property in a candidate for domestication, its daily pattern of activity is independent of the heat (unlike the eland, it does not stop eating when it gets too hot) and it has a naturally short daily feeding time. Both these behavioural attributes make controlling feeding easier. On the other hand, groups of oryx do not synchronize their activities, which presents some problems for management, but on balance, the oryx is a good candidate for domestication (Lewis, 1977).

9.4.2 SELECTION FOR DESIRED BEHAVIOURAL ATTRIBUTES

Selection for suitable behavioural qualities, whether aggressiveness in fighting cocks or tractability in gun dogs, has been practised for centuries without the guiding hand of ethology, on the basis of a familiarity with individual animals. Systematic studies of animals along ethological lines can provide some substitute for such intimacy in modern farming conditions. For example, ten minute observations of a number of cocks placed singly with a flock of eight hens allowed marked individual differences in courtship behaviour and in the frequency of mounting to be detected. These were then used as the basis for a selective breeding programme for males with high and low levels of mating; eleven generations of breeding from the two ends of the behaviour continuum produced significant effects in both directions (Siegel, 1965; Cook and Siegel, 1972).

9.4.3 CONTROLLING DISPERSAL AND MOVEMENT

The movement patterns of salmon must be understood in order to predict the return of introduced fish. Since the risk of predation is high during seaward migration and since migrating in groups reduces vulnerability, it is important to understand what determines the timing of this downstream journey. A comparison of two Atlantic salmon (*Salmo salar*) populations showed that fry from one site, 132 km from the sea, migrate in the autumn while those from another, only 42 km from the sea, migrate the following spring. It was suggested that this difference is a result of the higher energetic costs of overwintering in the first site, which is colder and in which resident fish lose weight during the winter. It may also be that early migration ensures that salmon from the upstream site reach the lower regions of the river system, where predators are abundant, at the same time as those from the downstream sites and thus find safety in numbers (Riddell and Leggett, 1981).

Although it is of commercial importance that small, young salmon reach the sea successfully, it is even more important that the fully grown adults return to places from which they can be harvested. Olfactory cues are important in the homing of Coho salmon (*Onchorhynchus kisutch*) (Hasler, 1960) and trans-portation experiments suggest that young salmon may learn the smell of their stream at the time when migration starts. Thus a long-term memory appears to be formed at an early stage which influences preferences in later life, a clear analogy with imprinting. Experimental demonstration of such a process was achieved by exposing salmon parr to morpholine (a chemical with a strong persistent smell) and releasing these, together with control fish which had been kept in tanks but not exposed, in equal numbers in several streams. Eighteen months later, when the fish were due to make their homeward migration for breeding, morpholine was introduced into a creek at a rate which produced concentrations similar to that used in the earlier exposure. Of the salmon which were trapped at the entrance to this creek, 1092 were from the experienced group and 143 were from the controls. Exposed fish arrived at the morpholine-smelling creek regardless of where they were released and even when the concentration used in the initial exposure was very small. Equal numbers of morpholine-treated and untreated fish returned to the same creek in an experiment performed later when no morpholine was released at the site (Cooper *et al.*, 1976). Finally, the EEG responses to morpholine of fish in the exposed group were much stronger than those of the controls (Cooper and Hasler, 1976). These results raised the possibility of controlling when the salmon migrate to the sea and where they return.

9.4.4 PROMOTING SURVIVAL

Young salmonids are attacked by a number of predatory birds and fish and their ability to avoid these will have a considerable impact on the economic success of commercial fisheries. The ethological literature suggests that the poor survival of hatchery reared fish may be a consequence of lack of experience of predators, although this is obviously not the only source of such an hypothesis. In an attempt to test this idea, two groups of hatchery reared sockeye salmon fry (*O. nerka*) were established, one of which experienced a single short encounter with a predator while the other remained naive. When the fish were subsequently exposed to a hunting rainbow trout in an artificial stream, 98% of the experienced fish but only 83% of the naive fish survived. This difference is a result of formation of compact schools by the experienced fish, which also showed lower general activity and greater reactivity to the predator than did the naive fish. Thus, brief exposure to a predator provides a possible, if costly, way of enhancing the viability of hatchery reared salmon. Since the effect of handling the fish was similar to the effect of exposure to a predator (90% of handled fish survive predation as opposed to 80% unhandled), some sort of physical manipulation may provide a substitute for direct experience (Ginetz and Larkin, 1976).

Ethological studies can help prevent disease among domestic animals; thus it is possible to get early warning of a disease by detecting subtle behavioural changes and this may allow a potential epidemic to be nipped in the bud. In addition, as any one who has the time and opportunity to observe domestic animals knows, given appropriate conditions animals behave in such a way as to promote their own wellbeing. For example, in a sufficiently large paddock, cows will avoid the lush green grass that grows around cowpats for long enough to ensure that any germs on them have died (Ekesbo, 1978), given enough space, pigs will feed and defecate in different areas and thus avoid infecting themselves (Wood-Gush and Stolba, 1981) and given the opportunity to groom themselves and their companions and to scratch and wallow will keep their skin in good condition (Van Putten, 1978). It is probably (though not necessarily) more economic to give the animals conditions in which they can look after themselves than to deprive them of these and then have to pay a vet to do the same things.

9.4.5 PROMOTING GROWTH

Because of its obvious relevance to productivity, what commercially important animals eat has been intensively studied and recently the results of such research have been interpreted in terms of optimal foraging theory. A series of observations and experiments on young Atlantic salmon prior to migration illustates this approach. The primary function of this stage in the complicated life cycle of the salmon is to grow and the more successfully this is achieved, the more likely the fish is to survive the rigours of its downstream migration. There is thus strong selection pressure on the young fish to feed efficiently and since in most cases their reproductive tissue is not developing, optimal foraging should maximize somatic growth. At this age, the salmon live in streams, feeding on the bottom as well as on food particles drifting in the current. Feeding on the drift is a much simpler strategy than those considered in many optimal foraging studies, since searching and handling time is minimal; however, it involves the energetic cost of maintaining a position in mid-current. Underwater observations showed that the distribution of wild salmon correlates positively with current speed and thus with the abundance of drift food, indicating that the fish established their feeding stations in areas of high food availability (Wankowsky and Thorpe, 1979a). Laboratory experiments in which salmon were fed on food particles of different sizes identified the food size which resulted in the highest growth rates; these range in diameter from 0.022–0.026 times their tail fork length (Wankowsky and

Thorpe, 1979b). As part of a broader study, a series of laboratory experiments, in which salmon in artificial streams were fed particles of various sizes one at a time, were then carried out during the summer, a time at which growth is rapid in the wild. Table 9.1 summarizes the percentage of food particles of different sizes which elicited a response and which were subsequently captured and ingested as well as the maximum distance from which a response was observed. The fish are clearly selective in the size of particle they will fixate and capture and in what they will swallow after capture, food particles between 0.018 and 0.051 fork lengths (which includes the optimal size identified in the previous experiment) being eaten preferentially although other sized particulae are taken occasionally (Wankowsky, 1981). Stomach analyses of wild salmon of this age showed that these fish feed predominantly, although again not exclusively, on food items in the same size range (Wankowsky, 1979). Thus, juvenile salmon appear to select food of a size which maximizes growth although they also sample food in other size categories. Such results make a contribution to the literature on optimal foraging theory but also have implications for selection of suitable sites for introducing fish stocks, for any provisioning that may be attempted and for predicting interactions between the introduced fish and the existing fauna.

Table 9.1 Applying optimal foraging theory to the feeding behaviour of salmon (after Wankowsky, 1981).

For prey passing through fixation zone			
Mean particle diameter (in fish lengths)	*Percentage of particles eliciting a response*	*Maximum overt response distance (in fish lengths)*	*Percentage of visible particles captured*
0.013	18	2.8	66
0.018	73	12.6	100
0.025	83	18.0	80
0.051	79	16.6	86
0.102	84	14.8	0

Feeding behaviour in domestic animals has also been the subject of applied behavioural research along ethological lines. To give a single example, the sequential relationships between eight different activities including feeding, drinking and standing at rest, were analysed in cows observed at different times of day; the results, which are presented in Fig. 9.1, show that not only does grazing occur at night as well as in the daytime but that at this time it is the dominant activity in the behavioural sequence (Low *et al.*, 1981). The management practice of putting cows on poor pasture during the night has been reassessed in the light of this sort of observation (Castle, Foot and Halley, 1950).

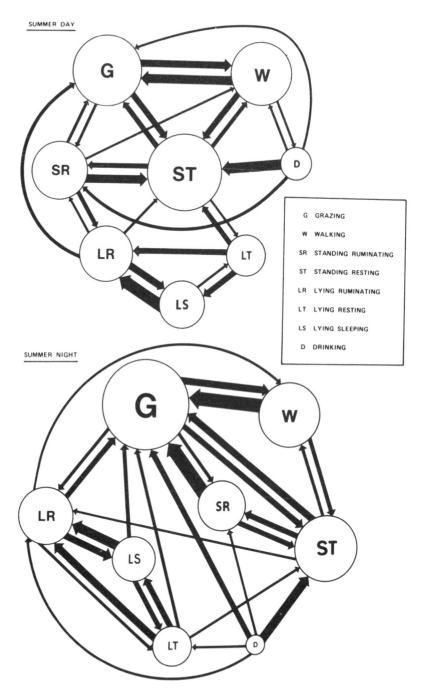

Figure 9.1 Applying ethological techniques to the behaviour of domestic animals; transition frequencies for various behaviour patterns shown by cows at different times of day. The diameter of the circles represents the frequency of occurrence of each act, the width of the lines represents the frequency of transitions between acts (from Low *et al.*, 1981, after Arnold and Dudzinsky, 1979).

Social relationships also have significant effects on feeding and growth. For example, dominance hierarchies have been described for most domestic species; whether or not this social system is observed under more natural conditions, dominant animals often interfere with attempts by their subordinates to obtain food if this is supplied in a restricted area. For example, when dairy cows were fed in pairs from a small trough, the subordinate animal was observed to feed for only seven seconds in a three minute observation period. This influence of rank on feeding was shown to depend on direct physical contact between the cows and the length of time spent feeding by the subordinate animal can be increased to over two minutes in three by placing a simple barrier across the trough and thus preventing head contact between the cows (Bouissou, 1970).

On the other hand, the strong social facilitation displayed by many gregarious animals when given sufficient opportunity to control their own behaviour can be used to promote feeding in livestock. For example, feeding on solid food by piglets immediately after weaning, a period when weight loss is common, was promoted by placing them in a cage next door to a litter which was still suckling; the weaned piglets began to feed whenever they heard their neighbours suckling (Kilgour, 1978).

However much animals eat, weight gain is not maximal if the conditions in which they are housed and the ways in which they are handled are stressful. In order to detect and reduce such stress, it is necessary to be familiar with the full behavioural repertoire of the species concerned, including their natural social structure. To this end, many detailed observational studies of domestic animals and their undomesticated relatives under unrestrained conditions have been carried out. Considering only the most important farm animals, wild and domestic pigs have been studied by Gundlach (1968) and Wood-Gush and Solba (1981), cows by Reinhardt and Reinhardt (1981), horses by Tyler (1972) and Collery (1974), sheep by Geist (1971), Grubb and Jewell (1966) and Arnold and Pahl (1974) and chickens by Kruijt (1964) and Wood-Gush and Duncan (1976).

Taking pigs as an example, a group of domesticated swine (consisting of one boar, several castrate males and adult females and a number of young) were observed over a long period in a large, hilly field containing a number of trees and bushes. The pigs exploited the space systematically, marking it at various points and using separate areas for feeding, defecating and sleeping. They slept in nests built of sticks and grass, with the opening face downhill. The group was highly structured along family lines, piglets forming long lasting social bonds with their mother and with their siblings, with whom they foraged, slept and played. Females detached themselves from the main group when they were about to give birth, building a small nest which they defended against the other pigs for about five days (Wood-Gush and Stolba, 1981; Stolba, 1982). The behaviour observed in these domesticated pigs was therefore complex and resembled that described for wild pigs by Gundlach (1968).

There is evidence that disturbing natural social organization by housing animals in isolation or disturbing established groups is stressful to the animals concerned. For example, milk yield dropped by 5% when strangers were introduced into a herd of dairy cows, although the precise nature of this effect is unclear (Sowerby and Polan, 1978). Most commercial pigfarms house fattening pigs and breeding sows separately, in extremely simple pens. In order to ensure that groups of sows farrow simultaneously and that fattening pigs therefore reach marketable size at the same time, the groups are frequently rearranged. On the basis of their observations of pigs in less constrained circumstances, Stolba and Wood-Gush have designed what they call an 'enriched pen' which incorporates the 'ethologically minimum housing needs'. The pen (which is quite small, requires no heating other than a farrowing lamp and is easy to clean) is divided into a roofed and an open section to simulate a forest border and has a large, sheltered nest area in the angle between two walls. A main defecation site is provided away from the nest, as well as a corridor which simulates tracks between bushes in which pigs defacate while foraging. In different parts of the pen are placed a levered bar and peat to form a rooting area, a rack with straw for nesting and a post for marking. The feeding stall is small, but has partitions to separate the animals, and, finally, one area is set aside for activity and another for escape. A group of breeding sows, two younger than the others, is kept permanently in the pen together with all their offspring (which are weaned naturally and remain in the group until they are removed for marketing). A familiar breeding boar is rotated between three or four such groups, spending about six weeks at a time in each pen. Under these conditions, the pigs show all the components of their normal repertoire, long lasting relationships between pigs are formed and the piglets grow extremely well, partly because they do not suffer the usual post-weaning weight loss. Thus given sufficient information about the natural behaviour of pigs, a housing system was devised which is practical and economical, which allows the pigs to behave naturally and which also promotes growth.

9.4.6 PROMOTING SUCCESSFUL REPRODUCTION

In these enriched pens, the females come into oestrus synchronously, perhaps because they frequently smell each others' urine; they can therefore all be mated during a single visit from the boar and their piglets are born and reach a suitable size for marketing at about the same time. Thus a condition which at present requires considerable rearrangement and disturbance of the pigs can be obtained by simply leaving them alone. In addition, the sows regularly come into oestrus during lactation, a rare occurrence in most management systems, and thus produce more litters.

The results of ethological research have been used to enhance reproductive output of domestic animals in other ways. Courtship behaviour is as important in persuading females to mate and in promoting the chances of successful fertilization in domestic animals as in wild ones. For example, there is a significant correlation between the number of times a boar noses a female before mounting her and the probability of conception, conception rate in sows that are courted prior to artificial insemination is 86.7%, as opposed to 62.1% in females which do not receive these attentions (Hemsworth, Beilhatz and Brown, 1978). Since the breeding system within which mating occurs is an important and probably adaptive aspect of reproduction, it is not surprising that the ratio of males to females when copulations are arranged for domestic animals is an important determinant of the outcome. For example, groups of 6, 12, 18 and 30 oestrus ewes were placed with a single ram and the number of females mounted, the number of times they were mounted and whether or not they conceived were recorded. In the largest group all 30 ewes were mated but each one was mounted infrequently; in addition, the percentage of conceptions dropped from 87% in the smallest to 56% in the largest group. The lower conception rate is thought to be a direct result of the smaller number of mountings each female received (Bryant and Tomkins, 1975).

Observations of the breeding behaviour of salmonids have shown that a proportion of males mature precociously, sneak fertilizations with females which are being courted by adult males, fail to migrate and probably die in the subsequent winter (Jones, 1959). The proportion of such precocial males can be as high at 60%; this represents a sizeable commercial loss since, however much the fish themselves may gain in fitness as a result of maturing precociously, they do not turn into useable adults. This loss is exaggerated by the fact that it is often the larger males in a group of young fish which mature precociously. Considerable research has therefore been aimed at identifying the factors which determine how many males mature early; water temperature is clearly one of these but genetically determined predispositions may also be involved (MacKinnon and Donaldson, 1976; Schmidt and House, 1979). Behavioural ecology could throw light on the balance of advantages and disadvantages which allows these two breeding strategies to coexist and may therefore indicate which factors are likely to be of importance; however, in this context, the direct, experimental approach of applied research is probably more informative and the flow of facts and ideas is likely to be from the applied fisheries scientist to the theoretical behavioural ecologist rather than in the opposite direction.

Finally, reproduction is unsuccessful if the young do not survive and ethological studies suggest certain ways in which their survival can be enhanced. In all domestic mammals which have been studied in unrestrained conditions, females which are about to give birth leave the main group and give birth alone. When they are denied this opportunity, they may be harassed during birth and the young may be stolen and harmed afterwards (Arnold and Morgan, 1975). During the period immediately after birth, mothers of all domestic species groom and clean their babies, often to the accompaniment of soft vocalizations (Selman, McEwan and Fischer, 1970). The importance of this early contact between mother and young is demonstrated by the fact that calves which are removed from their mothers soon after birth absorb immunoglobulins from colostrum less readily than do those which remain with their mothers for as little as 18 hours (Selman, McEwan and Fischer, 1971). Disruption of the bond between mother and young also affects the behaviour of domestic birds; for example, domestic chicks which were not brooded fought more often and more fiercely than those which were brooded normally, possibly because the mother hen is dominant over her brood and this suppresses aggression (Fält, 1978).

Thus, the systematic observation which is characteristic of, though not exclusive to, the ethological approach, has an important role to play in identifying the conditions under which production from commercially important animals will be at a maximum. In addition, concepts developed by ethologists and behavioural ecologists (the motivating effect of courtship and the role of pheromones in this process, the concept of imprinting during a sensitive period, the theory of optimal foraging and of the adaptive significance of mating systems) can add a new dimension to applied research into the behaviour of such animals and, perhaps, suggest areas where productivity might be improved.

9.5 Animal welfare

In what follows, it is assumed that certain animals experience aversive emotions which resemble those described in humans as suffering, a complex philosophical point which is not amenable to proof or disproof; if animals do not suffer, it makes no sense to talk about their welfare. It is also assumed that it matters if animals suffer, but that this is only of active concern if their suffering is a result of the things human do to them; this position is also open to argument. On the basis of these assumptions, one potential application of ethological research is in identifying and quantifying the signs of suffering in the animals that humans exploit, in determining the conditions which induce this state and in finding ways of reducing or removing it.

9.5.1 IDENTIFYING SUFFERING IN ANIMALS

The question of whether and how we can detect and measure suffering in animals has been discussed in some detail by Dawkins (1980) and will be considered fairly briefly here. There are a number of criteria that could be used to assess animal wellbeing. Overt ill health, whether this is the result of disease or of injury, means that the animal concerned is likely to be in pain and distress; on the other hand, if an animal is in good physical condition, this is often taken as a sign that its psychological condition is also good. Since activities concerned with body maintenance tend to have rather low priority in the behavioural repertoire (being carried out when other needs have been met; Fentress, 1968), this belief is not ill-founded. For example, a supple, pink skin in pigs is a sign that they have the conditions and the time in which to groom and therefore have no other pressing biological needs (Van Putten, 1978).

However, while a well groomed animal is probably not suffering severely, it may well be experiencing less acute, longer term discomfort or distress. For this reason, productivity is often taken into account in assessing animal well being, on the assumption that if an animal is putting on weight or reproducing as well as being in generally good health, its mental state must be satisfactory. Again there are some rational grounds for this belief, since growth can be stunted and breeding suppressed in otherwise healthy animals by a number of adverse features of the physical and social environment. However, growth and breeding can occur, albeit at a reduced rate, in animals which are experiencing chronic, low level distress, suggesting that productivity and mental wellbeing are therefore not synonymous.

A valuable concept in understanding the effects of slight but long term deficiencies in living conditions, is that of stress; there is a constellation of physiological changes which appears fairly consistently when vertebrate animals are exposed to a range of noxious conditions, from direct physical damage to prolonged exposure to an avoidance conditioning task. These changes, which are not precisely defined but which include a brief increase in autonomic activity and chronically enhanced ACTH and corticosteroid production, are said to be the result of stress. In the short term this is an adaptive response, mobilizing the body's resources for effective action in order to avoid damage, but in the long term the state can be detrimental. Since these physiological responses are shown in situations in which the animal is actually or potentially risking physical damage, it is reasonable to suppose that they are unpleasant and can therefore provide a way of detecting objectively whether and how much an animal is suffering. Such measures have been used to identify circumstances which produce stress in otherwise healthy animals. For example, corticosteroid levels are significantly enhanced in sheep following loading in trucks, dipping and shearing (Kilgour and De Langen, 1970).

However, the physiological bases of pain and stress are complex, variable and incompletely understood; in addition, since in the short term stress is an adaptive response, the fact that an animal shows these physiological symptoms may simply mean that its body's defence mechanisms are in good working order. Thus the presence of some or all of the physiological symptoms designated as the stress syndrome does not necessarily mean that an animal is suffering. In addition, the techniques for detecting these changes are intrusive, expensive and impractical when large numbers of animals are concerned, hence the search for behavioural indices of suffering in animals.

It can be argued that an animal which shows the complete repertoire of behaviour patterns typical of its species must be living in good conditions. In contrast, an animal which fails to do so, or is deprived of the opportunity to do so, is in adverse conditions and presumably suffering, as is one which shows excessively high levels of certain components of the repertoire or which performs completely abnormal behaviour patterns. Provided that a full description is available of the way animals behave in unconstrained conditions, we can recognize when an individual is behaving abnormally and thus, if these arguments are correct, when it suffers.

The two main assumptions on which this argument rests are that an animal's life in its natural habitat is free from distress and that failure to perform a natural behaviour pattern or performance of an unnatural one is accompanied by unpleasant emotions. The first of these assumptions is almost certainly incorrect and the second is a very complex issue. Whether or not an animal suffers when deprived of the need or the opportunity to perform natural behaviour patterns depends on the way in which motivational systems are organized. According to control theory models, behaviour is designed to bring some variable to an optimum level (see page 80) and failure to perform the behaviour patterns which bring this about may mean that this state is already attained in which case there is no reason to expect the animal to be distressed. However, if a particular behaviour pattern is controlled by action specific energy accumulating with time since it was last shown (Lorenz, 1950 and see page 6), then the animal will inevitably become motivated to perform the activity in question; if the natural releasing stimulus is absent or if physical conditions prevent expression of the behaviour, the activated drive will be thwarted. According to classical ethological theory, in these conditions displacement activities, ambiguous movements and other apparently inappropriate and compulsive actions occur. If this is how motivation works, performance of such abnormal behaviour by domestic animals is a sign that an activated drive is thwarted and that the animal concerned is frustrated and probably suffering.

While it may be distressing to read of hens which are ready to lay pacing about in cages with bare floors, unable to find a suitable nest site, Lorenz's picture of motivation is no longer widely accepted and a caged animal is not necessarily a collection of thwarted drives. Even if this were the case, motivational arousal in the absence of the opportunity to perform the relevant behaviour is not necessarily accompanied by mental distress, although since the systems that control how animals behave are the product of natural selection this may well be the case. To simplify a complex argument, pain and suffering are assumed to be adaptations which ensure that an animal reacts quickly and effectively to important features of its internal and external environment; we must therefore expect these mental states to occur when some pressing biological need is experienced, whether this is to avoid a predator, to take cover in a strange environment, to get food after a period of deprivation or to mate when hormone levels are high. According to this line of reasoning, the behaviour shown in such circumstances is therefore that which accompanies suffering and can provide an index of wellbeing, or lack of it, for use in other circumstances.

Thus if an animal's behaviour is recorded in a range of naturally occurring conditions from those in which all needs are met to those in which strong needs are present, those activities which signify comfort and distress in the species concerned can be identified. If such behavioural signs of distress correlate with the physiological signs of stress, the identification receives support and behavioural observation can potentially provide a substitute for these more expensive and intrusive techniques. However, this argument is based on assumptions about the way natural selection works on motivational systems and performance of such behavioural correlates of physiological stress does not necessarily mean that an animal is experiencing unpleasant emotions.

Suffering is an aversive mental state; in other words, by definition, animals will avoid conditions in which they suffer. This suggests an alternative way of using an animal's behaviour to find out about its mental state, and one which is based on the ideas and methods of experimental psychology rather than on those of ethology; an animal is assumed to be suffering if it makes efforts to change its state (Dawkins, 1980). On this basis, if it learns a task or works hard in order to get away from a certain environment then this environment is aversive and the animal suffers if forced to remain in it. On the other hand, if it learns in order to obtain access to a certain environment then this is reinforcing and the animal is in a state of mental wellbeing when allowed to remain in it. Pigs will learn to place their snouts in particular positions in order to turn a light on or off and, under these conditions, they will work so as to keep the light on for about 70% of the time, with bouts of illumination being distributed throughout the test period. Thus pigs avoid constant light and constant darkness and choose intermediate periods of illumination. According to the argument outlined above, they suffer in constant light or dark but are content in a mixture of these two conditions (Baldwin and Meese, 1977).

This conclusion only holds if animals work for or choose what is good for them, which has been questioned (Duncan, 1977). There is ample evidence that animals, including domesticated species, make decisions about when, where and on what to feed in a way which enhances their fitness (see page 169) and that many wild animals choose to live in habitats in which they flourish (see page 166) Domestic animals may have lost this ability, but since they retain many other aspects of the complex behaviour of their wild ancestors, they may well still show rational preferences. A combination of a preference test with ethological and physiological recording of the animal's state in the different conditions may allow this issue to be resolved.

9.5.2 ALLEVIATING ANIMAL SUFFERING

By applying the various procedures described above (to which the techniques and concepts of ethology make a real but limited contribution) in a range of physical and social environments, it is possible to find out what exactly it is that is the source of the suffering. Assuming that the animal's wellbeing is of importance, the next step is to find a way of removing the cause of the suffering from the environment; this is a technical question, although a knowledge of natural behaviour may suggest likely sources of suffering and observing and analysing behaviour is still necessary to check whether the attempt has been successful. The enriched pig pen designed by Wood-Gush and Stolba, and its effect on the behaviour of the pigs have already been described. Similarly, Bareham has designed a hen cage with a nest box containing litter which allowed the hens to scratch and dust as well as providing a more satisfactory place to lay. In these new cages, the hens showed fewer abnormal behaviour patterns, had smaller adrenal glands and laid heavier eggs (Bareham, 1976).

9.6 Conservation

Since destruction of an animal's natural habitat and reduction of its numbers to the brink of extinction presumably causes distress, attempts to conserve the environment thus represent one way of enhancing the welfare of animals, although there are also aesthetic and economic considerations. A knowledge of ecological principles is obviously essential for this exercise, but information about the behaviour of animals and the ways in which this influences and is influenced by environmental conditions is also of value.

In order to understand the impact of human activities on the distribution and abundance of a particular animal species it is necessary to know its movement patterns, habitat preferences, what it chooses to eat and how flexible these requirements are. In addition, whether it lives in groups or alone, whether there is a reservoir of potentially breeding adults and how the animal sets about finding a mate and raising young will all determine the impact of disturbances of their natural habitat. The same sort of information is also necessary for the rational design and management of nature reserves. For example, failure to allow for the movement patterns of elephants as they search for food has led to problems in confining these animals to areas in which they are protected; corridors of uncultivated land between game reserves may help to solve the problem. If social mechanisms exist by which the breeding rate is reduced when the food supply falls, these will solve the problem of overgrazing by elephants naturally without the need for human intervention. However, observation of the behaviour of elephants indicates that such behavioural mechanisms for population control do not exist in this species, suggesting that selective culling may be the only solution to the problem of over-grazing (Douglas-Hamilton and Douglas-Hamilton, 1975).

Breeding in zoos with subsequent release into suitable environments has a major role to play in the conservation of species which have been brought to the edge of extinction but such programmes often fail through lack of detailed information about the behaviour of the species concerned, and especially about their social organization. For example, in captive lion tamarins, sub-adult females are often killed by their mother as they approach maturity, a time when they would normally disperse from their natal group in the wild. The importance of knowing about the size of group in which animals live naturally is illustrated by the fact that cheetahs and elephant shrews breed better if caged alone, while short-nosed bats fail to breed successfully in small groups, probably because thermoregulation is inefficient. The composition of the captive group is also important; for example, in wild talapoin monkeys males and females usually live in separate groups and the males may be killed if the two sexes are caged together. On the other hand, since lion tamarins live in extended family groups with several non-breeding helpers, it is relatively easy to introduce strange animals into an existing group, providing they are not in breeding condition. Long-term social bonds, especially those based on kinship are central to the social system of lions and a new breeding colony of these animals is probably best based on groups of familiar, related males. In contrast, both female and male wolves disperse from their natal pack before mating and a pair of unrelated strangers is the best foundation for a colony in this species. Dominance relationships within a wolf pack are fairly rigid and as a result the subordinate animals do not often breed successfully, thus limiting the reproductive potential of a single pack. On the other hand, competition between males may have a stimulating effect on both sexes and as a consequence breeding failure in isolated pairs may result in species such as the gorilla in which a competition over status is a feature of the natural social organization. Housing conditions which deprive the animals of the opportunity to choose between prospective mates may interfere with breeding, especially in monogamous species. Lion tamarins can be kept in groups in which a female has a choice between two males, without excessive levels of aggression and with successful breeding.

Finally, the natural manner in which the young are raised is also important. For example, young tree shrews are normally left in an isolated nest and suckled at fairly long intervals; if the mother is unable to leave her young she will often kill them. In contrast, in the wild, young lion tamarin are looked after by their father and by other adult helpers as well as by mothers and zoo conditions should allow for these relationships (all examples from Kleiman, 1980).

The success of a subsequent release programme also depends on a detailed knowledge of the animals' biology, including their behaviour. If the released animals are to flourish when returned to their natural habitat, it is important that their genetic constitution is unaltered by the period of captivity. This means that selection in favour of animals which flourish in captivity must be avoided and that breeding programmes be arranged to mimic natural levels of inbreeding. For example, take-over of groups of breeding females by wandering males, and subsequent killing of existing babies, have been described in lions (Bertram, 1976) and in several species of colobine monkeys (Blaffer-Hrdy, 1977). Given the importance of keeping the gene pool natural, new males must be introduced into captive groups of these species but introduction of a new male should be delayed for some time after the old male has been removed to allow vulnerable young animals to be weaned, even if this means a short-term reduction in breeding output (Kleiman, 1980).

The lack of experience of the natural environment which animals bred and reared in captivity suffer puts them at a disadvantage when they are subsequently released. However, given a sufficient knowledge of the factors which determine the development of behaviour in the species concerned, this can be corrected to some extent. For example, hand-reared masked bob white quails (*Colinus virginianus*) were subjected to simulated attacks from a variety of predators before being released; they were set free in the company of a wild-reared, vasectomized male of a similar strain which was familiar with the natural habitat. Both these procedures were designed to increase their chances of surviving in an unfamiliar, hostile environment and the reintroduction programme has been successful (Campbell, 1980).

Information about the natural behaviour of endangered species is therefore of value in attempts to supplement declining numbers with zoo-reared animals and in the design and management of protected areas in which the surviving individuals can be preserved. Unfortunately, by definition, this information is hard to obtain and the interference caused while collecting it may be detrimental to the animals concerned. However, given information about the behaviour of related species and of other animals living in similar habitats, general sociobiological principles about the relationship between social structure and the environment can be used to supplement observations made on captive members of the endangered species itself.

9.7 Human behaviour

Since it is of absorbing interest as well as of considerable practical importance, the way human beings behave has been the subject of intensive study by sociologists, political theorists, military tacticians, anthropologists, psychiatrists and psychologists. Given the existence of these specialist disciplines devoted entirely to the subject, can ethology add anything to what we already know about human behaviour? This final section will consider briefly, by means of a few examples, what ethology can and cannot contribute in this context. A comprehensive discussion on this subject is provided by Hinde (1982).

9.7.1 APPLYING ETHOLOGICAL TECHNIQUES TO HUMAN BEHAVIOUR

The ethological approach differs from more conventional techniques for studying human behaviour in that it is non-intrusive, involving observation rather than experiments, questionnaires or interviews; in addition, the categories of behaviour selected for analysis are individual movement patterns such as bite and touch, rather than more global, interpretive concepts such as hostility and affiliation. The relationships between these items of behaviour are then investigated by studying their correlations and their sequential relationships.

This approach was first used to study young children, for the obvious reason that language is less important in their social relationships than it is for older children and adults. The classic study in this area was carried out by Blurton-Jones (1972) on children in a pre-school nursery. Each child was observed for a period of 5 minutes on 15 separate occasions and the occurrence of 22 behaviour patterns (e.g. push at, hit, smile, pucker face, fixate) recorded. The structure of the children's behaviour was studied by calculating the correlation between the various actions, across each child per observation period. The correlations were then investigated by means of a principle components analysis which identified groups of related behaviour patterns; for example, wrestle, hit at, jump, run, and laugh loaded positively and work loaded negatively on the same component which was labelled 'rough and tumble play'. Pucker face, fixate, grab, take and push represent another group of inter-related behaviour patterns which was labelled 'aggression'. This careful study provides information about the way in which social interactions are organized in young children, thus supplementing and extending existing information, for example by stressing the distinction between hitting in play context and pushing in an aggressive context.

Developmental psychologists and psychiatrists subsequently added these observational techniques to the existing battery of methods for studying human behaviour. For example, as part of a wider scale study of mental development in children with Down's syndrome, Charlesworth (1978b) studied 'intelligent behaviour in the natural habitat' by observing what young children did as they moved about freely in their own homes. The behaviour of the children was sampled regularly and described in terms of 14 categories, such as play, look at, eating and caring for the body; at the same time a continuous narrative was recorded of naturally occurring problems that the child encountered, what it was doing at the time, the nature of the problem, the response to it and the outcome. This produced an enormous amount of data and, among the results, it transpired that Down's syndrome children experience blocking conditions less frequently than normal children, that the kind of blocking tends to be different (Down's syndrome children encounter shorter, less complex problems), and that parents intervene less in the problem-solving process. This study is primarily of interest to developmental psychologists and doctors, but in that it used observation of movements rather than application of tests and questionnaires, it owes something to ethology.

Many recent studies have involved detailed observation of interactions between mothers and young children. For example, Brown et al. (1975, quoted in Bakeman, 1978) observed 45 mothers with their new born babies during feeding sessions, recording among other behaviour patterns, infant activity and maternal care giving. The frequencies of these two behaviour patterns are positively correlated, which could mean that infant activity elicits care giving or vice versa.

Figure 9.2 shows the probability of infant activity occurring at a particular point (the criterion interval) given that care giving occurred in earlier sampling intervals, with lags ranging from 1–10 intervals, and the equivalent probabilities for the performance of care giving following an episode of infant activity. The conditional probability of both acts increases following performance of the other, indicating that these have mutual stimulatory effects. However, the probability levels are highest for infant activity following a bout of care giving, indicating that the effect of maternal behaviour on the child is the stronger influence. The fact that systematic observation of mother–child interactions provides one of the more reliable predictors of subsequent child abuse and neglect demonstrates the practical importance of such detailed behavioural analyses (Gray *et al.*, 1977).

The non-verbal behaviour of adults can also be studied in this way; for example, patients with different depressive conditions show recognizably distinct constellations of behaviour patterns which vary with the stages of the depressive cycle and can be used as sensitive indicators of the subject's mental condition (Ekman and Friesen, 1974).

The advantages of the ethological approach to the study of human behaviour are that it forces observers to become familiar with their subjects and that it encourages a degree of objectivity; a mother either touches her child or she does not, but whether she is warm or cold towards it is a matter of opinion. In addition, focussing on small-scale behavioural events sometimes allows behavioural

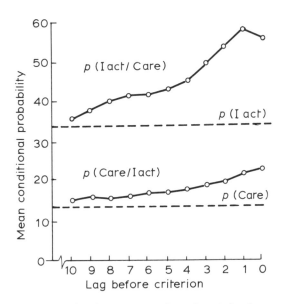

Figure 9.2 Using ethological techniques to study mother–infant interaction in humans; changes in the probability of occurrence of infant activity in the period following a bout of care giving (*p* (IACT/CARE)) and vice versa (*p* (CARE/IACT)). Dashed lines give base level probability of the two acts (after Brown *et al.*, 1975).

358   *The Study of Animal Behaviour*

features to be identified which might otherwise be missed (hitting with a relaxed face is different from hitting with a puckered face), as well as giving information about the causal relationships between different items (care giving by the mother has a stronger effect on infant activity than vice versa). When used in combination with analytical techniques for determining the relationships between a number of distinct behaviour patterns, the ethological approach can provide information at a fairly high level about how behaviour in humans is organized. This may simply confirm or extend what is already known but it can provide new insights into the way we behave and into the nature of behavioural abnormalities.

On the other hand, itemizing individual movements has a number of draw-backs: it is time consuming to learn and to apply, the enormous quantities of data it generates are unwieldy and patterns at higher levels may be obscured. Technical advances in data collection and analysis can go some way towards solving these problems. More seriously, techniques which accurately describe and measure social behaviour in animals may be inadequate for describing the subtle and complex ways that humans interact, even when language is not important. To characterize a relationship between two people we must know how often they interact, the kind of behaviour they show, how much of it they show, how the interactions are patterned in time and space and how they are influenced by physical and social context. It is also necessary to know about the quality of the relationship, whether it is reciprocal or not, whether is it affectionate or not and so on. Ethological methods and concepts can provide some but not all of the information necessary to describe and measure this complexity. Hinde (1979) has developed a hierarchical scheme for describing and measuring the ways in which behavioural interactions make up relationships and how these in turn combine to produce social organization; this scheme is based on an amalgamation of ethological and psychological techniques.

Finally, while the fact that people speak can be accommodated in the etho-logical approach to a certain extent by incorporating behavioural categories such as vocalize or shout, and while humans have a rich repertoire of non-verbal behaviour which can be investigated by observation alone, the involvement of language adds a new dimension to social interactions which may completely alter the relationships identified by studies of overt behaviour alone. Thus observation of discrete items of behaviour in undisturbed encounters has its limitations as a technique for investigating human behaviour.

9.7.2 ETHOLOGICAL CONCEPTS AS A SOURCE OF HYPOTHESES ABOUT HUMAN BEHAVIOUR

The theories developed by ethologists and discussed in this book provide a source of testable hypotheses about the determinants of human behaviour. During courtship, male and female gulls stand parallel to each other and periodically turn their heads away from their partner. In this context the female gull is believed to be in a motivational conflict between a tendency to approach and a tendency to flee while the male is simultaneously motivated to attack and to mate; head flagging is seen as a reflection of these motivational conflicts. Tinbergen has carried out a series of observations in the ethological tradition to see whether this concept, which has made sense of a number of apparently incongruous behaviour patterns in animals, can throw any light on the immediate causes of the abnormal behaviour shown by autistic children, in particular, on withdrawal, avoidance of eye contact and behavioural stereotypies. A model in which autism is seen as an extreme and self-reinforcing form of an approach–avoidance conflict which all children experience when they encounter a stranger provides an internally consistent explanation of some of the behavioural manifestations of the condition and suggests a method of treatment which has been used successfully in a number of cases (Tinbergen and Tinbergen, 1972, 1976).

Similarly, the concept of imprinting during a sensitive period provides a useful framework within which to interpret some cases of disruption of the mother–infant bond (Bowlby, 1980). This idea stimulated a considerable amount of research; for example, increasing the amount of contact between mothers and babies 36 hours after birth is found to have a long-term, beneficial effect on the behaviour of both mother and child (de Chateau and Wiberg, 1977). The concept of early bonding also suggested ways in which an existing unsatisfactory relationship between a mother and her baby can be improved (Shapiro, Fraiberg and Adelson, 1976). Granted that Bowlby initially overstated the importance of a fixed, critical period for bonding and underestimated the importance of relationships between a baby and its father and other caring adults, the suggestion that the ethological concept of imprinting might be applied also to humans has helped in understanding a problem in child care which causes considerable suffering to both parents and children.

The study of the adaptive significance of animal behaviour has been revolutionized by the concept of inclusive fitness (Hamilton, 1964). Several attempts have been made to find out whether this idea can be applied to humans. For example, the women of the Kalahari !Kung tribe give birth on average once every four years, probably as a result of suppressed ovulation during lactation. Blurton-Jones and Sibly (1978) carried out a cost–benefit analysis of the kind used in behavioural ecology to find out whether this birth interval maximizes the life time reproductive output of the women concerned. The benefit of frequent births is obviously a greater rate of reproduction; however, frequent breeding imposes costs, the most serious of which is in terms of having to carry a heavier burden of food and children during foraging trips. Using data on survival, growth and nutritional needs of !Kung babies, and observing how often and how far children of different ages are carried, the back loads the mother must carry to feed her family was calculated for different birth intervals (Fig. 9.3). This increases sharply when the birth interval drops below four years; the weights

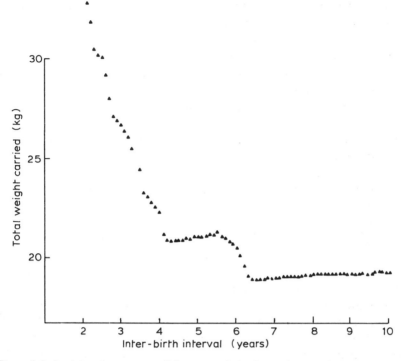

Figure 9.3 Applying the concept of fitness maximization to human characteristics; the maximum back load carried on foraging trips by !Kung women for different birth intervals (from Blurton-Jones and Sibly, 1978).

involved would impose serious heat stress during the dry season when the temperature is high and food is scarce. The success of this analysis implies that the observed spacing may well maximize fitness and that the upper limit on breeding rate is probably imposed by the risk of heat stress while collecting food in the dry season.

Kinship is an important feature of all human cultures, but the great complexity and variety of kinship systems and the frequent lack of close biological relatedness among individuals who are given the status of kin, would appear to rule out the possibility of using the concept of kin selection to explain the distribution of aid in human societies (Sahlins, 1976). However, where biological relatedness is known precisely, from genealogies and from blood typing, there is evidence that aggression is lower between groups which are related than between those which are unrelated and that relatives tend to come to each others' aid during fights and at other times (Chagnon, 1981). Kin selection as it applies to the relationship between parents and their offspring predicts that where certainty of paternity is low, a male may do better to invest in the children of his full sisters in preference to his own sons and daughters, since on average they will be more closely related to him; cross-cultural comparisons indicate that uncles do tend to care for their nephews and nieces in societies in which women mate promiscuously (Alexander, 1977).

While these results imply that the concept of kin selection can be applied to human aid-giving behaviour, because such a variety of cultural systems exist, many examples of correlations between altruism and kinship are required before this point can be argued convincingly. In addition, our ignorance of the adaptive significance of behaviour is almost complete and where predictions from inclusive fitness theory are not met, a plausible explanation can always be found for the discrepancy. This does not invalidate the application of concepts derived from studies of non-human animals to human behaviour, but it does illustrate the importance of collecting facts as well as applying theories.

9.7.3 MAKING DIRECT USE OF THE FACTS COLLECTED BY ETHOLOGISTS

In the attempt to identify a natural and biologically determined behavioural repertoire of the human species, should such a thing exist, the application of ethological concepts grades into the direct use of ethological facts. To give a reasonably modern example, the widespread occurrence of territorial behaviour in animals led to the claim that defence of space is a biologically determined characteristic of the human male (Ardrey, 1966).

A more respectable role for facts about animals in the search for an understanding of human behaviour, but one which is based on the same assumptions, is the use of particular animal species as models for people. Animal models are used either because initial investigation of a (presumably) simple system is a useful step in analysis of a more complex, but similar, one or because performing experiments on humans is technically difficult and/or ethically unjustifiable.

The intensive study of social organization in rhesus monkeys which has been carried out by Hinde and his collaborators provides an example of the use of animals as model humans where experiments on the latter would be unacceptable. At least one aim of this study was to collect information about the effects of interference with the mother−infant bond; this may help in assessing the influence of various child-rearing practices on the development of behaviour in humans. To summarize some of their results, separation from the mother produced both short term distress and long term alterations in the behaviour of young rhesus monkeys; up to a year later, monkeys which had been separated from their mothers initiated more contact with them than did control monkeys. The magnitude of this effect depended strongly on the conditions in which the separation occurred (it was more marked if the mother was removed, leaving the baby in the social group than in the converse situation), and on the nature of the relationship between the baby and its mother (those with closer, less stressful relationships were less affected by the separation) (Hinde and McGinnis, 1977).

In addition to their obvious theoretical importance, these results would seem to be of direct practical value, since experimental removal of human babies from their mothers is out of the question. However, it might well be possible to extract information about the effects of such separation from direct observation of humans, by using techniques such as multiple regression, in which the effects of variables which cannot be controlled experimentally can be allowed for statistically.

Given an ideal model species, the results of such studies might be related directly to humans; however, since the models are never ideal, a more valid use of facts about animal behaviour is to derive from them general rules which can then be applied to humans (Hinde, 1981). Behavioural ecologists have identified consistent relationships between behavioural and ecological parameters; for example, group size and movement patterns can be related to food abundance and distribution (Jarman, 1974; Clutton-Brock and Harvey, 1977). Since the human species inhabits such a wide range of different environments it is not easy to use these rules to make deductions about human behaviour. However, in other cases, comparison is between behavioural features and some measurable aspect of the morphology or physiology of the species concerned; any principles that these generate are easier to apply to people. For example, for a number of primate species we know the weight of the body and testes and whether the animals live in multi-male groups, single male harems or monogamous pairs. When these morphological and behavioural variables are compared, a systematic relationship emerges (Fig. 9.4); genera which live in multi-male groups have significantly

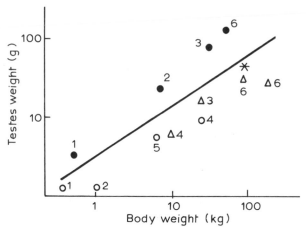

Figure 9.4 Applying rules about animal behaviour to humans; the relationship between testes weight, body weight and mating systems in primates, showing fitted regression line and the position of some representative examples (after Harcourt *et al.*, 1981); where * is *Homo sapiens*, ● is multi-male groups, o is monogamous groups, △ is single male harems, 1 is *Callithricidae*, 2 is *Cebidae*, 3 is *Cercopithicinae*, 4 is *Colobinae*, 5 is *Hylobatidae* and 6 is *Pongidae*.

heavier testes in relation to their body weight than do those which live in single male groups or monogamous pairs. The suggested explanation is that males in multi-male groups have the opportunity to enhance their fitness by mating many times and can therefore use a good sperm supply. When the position of the human male is plotted on the graph of testes weight against body weight, he falls among the monogamous and single male genera; if the rule which relates these morphological and behavioural factors in non-human primates applies to our own species, this result means that our natural social orgnization, that for which selection has adapted us, is not the multi-male group (Harcourt *et al.*, 1981).

The validity of such direct application of facts about animals to humans depends on the assumption that it is reasonable to extrapolate from animals to people, that the behaviour will be the same or at least tht the rules relating behaviour to physiology apply in both cases. The theoretical rationale for this assumption is that, since all modern species are the product of evolution, human beings shared a common ancestor with other species and have retained certain characteristics of that ancestor in common with its other descendants. The traits in question may be the possession of a pentadactyl limb, the way action potentials pass along nerves or gonads which produce sperm at a particular rate.

This approach raises a number of problems, most of which are exacerbated where the behaviour of human beings is concerned. Thus, it is not always easy to decide from which species facts can best be extrapolated or which group of species should be used to generate rules about behaviour. In attempting to identify natural human social behaviour, should we look to the chimpanzee and the gorilla which are our nearest living relatives, to savannah baboons which live in an environment similar to that of the early hominids or to cape hunting dogs which are also communal hunters? The problem arises because although they share a common ancestor, related species may be specialized for different ways of life. For example, the effects of separating young bonnet macaques (*Macaca radiata*) from their mother are less drastic than the effects of the same treatment in rhesus monkeys, possibly because of the greater involvement of other adults in care of the young in this species. It is not clear which of these two species provides the best model of the effects of disruption of the mother–offspring bond in humans (Hinde, 1982). In the face of such variation in behaviour between closely related primate species, Wilson (1975) suggests that only traits which are relatively invariant in this group, such as a prolonged and close mother–offspring bond should be used in reconstructing our natural behavioural repertoire.

The lability of behavioural traits in the face of environmental variation also complicates the process of extrapolating between species. Humans have a uniquely developed capacity for behavioural modification by learning and are exposed from birth to a complex cultural system. Whether or not the way animals behave is of any relevance to what people do depends on the nature of this cultural process; this is a question which can only be solved by anthropological study, although observations on cultural propagation in non-human animals may provide some relevant information. To simplify a large and growing literature, four broadly distinct positions on this issue can be recognized.

1. That human behaviour, including complex social interactions, is determined by strong biological predispositions which are the end product of natural selection and which have been inherited from our primate ancestors. According to this view, learning and culture produce variation about a biologically adapted mean which can be identified by judicious cross-species comparison and which we ignore at our peril.

There are any number of examples which could be quoted to illustrate this general position; the following extract from Wilson's book (1975, page 565) is quoted slightly out of context but accurately reflects his approach. '. . . it is reasonable to conclude that territoriality is a general trait of hunter–gatherer societies . . . these relatively primitive societies do not differ basically in their strategy of land tenure from many mammalian species . . . Moreover, in obedience to the rules of ecological efficiency, the home ranges and territories were probably large and the population density correspondingly low . . . Part of man's problem is that his intergroup responses are still crude and primitive, and inadequate for the extended extraterritorial relationships that civilization has thrust upon him. The unhappy result is . . . tribalism in the modern sense . . . fearful of the hostile groups around them, the 'tribe' refuses to concede to the common good . . . Justice and liberty decline . . . Xenophobia becomes a political virtue. . . the treatment of nonconformists within the group grows harsher.'

According to this position, informed and cautious extrapolation of facts about primate behaviour can be used as a direct source of information about human behaviour.

2. That culture is an important determinant of human behaviour but, being the product of the human brain, is itelf a result of natural selection. Cultural traits which promote the inclusive fitness of the individuals involved will be perpetuated while those which fail to do so will disappear, a process which is brought about partly by adaptive constraints on human learning abilities. Thus '. . . to the extent that culturally acquired information elevates individual fitness, there will be selection in favour of humans who are able to absorb this information more completely, rapidly and with less expenditure of effort than others. Conversely, if a cultural practice reduces inclusive fitness, individuals who are UNABLE to learn it should enjoy a selective advantage' (Alcock, 1979). On this view, while cultural modification reduces the relevance of facts about animals to complex behavioural traits in humans, the latter can usefully be viewed in the light of the concept of maximization of inclusive fitness.

3. That the cultural system in which development occurs is an important determinant of human behaviour but it is the result of a process of cultural evolution which is analogous to rather than a product of Darwinian natural selection. Cultural practices spread or die out according to their capacity to

propagate themselves and this is not necessarily dependent on their impact on inclusive fitness. For example, Dawkins develops a picture of cultural evolution via the spread of memes, cultural equivalents of genes replicating in the brains of human beings and writes 'We do not have to look for conventional biological survival values of traits like religion, music, and ritual dancing, though these may also be present . . . We do not even have to posit a genetic advantage in imitation, though this would certainly help. All that is necessary is that the brain should be *capable* of imitation: memes will then evolve which exploit this capacity to the full' (Dawkins, 1977). According to this view, the only contribution that biology can make to an understanding of the many behavioural traits which are subject to cultural modification in humans is to provide an analogy which may help us to understand how cultural systems evolve.

4. That culture is all important in determining human behaviour and that the form it takes is arbitrary. Any influence of our evolutionary past is at the level of very broad predispositions and while animal behaviour may provide information about the very simplest human behaviour patterns, it has nothing at all to tell us about human social responses and human social institutions. For example, 'The reason why human social behaviour is not organized by the individual maximization of genetic interest is that human beings are not socially defined by their organic qualities but in terms of symbolic attributes . . .' (Sahlins, 1976). '. . . we know of no relevant constraints placed on social processes by human biology. There is no evidence from ethnography, archaeology or history that would enable us to circumscribe the limits of possible human social organization' (Sociobiology Study Group of Science for the People, 1976).

Evidence from a variety of sources such as heritability estimates of human psychological propensities and cross-cultural similarities in facial expressions, indicates that inherited predispositions to behave in a particular way do exist in humans and may be fairly specific. Similarly, the success of some attempts to apply the theory of kin selection of culturally determined traits, indicates that the latter may be an additional source of adaptive behaviour in humans. However, such results are rare and apply to fairly simple behavioural traits; most aspects of human society and social institutions cannot easily be related to biology.

9.7.4 SOCIOBIOLOGY AND HUMAN BEHAVIOUR

These issues concern the application of what is usually called sociobiological theory to human behaviour. The shortcomings of this approach as it is often practised (the naïvety of its aims, the oversimple picture of the development of behaviour and the lack of precise information about the costs and benefits of behaviour, see page 271), are all magnified where human behaviour is concerned. These points are generally recognized; thus Wilson discusses at length the problem of extrapolating from animals to man where labile traits such as the intensity and form of territorial defence are concerned, while Barash stresses the fact that sociobiologists '. . . do not necessarily advocate biological determinism of human behaviour' (Barash, 1977). However, Wilson procedes to discuss the biologically determined human condition for the very same labile traits while, to give just one example, Barash suggests that '. . . too much competence and accomplishment by a woman is often threatening to a prospective male partner' this being a 'basic adaptive inclination' which is 'insensitive to personal conditions . . . which are themselves too recent to have been acted on by natural selection' (Barash, 1977).

Merely acknowledging the need for caution in extrapolating from animals to people is not sufficient; it is necessary to put this principle into practice. Nor is it sufficient to recognize that the pervasive influence of cultural background on the development of our behaviour means that genes can do no more than predispose us to behave in particular ways; this complexity must be incorporated into sociobiological theory when this is applied to humans. When these things are done, the carefully researched theories which have been successful in explaining animal behaviour may provide new insights into the way humans behave.

References

Alatalno, R.V., Carlson, A., Lundberg, A. and Ulfstrand, S. (1981) The conflict between male polygamy and female monogamy; the case of the pied flycatcher, *Ficedula hypoleuca. Amer. Nat.,* 117, 738–753.

Albright, J.L. (1976) The starling–its history–its nature–its control around animal houses. *Confinement,* 1, 14–19.

Alcock, J. (1979) *Animal Behaviour: an Evolutionary Approach,* 2nd edn, Sunderland, Massachusetts.

Alcock, J., Eickwort, E.C. and Eickwort, K.R. (1977) The reproductive behaviour of *Anthidium maculosum* and the evolutionary significance of multiple copulations by females. *Behav. Ecol. Syst.,* 2, 385–396.

Alexander, R.D. (1974) The evolution of social behaviour. *An. Rev. Ecol. Syst.,* 5, 325–383.

Alexander, R.D. (1977) Natural selection and the analysis of human sociality; in *Changing Scenes in Natural Sciences* (ed. G.E. Goulden), Philadelphia Acad. Nat. Sci., Special Publication 12, pp. 283–337.

Alexander, R.D. and Borgia, G. (1979) On the origin and basis of the male female phenomenon; in *Sexual Selection and Reproductive Competition in Insects* (eds M.S. Blum and N.A. Blum), Academic Press, New York, pp. 417–440.

Altmann, S.A. (1965) Sociobiology of Rhesus monkeys. II Stochastics of social communication. *J. Theoret. Biol.,* 8, 490–522.

Anderson, W.W. and McGuire, P. (1978) Mating patterns and mating success of *Drosophila pseudobscura* karyotypes in large experimental populations. *Evol.,* 32, 416–423.

Andersson, M. (1980) Female choice selects for extreme tail length in a widow bird. *Nature,* 229, 818–820.

Archer, J. (1976) The organisation of aggression and fear in vertebrates; in *Perspectives in Ethology – Vol. 2* (eds P.P.G. Bateson and P. Klopfer), Plenum Press, New York, pp. 231–298.

Ardrey, R. (1966) *The Territorial Imperative: A Personal Inquiry into the Animal Origins of Property and Nations,* Atheneum, New York.

Arnold, G.W. and Dudzinsky, M.L. (1979) *Behaviour of Free-ranging Domestic Animals,* Elsevier, Amsterdam/Oxford.

Arnold, G.W. and Morgan, P.D. (1975) Behaviour of the ewe and lamb at lambing and its relation to lamb mortality. *App. Anim. Ethol.,* 2, 25–46.

Arnold, G.W. and Pahl, P.J. (1974) Some aspects of social behaviour in domestic sheep. *Anim. Behav.,* 22, 592–600.

Arnold, S.J. (1972) The evolution of courtship behaviour in salamanders. Ph.D. Thesis, University of Michigan.

Baerends, G.P. (1970) A model of the functional organisation of incubation behaviour in the herring gull. *Behav. Suppl.*, **17**, 261–312.

Baerends, G.P. (1971) The ethological analysis of fish behaviour; in *Fish Physiology Vol. VI* (eds W.S. Hoar and D.J. Randall), Academic Press, New York, pp. 279–370.

Baerends, G.P. and Drent, R.H. (1982) The herring gull and its eggs. Part II. The responsiveness to egg features. *Behaviour*, **82**, 1–416.

Baerends, G.P. and Kruijt, J.P. (1973) Stimulus selection; in *Constraints on Learning* (eds R.A. Hinde and J. Stevenson-Hinde), Academic Press, London, pp. 23–50.

Baerends, G.P., Blokzijl, G.J. and Kruijt, J.P. (1982) The processing of heterogeneous information of egg features inducing the retrieval response. *Behaviour*, **82**, 212–224.

Baerends, G.P., Drent, R.H., Glas, P. and Groenewold, H. (1970) An ethological analysis of incubation behaviour in the herring gull. *Behav. Suppl.*, **17**, 135–235.

Bakeman, R. (1978) Untangling streams of behaviour: sequential analysis of observational data; in *Observing Behaviour Vol. II* (ed. G.P. Sackett), University Park Press, Baltimore, pp. 63–78.

Baker, A.E. (1981) Gene flow in house mice: introduction of a new allele into free-living populations. *Evol.*, **35**, 243–258.

Baker, M.C. (1978) Flocking and feeding in the great tit *Parus major* – an important consideration. *Amer. Nat.*, **112**, 779–781.

Baker, M.C. and Marler, P. (1980) Behavioural adaptations that constrain the gene pool in vertebrates; in *Evolution of Social Behaviour* (ed. H. Markl), Verlag Chemie GbmH, Weinheim, pp. 59–80.

Baker, M.C. and Medwaldt, R. (1978) Song dialects as barriers to dispersal in white crowned sparrows, *Zonotrichia leucophrys nuttali. Evol.*, **32**, 712–722.

Baker, M.C., Thompson, D.B., Sherman, G.L., Cunningham, M.A. and Tomback, D.F. (1982) Allozyme frequencies in a linear series of song dialect populations. *Evol.*, **36**, 1020–1029.

Baker, R.R. (1978) *Animal Migration*, Hodder and Stoughton, London.

Baldwin, B.A. and Meese, G.B. (1977) Sensory reinforcement and illumination preference in the domesticated pig. *Anim. Behav.*, **25**, 497–507.

Balph, D.E., Innis, G.S. and Balph, M.H. (1980) Kin selection in Rio Grande turkeys: a critical reassessment. *Auk*, **97**, 854–859.

Barash, D.P. (1977) *Sociobiology and Behaviour*, Elsevier, New York.

Bareham, J.R. (1976) A comparison of the behaviour and production of laying hens in experimental and conventional battery cages. *Appl. Anim. Ethol.*, **2**, 291–303.

Barlow, G. (1977) Modal action patterns; in *How Animals Communicate* (ed. T.A. Sebeok), Indiana Univ. Press, Bloomington, pp. 98–134.

Barrett, P. and Bateson, P.P.G., (1978) The development of play in cats. *Behaviour*, **66**, 106–120.

Bartz, S.H. (1979) Evolution of eusociality in termites. *Proc. Natl. Acad. Sci.*, **76**, 5764–5768.

Bastock, M.A. (1956) A gene mutation which changes a behaviour pattern. *Evol.*, **10**, 421–439.

Bateman, A.J. (1948) Intrasexual selection in *Drosophila. Heredity*, **2**, 349–368.

Bateson, P.P.G. (1976) Rules and reciprocity in the development of behaviour; in *Growing Points in Ethology* (eds P.P.G. Bateson and R.A. Hinde), Cambridge Univ. Press, pp. 401–421.

Bateson, P.P.G. (1978a) Early experience and sexual preferences; in *Biological Determinants of Sexual Behaviour* (ed. J. Hutchison), Wiley, Chichester, pp. 29–53.

Bateson, P.P.G. (1978b) How does behaviour develop? in *Perspectives in Ethology, 3* (eds P.P.G. Bateson and P.H. Klopfer), Plenum Press, New York, pp. 55–66.

Bateson, P.P.G. (1979) How do sensitive periods arise and what are they for? *Anim. Behav.*, 27, 470–486.

Bateson, P.P.G. (1981a) Ontogeny of behaviour. *Br. Med. Bull.*, 37, 159–164.

Bateson, P.P.G. (1981b) Discontinuities in development; in *Behavioural Development* (eds K. Immelmann, G.W. Barlow, L. Petrinovich and M. Main), Cambridge Univ. Press, pp. 281–295.

Bayliss, J.R. (1981) The evolution of parental care in fishes with reference to Darwin's rule of male sexual selection. *Env. Biol. Fish*, 6, 223–252.

Bearder, S.K. and Martin, R.D. (1980) The social organisation of a nocturnal primate revealed by radiotracking; in *A Handbook on Biotelemetry and Radiotracking* (eds C.J. Amlaner and D.W. Macdonald), Pergamon Press, Oxford, pp. 633–649.

Beecher, M.D. and Beecher, I.M. (1979) Sociobiology of bank swallows: reproductive strategies of the male. *Science*, 205, 1282–1285.

Bekoff, A. (1976) Ontogeny of leg motor output in the chick embryo: a neural analysis. *Brain Res.*, 106, 271–291.

Bekoff, A. (1978) A neuroethological approach to the study of the ontogeny of coordinated behaviour; in *The Development of Behaviour* (eds G.M. Burghart and M. Bekoff), Garland Press, New York, pp. 19–41.

Bekoff, A. (1981) Behavioural embryology in birds and mammals: neuroembryological studies of the development of motor behaviour; in *Behavioural Development* (eds K. Immelmann, G. Barlow, L. Petrinovich and M. Main), Cambridge Univ. Press, pp. 152–163.

Belovsky, G.E. and Jordan, P.A. (1978) Time–energy budget of a moose. *Theoret. Pop. Biol.*, 14, 76–104.

Bentley, D.R. and Hoy, R.R. (1970) Post embryonic development of adult motor patterns in crickets: a neural analysis. *Science*, 170, 1409–1411.

Bentley, D.R. and Hoy, R.R. (1972) Genetic control of the neural network generating cricket (*Teleogryllus gryllus*) song patterns. *Anim. Behav.*, 20, 478–492.

Benton, C., Khan, F., Monaghan, P., Richards, W.N. and Shedden, C.B. (1983) The contamination of a major water supply by gulls (*Larus* sp.) – a study of the problem and remedial action taken. *Water Research*, 17, 789–798.

Benzer, S. (1973) Genetic dissection of behaviour. *Sci. Amer.*, 299, 24–37.

Berg, C.J. (1978) Development and evolution of behaviour in molluscs, with emphasis on changes in stereotypy; in *The Development of Behaviour* (eds G.M. Burghardt and M. Bekoff), Garland Press, New York, pp. 3–17.

Bergman, G. (1980) Single-breeding versus colonial breeding in the Caspian tern *Hydroprogne caspia*, the common tern *Sterna hirundo* and the arctic tern *Sterna paradisaea*. *Ornis Fenn*, 57, 141–152.

Berthold, P. and Querner, U. (1981) Genetic basis of migratory behaviour in European warblers. *Science*, 212, 77–79.

Bertram, B.C.R. (1976) Kin selection in lions and in evolution; in *Growing Points in Ethology* (eds P.P.G. Bateson and R.A. Hinde), Cambridge Univ. Press, pp. 281–301.

Bertram, B.C.R. (1978) Living in groups: predators and prey; in *Behavioural Ecology* (eds J.R. Krebs and N.B. Davies), Blackwell Scientific Publications, Oxford, pp. 64–96.

Bertram, B.C.R. (1980) Vigilance and group size in ostriches. *Anim. Behav.*, 28, 278–286.

Blaffer-Hrdy, S. (1977) *The Langurs of Abu*, Harvard Univ. Press, Cambridge, Mass.

Blair, W.F. (1958) Mating calls in the speciation of anuran amphibians. *Amer. Nat.*, 92, 27–51.

Blaustein, A.R. and O'Hara, R.K. (1981) Genetic control for sibling recognition. *Nature*, 290, 246–248.

Blurton-Jones, N. (1972) Categories of child–child interaction; in *Ethological Studies of Child Behaviour* (ed. N. Blurton-Jones), Cambridge Univ. Press, pp. 97–127.

Blurton-Jones, N. and Sibly, R. (1978) Testing adaptiveness of culturally determined behaviour; in *Human Behaviour and Adaptation* (eds V. Reynolds and N. Blurton-Jones), Taylor and Francis, London, pp. 135–157.

Boehm, C. (1978) Rational preselection from hamadryas to *Homo sapiens*; the place of decisions in the adaptive process. *Amer. Anthrop.*, 80, 265–296.

Boorman, S.A. and Levitt, P.R. (1980) *The Genetics of Altruism*, Academic Press, New York.

Borchers, H.-W. and Ewert, J.-P. (1979) Correlation between behavioural and neuronal activities of toads *Bufo bufo* in response to moving configurational prey stimuli. *Behav. Proc.*, 4, 99–106.

Borgia, G. (1979) Sexual selection and the evolution of mating systems; in *Sexual Selection and Reproductive Competition in Insects* (eds M.S. Blum and N.A. Blum), Academic Press, New York, pp. 19–80.

Borgia, G. (1981) Mate selection in the fly *Scatophaga stenoraria*: female choice in a male controlled system. *Anim. Behav.*, 29, 71–80.

Bouissou, M.F. (1971) Effect de l'absence d'informations optiques et de contact physique sur la manifestation des relations hiérarchiques chez les bovins domestiques. *Ann. Biol. Anim. Biochem. Biophys.*, 11, 191–198.

Bowlby, J. (1980) By ethology out of psycho-analysis: an experiment in interbreeding. *Anim. Behav.*, 28, 649–656.

Bradbury, J.W. (1981) The evolution of leks; in *Natural Selection and Social Behaviour* (eds R.D. Alexander and D.W. Tinkle), Chiron Press, New York, pp. 138–169.

Bray, O.E., Kennelly, J.J. and Guarino, J.L. (1975) Fertility of eggs produced on territories of vasectomized red-winged blackbirds. *Wilson Bull.*, 85, 187–195.

Breakefield, X.O. (1979) *Neurogenetics: Genetic Approaches to the Nervous System*. Elsevier, North Holland.

Brenner, S. (1973) The genetics of behaviour. *Br. Med. Bull.*, 29, 269–271.

Broadhurst, P.L. (1979) The experimental approach to behavioural evolution; in *Theoretical Advances in Behaviour Genetics* (eds J.R. Royce and L.P. Mos), Sijhoff and Nordhoff, Alphenaan den Rijn, Netherlands, pp. 43–95.

Brockmann, H.J., Grafen, A. and Dawkins, R. (1979) Evolutionarily stable nesting strategy in a digger wasp. *J. Theoret. Biol.*, 77,. 473–496.

Broom, D.M. (1981) *Biology of Behaviour*, Cambridge Univ. Press.

Brown, J.H., Lieberman, G.A. and Dengler, W.F. (1972) Woodrats and Cholla:

dependence of a small mammal population on the density of cacti. *Ecology*, 53, 310–313.

Brown, J.L. (1975) *The Evolution of Behaviour*, Norton, New York.

Brown, J.L. (1978) Avian communal breeding systems. *An. Rev. Ecol. Syst.*, 9, 123–155.

Brown, J.L. and Brown, E.R. (1981) Extended family system in a communal bird. *Science*, 211, 959–960.

Brown, J.V., Bakeman, R., Snyder, P.A., Frederickson, W.T., Morgan, S.T. and Hepler, R. (1975) Interactions of black inner-city mothers with their newborn infants. *Child Dev.*, 46, 667–686 (reanalysed data quoted in Bakeman (1978)).

Brown, R.E. and McFarland, D.J. (1979) Interaction of hunger and sexual motivation in the male rat: a time-sharing approach. *Anim. Behav.*, 27, 887–896.

Bryant, M.J. and Tomkins, T. (1975) The flock-mating of progestagen synchronised ewes 1. The influence of ram–to–ewe ratio on mating behaviour and lambing performance. *Amin. Prod.*, 20, 381–390.

Burnet, B. and Connolly, K. (1974) Activity and sexual behaviour in *Drosophila melanogaster*; in *The Genetics of Behaviour* (ed. J.H.F. Van Abeelen), North Holland Publ. Co., Amsterdam, pp. 201–258.

Bush, G.L. (1978) Planning a rational quality control programme for the screw-worm fly; in *The Screwworm Problem* (ed. R.H. Richards), University of Texas Press, Austin, pp. 37–47.

Buzin, C.H., Dewhurst, S.A. and Seecof, R.L. (1978) Temperature sensitivity and neuron differentiation in embryonic cell cultures from the *Drosophila* mutant *shibire (tgl)*. *Dev. Biol.*, 66, 442–456.

Bygott, J.D., Bertram, B.C.R. and Hanby, J.P. (1979) Male lions in large coalitions gain a reproductive advantage. *Nature*, 282, 839–841.

Cade, W. (1979) The evolution of alternative male reproductive strategies in field crickets; in *Sexual Selection and Reproductive Competition in Insects* (eds M.S. Blum and N.A. Blum), Academic Press, New York, pp. 343–379.

Cade, W.H. (1981) Alternative mating strategies: genetic differences in crickets. *Science*, 212, 563–564.

Campbell, S. (1980) Is reintroduction a realistic goal? in *Conservation Biology* (eds M.E. Soule and B.A. Wilcox), Sinauer, Sunderland, Mass., pp. 263–269.

Caprianica, R.R., Frishkopf, L.-S. and Nevo, E. (1973) Encoding of geographical dialects in the auditory system of the cricket frog. *Science*, 182, 1272–1275.

Caraco, T. (1979) Time budgeting and group size a theory (and a test of a theory). *Ecology*, 60, 611–627.

Caraco, T., Martindale, S. and Pulliam, H.R. (1980) Avian flocking in the presence of a predator. *Nature*, 285, 400–401.

Caraco, T., Martindale, S. and Whittam, T.S. (1980) An empirical demonstration of risk sensitive preferences. *Anim. Behav.*, 28, 820–831.

Caro, T. (1981) Predatory behaviour and social play in kittens. *Behaviour*, 76, 1–24.

Caryl, P. (1979) Communication by agonistic displays: what can games theory contribute to ethology? *Behaviour*, 68, 136–169.

Caryl, P. (1981a) Animal signals: a reply to Hinde. *Anim. Behav.*, 30, 240–244.

Caryl, P. (1981b) Escalated fighting and the war of nerves: games theory and animal conflict; in *Perspectives in Ethology Vol. 4* (eds P.P.G. Bateson and P.H. Klopfer) Plenum Press, London, pp. 199–224.

Castle, K.E., Foot, A.S. and Halley, R.J. (1950) Some observations of the behaviour of dairy cattle with particular reference to grazing. *J. Dairy Res.*, **17**, 215–229.

Catchpole, C.K. (1979) *Vocal Communication in Birds*, Edward Arnold, London.

Catchpole, C.K. (1980) Sexual selection and the evolution of complex songs among European warblers of the genus *Acrocephalus. Behaviour*, **74**, 149–166.

Cavalli-Sforza, L.L. and Feldman, M.W. (1978) Darwinian selection and altruism. *Theoret. Pop. Biol.*, **14**, 268–280.

Cazala, P. and Guenet, J.L. (1980) The recombinant inbred strains: a tool for the genetic analysis of differences observed in the self stimulation behaviour of the mouse. *Physiol. Behav.*, **24**, 1057–1060.

Chagnon, N.A. (1981) Terminological kinship, genealogical relatedness and village fissioning among the Yanomamo indians; in *Natural Selection and Social Behaviour* (eds R.D. Alexander and D.W. Twinkle), Chiron Press, New York, pp. 490–508.

Chalmers, N.R. (1980) Developmental relationships among social, manipulatory, postural and locomotor behaviours in olive baboons, *Papio anubis. Behaviour*, **74**, 22–37.

Charlesworth, B. (1978a) Some models of the evolution of altruistic behaviour between siblings. *J. Theoret. Biol.*, **72**, 297–319.

Charlesworth, B. (1980) Models of kin selection; in *The Evolution of Social Behaviour* (ed. H. Markl), Weinheim: Verlag Chemie GmbH, pp. 11–26.

Charlesworth, W.R. (1978b) Ethology: its relevance for observational studies of human adaptation; in *Observing Behaviour Vol. 1* (ed. G.P. Sackett), Univ. Park Press, Baltimore, pp. 7–32.

Charnov, E.L. (1976) Optimal foraging theory: the marginal value theorem. *Theoret. Pop. Biol.*, **9**, 129–136.

Charnov, E.L. and Krebs, J.R. (1974) The evolution of alarm calls: altruism or manipulation? *Amer. Nat.*, **109**, 107–112.

de Chateau, P. and Wiberg, B. (1977) Long-term effects of mother-infant behaviour of extra contact during the first hour post-partum. *Acta Paediatr. Scan.*, **66**, 137–151.

Cheng, K.M., Shoffner, R.N. and Phillips, R.E. (1979) Early imprinting in wild and game farm mallards (*Anas platyrhynchos*): genotype and arousal. *J. Comp. Physiol. Psychol.*, **93**, 929–938.

Cheng, M.F. (1979) Progress and prospect in ring dove research: a personal view. *Adv. St. Behav.*, **9**, 97–129.

Clayton, D.L. and Paietta, J.V. (1972) Selection for circadian eclosion time in *Drosophila melanogaster. Science*, **178**, 994–995.

Clutton-Brock, T.H. (1975) Feeding behaviour of red colobus and black and white colobus in east Africa. *Folia Primat.*, **23**, 165–207.

Clutton-Brock, T.H. and Harvey, P.H. (1977) Primate ecology and social organisation. *J. Zool.*, **183**, 1–39.

Clutton-Brock, T.H., Albon, S.D., Gibson, R.M. and Guiness, F.E. (1979) The logical stag: adaptive aspects of fighting in red deer (*Cervus elaphus*). *Anim. Behav.*, **27**, 211–225.

Cohen, S. and McFarland, D.J. (1979) Time-sharing as a mechanism for the control of behaviour sequences during the courtship of the three-spined stickleback (*Gasterosteus aculeatus*). *Anim. Behav.*, **27**, 270–283.

Colgan, P. (1978) Modelling; in *Quantitative Ethology* (ed. P.W. Colgan), Wiley, New York, pp. 313–326.

Collery, L. (1974) Observations of equine animals under farm and feral conditions. *Equine Vet. J.*, **6**, 170–173.

Collins, A.M. (1979) Genetics of the response of the honeybee to an alarm chemical, isopentyl acetate. *J. Apic. Res.*, **18**, 285–291.

Cook, W.T. and Siegel, P.B. (1974) Social variables and divergent selection for mating behaviour in male chickens. *Anim. Behav.*, **22**, 390–396.

Cooke, F. (1978) Early learning and its effects on population structure. Studies of a wild population of snow geese. *Z. Tierpsychol.*, **46**, 344–358.

Cooper, J.C. and Hasler, A.D. (1976) Electrophysiological studies of morpholine-imprinted coho salmon (*Onchorhynchus kisutch*) and rainbow trout (*Salmo gairdneri*). *J. Fish. Res. Bd. Can.*, **33**, 688–694.

Cooper, J.C., Scholz, A.J., Horrall, R.M., Hasler, A.D. and Madison, D.M. (1976) Experimental confirmation of the olfactory hypothesis with homing, artificially imprinted coho salmon (*Onchorhynchus kisutch*). *J. Fish. Res. Bd. Can.*, **33**, 703–710.

Coulson, J.C. (1966) The influence of the pair bond and age on the breeding biology of the kittiwake gull, *Rissa tridactyla. J. An. Ecol.*, **35**, 269–279.

Cowie, R.J. (1977) Optimal foraging in great tits (*Parus major*). *Nature*, **268**, 137–139.

Cowling, D.E. (1980) The genetics of *Drosophila melanogaster* courtship song – diallel analysis. *Heredity*, **45**, 401–403.

Craig, J.V. (1981) *Domestic Animal Behaviour*, Prentice Hall, New Jersey.

Cronin, E.W. and Sherman, P.W. (1977) A resource based mating system: the orange rumped honey guide. *Living Bird*, **15**, 5–32.

Crook, J.H. (1964) The evolution of social organisation and visual communication in the weaver birds. *Behav. Suppl.*, **10**, 1–178.

Cullen, E. (1960) Experiments on the effects of social isolation on reproductive behaviour in the three-spined stickleback. *Anim. Behav.*, **8**, 235.

Cullen, J.M., Shaw, E. and Baldwin, H. (1965) Methods for measuring the three-dimensional structure of fish schools. *Anim. Behav.*, **13**, 534–543.

Culotti, J.G., Von Ehrenstein, G.V., Culotti, M.R. and Russel, R.L. (1981) A second class of acetylcholinesterase deficient mutants of the nematode *Caenorhabditis elegans. Genetics*, **97**, 281–305.

Daan, S. and Slopsema, S. (1978) Short-term rhythms in foraging behaviour of the common vole, *Microtus arvalis. J. Comp. Physiol.*, **127**, 215–227.

Daan, S. and Tinbergen, J. (1979) Young guillemots (*Uria lomvia*) leaving their Arctic breeding cliffs: a daily rhythm in numbers and risk. *Ardea*, **67**, 96–100.

Daly, J.C. (1981) Effects of social organisation and environmental diversity on the genetic structure of a population of wild rabbits *Oryctolagus cuniculus. Evol.*, **35**, 689–706.

Dane, B. and Van der Kloot, W.G. (1964) An analysis of the display of the goldeneye duck (*Bucephala clangula L.*). *Behaviour*, **22**, 282–328.

Daniels, R.A. (1979) Nest guard replacement in the antarctic fish *Harpagifer bispinis*: possible altruistic behaviour. *Science*, **205**, 831–833.

Darwin, C. (1871) *The Descent of Man and Selection in Relation to Sex.* John Murray, London.

Davidson, D.W. (1978) Experimental tests of the optimal diet in two social insects. *Behav. Ecol. Sociobiol.*, **4**, 35–41.

Davies, N.B. and Halliday, T.R. (1978) Deep croaks and fighting assessment in toads *Bufo bufo. Nature*, **274**, 683–685.

Davies, S.J.J.F. (1970) Patterns of inheritance in the bowing display and associated behaviour of some hybrid *Streptopelia* doves. *Behaviour*, 36, 187–214.

Davies, W.G. (1978) Cluster analysis applied to the classification of postures in the Chilean flamingo (*Phoenicopterus chilensis*). *Anim. Behav.*, 26, 381–388.

Dawkins, M. (1974) Behavioural analysis of co-ordinated feeding movements in the gastropod *Lymnaea stagnalis*. *J. Comp. Physiol.*, 92, 255–271.

Dawkins, M.S. (1980) *Animal Suffering: The Science of Animal Welfare*, Chapman and Hall, London.

Dawkins, M. and Dawkins, R. (1974) Some descriptive and explanatory stochastic models of decision making; in *Motivational Control Systems Analysis* (ed. D.J. McFarland), Academic Press, London, pp. 119–168.

Dawkins, R. (1976) Hierarchical organisation; in *Growing Points in Ethology* (eds P.P.G. Bateson and R.A. Hinde), Cambridge Univ. Press, pp. 7–54.

Dawkins, R. (1977) *The Selfish Gene*, Oxford University Press, London.

Dawkins, R. and Carlisle, T.R. (1976) Parental investment, mate desertion and a fallacy. *Nature*, 262, 131–133.

Dawkins, R. and Dawkins, M. (1973) Decisions and the uncertainty of behaviour. *Behaviour*, 45, 83–103.

Dawkins, R. and Dawkins, M. (1976) Hierarchical organisation and postural facilitation: rules for grooming in flies. *Anim. Behav.*, 24, 739–755.

De Groot, P. (1980) Information transfer in a socially roosting weaver bird (*Quelea quelea*); an experimental study. *Anim. Behav.*, 28, 1249–1254.

Denno, R.F., Paupp, M.J., Tallamy, W. and Reichelderfer, C.F. (1980) Migration in heterogeneous environments: differences in habitat selection between the wing forms of the dimorphic planthopper *Prokelisia marginata. Ecology*, 61, 859–867.

De Ruiter, L., Wiepkema, P.R. and Veening, J.G. (1974) Models of behaviour and the hypothalamus. *Progr. Brain Res.*, 41, 481–508.

Dilger, W. (1962) Behaviour and genetics; in *Roots of Behaviour* (ed. E.L. Bliss), Harper and Bros., New York, pp. 35–47.

Douglas-Hamilton, I. and Douglas-Hamilton, O. (1975) *Among the Elephants*, Collins, London.

Downhower, J.F. and Armitage, K.B. (1971) The yellow bellied marmot and the evolution of polygamy. *Amer. Nat.*, 105, 355–370.

Downhower, J.F. and Brown, L. (1980) Mate preferences of female mottled sculpins, *Cottus bairdi. Anim. Behav.*, 28, 728–734.

Drent, R.H., Postuma, K.H. and Joustra, T. (1970) The effect of egg temperature on incubation behaviour in the herring gull. *Behav. Suppl.*, 17, 235–260.

Duncan, I.J.H. (1977) Behavioural wisdom lost. *Appl. Anim. Ethol.*, 3, 193–194.

Dunford, C. (1977) Kin selection for ground squirrel alarm calls. *Amer. Nat.*, 111, 782–785.

Dunn, E. (1977) Predation by weasels (*Mustela rivalis*) on breeding tits (*Parus* spp.) in relation to the density of tits and rodents. *J. Anim. Ecol.*, 46, 633–652.

Ebersole, J.P. (1980) Food density and territory size: an alternative model and a test on the reef fish *Eupomacentrus leucostrictus. Amer. Nat.*, 115, 492–509.

Ehrman, L. and Parsons, P.A. (1981) *Behavioural Genetics and Evolution*, McGraw-Hill Book Co., New York.

Eibl-Eibesfeldt, I. (1951) Beobachtungen zur Fortpflanzungsbiologie und Jungendent-wicklung des Eichhörnchens (*Sciurus vulgaris*). *Z. Tierpsychol.*, **8**, 370–400.

Ekesbo, I. (1978) Ethics, ethology and animal health in modern Swedish livestock pro-duction; in *The Ethology and Ethics of Farm Animal Production* (ed. D.W. Folsch), Birkhauser Verlag, Basel, pp. 46–50.

Ekman, P. and Friesen, W.V. (1974) Non-verbal behaviour and psychopathology; in *The Psychology of Depression: Contemporary Theory and Research* (eds R.J. Friedman and M.M. Katz), Winston and Sons, Washington, D.C., pp. 203–232.

Eleftheriou, B.E., Bailey, D.W. and Denenberg, V.H. (1974) Genetic analysis of fighting behaviour in mice. *Physiol. Behav.*, **13**, 773–777.

Elner, R.W. and Hughes, R.N. (1978) Energy maximisation in the diet of the shore crab, *Carcinus maenas. J. Anim. Ecol.*, **47**, 103–116.

Elsner, N. and Popov, A.V. (1978) Neuroethology of acoustic communication. *Adv. Ins. Phys.*, **13**, 229–355.

Emlen, S.T. and Oring, L.W. (1977) Ecology, sexual selection and the evolution of mating systems. *Science*, **197**, 215–223.

Erckmann, W.J. (1983) The evolution of polyandry in shorebirds: an evaluation of hypotheses; in *Social Behaviour of Female Vertebrates* (ed. S.K. Wasser), Academic Press, New York, pp. 113–168.

Erickson, K.J. and Martnez-Vargas, M.C. (1975) The hormonal basis of cooperative nest building; in *Neural and Endocrine Aspects of Behaviour of Birds* (eds P. Wright, P.G. Caryl and D.M. Vowles), Elsevier, Amsterdam, pp. 91–109.

Ewert, J.P. (1980) *Neuroethology. An Introduction to the Neurophysiological Fundamentals of Behaviour*, Springer-Verlag, Berlin.

Ewert, J.P. and Burghagen, H. (1979) Configurational prey selection by *Bufo, Alytes, Bombina* and *Hyla. Brain, Behav. Evol.*, **16**, 157–175.

Ewert, J.P. and Kehl, W. (1978) Configurational prey selection by individual experience in the toad, *Bufo bufo. J. Comp. Physiol.*, **126**, 105–114.

Ewing, A.W. (1969) The genetic basis of sound production in *Drosophila pseudobscura* and *D. persimilis. Anim. Behav.*, **17**, 555–560.

Ewing, A.W. (1975) Studies of the behaviour of cyprinodont fish II. The evolution of aggressive behaviour in the old world rivulins. *Behaviour*, **52**, 172–195.

Fagen, R.M. (1978) Repertoire analysis; in *Quantitative Ethology* (ed. P. Colgan), Wiley, New York, pp. 25–42.

Falconer, D.S. (1981) *Introduction to Quantitative Genetics*, 2nd edn, Longmans, London.

Fält, B. (1978) Differences in aggression between brooded and non-brooded domestic chicks. *Appl. Anim. Ethol.*, **4**, 211–221.

Farish, D.J. (1972) The evolutionary implications of quantitative variation in the grooming behaviour of the hymenoptera. *Anim. Behav.*, **20**, 662–676.

Farr, J.A. (1975) The role of predation in the evolution of social behaviour of natural populations of the guppy *Poecilia reticulata. Evol.*, **29**, 151–158.

Fentress, J.C. (1968) Interrupted ongoing behaviour in two species of vole (*Microtus agrestis* and *Clethrionomys brittanicus*). *Anim. Behav.*, **16**, 154–167.

Fentress, J.C. (1973) Development of grooming in mice with amputated forelimbs. *Science*, **179**, 704–705.

Fentress, J.C. (1976) Behavioural networks and the simpler systems approach; in *Simpler Networks and Behaviour* (ed. J.C. Fentress), Sinauer, Sunderland, Massachusetts, pp. 5–20.

Fentress, J.C. (1978) *Mus musicus*: the developmental orchestration of selected movement patterns in mice; in *The Development of Behaviour* (eds G.M. Burghardt and M. Bekoff), Garland Press, New York, pp. 321–342.

Fentress, J.C. (1981) Order in ontogeny: relational dynamics; in *Behavioural Development* (eds K. Immelmann, G. Barlow, L. Pertinovich and M. Main), Cambridge Univ. Press, pp. 338–371.

Fentress, J.C. and Stilwell, F.P. (1973) Grammar of a movement sequence in inbred mice. *Nature*, **244**, 52–53.

Ferguson, M.M. and Noakes, D.L. (1982) Genetics of social behaviour in charrs (*Salvelinus* spp.). *Anim. Behav.*, **30**, 128–134.

Ferron, J. (1980) Ontogenese du comportement de l'Ecureile roux (*Tamiasciurus hudsonicus*). *Can. J. Zool.*, **58**, 1090–1099.

Fix, A.G. (1978) The role of kin structured migration in genetic microdifferentiation. *Ann. Hum. Genet.*, **41**, 329–339.

Ford, R.G. and Krumme, D.W. (1979) The analysis of space use patterns. *J. Theoret. Biol.*, **76**, 125–155.

Forester, D.C. (1979) The adaptiveness of parental care in *Desmognathus ochrophaeus*. *Copeia*, 332–341.

Foster, W.A. and Treherne, J.E. (1981) Evidence for the dilution effect in the selfish herd from fish predation on a marine insect. *Nature*, **293**, 466–467.

Franck, D. (1974) The genetic basis of evolutionary change in behaviour patterns; in *The Genetics of Behaviour* (ed. J.H.F. van Abeelen), North Holland Publ. Co., Amsterdam, pp. 119–140.

Fretwell, S.D. and Lucas, H.L. (1970) On territorial behaviour and other factors influencing habitat distribution in birds. I. Theoretical development. *Acta. Biotheor.*, **19**, 16–36.

Fulker, D.W. (1966) Mating speed in male *Drosophila melanogaster*: a psychogenetic analysis. *Science*, **151**, 203–205.

Gale, J.S. and Eaves, L.J. (1975) Logic of animal conflict. *Nature*, **254**, 463–464.

Garcia, J., Ervin, F.R. and Koelling, R.A. (1966) Learning with prolonged delay of reinforcement. *Psychonom. Sci.*, **5**, 121–122.

Gatz, J. 1981. Non-random mating by size in American toads, *Bufo americanus. Anim. Behaviour*, **29**, 1004–1012.

Gee, J.H. (1969) Effect of daily synchronisation of sexual activity on mating success in laboratory population of two species of *Dacus* (Diptera). *Austr. J. Zool.*, **17**, 619–624.

Geist, V. (1971) *Mountain Sheep. A Study in Behaviour and Evolution.* Univ. of Chicago press.

Geist, V. (1974) On fighting strategies in animal conflict. *Nature*, **250**, 354.

Gibson, R. (1980) Optimal prey size selection by three spined sticklebacks (*Gasterosteus aculeatus*): a test of the apparent size hypothesis. *Z. Tierpsychol.*, **52**, 291–307.

Gilbert, D.G., Richmond, R.C. and Sheehan, K.B. (1981) Studies of esterase-6 in *Drosophila melanogaster*. VII. Remating times of females inseminated by males having active or null alleles. *Behav. Genet.*, **11**, 195–208.

Gilbert, L.E. (1976) Postmating female odour in *Heliconius* butterflies: a male contributed anti-aphrodisiac? *Science*, **193**, 419–420.

Gill, F.B. and Wolf, L.L. (1975) Economics of feeding territoriality in the goldenwinged sunbird. *Ecology*, **56**, 333–345.

Ginetz, R.M. and Larkin, P.A. (1976) Factors affecting rainbow trout (*Salmo gairdneri*) predation on migrant fry of sockeye salmon (*Onchrhynchus nerka*). *J. Fish. Res. Bd. Can.*, 33, 19–24.

Golani, I. (1976) Homeostatic motor processes in mammalian interactions: a choreography of display; in *Perspectives in Ethology Vol. 2* (eds P.P.G. Bateson and P. Klopfer), Plenum Press, New York, pp. 69–134.

Goss-Custard, J.D. (1970) Feeding dispersion in some overwintering wading birds; in *Social Behaviour in Birds and Mammals* (ed. J.H. Crook), Academic Press, London, pp. 3–34.

Goss-Custard, J.D. (1981) Feeding behaviour of redshank *Tringa totanus* and optimal foraging theory; in *Foraging Behaviour* (eds A.C. Kamil and T.D. Sargent), Garland Press, New York, pp. 115–133.

Gottlieb, G. (1971) *Development of Species Identification in Birds.* Univ. of Chicago Press.

Gottlieb, G. (1976) The roles of experience in the development of behaviour and the nervous system; in *Studies of the Development of Behaviour and the Nervous System Vol. 3* (ed. G. Gottleib), Academic Press, New York, pp. 1–35.

Gove, D.H. (1979) A comparative study of snake and lizard tongue flicking; an evolutionary hypothesis. *Z. Tierpsychol.*, 51, 58–76.

Grafen, A. (1979) The hawk–dove game played between relatives. *Anim. Behav.*, 27, 905–907.

Grant, B., Burton, S., Contoreggi, C. and Rothstein, M. (1980) Outbreeding via frequency dependent mate selection in the parasitoid wasp, *Nasonia vitripennis. Evol.*, 34, 983–992.

Gray, G.D., Kenney, A.M. and Dewsbury, D.A. (1977) Adaptive significance of the copulatory behaviour pattern of male meadow voles (*Microtus pennsylvanicus*) in relation to induction of ovulation and implantation in females. *J. Comp. Physiol. Psychol.*, 91, 1308–1319.

Gray, J.D., Cutler, C.A., Dean, J.G. and Kempe, C.H. (1979) Prediction and prevention of child abuse and neglect. *J. Soc. Issues*, 35, 127–139.

Gray, L. (1979) Feeding diversity in deermice. *J. Comp. Physiol. Psychol.*, 93, 1118–1126.

Greenberg, L. (1979) Genetic component of bee odour in kin recognition. *Science*, 206, 1095–1097.

Greig-Smith, P.W. (1982) Song rates and parental care by individual male stonechats (*Saxicola torquata*). *Anim. Behav.*, 30, 245–252.

Gromko, M.H. and Pyle, D.W. (1978) Sperm competition, male fitness and repeated mating by female *Drosophila melanogaster. Evol.*, 32, 588–593.

Gross, M.R. and Charnov, E.L. (1980) Alternative male life histories in bluegill sunfish. *Proc. Natl. Acad. Sci.*, 77, 6937–6940.

Gross, M.R. and Shine, R. (1981) Parental care and mode of fertilisation in ectothermic vertebrates. *Evol.*, 35, 775–793.

Grubb, P. and Jewell, P.A. (1966) Social grouping and home range in feral Soay sheep. *Symp. Zool. Soc. Lond.*, 18, 179–210.

Grubb, T.C. (1978) Weather-dependent foraging rates of wintering woodland birds. *Auk*, 95, 370–376.

Grubb, T.C. and Greenwald, L. (1982) Sparrows and a brushpile: foraging responses to different combinations of predation risk and energy cost. *Anim. Behav.*, 30, 637–640.

Gundlach, H. (1968) Brutfursorge, Brutpflege, Verhaltensontogenese und Takesperiodik beim Europaischen Wildschwein (*Sus scrofa*). *Z. Tierpsychol.*, **25**, 955–995.

Gurney, M.E. (1981) Hormonal control of cell form and number in the zebra finch nervous system. *J. Neuroscience*, **1**, 658–673.

Güttinger, H.R. (1981) Self-differentiation of song organisation rules by deaf canaries. *Z. Tierpsychol.*, **56**, 323–340.

Gwinner, E. (1971) A comparative study of circannual rhythms in warblers; in *Biochronometry* (ed. M. Menaker), National Academy of Science, Washington, pp. 405–427.

Gwinner, E. and Wiltschko, W. (1978) Endogenously controlled changes in migratory direction of the garden warbler, *Sylvia borin*. *J. Comp. Physiol.*, **125**, 267–273.

Gwynne, D.T. (1981) Sexual difference theory: mormon crickets show role reversal in mating. *Science*, **213**, 779–780.

Hahn, M.E. (1971) Social relationships and their development in two strains of *Mus musculus. Diss. Abst. Int.*, **32**, 585.

Hailman, J.P. (1967) The ontogeny of an instinct. *Behav. Suppl.*, **15**, 1–159.

Hailman, J.P. (1976) Uses of the comparative study of behaviour; in *Evolution, Brain and Behaviour. Persistent Problems* (eds R.B. Masterton, W. Hodos and H. Jerison), Erlbaum Associates, Hilsdale, New Jersey, pp. 13–22.

Hall, J.C. (1978) Courtship among males due to a male sterile mutation in *Drosophila melanogaster. Behav. Genet.*, **8**, 125–141.

Hall, J.C. (1979) Control of male reproductive behaviour by the central nervous system of *Drosophila*: dissection of a courtship pathway by genetic mosaics. *Genetics*, **92**, 437–457.

Hall, J.C. and Greenspan, R.J. (1979) Genetic analysis of *Drosophila* neurobiology. *Ann. Rev. Genet.*, **13**, 127–195.

Halliday, T.R. (1975) An observational and experimental study of sexual behaviour in the smooth newt, *Triturus vulgaris. Anim. Behav.*, **23**, 291–322.

Halliday, T.R. (1976) The libidinous newt: an analysis of variations in the sexual behaviour of the male smooth newt, *Triturus vulgaris. Anim. Behav.*, **24**, 398–414.

Hamilton, W.D. (1964) The genetical theory of social behaviour. *J. Theoret. Biol.*, **7**, 1–52.

Hamilton, W.D. (1967) Extraordinary sex ratios. *Science.*, **156**, 477–485.

Hamilton, W.D. (1971) Geometry for the selfish herd. *J. Theoret. Biol.*, **31**, 295–311.

Hamilton, W.D. (1979) Wingless and fighting males in fig wasps and other insects; in *Sexual Selection and Reproductive Competition in Insects* (eds M.S. Blum and N.A. Blum), Academic Press, London, pp. 167–220.

Hamilton, W.D. and May, R.M. (1977) Dispersal in stable habitats. *Nature*, **269**, 578–581.

Hamilton, W.D., Henderson, P.A. and Moran, N.A. (1981) Fluctuation of environment and coevolved antagonist polymorphism as factors in the maintainence of sex; in *Natural Selection and Social Behaviour* (eds R.D. Alexander and D.W. Tinkle), Chiron Press, New York, pp. 363–381.

Harcourt, A.H., Harvey, P.H., Larson, S.G. and Short, R.V. (1981) Testis weight, body weight and breeding system in primates. *Nature*, **293**, 55–57.

Harlow, H.F. and Harlow, M.K. (1965) The affectional systems; in *Behaviour of Nonhuman Primates II* (eds A.M. Schrier, H.F. Harlow and F. Stollnitz), Academic Press, New York, pp. 287–334.

Harmon, L.D. (1964) Problems in neural modelling; in *Neural Theory and Modelling* (ed. R.F. Reiss), Stanford Univ. Press, pp. 9–30.

Hasler, A. (1960) Guideposts of migrating fishes. *Science,* 132, 785–792.

Hassell, M.P. (1979) Non-random search in predator–prey models. *Fortschr. Zool.,* 25, 311–330.

Hassell, M.P. and May, R.M. (1974) Aggregation of predators and insect parasites and its effect on stability. *J. An. Ecol.,* 43, 567–594.

Heiligenberg, W. (1973) Random processes describing the occurrence of behaviour patterns in a cichlid fish. *Anim. Behav.,* 21, 169–182.

Heiligenberg, W. (1974) Processes governing behavioural states of readiness. *Adv. St. Behav.,* 5, 173–200.

Heiligenberg, W. (1976) A probabilistic approach to the motivation of behaviour; in *Simpler Networks and Behaviour* (ed. J.C. Fentress), Sinauer, Sunderland, Massachusetts, pp. 301–313.

Heinrich, B. (1979a) *Bumblebee Economics,* Harvard University Press.

Heinrich, B. (1979b) 'Majoring' and 'minoring' by foraging bumblebees, *Bombus vagans*: an experimental analysis. *Ecology,* 60, 245–255.

Heinsenberg, M. and Buchner, E. (1977) The role of retinula cell types in visual behaviour of *Drosophila melanogaster. J. Comp. Physiol.,* 117, 127–162.

Heller, R. and Milinski, M. (1979) Optimal foraging of sticklebacks on swarming prey. *Anim. Behav.,* 27, 1127–1241.

Hemsworth, P.H., Beilharz, R.G. and Brown, W.J. (1978) The importance of the courting behaviour of the boar on the success of natural and artificial mating. *Appl. Anim. Ethol.,* 4, 341–347.

Hilborn, R. (1975) Similarities in dispersal tendencies among siblings in four species of vole. *Ecology,* 56, 1221–1225.

Hinde, R.A. (1970) *Animal Behaviour,* 2nd edn, McGraw-Hill, New York.

Hinde, R.A. (1975) The concept of function; in *Function and Evolution of Behaviour* (eds G. Baerends, C. Beer and A. Manning), Clarendon Press, Oxford, pp. 3–15.

Hinde, R.A. (1979) *Towards Understanding Relationships,* Academic Press, London.

Hinde, R.A. (1981) Animal signals: ethological and games theory approaches are not incompatible. *Anim. Behav.,* 29, 535–542.

Hinde, R.A. (1982) *Ethology,* Oxford Univ. Press.

Hinde, R.A. and McGinnis, I. (1977) Some factors influencing the effects of temporary mother–infant separation – some experiments with rhesus monkeys. *Psychol. Med.,* 7, 197–212.

Hirsch, J. (1967) *Behaviour Genetic Analysis,* McGraw-Hill, New York.

Hodgekin, J. (1983) Male phenotypes and mating efficiency in *Caenorhabdihs elegans. Genetics,* 103, 43–64.

Hölldobler, B. and Lumsden, C.J. (1980) Territorial strategies in ants. *Science,* 210, 732–739.

Hörmann-Heck, S.V. (1957) Untersuchungen über den Erbgang einiger Verhaltensweisen bei Gryllenbastarden (*Gryllus campestris×Gryllus bimaculatus*). *Z. Tierpsychol.,* 14, 137–183.

Hotta, Y. and Benzer, S. (1972) Mapping of behaviour in *Drosophila* mosaics. *Nature,* 240, 527–535.

Hotta, Y. and Benzer, S. (1976) Courtship in *Drosophila* mosaics: sex specific foci for sequential action patterns. *Proc. Natl. Acad. Sci.*, **73**, 4145–4158.

Houston, A.I. (1980) Godzilla v. the creature from the black lagoon – ethology v. psychology; in *The Analysis of Motivational Processes* (eds F.M. Toates and T.R. Halliday), Academic Press, London, pp. 297–318.

Houston, A.I. and McFarland, D.J. (1976) On the measurement of motivational variables. *Anim. Behav.*, **24**, 459–475.

Houston, A.I., Halliday, T.R. and McFarland, D.J. (1977) Towards a model of the courtship of the smooth newt, *Triturus vulgaris*. *Med. Biol. Eng. Comp.*, **15**, 49–61.

Hover, E.L. and Jenssen, T.A. (1976) Descriptive analysis and social correlates of agonistic displays of *Anolis limnifrons*. *Behaviour*, **58**, 173–191.

Howard, J.C. (1977) H-2 and mating preferences. *Nature*, **266**, 406–408.

Howard, R.D. (1978) The influence of male defended oviposition sites on early embryo mortality in bullfrogs. *Ecology*, **59**, 789–798.

Howell, D.J. (1979) Flock foraging in nectar feeding bats: advantages to the bats and to the host plants. *Amer. Nat.*, **114**, 23–49.

Hoy, R.R. and Paul, R.C. (1973) Genetic control of song specificity in crickets. *Science*, **180**, 82–83.

Hoy, R.R., Hahn, J. and Paul, R.C. (1977) Hybrid cricket auditory behaviour: evidence for genetic coupling in animal communication. *Science*, **195**, 82–83.

Huck, V.W., Banks, E.M. and Wang, S.C. (1981) Olfactory discrimination of social status in the brown lemming. *Behav. Neur. Biol.*, **33**, 364–371.

Humphrey, N.K. (1976) The social function of intellect; in *Growing Points in Ethology* (eds P.P.G. Bateson and R.A. Hinde), Cambridge Univ. Press, pp. 303–317.

Hunt, G.L. and Hunt, M.W. (1976) Gull chick survival: the significance of growth rates, timing of breeding and territory size. *Ecology*, **57**, 62–75.

Huntingford, F.A. (1976) An investigation of the territorial behaviour of the three spined stickleback (*Gasterosteus aculeatus*) using principal components analysis. *Anim. Behav.*, **24**, 822–834.

Immelmann, K. (1969) Song development in the zebra finch and other *Estrildid* finches; in *Bird Vocalisations* (ed. R.A. Hinde), University Press, Cambridge, pp. 61–74.

Jacques, A.R. and Dill, L.M. (1980) Zebra spiders may use uncorrelated asymmetries to settle contests. *Amer. Nat.*, **116**, 899–901.

Jaisson, P. (1980) Environmental preference induced experimentally in ants. *Nature*, **286**, 388–389.

Jarman, P.J. (1974) The social organisation of antelope in relation to their ecology. *Behaviour*, **48**, 215–267.

Jenni, D.A. and Collier, G. (1972) Polyandry in the American jacana. *Auk*, **89**, 743–765.

Jenssen, T.A. (1978) Display diversity in anole lizards and problems of interpretation; in *Behaviour and Neurology of Lizards* (eds N. Greenberg and P.D. MacLean) N.I.M.H. Publ., pp. 269–286.

Johnson, M.H. and Everitt, B.J. (1980) *Essential Reproduction*, Blackwell Scientific Publications, Oxford.

Jones, J.W. (1959) *The Salmon*, Collins, London.

Jumars, P.A., Thistle, D. and Jones, M.L. (1977) Detecting two-dimensional spatial structure in biological data. *Oecologia*, **28**, 109–123.

Kallman, D. and Schreibman, M.P. (1973) A sex-linked gene controlling gonadotrop differentiation and its significance in determining the age of sexual maturation and size of the platyfish, *Xiphophorus maculatus. Gen. Comp. End.*, 21, 287–304.

Karlson, P. and Lüscher, M. (1959) Pheromones: a new term for a class of biologically active substances. *Nature*, 183, 55–56.

Kasang, G. and Kaissling, K.E. (1972) Specificity of primary and secondary olfactory processes in *Bombyx* antennae; in *Proceedings of the 4th International Symposium on Olfaction and Taste. Seeweisen, Germany. 1971* (ed. D. Schneider), Wissenschafliche Verlagsgesellschaft MBH, Stuttgart, pp. 200–206.

Kenward, R.E. (1978) Hawks and doves: attack success and selection in goshawk flights at woodpigeon. *J. An. Ecol.*, 47, 449–460.

Kessel, E.L. (1955) The mating activities of balloon flies. *Syst. Zool.*, 4, 97–104.

Keverne, E.B. (1976) Sexual receptivity and attractiveness in the female rhesus monkey. *Adv. St. Behav.*, 7, 155–200.

Kilgour, R. (1978) The application of animal behaviour and the humane care of farm animals. *J. Anim. Sci.*, 46, 1478–1486.

Kilgour, R. and De Langen, H. (1970) Stress in sheep resulting from farm management practices. *Proc. New Zealand Soc. Anim. Prod.*, 30, 65–76.

Kleiman, D.G. (1980) The sociobiology of captive propagation; in *Conservation Biology* (eds M.E. Soule and B.A. Wilcox), Sinauer, Sunderland, Mass, pp. 234–261.

Knowlton, N. (1980) Sexual selection and dimorphism in two demes of a symbiotic, pair-bonding snapping shrimp. *Evol.*, 34, 161–173.

Konishi, M. (1965) The role of auditory feedback in the control of vocalisation in the white-crowned sparrow. *Z. Tierpsychol.*, 22, 770–783.

Konopka, R.J. and Benzer, S. (1971) Clock mutants of *Drosophila melanogaster. Proc. Natl. Acad. Sci.*, 68, 2112–2116.

Koolhaas, J.M., Schuurman, T. and Wiepkema, P.R. (1980) The organisation of intra-specific agonistic behaviour in the rat. *Prog. Neurobiol.*, 15, 247–268.

Kovach, J.K. and Wilson, G.C. (1980) Behaviour and pleiotrophy: generalisation of gene effects in the colour preference of Japanese quail chicks. *Anim. Behav.*, 29, 746–759.

Kovach, J.K., Yeatman, F.R. and Wilson, G. (1980) Perception or preference? Mediation of gene effects in the colour choices of naive quail chicks. *Anim. Behav.*, 29, 760–770.

Kramm, K.R. (1980) Why circadian rhythms? *Amer. Nat.*, 116, 452–453.

Krebs, C.J. (1979) Dispersal, spacing behaviour and genetics in relation to population fluctuation in the vole *Microtus townsendii. Forschr. Zool.*, 25, 61–77.

Krebs, J.R. (1974) Colonial nesting and social feeding as strategies for exploiting food resources in the great blue heron (*Ardea herodias*). *Behaviour*, 51, 99–134.

Krebs, J.R. (1978) Optimal foraging: decision rules for predators; in *Behavioural Ecology* (eds J.R. Krebs and N. Davies), Blackwell Scientfic Publications, Oxford, pp. 23–63.

Krebs, J.R. and Davies, N.B. (1981) *Introduction to Behavioural Ecology*, Blackwell Scientific Publications, Oxford.

Krebs, J.R., Kacelnik, A. and Taylor, P. (1978) Test of optimal sampling by foraging great tits. *Nature*, 275, 27–31.

Krebs, J.R., MacRoberts, M.H. and Cullen, J.M. (1972) Flocking and feeding in the great tit, *Parus major* – an experimental study. *Ibis*, 114, 507–530.

Krebs, J.R., Ryan, J.C. and Charnov, E.L. (1974) Hunting by expectation or optimal foraging? A study of patch use by chickadees. *Anim. Behav.*, 22, 953–964.

Kroodsma, D.E. (1977) Correlates of song organisation among North American wrens. *Amer. Nat.*, 111, 995–1008.

Kroodsma, D.E. (1978) Aspects of learning in the ontogeny of bird song: where, from whom, when, how many, which and how accurately? in *The Development of Behaviour* (eds G.P. Burghart and M. Bekoff), Garland Press, New York, pp. 215–230.

Kroodsma, D.E. (1981) Ontogeny of bird song; in *Behavioural Development* (eds K. Immelmann, G.W. Barlow, L. Petrinovich and M. Main), Cambridge Univ. Press, pp. 518–532.

Kroodsma, D.E. and Pickert, R. (1980) Environmentally dependent sensitive periods for avian vocal learning. *Nature*, 288, 477–480.

Kruijt, J.P. (1964) Ontogeny of social behaviour in Burmese red jungle fowl (*Gallus gallus spacticeus*). *Behav. Suppl.*, 12, 1–201.

Kruijt, J.P., de Vos, G.J. and Bossema, I. (1972) The arena system of black grouse. *Proc. Int. Ornith. Congr.*, 15, 339–423.

Kruuk, H. (1972) *The Spotted Hyena*, Univ. of Chicago Press.

Kyriacou, C.P. (1981) The relation between locomotor activity and sexual behaviour in ebony strains of *Drosophila melanogaster*. *Anim. Behav.*, 29, 462–471.

Kyriacou, C.P. and Hall, J.C. (1980) Circadian rhythm mutations in *Drosophila melanogaster* affect short-term fluctuations in the male's courtship song. *Proc. Natl. Acad. Sci.*, 77, 6729–6733.

Kyriacou, C.P., Burnet, B. and Connolly, K.J. (1978) The behavioural basis of over-dominance in competitive mating success at the ebony locus in *Drosophila melanogaster*. *Anim. Behav.*, 26, 1195–1207.

Lacy, R.C. (1980) The evolution of eusociality in termites: a haplodiploid analogy. *Amer. Nat.*, 116, 449–451.

Le Boeuf, B.J. (1972) Sexual behaviour in northern elephant seals. *Behaviour*, 41, 1–26.

Lefebvre, L. (1981) Grooming in crickets: timing and hierarchical organisation. *Anim. Behav.*, 29, 973–984.

Lehrman, D.S. (1964) The reproductive behaviour of ring doves. *Sci. Amer.*, 211, 48–54.

Lehrman, D.S. (1970) Semantic and conceptual issues in the nature–nurture problem; in *Development and Evolution of Behaviour* (eds L.R. Aronsen, E. Tobach, D.S. Lehrman and J. S. Rosenblatt), Freeman, San Francisco, pp. 17–52.

Lester, L.J. and Selander, R.K. (1981) Genetic relatedness and the social organisation of *Polistes* colonies. *Amer. Nat.*, 117, 147–166.

Lewis, J.A. and Hodgkin, J.A. (1977) Specific neuroanatomical changes in chemosensory mutants of the nematode *Caenorhabditis elegans*. *J. Comp. Neurol.*, 172, 489–510.

Lewis, J.G. (1977) Game domestication for animal production in Kenya: activity patterns of eland, oryx, buffalo and zebu cattle. *J. Agric. Sci.*, 89, 551–563.

Lewontin, R.C. (1978) Adaptation. *Sci. Amer.*, 239, 156–169.

Lieberman, P. (1977) The phylogeny of language; in *How Animals Communicate* (ed. T.A. Sebeok), Indiana Univ. Press, pp. 3–25.

Liem, K.F. (1980) Adaptive significance of intra- and interspecific differences in the feeding repertoires of cichlid fishes. *Amer. Zool.*, 20, 295–314.

Liley, N.R. and Seghers, B.H. (1975) Factors affecting the morphology and behaviour of guppies in Trinidad; in *Function and Evolution of Behaviour* (eds G.P. Baerends, C. Beer and A. Manning), Clarendon Press, Oxford, pp. 92–118.

Lin, N. and Michener, C.D. (1972) Evolution of sociality in insects. *Q. Rev. Biol.*, 47, 131–159.

Lind, H. and Poulsen, H. (1963) On the morphology and behaviour of a hybrid between goosander and shelduck (*Mergus merganser* and *Tadorna tadorna*). *Z. Tierpsychol.*, **20**, 558–569.

Lindsley, D.L. and Grell, E.H. (1968) Genetic variants of *Drosophila melanogaster. Carnegia Instit. of Washington Publ. No. 627.*

Lloyd, M. and Dybas, H.S. (1966) The periodic cicada problem I. Population ecology. *Evol.*, **20**, 133–149.

Lorenz, K. (1937) The companion in the bird's world. *Auk*, **54**, 245–273.

Lorenz, K. (1941) Vergleichende Bewegungsstudien an Anatinen. *J. Ornith.*, **89**, 194–294.

Lorenz, K. (1950) The comparative method in studying innate behaviour. *Symp. Soc. Exp. Biol.*, **4**, 221–268.

Lorenz, K. (1966) *On Aggression*, Methuen, London.

Lorenz, K (1973) The fashionable fallacy of dispensing with description. *Naturwissensch.*, **60**, 1–9.

Lorenz, K. and Tinbergen, N. (1938) Taxis und Instinkthandlung in der Eirollbewegung der Graugans. *Z. Tierpsychol.*, **2**, 1–29.

Losey, G.S. (1978) Information theory and communication; in *Quantitative Ethology* (ed. P.W. Colgan), Wiley, New York, pp. 43–78.

Losey, G.S. (1982) Intra- and interspecific aggression by the central American midas cichlid fish, *Cichlasoma citrinellum. Behaviour*, **79**, 39–80.

Low, B.S. (1978) Environmental uncertainty and the parental strategies of marsupials and placentals. *Amer. Nat.*, **112**, 107–124.

Low, W.A., Tweedie, R.L., Edwards, C.B.H., Hodder, R.M., Malafant, K.W.J. and Cunningham, R.P. (1981) The influence of environment on daily maintenance behaviour of free ranging shorthorn cows in central Australia. *Appl. Anim. Ethol.*, **7**, 11–26.

Lund, R.D. (1978) *Development and Plasticity of the Brain*, Oxford Univ. Press, New York.

MacBean, I.T. (1970) The genetic control of quantitative characteristics in *Drosophila*. Ph.D. Thesis, La Trobe Univ.

McCauley, D.E. and Wade, M.J. (1978) Female choice and the mating structure of a natural population of the soldier beetle. *Evol.*, **32**, 771–775.

McCracken, G.F. and Bradbury, J.W. (1977) Paternity and genetic heterogeneity in the polygynous bat, *Phyllostomus hastatus. Science*, **198**, 303–306.

MacDonald, D. (1980) *Wildlife and Rabies*, Oxford Univ. Press.

MacDonald, D., Ball, F.G. and Hough, N.G. (1980) The evaluation of home range size and configuration using radiotracking data; in *A Handbook on Biotelemetry and Radiotracking* (eds C.J. Amlaner and D.W. MacDonald), Pergamon Press, Oxford, pp. 405–424.

McFarland, D.J. (1974) Time sharing as a behavioural phenomenon. *Adv. St. Behav.*, **5**, 201–227.

McFarland, D.J. and Houston, A. (1981) *Quantitative Ethology*, Pitman, London.

McGregor, P.K. and Krebs, J.R. (1982) Mating and song type in the great tit. *Nature*, **297**, 60–61.

Machlis, L. (1977) An analysis of the temporal patterning of pecking in chicks. *Behaviour*, **63**, 1–70.

McKay, T.F.C. and Doyle, R.W. (1978) An ecological–genetic analysis of the settling behaviour of a marine polychaete. i. Probability of settlement and gregarious behaviour. *Heredity*, 40, 1–12.

McKinney, F. (1978) Comparative approaches to social behaviour in closely related species of birds. *Adv. St. Behav.*, 8, 1–38.

MacKinnon, C.N. and Donaldson, E.M. (1976) Environmentally induced precocious sexual development in the male pink salmon (*Oncorhynchus gorbuscha*). *J. Fish. Res. Bd. Can.*, 33, 2602–2605.

Manning, A. (1961) Effects of artificial selection for mating speed in *Drosophila melanogaster*. *Anim. Behav.*, 9, 82–92.

Manning, A. (1968) The effects of artificial selection for slow mating speed in *Drosophila simulans* 1. The behavioural changes. *Anim. Behav.*, 16, 108–113.

Manning, A. (1979) *An Introduction to Animal Behaviour*, 3rd edn, Edward Arnold, London.

Marler, P. (1975) On strategies of behavioural development; in *Function and Evolution in Behaviour* (eds G.P. Baerends, C. Beer and A. Manning), Clarendon Press, Oxford, pp. 254–275.

Marler, P. (1976) Sensory templates in species specific behaviour; in *Simpler Networks and Behaviour* (ed. J.C. Fentress), Sinauer, Sunderland, Massachusetts, pp. 314–329.

Marler, P. and Hamilton, W.J. (1966) *Mechanisms of Animal Behaviour*, Wiley, New York.

Marler, P. and Sherman, V. (1983) Song structure without auditory feedback: emendations of the auditory template hypothesis. *J. Neurosci.*, 3, 517–531.

Marler, P. and Tamura, M. (1962) Song dialects in three populations of white crowned sparrows. *Condor*, 64, 368–377.

Marshall, L.D. and Alcock, J. (1981) The evolution of the mating system of the carpenter bee *Xylocopa varipunctata*. *J. Zool.*, 193, 315–324.

Massey, A. (1977) Agonistic aids and kinship in a group of pigtail macaques. *Behav. Ecol. Sociobiol.*, 2, 31–40.

Maynard Smith, J. (1964) Group selection and kin selection. *Nature*, 201, 1145–1147.

Maynard Smith, J. (1966) Sympatric speciation. *Amer. Nat.*, 100, 637–650.

Maynard Smith, J. (1974) The theory of games and the evolution of animal conflicts. *J. Theoret. Biol.*, 47, 209–221.

Maynard Smith, J. (1977) Parental investment: a prospective analysis. *Anim. Behav.*, 25, 1–9.

Maynard Smith, J. (1978a) *The Evolution of Sex*, Cambridge Univ. Press.

Maynard Smith, J. (1978b) The handicap principle – a comment. *J. Theoret. Biol.*, 70, 251–252.

Maynard Smith, J. (1979) Games theory and the evolution of behaviour. *Proc. Roy. Soc. B*, 205, 475–488.

Maynard Smith, J. (1981) Will a sexual population evolve towards an ESS? *Amer. Nat.*, 117, 1015–1018.

Maynard Smith, J. and Parker, G.A. (1976) The logic of asymmetric contests. *Anim. Behav.*, 24, 159–175.

Maynard Smith, J. and Price, G.R. (1973) The logic of animal conflict. *Nature*, 246, 15–18.

Mayr, E. (1978) Evolution. *Sci. Amer.*, 239, 38–47.

Meaney, M.J. and Stewart, J. (1981) A descriptive study of social behaviour in the rat (*Rattus norvegicus*). *Anim. Behav.*, 29, 34–45.

Metcalf, R.A. and Whitt, G.S. (1977) Intra-nest relatedness in the social wasp *Polistes metricus*. *Behav. Ecol. Syst.*, **2**, 339–360.

Metz, H. (1974) Stochastic models for the temporal fine structure of behaviour sequences; in *Motivational Control Systems Analysis* (ed. D.J. McFarland), Academic Press, London, pp. 5–86.

Meyerson, B.J. and Malmnas, E.O. (1978) Brain monoamines and sexual behaviour; in *Biological Determinants of Sexual Behaviour* (ed. J.B. Hutchison), Wiley, Chichester, pp. 521–554.

Milinski, M. (1979) An evolutionarily stable feeding strategy in sticklebacks. *Z. Tierpsychol.*, **51**, 36–40.

Milinski, M. and Heller, R. (1978) Influence of a predator on the optimal foraging behaviour of sticklebacks (*Gasterosteus aculeatus*). *Nature*, **275**, 642–644.

Mock, D.W. (1980) Communication strategies of great blue herons and great egrets. *Behaviour*, **72**, 156–170.

Moehlman, P.D. (1979) Jackal helpers and pup survival. *Nature*, **277**, 382–383.

Morgan, B.J.T., Simpson, M.J.A., Hanby, J.P. and Hall-Craggs, J. (1976) Visualizing interaction and sequential data in animal behaviour; theory and application of cluster analysis. *Behaviour*, **56**, 1–35.

Morris, D. (1952) Homosexuality in the ten-spined stickleback. *Behaviour*, **4**, 233–261.

Muckensturm, B. (1968) La significance de la livrée nuptiale de l'épinoche. *Rev. Comp. Anim.*, **3**, 39–64.

Nagel, V. (1971) Social organisation in a baboon hybrid zone. *Congr. Primat.*, **3**, 48–57.

Naylor, E. (1958) Tidal and diurnal rhythms of locomotory activity in *Carcinus maenus*. *J. Exp. Biol.*, **35**, 602–610.

Neill, S.R. St. J. and Cullen, J.M. (1974) Experiments on whether schooling by their prey affects the hunting behaviour of cephalopod and fish predators. *J. Zool.*, **172**, 549–569.

Nelson, K. (1965) After effects of courtship in the male three-spined stickleback. *Zeit. Vergl. Physiol.*, **50**, 569–597.

Nelson, K. and Hedgecock, D. (1977) Electrophoretic evidence of multiple paternity in the lobster *Homarus americanus*. *Amer. Nat.*, **111**, 361–363.

Nesbitt, M.N. (1978) Attempts at locating the site of action of genes controlling behaviour; in *Genetic Mosaics and Chimeras in Mammals* (ed. L.B. Russel), Plenum Press, New York, pp. 51–58.

Neumann, D. (1975) Lunar and tidal rhythms in the development and reproduction of inter-tidal organisms; in *Physiological Adaptation to the Environment* (ed. F.J. Vernberg), Intext Educational Publ., New York, pp. 451–463.

Neumann, D. and Heimbach, F. (1979) Time cues for semi-lunar reproductive rhythms in European populations of *Clunio marinus*. The influence of tidal cycles of mechanical disturbances; in *Cyclic Phenomena in Marine Plants and Animals* (eds E. Naylor and R.G. Hartnoll), Pergamon Press, Oxford, pp. 423–434.

Nissani, M. (1977) Gynandromorph analysis of some aspects of sexual behaviour of *Drosophila melanogaster*. *Anim. Behav.*, **25**, 555–566.

Northup, L.R. (1977) Temporal patterning of grooming in three lines of mice; some factors influencing control levels of a complex behaviour. *Behaviour*, **61**, 1–25.

Nottebohm, F. (1968) Auditory experience and song development in the chaffinch (*Fringilla coelebs*). *Ibis*, **110**, 549–568.

Nottebohm, F. (1980) Brain pathways for vocal learning in birds. A review of the first 10 years. *Progr. Psychobiol. Physiol. Psychol.*, **9**, 85–124.

Novy, J.E. (1978) Operation of a screwworm eradication programme; in *The Screwworm Problem* (ed. R.H. Richards), University of Texas Press, Austin.

Oatley, K. and Toates, F.M. (1969) The passage of food through the gut of rats and its uptake of fluid. *Psychonom. Sci.*, **16**, 225–226.

O'Brien, W.J., Slade, N.A. and Vinyard, G.L. (1976) Apparent size as the determinant of prey selection by bluegill sunfish (*Lepomis macrochirus*). *Ecology*, **57**, 1304–1311.

Oden, N. (1977) Partitioning dependence in non-stationary behavioural sequences; in *Quantitative Methods in Animal Behaviour* (ed. B. Hazlett), Atheneum, New York, pp. 203–220.

O'Donald, O. (1980) *Genetic Models of Sexual Selection*, Cambridge Univ. Press.

Oosterhoff, L.M. (1977) Variation in growth rate as an ecological factor in landsnails, *Cepea nemoralis. Neth. J. Zool.*, **27**, 1–8.

Oppenheim, R.W. (1974) The ontogeny of behaviour in the chick embryo. *Adv. St. Behav.*, **5**, 133–172.

Orians, G.H. (1969) On the evolution of mating systems in birds and mammals. *Amer. Nat.*, **103**, 589–603.

Otte, D. (1974) Effects and functions in the evolutions of signalling systems. *Ann. Rev. Ecol. Syst.*, **5**, 385–417.

Owings, D.H. and Lockard, R.B. (1971) Different nocturnal activity patterns of *Peromyscus californicus* and *Peromyscus eremicus* in lunar lighting. *Psychonom. Sci.*, **22**, 63–64.

Packer, C. (1977) Reciprocal altruism in *Papio anubis. Nature*, **265**, 441–443.

Packer, C. and Pusey, A.E. (1982) Cooperation and competition within coalitions of male lions: kin selection or games theory? *Nature*, **296**, 740–742.

Parker, G.A. (1978) Searching for mates; in *Behavioural Ecology* (eds J.R. Krebs and N. Davies), Blackwell Scientific Publications, Oxford, pp. 214–244.

Parker, G.A. (1979) Sexual selection and sexual conflict; in *Sexual Selection and Reproductive Competition in Insects* (eds M.S. Blum and N.A. Blum), Academic Press, New York, pp. 123–166.

Parker, G.A. and Stuart, R.A. (1976) Animal behaviour as a strategy optimiser. *Amer. Nat.*, **110**, 1055–1076.

Parker, G.A., Baker, R.R. and Smith, V.G.F. (1972) The origin and evolution of gamete dimorphism and the male female phenomenon. *J. Theoret. Biol.*, **36**, 529–553.

Parry, V. (1973) The auxiliary social system and its effects on territory and breeding in kookaburras. *Emu*, **73**, 81–100.

Partridge, B. (1980a) The effect of school size on the structure and dynamics of minnow schools. *Anim. Behav.*, **28**, 68–77.

Partridge, L. (1980b) Mate choice increases a component of offspring fitness in fruit flies. *Nature*, **283**, 290–291.

Patton, J.L. and Feder, J.H. (1981) Microspatial genetic heterogeneity in pocket gophers; non-random breeding and genetic drift. *Evol.*, **35**, 912–920.

Pengelley, E. and Asmundson, S. (1971) Annual biological clocks. *Sci. Amer.*, **224 (4)**, 72–79.

Perrill, S.A., Gerhardt, H.C. and Daniel, R. (1978) Sexual parasitism in the green tree frog (*Hyla cinerea*). *Science*, **200**, 1179–1180.

Pielou, E.C. (1974) *Population and Community Ecology. Principles and Methods*, Gordon and Breach, New York.

Pitcher, T.J. (1973) The three-dimensional structure of schools in the minnow *Phoxinus phoxinus*. *Anim. Behav.*, **21**, 673–686.

Pittendrigh, C.S. (1956) Adaptation, natural selection and behaviour; in *Behaviour and Evolution* (eds A. Roe and G.G. Simpson), Yale Univ. Press, New Haven, pp. 390–427.

Pittendrigh, C.S. (1966) The circadian oscillation in *Drosophila pseudobscura* pupae; a model for the photoperiodic clock. *Z. Planzenphysiol.*, **54**, 275–307.

Pittendrigh, C.S. and Daan, S. (1976) A functional analysis of circadian pacemakers in nocturnal rodents; IV. Entrainment: pacemakers as clock. *J. Comp. Physiol.*, **106**, 291–331.

Pleszczynska, W. (1978) Microgeographic prediction of polygyny in the lark bunting. *Science*, **201**, 935–937.

Pleszczynska, W. and Hansell, R.I.C. (1980) Polygyny and decision theory: testing a model in lark buntings (*Calamospiza melanocorys*). *Amer. Nat*, **116**, 821–830.

Plomin, R.J. and Manosevitz, M. (1974) Behavioural polytypism in wild *Mus musculus*. *Behav. Genet.*, **4**, 145–157.

Plomin, R.J., DeFries, J.C. and McClearn, G.E. (1980) *Behavioural Genetics; a Primer*. Freeman, San Francisco.

Pollack, G.S. and Hoy, R.R. (1979) Temporal pattern as a cue for species-specific calling song recognition in crickets. *Science*, **204**, 429–432.

Potter, D.A. (1981) Agonistic behaviour in male spider mites: factors affecting frequency and intensity of fighting. *Ann. Ent. Soc. Amer.*, **74**, 138–143.

Price, P.H. (1979) Developmental determinants of structure in zebra finch song. *J. Comp. Physiol. Psychol.*, **93**, 260–277.

Pringle, J.W.S. (1964) Input and output elements of behaviour models; in *Neural Theory and Modelling* (ed. R.F. Reiss), Stanford Univ. Press, pp. 31–42.

Pyke, G.H. (1978a) Optimal foraging in hummingbirds; testing the marginal value theory. *Amer. Zool.*, **18**, 739–752.

Pyke, G.H. (1978b) Optimal foraging: movement patterns of bumblebees between inflorescences. *Theoret. Pop. Biol.*, **13**, 72–98.

Pyke, G.H. (1978c) Optimal foraging in bumblebees and coevolution with their plants. *Oecologia*, **36**, 281–293.

Pyle, D.W. and Gromko, M.H. (1978) Repeated mating by female *Drosophila melanogaster*: the adaptive importance. *Experientia*, **34**, 449–450.

Pyle, D.W. and Gromko, M.H. (1981) Genetic basis for repeated mating in *Drosophila melanogaster*. *Amer. Nat.*, **117**, 133–146.

Rand, W.M. and Rand, A.S. (1976) Agonistic behaviour in nesting iguanas: a stochastic analysis of dispute settlement dominated by the minimisation of energy lost. *Z. Tierpsychol.*, **40**, 279–299.

Rapport, D.J. (1981) Foraging behaviour of *Stentor coerulens*: a microeconomic interpretation; in *Foraging Behaviour* (eds A.C. Kamil and T.D. Sargent), Garland Press, New York, pp. 77–94.

Reinhardt, V. and Reinhardt, A. (1981) Cohesive relationships in a cattle herd (*Bos indicus*). *Behaviour*, **77**, 121–150.

Rendel, J.M. (1951) Mating of ebony, vestigial and wildtype *D. melanogaster* in light and dark. *Evol.*, **5**, 226–230.

Richards, A. (1974) Intra-specific variation in the social organisation and ecology of *Propithecus verreauxi*. *Folia Primat.*, **22**, 178–207.

Riddell, B.E. and Leggett, W.C. (1981) Evidence of an adaptive basis for geographic variation in body morphology and time of downstream migration of juvenile atlantic salmon (*Salmo salar*). *Can. J. Fish. Aqu. Sci.*, **38**, 308–320.

Robertson, R.J. and Biermann, G.C. (1979) Parental investment strategies determined by expected benefits. *Z. Tierpsychol.*, **50**, 124–128.

Röell, A. (1978) Social behaviour of the jackdaw, *Corvus monedula*, in relation to its niche. *Behaviour*, **64**, 1–124.

Rood, J.P. (1978) Dwarf mongoose helpers at the den. *Z. Tierpsychol.*, **48**, 277–287.

Roper, T.J. (1978) A possible function for time sharing. *Anim. Behav.*, **26**, 1277–1278.

Rosenzweig, M.L. (1979) Optimal habitat selection in two-species competitive situations. *Fortsch. Zool.*, **25**, 283–295.

Rothenbuhler, W.C. (1964) Behaviour genetics of nest cleaning in honey bees. 4. Responses of F1 and backcross generations to disease killed brood. *Amer. Zool.*, **4**, 111–123.

Rowe, F.P. and Redfern, R. (1969) Aggressive behaviour in related and unrelated wild housemice (*Mus musculus*). *Ann. Appl. Biol.*, **64**, 425–431.

Rowley, I. (1965) The life history of the superb blue wren. *Emu*, **64**, 251–297.

Rowley, I. (1981) The communal way of life of the splendid wren, *Malurus splendens*. *Z. Tierpsychol.*, **55**, 228–267.

Russel, W.M.S., Mead, A.P. and Hayes, J.S. (1954) A basis for the quantitative study of the structure of behaviour. *Behaviour*, **6**, 153–205.

Ryan, M.J., Tuttle, M.D. and Rand, A.S. (1982) Bat predation and sexual advertisement in a neotropical anuran. *Amer. Nat.*, **119**, 136–139.

Sachs, B.D. and Meisel, R.L. (1979) Pubertal development of penile reflexes and copulation in male rats. *Psychoneuroend.*, **4**, 287–296.

Sahlins, M. (1976) *The Use and Abuse of Biology*, Univ. of Michigan Press, Ann Arbor.

Sakaluk, S.K. and Cade, W.H. (1980) Female mating frequency and progeny production in single and doubly mated house and field crickets. *Can. J. Zool.*, **58**, 404–411.

Schemmel, C. (1980) Studies on the genetics of feeding behaviour in the cave fish *Astyanax mexicanus*. An example of apparent monofactorial inheritance by polygenes. *Z. Tierpsychol.*, **53**, 9–22.

Schenkel, R. (1956) Zur Deutung der Phasianidenbalz. *Ornithol. Beobacht.*, **53**, 182.

Schilcher, F. von (1977) A mutation which changes courtship song in *Drosophila melanogaster*. *Behav. Genet.*, **7**, 251–259.

Schilcher, F. von and Hall, J.C. (1979) Neural topography of courtship in sex mosaics of *Drosophila melanogaster*. *J. Comp. Physiol.*, **129**, 85–95.

Schleidt, W.M. (1973) Tonic communication: continual effects of discrete signs in animal communication. *J. Theoret. Biol.*, **42**, 359–386.

Schmidt, S.P. and House, E.W. (1979) Precocious sexual development in hatchery-reared and laboratory-maintained male steelhead trout (*Salmo gairdneri*). *J. Fish. Res. Bd. Can.*, **36**, 90–93.

Seghers, B. (1974) Schooling behaviour in the guppy (*Poecilia reticulata*): an evolutionary response to predation. *Evol.*, **28**, 486–489.

Seilacher, A. (1967) Fossil behaviour. *Sci. Amer.*, **217**, 72–80.

Selander, R.K. (1970) Behaviour and genetic variation in natural populations. *Amer. Zool.*, **10**, 53–66.

Selman, I.E., McEwan, A.D. and Fisher, E.W. (1970) Studies of natural suckling behaviour in cattle during the first 8 hours post-partum. *Anim. Behav.*, **18**, 276–289.

Selman, I.E., McEwan, A.D. and Fisher, E.W. (1971) Absorption of immune lactoglobulin by newborn dairy calves. *Res. Vet. Sci.*, **12**, 205–210.

Sevenster, P. (1973) Incompatibility of response and reward; in *Constraints on Learning* (eds R.A. Hinde and J. Stevenson-Hinde), Academic Press, London, pp. 265–283.

Sevenster, P. and Goyens, J. (1975) Expérience sociale et role du sexe dans l'ontogenese de l'aggressivité chez l'épinoche (*Gasterosteus aculeatus*). *Neth. J. Zool.*, **25**, 195–205.

Sevenster, P. and t'Hart, M. (1974) A behavioural variant in the three-spined stickleback; in *The Genetics of Behaviour* (ed. J.H.F. van Abeelen), North Holland Publ. Co., Amsterdam, pp. 141–165.

Seyfried, T.N., Yu, R.K. and Glaser, G.H. (1980) Genetic analysis of audiogenic seizure susceptibility in C57BL/6J (B6) and DBA/2J(D2) recombinant inbred strains of mice. *Genetics*, **94**, 701–718.

Shapiro, V., Fraiberg, S. and Adelson, E. (1976) Infant–parent psychotherapy on behalf of a child in a critical motivational state. *J. Child Psychol. Psychiatry*, **7**, 179–197.

Sherman, P.W. (1977) Nepotism and the evolution of alarm calls. *Science*, **197**, 1246–1253.

Shields, W.M. (1980) Ground squirrel alarm calls: nepotism or parental care? *Amer. Nat.*, **116**, 599–603.

Shine, R. (1979) Sexual selection and sexual dimorphism in the amphibia. *Copeia*, pp. 297–306.

Shire, J.G.M. (1979) Genetic variation in hormone systems. *Boca Raton*, CRC Press, Florida.

Sibly, R. (1975) How incentive and deficit determine feeding tendency. *Anim. Behav.*, **23**, 437–446.

Sibly, R. and Calow, P. (1983) An integrated approach to life-cycle evolution using selective landscapes. *J. Theoret. Biol.*, **102**, 527–547.

Sibly, R. and McCleery, R.H. (1976) The dominance boundary method of determining motivational state. *Anim. Behav.*, **24**, 108–124.

Sibly, R. and McFarland D.J. (1976) On the fitness of behavioural sequences. *Amer. Nat.*, **110**, 601–617.

Siegel, P.B. (1965) Genetics of behaviour: selection for mating ability in chickens. *Genetics*, **52**, 1269–1277.

Sih, A. (1980) Optimal behaviour: can foragers balance two conflicting demands. *Science*, **210**, 1041–1043.

Slater, P.J.B. (1973) Describing sequences of behaviour; in *Perspectives in Ethology, Vol. 1* (eds P.P.G. Bateson and P.H. Klopfer), Plenum Press, New York, pp. 131–153.

Smith, J.N.M. (1974) The food searching behaviour of two European thrushes I. Description and analysis of search paths. *Behaviour*, **48**, 276–302.

Smith-Gill, S.J. and Berven, K.A. (1980) *In vitro* fertilisation and assessment of male reproductive potential using mammalian GTRH to induce spermiation in *Rana sylvatica*. *Copeia*, 723–728.

Sociobiology Study Group (1976) Sociobiology – another biological determinism. *Bioscience*, **26**, 182–186.

Sokolowski, M.B. (1980) Foraging strategies on *Drosophila melanogaster*: a chromosomal analysis. *Behav. Genet.*, **10**, 291–302.

Southwood, T.R.E. (1978) *Ecological Methods*, 2nd edn, Chapman and Hall, London.

Sowerby, M.E. and Polan, C.E. (1978) Milk production response to shifting cows between intraherd groups. *J. Dairy Sci.*, **61**, 445–460.

Stacey, P.B. (1979) Habitat saturation and communal breeding in the acorn woodpecker. *Anim. Behav.*, **27**, 1153–1166.

Stearns, S.C. (1980) A new view of life history evolution. *Oikos*, **35**, 266–281.

Steinberg, J.B. (1977) Information theory; in *Quantitative Methods in Animal Behaviour* (ed. B. A. Hazlett), Academic Press, New York, pp. 47–74.

Steinberg, J.B. and Conant, R.C. (1974) An information analysis of inter-male behaviour of the grasshopper *Chortophaga viridifasciata*. *Anim. Behav.*, **22**, 617–627.

Steinbock, R.T. (1976) *Palaeopathological Diagnosis and Interpretation. Bone Diseases in Ancient Human Populations*. Charles C. Thomas, Springfield, Illinois.

Stokes, A.W. (1962) Agonistic behaviour among blue tits at a winter feeding station. *Behaviour*, **19**, 118–138.

Stolba, A. (1982) Designing pig housing conditions according to patterns of social structure. *Proc. Perth Pig Conf.*, 11–24.

Syren, R.M. and Luykx, P. (1977) Permanent segmental interchange complex in the termite *Incisitermes schwarzi*. *Nature*, **266**, 167–168.

Szabad, J. and Fajszi, C. (1982) Control of female reproduction in *Drosophila*: genetic dissection using gyandromorphs. *Genetics*, **100**,. 61–78.

Taylor, C.E. (1976) Genetic variation in heterogeneous environments. *Genetics*, **73**, 887–894.

Taylor, C.E. and Powell, J.R. (1977) Microgeographic differentiation of chromosomal and enzyme polymorphisms in *Drosophila persimilis*. *Genetics*, **85**, 681–695.

Taylor, L.R. and Kalmus, H. (1954) Dawn and dusk flight of *Drosophila subobscura*. *Nature*, **174**, 221–222.

Taylor, R.J. (1977) The value of clumping to prey: experiments with a mammalian predator. *Oecologia*, **30**, 285–294.

Thornhill, R. (1980) Mate choice in *Hylobittacus apicalis* and its relation to some models of female choice. *Evol.*, **34**, 519–538.

Thornhill, R. (1981) *Panorpa* scorpionflies: systems for understanding resource defence polygyny and alternative male reproductive efforts. *Ann. Rev. Ecol. Syst.*, **12**, 355–368.

Thorpe, W.H. (1958) The learning of song patterns by birds, with especial reference to the song of the chaffinch, *Fringilla coelebs*. *Ibis*, **100**, 535–570.

Thorpe, W.H. (1961) *Bird Song*, Cambridge Univ. Press, Cambridge.

Thorpe, W.H. (1979) *The Origins and Rise of Ethology*, Heinemann, London.

Tilson, R.L. and Norton, P.M. (1981) Alarm duetting and pursuit deterrence in an African antelope. *Amer. Nat.*, **118**, 455–462.

Tinbergen, N. (1951) *The Study of Instinct*, Oxford Univ. Press, London.

Tinbergen, N. (1953) *Social Behaviour in Animals*, Methuen, London.

Tinbergen, N. (1959) Comparative studies of the behaviour of gulls (*Laridae*) – a progress report. *Behaviour*, **15**, 1–70.

Tinbergen, E.A. and Tinbergen, N. (1972) Early infant autism – an ethological approach. *Z. Tierpsychol., Suppl.* **10**, 1–53.

Tinbergen, E.A. and Tinbergen, N. (1976) The aetiology of childhood autism: a criticism of the Tinbergen's theory: a rejoinder. *Psychol. Med.,* **6**, 545–549.

Tinbergen, N., Broekhuysen, G.J., Feekes, F., Houghton, J.C., Kruuk, H. and Szuk, E. (1962) Eggshell removal by the blackheaded gull (*Larus ridibundus L.*); a behavioural component of camouflage. *Behaviour,* **19**, 74–117.

Toates, F.M. (1980) *Animal Behaviour: A Systems Approach,* John Wiley, Chichester.

Toates, F.M. and Booth, D.A. (1974) Control of food intake by energy supply. *Nature,* **251**, 710–711.

Toates, F.M. and O'Rourke, C. (1978) Computer simulation of male rat sexual behaviour. *Med. Biol. Eng. Comp.,* **16**, 98–104.

Tomkins, L. and Hall, J.C. (1983) Identification of brain sites controlling female receptivity in mosaics of *Drosophila melanogaster. Genetics,* **103**, 179–195.

Treisman, M. (1975) Predation and the evolution of gregariousness. *Anim. Behav.,* **23**, 779–800.

Trivers, R.L. (1971) The evolution of reciprocal altruism. *Q. Rev. Biol.,* **46**, 35–57.

Trivers, R.L. (1972) Parental investment and sexual selection; in *Sexual Selection and the Descent of Man* (ed. B. Campbell), Aldine, Chicago, pp. 136–179.

Trivers, R.L. (1974) Parent–offspring conflict. *Amer. Zool.,* **14**, 249–264.

Trivers, R.L. (1976) Sexual selection and resource-accruing abilities in *Anolis garmani. Evol.,* **30**, 253–269.

Trivers, R.L. and Hare, H. (1976) Haplodiploidy and the evolution of the social insects. *Science,* **191**, 249–263.

Truax, R.E. and Siegel, P.B. (1981) An autosomal allelic series of plumage colour in Japanese quail. *J. Hered.,* **72**, 61–62.

Tychsen, P.H. and Fletcher, B.S. (1971) Studies on the rhythm of mating in the Queensland fruit fly, *Dacus tryoni. J. Insect Physiol.,* **17**, 2139–2156.

Tyler, S. (1972) The behaviour and social organisation of the New Forest ponies. *Anim. Behav. Mon.,* **5**, 87–196.

Van der Bercken, J.H.L. and Cools, A.R. (1980a) Information-statistical analysis of social interaction and communication: an analysis of variance approach. *Anim. Behav.,* **28**, 172–188.

Van der Bercken, J.H.L. and Cools, A.R. (1980b) Information-statistical analysis of factors determining ongoing behaviour and social interaction in Java monkeys (*Macaca fascicularis*). *Anim. Behav.,* **28**, 189–200.

Van Putten, G. (1978) Comfort behaviour in pigs: information for their wellbeing; in *The Ethology and Ethics of Farm Animal Production* (ed. D.W. Fölsch), Birkhäuser-Verlag, Basel, pp. 70–76.

Van Rhijn, J.G. (1973) Behavioural dimorphism in male ruffs *Philomachus pugnax. Behaviour,* **47**, 153–229.

Van Rhijn, J.G. (1981) Units of behaviour in the black-headed gull, *Larus ridibundus L. Anim. Behav.,* **29**, 586–597.

Van Rhijn, J.G. and Vodegal, R. (1980) Being honest about ones intentions: an ESS for animal conflicts. *J. Theoret. Biol.,* **85**, 623–641.

Vauclair, J. and Bateson, P.P.G. (1975) Prior exposure to light and pecking accuracy in chicks. *Behaviour,* **52**, 196–201.

Vehrencamp, S. (1978) The adaptive significance of communal nesting in groove-billed anis (*Crotophaga sulcirostris*). *Behav. Ecol. Sociol.*, **4**, 1–33.

Verner, J. and Willson, M.F. (1966) The influence of habitats on mating systems of North American passerine birds. *Ecology*, **47**, 143–147.

Vietze, P.M., Abernathy, S.R., Ashe, M.L. and Faulstich, G. (1978) Contingency interactions between mothers and their developmentally delayed infants; in *Observing Behaviour, Vol. 1* (ed. G.P. Sackett), University Park Press, Baltimore, pp. 115–132.

Waddington, K.D. and Heinrich, B. (1981) Patterns of movement and floral choice by foraging bees; in *Foraging Behaviour* (eds A.C. Kamil and T.D. Sargent), Garland Press, New York, pp. 215–230.

Wankowsky, J.W.J. (1979) Morphological limitation, prey size selection and growth response of juvenile atlantic salmon (*Salmo salar*). *J. Fish. Biol.*, **14**, 89–100.

Wankowsky, J.W.J. (1981) Behavioural aspects of predation by juvenile atlantic salmon (*Salmo salar L.*) on particulate drifting prey. *Anim. Behav.*, **29**, 557–571.

Wankowsky, J.W.J. and Thorpe, J.E. (1979a) Spatial distribution and feeding in atlantic salmon, *Salmo salar L.* juveniles. *J. Fish. Biol.*, **14**, 239–247.

Wankowsky, J.W.J. and Thorpe, J.E. (1979b) The role of food particle size in the growth of juvenile atlantic salmon (*Salmo salar*). *J. Fish. Biol.*, **14**, 351–370.

Ward, S. (1977) Invertebrate neurogenetics. *Ann. Rev. Genet.*, **11**, 415–450.

Watts, C.R. and Stokes, A.W. (1971) The social order of turkeys. *Sci. Amer.*, **224**, 112–118.

Weatherhead, P.J. (1979) Do savanah sparrows commit the concord fallacy? *Behav. Ecol. Sociobiol.*, **5**, 373–381.

Weigel, R.N. (1981) The distribution of altruism among kin: a mathematical model. *Amer. Nature*, **118**, 191–201.

Werner, E.E. and Hall, D.J. (1974) Optimal foraging and the size selection of prey by the bluegill sunfish (*Lepomis macrochirus*). *Ecology*, **55**, 1042–1052.

Werner, E.E. and Hall, D.J. (1979) Foraging efficiency and habitat switching in competing sunfish. *Ecology*, **60**, 256–264.

West, M.J. and King, H.P. (1980) Enriching cowbird song by deprivation. *J. Comp. Physiol. Psychol.*, **94**, 263–270.

West-Eberhard, M.J. (1975) The evolution of social behaviour by kin selection. *Q. Rev. Biol.*, **50**, 1–33.

West-Eberhard, M.J. (1979) Sexual selection, social competition and evolution. *Proc. Amer. Phil. Soc.*, **123**, 222–234.

Whitham, T.G. (1980) The theory of habitat selection: examined and extended using *Pemphigus* aphids. *Amer. Nat.*, **115**, 449–466.

Wicklund, C.G. and Andersson, M. (1980) Nest predation selects for colonial breeding among fieldfares *Turdus pilaris. Ibis*, **122**, 363–366.

Wilbur, H.M., Rubenstein, D.I. and Fairchild, L. (1978) Sexual selection in toads: the roles of female choice and male body size. *Evol.*, **32**, 264–270.

Wiley, R.H. (1973) The strut display of the male sage grouse: a fixed action pattern. *Behaviour*, **47**, 129–152.

Wiley, R.H. (1974) Evolution of social organisation and life history patterns among grouse. *Q. Rev. Biol.*, **49**, 201–227.

Williams, B.G. and Naylor, E. (1967) Spontaneously induced rhythm of tidal periodicity in laboratory reared *Carcinus. J. Exp. Biol.*, **47**, 229–234.

Willows, A.O.D., Dorsett, D.A. and Hoyle, G. (1973) The neuronal basis of behaviour in *Tritonia* III. Neuronal machanisms of a fixed action pattern. *J. Neurobiol.*, **4**, 255–285.

Wilson, E.O. (1971) *The Insect Societies*, Harvard Univ. Press, Cambridge, Mass.

Wilson, E.O. (1975) *Sociobiology. The New Synthesis*, Harvard Univ. Press, Cambridge Mass.

Wilson, R., Burnet, B., Eastwood, L. and Connolly, K. (1976) Behavioural pleiotropy of the yellow gene in *Drosophila melanogaster. Genet. Res.*, **28**, 75–88.

Wine, J.J. and Krasne, F.B. (1982) The cellular organisation of crayfish escape behaviour; in *The Biology of Crustacea, Vol. 4* (eds D.C. Sandeman and H.L. Atwood), Academic Press, New York, pp. 242–292.

Wood-Gush, D.G.M. and Duncan, I.J.H. (1976) Some behavioural observations on domestic fowl in the wild. *Appl. Anim. Ethol.*, **2**, 255–268.

Wood-Gush, D.G.M. and Stolba, A. (1981) The assessment of behavioural needs of pigs under free-range and confined conditions. *Appl. Anim. Ethol.*, **7**, 380–389.

Wood-Gush, D.G.M., Duncan, I.J.H. and Fraser, D. (1975) Social stress and welfare problems in agricultural animals; in *The Behaviour of Domestic Animals*, 3rd edn (ed. E.S.E. Hafez), Ballière-Tindall, London, pp. 182–202.

Wu, M.H., Holmes, W.G., Medina, S.R. and Sackett, C.P. (1980) Kin preferences in infant *Macaca nemestrina. Nature*, **285**, 225–227.

Wyman, R.L. and Ward, J.A. (1973) The development of behaviour in the cichlid fish *Etroplus maculatus. Z. Tierpsychol.*, **33**, 461–491.

Wynne-Edwards, V.C. (1962) *Animal Dispersal in Relation to Social Behaviour*, Oliver and Boyd, Edinburgh.

Yamazaki, K., Boyse, E.A., Miké, V., Thaler, H.T., Mathieson, B.J., Abbott, J., Boyse, J., Zayas, Z.A. and Thomas, L. (1976) Control of mating preferences in mice by genes in the major histocompatibility locus. *J. Exp. Med.*, **144**, 1324–1335.

Yokoyama, S. and Felsenstein, J. (1978) A model of kin selection for an altruistic trait considered as a quantitative character. *Proc. Natl. Acad. Sci.*, **75**, 420–422.

Youthed, G.J. and Moran, V.C. (1969) The lunar-day activity rhythm of myrmeleontid larvae. *J. Ins. Physiol.*, **15**, 1259–1271.

Zach, R. and Falls, J.B. (1979) Foraging and territoriality of male ovenbirds in a heterogeneous habitat. *J. Anim. Ecol.*, **48**, 33–52.

Zahavi, A. (1975) Mate selection – a selection for a handicap. *J. Theoret. Biol.*, **53**, 205–214.

Zeveloff, S.I. and Boyce, M.S. (1980) Parental investment and mating systems in mammals. *Evol.*, **34**, 973–982.

Zouros, E. (1981) The chromosomal basis of sexual isolation in two siblings species of *Drosophila. Genetics*, **97**, 703–718.

Author index

400   *Author index*

Yu, R.K., 322

Zach, R., 169

Zahavi, A., 226
Zeveloff, S.I., 240
Zouros, E., 310, 334

Species index

Ground squirrel (*continued*)
  Spermophilus beldingi (Belding's ground
    squirrel), 253, 261
  Spermophilus tereticaudus (round-tailed
    ground squirrel), 261
Groove-billed ani
  Crotophaga sulchirostris, 143, 152, 153, 256
Guillimot
  Uria lomvia, 163
Gull
  Larus spp., 16, 163, 189, 359
  Larus argentatus (herring gull), 59, 67, 71, 77,
    340
  Larus atricilla (laughing gull), 107, 108
  Larus ridibundus (black-headed gull), 2, 21
    159
  Rissa tridactyla (kittiwake), 209, 226
Guppy
  Poecilia reticulata, 140, 147, 245, 334

Hanging fly
  Mecoptera, 211
  Bittacus apicalis, 220
  Bittacus strigosus, 223
  Hylobittacus bittacus, 223
  Panorpa spp., 230, 231
  Panorpa latipennis, 226
Harris' hawk
  Parbuteo unicinctus, 252
Hummingbird
  Selasphorus spp., 172
Human
  Australopithecus, 278
  Homo sapiens, 10, 276, 356–367
  Neanderthal, 278
Hyena
  Crocuta crocuta, 249
Hymenoptera, 262, 265, 285

Impala
  Aepyceros melampus, 209
Indigo bird, 137
Isoptera, 262, 267

Jacana
  Jacana spinosa, 208, 219
Jackdaw
  Corvus monedula, 34
Junco
  Junco phaeonotus (Arizona/yellow-eyed
    junco), 106, 126, 184, 252
Jungle fowl
  Gallus gallus spadiceus, 114

Kangaroo, 237

Kangaroo rat
  Dipodomys agilus, 25
  Dipodomys merii, 292
  Dipodomys ordii, 292
Kestrel
  Falco tinnunculus, 163
Klipspringer (antelope)
  Oreotragus oreotragus, 256
Kob
  Adenota kob, 209
Kookaburra
  Dacelo gigas, 141

Lark, 278
Lark bunting
  Clamospiza melanocorys, 189, 209, 213
Lemming, 163
Lion
  Panthera leo, 214, 249, 254, 261, 267, 335, 355
Lizard
  Anolis limnifrons, 13, 18, 20
  Anolis nebula, 24
  Iguana iguana, 37, 197, 230
Lobster
  Homarus americanus, 211

Marine midge
  Clunio marinus, 161, 162, 165
Mexican jay
  Phelocoma ultramarina, 267
Minnow
  Phoxinus phoxinus, 29
Monkey
  Colobinae spp., 363
  Colobus badius (red colobus), 245
  Colobus guereza (black and white colobus), 245
  Leontopithecus rosalis (lion tamarin), 355
  Macaca fascicularis (Java monkey), 41
  Macaca mulatta (rhesus macaque), 362
  Macaca nemestrina (pigtailed macaque), 261
  Macaca radiata (bonnet macaque), 362
  Miopithecus talapoin (Talapoin monkey), 355
  Propithecus verreauxi, 273
Moose
  Alces alces, 181
Mosquito
  Anopheles bambusicolus, 294
Mosquito fish
  Gambusia affinis, 272
Mottled sculpin
  Cottus bairdi, 223
Mouse
  Mus musculus, 15, 111, 114, 227, 295, 312,
    317, 318, 319, 322, 325, 327, 328, 330,
    334

Nematode
Caenorhabditis elegans, 313, 327, 329, 333
Newt
Triturus vulgaris, 37, 67, 86, 97

Ocean skater
Halobates robustus, 247
Oryx
Oryx beisa, 342
Ostrich
Struthio camelus, 345
Ovenbird
Seiurus aurocapillus, 169

Parrot
Agapornis fischeri, 302
Agapornis roseicolis, 302
Peacock
Pavo pavo, 8, 289, 290
Periodic cicada
Magicada spp., 160
Phalarope
Phalaropus spp., 209, 215
Pheasant
Lophophorus impeyanus (impayan pheasant), 8, 289
Polyplectron bicalcaratum (peacock pheasant), 8, 289
Pied flycatcher
Ficedula hypoleuca, 215, 235
Pig
Sus scrofa, 344, 347, 348, 354
Pigeon
Columba palumbris, 245, 247
Pilchard
Harengula spp., 29
Pippet, 278
Planthopper
Prokelisia marginata, 166
Pocket gopher
Thomomys bottae, 295
Polychaetes
Armandia spp., 28
Spirorbis borealis, 168
Pomacentrid fish
Eupomacentrus leucostrictus, 191

Quail
Colinus virginianus (masked bob-white quail), 356
Coturnix coturnix japonica (Japanese quail), 137, 227, 299, 324

Rabbit
Oryctolagus cuniculus, 298

Rat
Rattus exulans, 25
Rattus norvegicus (domestic rat), 83, 85, 101, 116, 119, 136
Red deer
Cervus elephas, 45, 201, 202
Redshank
Tringa totanus, 181, 249
Red winged black bird
Agelaius phoeniceus, 126, 209, 210, 240, 335
Rivulin fish, 283
Rock ptarmigan
Lagopus urophasianus, 208
Ruff
Philomachus pugnax, 138, 209, 230, 231

Sage grouse
Centrocercus urophasianus, 23, 45
Salamander
Ambystoma maculatus, 41, 218
Desmognathus ocrophaeus, 237
Plethodon jordani, 41, 218
Salmonids
Onchorhynchus kisutch (Coho salmon), 343
Onchorhynchus nerka (Sockeye salmon), 343
Salmo gairdneri (rainbow trout), 343
Salmo salar (Atlantic salmon), 342, 344
Salvelinus fontinalis (brook char), 307, 334
Salvelinus namaycush (lake char), 307, 334
Sandpiper
Calidrininae, 208, 215
Screwworm
Cochliomyia hominivorax, 339
Shore crab
Carcinus maenus, 160, 161
Silk moth
Bombyx mori, 339
Snakes, 283
Snapping shrimp
Alpheus armatus, 211, 219, 290
Soldier beetle
Chauliognathus pennsylvanicus, 221
Sparrow
Melospiza melodia (song sparrow), 126, 129
Melospiza georgiana (swamp sparrow), 129
Zonotricha leucophrys (white crowned sparrow), 126, 128, 137, 296
Passerculus sandwichensis (savannah sparrow), 241
Passerella iliaca (fox sparrow), 273
Spider mite
Tetranychus urticae, 220
Squirrel
Tamiasciurs hudsonicus (red squirrel), 121, 136
Starling
Sternus vulgaris, 337

Subject index